Introduction to Hard Disk Management

JACKIE FOX
MARTIN WATERHOUSE

Introduction to Hard Disk Management

Copyright © 1992 by Que® Corporation

Library of Congress Catalog No.: 91-68375

ISBN: 0-88022-897-0

95 94 93 92   8 7 6 5 4 3 2 1

Interpretation of the printing code: the rightmost double-digit number is the year of the book's printing; the rightmost single-digit number, the number of the book's printing. For example, a printing code of 92-1 shows that the first printing of the book occurred in 1992.

Publisher: Lloyd J. Short

Associate Publisher: Rick Ranucci

Product Development Manager: Thomas H. Bennett

Acquisitions Editor: Chris Katsaropoulos

Book Designers: Scott Cook and Michele Laseau

Production: Jeff Baker, Claudia Bell, Scott Boucher, Paula Carroll, Michelle Cleary, Christine Cook, Keith Davenport, Terri Edwards, Mark Enochs, Brook Farling, Kate Godfrey, Carrie Keesling, Betty Kish, Bob LaRoche, Loren Malloy, Cindy L. Phipps, Linda Quigley, Caroline Roop, Linda Seifert, Sandra Shay, Kevin Spear, Angie Trzepacz, Julie Walker, Lisa Wilson, Allan Wimmer

CREDITS

Product Director
Brenda Carmichael

Production Editors
Kelly Currie
Kelly D. Dobbs
H. Leigh Davis

Technical Editor
John Tyler Fosdick III

Composed in *Cheltenham* and *MCPdigital*
by Que Corporation

DEDICATION

For Bruce
—J.F.

Thanks to my mum ("Way to go Jimmie") and my dad ("Right-on Commander").
—M.W.

Jackie Fox is a former senior writer for *PC Today* and *PC Novice* magazines. She also has written about technology for the *Omaha World-Herald* and *Writer's Digest* and has written user documentation and help screens for a variety of software programs. She currently is employed in Omaha, Nebraska, as a technical writer with Custom Computing Corporation, which develops software for the financial and medical fields. Her first computer was an Apple IIE, which sat untouched for three months while she worked up sufficient nerve to get near it.

Martin Waterhouse works for a major oil company and supervises a group of individuals best described as "technology evangelists." He has a background in Information Technology spanning 15 years and has written professionally for five years on a variety of PC-related topics from operating systems to object-oriented programming. His previous credits include *MS-DOS Power User's Guide, Vol. II*, and magazine pieces for *PC Today*, *Pacer*, and *LAN News*.

TRADEMARK ACKNOWLEDGMENTS

ACKNOWLEDGMENTS

I would like to thank the following people who contributed to the publishing of *Introduction to Hard Disk Management*:

Thanks to **Chris Katsaropoulos**, **Brenda Carmichael**, **Tim Stanley**, and **Kelly Currie** of Que Corporation — Chris for contacting me in the first place and Brenda, Tim, and Kelly for having the patience of a dozen saints. Special thanks to **Martin Waterhouse** for making the whole process seem a little less strange and for providing a calming influence during one particularly frustrating moment.

Thanks to **Steve Mann** of the Software Workshop for being my first mentor and encouraging me when I was tempted to doubt myself. Thanks also to **Mike Reith** of Con Brio Software, **Tim Gilderson**, and **Susan Mackall** for their ongoing support and to **Bob Katzive** of Disk/Trend and **Brian Ziel** of Seagate Technology. Special thanks to **Winn Rosch**.

For technical assistance on the finer points of drive controllers and interfaces, thanks to **John Cuda**, director of engineering at Microscience, and **Charles Marslett**, staff engineer with STB Systems. Thanks must also go to **Jonathan Bloom** of McGrath Power West for giving me John's phone number and for always being there when I have questions.

Finally, special thanks must go to my husband **Bruce** for doing far more than his share of packing, because this project coincided with an out-of-town move.

Jackie Fox

Acknowledgment for his support in writing this book goes to **David Stuk** for his valuable insight and help with the glossary.

Special thanks for product assistance go to

> Gibson Research
> Fifth Generation Systems
> Symantec
> Gazelle Systems Inc.
> Fischer International
> Addstor

Martin Waterhouse

CONTENTS AT A GLANCE

Introduction 1

I Hard Disk Basics

1 A Hard Disk Primer 9
2 Choosing a Hard Disk: Self-Defense for Buyers 29

II Operating System and Environment Basics

3 Understanding How DOS Works
with the Hard Disk 49
4 Managing Your Hard Disk in the Graphical Era 71

III Organizing Your Disk with Files and Directories

5 Keeping Files Organized 91
6 Working with Directories on Your Hard Disk.............123
7 Using Batch Files and Macros 141

IV Fine-Tuning Your Hard Disk's Performance

8 Using Memory To Speed Up Your Disk 179
9 Exploring Hard Disk Fitness Programs 199

V Keeping Your Hard Disk Secure

10 Understanding the Importance of Backing Up 223
11 Preventing Trouble 247
12 Raiders of the Lost Data 265
13 Keeping Your Data Confidential 287
14 Immunizing Your PC against Viruses 309
15 Understanding Data Compression 333

Appendixes

A DOS Commands...353
B Some Program Files You Can Live Without 391
C Some Common Errors 393

Glossary 397
Index 407

TABLE OF CONTENTS

Introduction 1

    What To Expect from This Book 1
    What Not To Expect from This Book 3
    How This Book Is Organized 3
    Conventions Used in This Book 5

I Hard Disk Basics

1 A Hard Disk Primer 9

    Learning Some Computer Basics 9
        Examining the Motherboard 10
        Examining the Bus 10
        Examining the Microprocessor 11
            The Arithmetic Logic Unit (ALU) 11
            The Central Processing Unit (CPU) 12
            The Intel Chip Family 12
    Learning about Bits, Bytes, and Beyond 13
    Exploring the History and Evolution
       of the Hard Disk 14
    Comparing Data Storage Methods 15
        Comparing RAM to Magnetic Storage 15
        Comparing Floppy Drives to Hard Drives 16
    Examining the Physical Structure of the Hard Disk 16
    Understanding How the Hard Disk Stores Data 19
        Examining the Head Actuator 19
        Understanding the Controller's Role 20
        Reading from and Writing to Disk 21
        Watching Out for Head Crashes 22
    Examining Types of Hard Drives 23
        Comparing Device-Level
           and System-Level Interfaces 23
        Examining the ST-506/412 Interface 24
        Examining the ESDI
           (Enhanced Small Device Interface) 25
        Examining the SCSI
           (Small Computer Systems Interface) 25
        Examining the IDE
           (Integrated Drive Electronics) Interface............26
    Summary 27

2 Choosing a Hard Disk: Self-Defense for Buyers **29**

Deciding How Much Storage You Need 29
Measuring Speed and Performance 31
  Checking the Data Transfer Rate 31
  Understanding Average Access Time 32
  Analyzing the Mean Time
    Between Failures (MTBF) 33
  Measuring Track-to-Track Seek Time 33
Understanding How the Interleave
  Affects Performance....................................33
Considering Disk Caches and Buffers 35
Comparing Internal to External Drives 37
Looking at Price per Megabyte 38
Replacing Your Disk or Adding a Second Disk............38
  Ensuring Compatibility among Components........38
  Remembering the BIOS 39
  Matching the Data Transfer Rate to Your PC 40
  Considering the Form Factor Fit 41
Considering Alternative Storage Technologies...........41
  Using Hard Disk Cards................................41
  Using Removable Hard Disks.........................42
  Exploring Optical Technologies 42
    CD-ROM 43
    WORMs and Rewritable Technologies 43
    Looking at the Pros and Cons.....................44
Summary 44

II Operator System and Environment Basics

3 Understanding How DOS Works with the Hard Disk **49**

Understanding the Role of the Operating System 49
Examining the Central Components
  of an Operating System 50
  Examining the BIOS....................................51
  Examining the Kernel 51
  Examining the Command Interpreter 52
  Examining the Utilities 53
Looking at Some Operating Systems 54
  Looking at DOS: Disk Operating System 54
    Having a Quick DOS History Lesson 54
    Noting Changes in DOS 5.0 55
  Looking at OS/2 56

Looking at UNIX 57
Looking at the Mac System 58
Preparing the Hard Disk To Work with DOS 59
Performing the Low-Level Format 60
Setting Up Disk Partitions 60
Performing the High-Level Format 63
The Boot Record 64
The File Allocation Table 66
The Root Directory 68
Summary 68

4 Managing Your Hard Disk in the Graphical Era 71

Looking at the Two Interfaces of DOS 72
Exploring the Features of the DOS Shell 74
Navigating the DOS Shell 76
Changing the Look of the DOS Shell 78
Looking at the Advantages of a GUI 80
Exploring Microsoft Windows 81
Looking at Commercial DOS Shells 84
Looking at Q-DOS 3 85
Looking at DESQview 86
Deciding whether You Need
a Third-Party Shell 87
Summary 88

III Organizing Your Disk with File and Directories

5 Keeping Files Organized 91

What Is a File? 92
Using File Names and Extensions 92
Examining Types of Files 94
Looking at Program Files 94
Looking at Data Files and Text Files 94
Looking at Other File Types 95
Understanding Other File Attributes 96
Displaying File Lists 97
Using Wild Cards When Working with Files 100
Selecting Files 101
Selecting Individual Files 101
Selecting Multiple Files 102
Selecting All Files in a Directory 104
Selecting Files across Directories 105

Viewing Files 106
Searching for Files 108
Copying Files 110
   Using the File Menu To Copy Files 110
   Using the Dual File List To Copy Files 112
   Using the Mouse To Copy Files to
     a Different Directory 114
   Copying Files in Windows 114
   Using the DOS Command Line To Copy Files 116
Moving Files 116
Deleting Files 118
Renaming Files 120
Summary 121

6 Working with Directories on Your Hard Disk **123**

Viewing a Sample Directory 124
Developing a Strategy 125
Understanding How Directories Work 127
   Understanding Hierarchical Directories 127
   Understanding Paths 129
   Understanding the Current Directory 130
   Changing the Prompt To Reflect
     the Current Directory 131
Managing Your Directories 132
   Navigating the Directory Structure 132
   Using Absolute and Relative Paths 132
   Expanding and Collapsing Branches
     in the Directory Tree 133
   Creating Directories 135
   Renaming Directories 137
   Removing Directories 138
Keeping Directories Organized 139
Summary 140

7 Using Batch Files and Macros **141**

What Are Batch Files? 141
   Examining Batch File Structure 142
   Understanding Why You Should Use Batch Files 143
Creating Batch Files 145
   Creating Batch Files with COPY CON 145
   Creating Batch Files with EDLIN
     (DOS 2.X through 5.0) 147

Creating Batch Files with EDIT
(DOS 5.0) 151
Creating Batch Files with Other Text Editors 152
Running Batch Files 153
Examining Commands and Features
Specific to Batch Files 153
Using Parameters 155
Controlling the Display with ECHO 156
Adding Remarks with REM 157
Halting Processing with PAUSE 158
Setting Conditions with IF 158
Shifting Parameters with SHIFT 159
Manipulating Parameters with FOR..IN..DO 160
Examining Some Ways To Use Batch Files 160
Using Batch Files To Help Organize Your Disk ... 161
Using Batch Files for Housekeeping Chores 162
Using Batch Files To Create
a Simple Menu System 163
Understanding AUTOEXEC.BAT 164
Knowing What To Include in AUTOEXEC.BAT 165
Knowing the Rules for a Fast Path 167
Exploring Alternatives to Batch Programs 169
Using DOSKEY 171
Accessing DOSKEY Commands 171
Learning How To Create DOSKEY Macros 172
Creating Batch Files with DOSKEY 174
Looking at Alternatives to DOSKEY Macros 175
Summary 176

IV Fine-Tuning Your Hard Disk's Performance

8 Using Memory To Speed Up Your Disk 179

Determining the Amounts and Kinds of Memory
You Can Use 180
Understanding Addressable Memory 180
Using Conventional Memory 182
Using Upper Memory 182
Using Expanded Memory 183
Using Extended Memory 184
Examining DOS 5.0's Memory-Management
Improvements 185
Using HIMEM.SYS 185
Using EMM386.EXE 186

Optimizing the Number of Buffers 187
Working with RAM Disks 189
    Creating a RAM Disk 189
    Copying Files to the RAM Disk 191
Working with Disk Caches 192
    Using DOS and Windows Caches 194
    Using Commercial Caches 195
    Using Hardware Caches 196
Summary 197

9 Exploring Hard Disk Fitness Programs **199**

What Is Disk Optimization? 200
Understanding Why Disks Need Optimizing 201
Dealing with Fragmentation 202
    Understanding How Disks Become Fragmented . 202
    Looking at How Defragmentation Works 205
    Understanding Why Defragmentation
        Is Important 206
Understanding How the Interleave
    Affects Performance 206
Examining Some Disk-Fitness Utilities 208
    Using PC Tools Compress 209
    Using the Revitalize Option
        in PC Tools DiskFix 210
    Using the Norton Utilities
        Speeddisk Command 211
    Using the Norton Utilities
        Calibrate Command 212
    Using FastTrax 213
    Using Gazelle's Optune 215
    Using SpinRite II 216
Summary 220

V Keeping Your Hard Disk Secure

10 Understanding the Importance of Backing Up **223**

Deciding Where To Keep Your Backups 225
Deciding How OftenYou Should Back Up 226
Backing Up with DOS 226
    Examining COPY and Its Shortcomings 227
    Working with XCOPY 228

Working with BACKUP and RESTORE 230
Using Commercial Backup Programs 234
Using FastBack Plus 234
Using Back-It 4 237
Using Norton Backup 240
Using Central Point Backup 243
Making Tape Backups 244
Summary 246

11 Preventing Trouble 247

Ensuring a Healthy Environment
for Your Hard Disk 247
Examining Factors That Cause Trouble 248
Heat 249
Nonparked Heads 249
Vibration 249
Impact 250
Power Fluctuations 250
Magnetic Fields 251
Deciding Whether To Leave Your Machine
Running or Turn It Off 251
Protecting Your Data from Yourself 252
Making Files Read-Only 252
Hiding Files 253
Using the DOS Shell To Display
and Change Attributes 255
Using the Windows File Manager To Display
and Change Attributes 256
Performing Hard Disk Checkups
with Disk Analyzers 257
Using the CHKDSK Command 257
Using the Norton Utilities 258
Using PC Tools 261
Using the MIRROR Command in DOS 5.0 264
Summary 264

12 Raiders of the Lost Data 265

Understanding Why Lost Data Isn't Really Lost 266
Understanding Why Unformatting Is Possible 268
Examining the MIRROR Command 269
Using DOS's UNDELETE Command 270
Using UNDELETE with MIRROR 271

Using UNDELETE without MIRROR 273
Recovering from an Accidental Format
  with UNFORMAT 273
  Using UNFORMAT with MIRROR 275
  Verifying MIRROR Information 276
  Using UNFORMAT without MIRROR 277
Repairing Damaged DOS Structures 278
  Knowing Which Error Messages
  Indicate Disk Trouble 279
  Looking for FAT Trouble 279
  Performing CPR for Structural Damage 280
    Using PC Tools DiskFix 281
    Using the Norton Disk Doctor 282
  Using MIRROR To Recover
  Partition Information 283
Repairing Damaged Spreadsheet and Text Files 284
Deciding Whether To Use
  the DOS RECOVER Command 284
Summary 285

13 Keeping Your Data Confidential **287**

Examining Your Basic Security Options 288
  Using Floppies 288
  Using Removable Hard Disks 289
Understanding Why Erasing and Deleting Files
  Isn't Enough 289
Wiping Data from the Disk 291
  Using Norton's WipeInfo 291
  Using PC Tools Wipe 293
Examining Some Password Dos and Don'ts 294
Exploring Some Data-Protection Programs 295
  Using Security Options in PC Tools 295
    Using PC Secure 296
    Using Data Monitor 297
  Using Security Options in Norton Utilities 298
    Using Disk Monitor 298
    Using Diskreet 299
  Using Fifth Generation Systems' DiskLock 300
  Using Watchdog 302
    Restricting and Controlling Access 302
    Protecting Data and Files 302
    Protecting Resources 302
    Protecting against Boots and Formats 303
    Protecting Old Memory and Files 303

Protecting against Viruses 303
Keeping an Audit Trail 303
Using Systems with Built-in Protection 304
Examining Compaq's Security Features 304
Examining AST Research's Security Options 305
Examining IBM's Security Options 305
Exploring Other Hardware Options 306
Summary 307

14 Immunizing Your PC against Viruses **309**

Examining Threats to Your System 309
What Is a Virus? 310
Understanding How Viruses Manifest and Spread 311
Looking at Boot Infectors 311
Looking at Program Infectors 312
Looking at Cloaked Infectors 313
Preparing a Virus Avoidance Checklist 314
Checking for Viruses 315
Watching for the Signs 315
Eliminating Other Causes 316
Getting Rid of Viruses 317
Using Virus Protection and Recovery Utilities 318
Examining Norton AntiVirus for DOS 318
Testing for Viruses while Booting 319
Using Norton AntiVirus 319
Scanning for Viruses with
Norton AntiVirus 320
Inoculating/Uninoculating 321
Using Virus Clinic 322
Using Global Settings 322
Using Intercept 323
Using Password-Protection Access 323
Keeping Up with New Viruses 323
Examining Norton AntiVirus for Windows..........324
Examining Central Point Anti-Virus 324
Examining Fifth Generation's Untouchable 326
Examining McAffee Associates
Viruscan Series 328
Scan 328
Scan for Windows (Wscan) 329
Clean 329
Vshield 330
Summary 331

15 Understanding Data Compression 333

    Defining Data Compression 334
    Understanding How Data Compression Works 335
    Being Wary of Multiple Compressions 336
    Looking at Compression's Effectiveness 336
    Determining When You Should Use Compression 338
    Examining Software Solutions 338
        Looking at LHARC 339
        Looking at ARC 340
        Looking at PKZIP 340
        Looking at PAK 342
        Looking at ZOO 343
        Looking at PKLITE 345
        Looking at SuperStor 345
        Looking at Stacker 348
    Using Data Compression with a RAM Disk 349
    Exploring Hardware Options 350
    Summary 351

Appendixes

A DOS Commands 353

B Some Program Files You Can Live Without 391

C Some Common Errors 393

    Looking at Some DOS Error Messages 393
    Encountering Other Problems 396

Glossary 397

Index 407

Introduction

People often say that the microprocessor is the computer's brain. If that statement is true, then the humble, often-overlooked hard disk is the computer's heart.

Although the microprocessor determines how much information your computer can handle and how quickly it can process that information, the hard disk determines how much information your computer can store. And having enough space is what most computer users care about. The computer industry often focuses on a computer's speed, but people in the real world are far more concerned with keeping all the data they need close at hand—and conveniently accessible. That's where hard disks come in. Without a hard disk, you have to load software every time you start your computer. This cumbersome task slows you down and nullifies the advantage that computers are supposed to offer—making your work easier.

Like computers in general, however, hard disks are not magic. They haven't (yet) reached the point at which they determine the best place to store your annual report or your spreadsheet. That decision must come from you. And *Introduction to Hard Disk Management* can help you make that decision and many more. Being familiar with the workings of your hard disk is critical to making the most of the equipment you have and solving problems as they come along.

What To Expect from This Book

This book is full of tips for selecting, replacing, organizing, fine-tuning, and securing your hard disk so that it can do its job more efficiently.

You may be surprised to find that you can accomplish a great deal without investing in any special software. Planning has much to do with it. Organizing your hard disk isn't all that different from organizing your desk or your linen closet. You just need to know a few quirks about the ways computers operate, and the rest is common sense.

Chief among those quirks is the way DOS operates. DOS stands for *Disk Operating System*, the basic instructional software that comes with your computer. As the name implies, DOS controls all the computer's operations, which includes acting as a liaison between your application programs and your computer.

Without DOS, your spreadsheet program and word processing program would have to contain their own instructions for communicating with the computer's display screen or hard drive. DOS also acts as a liaison for you, the user. You don't need to speak the low-level machine language the computer understands in order to get it to do something— DOS handles that for you. Because it has such a central role, much of the discussion in this book is devoted to familiarizing you with DOS operations.

DOS can help you organize the data you keep on your hard disk, but some good specialty software programs also can help you keep your disk organized. Other programs help you keep the physical disk itself healthy and alert you to signs of trouble. This book doesn't play favorites or make any endorsements, but the text does include discussions of some of the most popular and highly rated programs available today.

Knowing how to use DOS to organize your disk is an important component of good disk management, but you have to buy a disk before you can manage it. After you start shopping around for a computer and disk drive, you're likely to be bombarded with acronyms, such as IDE, MTBF, and ESDI, or equally baffling phrases, such as data transfer rate and seek times. This book helps you understand what those terms mean and how they affect disk performance.

After you become more comfortable with what your computer can do, you may want to go beyond file and directory management. Later chapters discuss ways to use memory in place of a disk drive. (Don't worry; it's much less hassle than you might think. You don't have to be a programming genius to do it.) Also discussed are programs that can analyze your hard disk and fine-tune it for optimum performance.

Another way to get more from your disk is to compress the data you store on it, so different data-compression programs and techniques are discussed in this book as well. Finally, you look at ways to keep your data safe from accidental disk crashes and viruses.

You can do all these things without acquiring a computer science degree or taking out a second mortgage to pay for your investment in hardware and software. Consider this book the hard disk equivalent of a driver's education course. It doesn't prepare you to drive in the Grand Prix; it does, however, help you practice defensive driving in the traffic you encounter every day.

What Not To Expect from This Book

Introduction to Hard Disk Management covers DOS only in its role of keeping the information on your disk organized. The purpose of this book is not to make you a DOS expert. You can find plenty of DOS books on the market to help you accomplish that goal (*Using MS-DOS 5*, *Que's MS-DOS 5 User's Guide*, and *Turbocharging MS-DOS*, all from Que Corporation, to name a few). Nor will this book turn you into a hard disk hot rod. The goal is to show you how to perform routine maintenance, not to turn you into a mechanic. Part of the reason computers can be so scary is that people think they have to learn how to take one apart in order to use it. Although many books and articles are written as if that were the case, it simply isn't.

If you find that this book whets your appetite, and you want to dig deeper into hard disks and computers, you may want to check out Scott Mueller's excellent book, *Upgrading and Repairing PCs*, 2nd Edition, which also is published by Que Corporation.

How This Book Is Organized

It seems only fair that a book preaching the virtues of organizing your hard disk should give you some clue as to how the book itself is organized. The book is divided into the following parts:

> Part I: Hard Disk Basics
> Part II: Operating System and Environment Basics
> Part III: Organizing Your Disk with Files and Directories
> Part IV: Fine-Tuning Your Hard Disk's Performance
> Part V: Keeping Your Hard Disk Secure

Part I is meant to get you up to speed on hard disks. Chapter 1, "A Hard Disk Primer," familiarizes you with the basics of disk operation and also introduces you to different types of hard disks. Chapter 2, "Choosing a Hard Disk: Self-Defense for Buyers," offers you a guide to the industry jargon used by salespeople; tips on selecting the right kind of hard disk, including what you do and do not need to worry about; information about what to do if you need to upgrade; and news about alternative storage technologies you may want to consider.

Part II discusses the role of the operating system. Chapter 3, "Understanding How DOS Works with the Hard Disk," introduces you to the role DOS plays in hard disk management, from the time you turn on the computer to the moment you ask for a file. You also are introduced to the *graphical user interface* (GUI) in Chapter 4, "Managing Your Hard Disk in the Graphical Era." A GUI is an environment that uses a mouse and pull-down menus rather than typed commands. The emphasis is on the DOS Shell and Microsoft Windows. Knowing how to navigate graphical environments is important because more and more often, computers ship with Windows, the DOS Shell, or both.

For that reason, when you get to Part III, "Organizing Your Disk with Files and Directories," you see that the examples focus on the DOS Shell and also include tips for Windows. For those of you who have an older version of DOS or who simply prefer working from the command line, some tips on using the DOS command line also are included.

Chapter 5, "Keeping Files Organized," and Chapter 6, "Working with Directories on Your Hard Disk," introduce you to the concepts of files and directories and then show you steps for keeping them organized. The final chapter in this section, Chapter 7, "Using Batch Files and Macros," introduces you to batch files and macros. Because the subject of batch files in particular can go well beyond the introductory level of this book, Chapter 7 eases you into the topic by providing a couple of simple examples to give you a feel for what batch files and macros can do. If you want to dig deeper, you can check out some other books, such as *Batch Files and Macros Quick Reference* and *Que's MS-DOS 5 User's Guide*, both by Que Corporation.

If you read only Parts I through III, you are well on the road to an organized hard disk. But if you want to get the most from your hard disk, you will be interested in Part IV, "Fine-Tuning Your Hard Disk's Performance." Chapter 8, "Using Memory To Speed Up Your Disk," explores the mysteries of memory and how it can help speed up your hard disk's performance. Chapter 9, "Exploring Hard Disk Fitness Programs," looks at a variety of fitness programs for your disk, ranging from products that clean up the space on your disk to products that tune up the disk surface itself.

Part V explains how to keep the data on your hard disk secure from accidental erasure, nosy coworkers, and viruses.

Chapter 10, "Understanding the Importance of Backing Up," discusses the significance of backing up your data so that if something does happen, you don't lose everything. The chapter discusses developing a backup strategy as well as tips for using DOS or commercial programs.

Chapter 11, "Preventing Trouble," offers a variety of tips on preventing data loss, ranging from using power supplies that protect your PC in case of electrical glitches, to using disk diagnostics programs that can tell you whether your hard disk is showing potentially harmful symptoms.

Chapter 12, "Raiders of the Lost Data," shows you how to get your data back if preventive measures don't work and you accidentally erase a file or an entire disk. In addition to dealing with erased files, Chapter 12 explains how to repair damaged files.

Chapter 13, "Keeping Your Data Confidential," shows you how to keep your private data private, and Chapter 14, "Immunizing Your PC against Viruses," explains what viruses are and shows you how to protect your PC from infection.

Finally, Chapter 15, "Understanding Data Compression," explains how to fit more data on your disk by using compression techniques and compares hardware and software data compression.

Introduction to Hard Disk Management also contains three appendixes and a glossary of computer terms. Appendix A covers basic DOS commands. Appendix B points out some unnecessary program files that you can remove from your hard disk to gain more space. And Appendix C deciphers many of the common error messages you may see as you work on your hard disk.

Conventions Used in This Book

In this text, file names and operating system commands are shown in all uppercase letters, as in a file named LETTER.TXT or the DOS directory command DIR. The caps are for emphasis in the text only; DOS is not case-sensitive.

If you need to press a special key combination, the keys are shown in the text with hyphens. Ctrl-F6, for example, means hold down the Ctrl key and press the F6 function key. Ctrl-Alt-Del means hold down the Ctrl key and then press the Alt and Del keys.

Significant words or phrases mentioned for the first time are shown in *italic* characters, and anything that you're supposed to type is shown in **boldface** characters. All on-screen messages appear in a special typeface.

Throughout the book, the assumption is that you're working from the DOS Shell. Special icons, however, call your attention to alternative instructions for working with Microsoft Windows and the DOS command line.

The Windows icon looks like this:

The DOS command line icon looks like this:

If you want to work from Windows or the DOS command line, keep an eye out for these icons in the margin.

Learning about your computer should be a pleasant experience, and you should have fun while you learn to work with your hard disk. In fact, consider the following your first homework assignment: *Please remember that mastering your hard disk isn't an all-or-nothing proposition.* You didn't learn how to speak Spanish or German fluently in one lesson, but you did learn to say, "Buenos dios, me llamo es Lupe" (or Olga, or whatever name the teacher made you use). Learning about your hard disk and computer is exactly the same. First you learn how to say Hello, then you learn how to ask for and give directions, and before you know it, you may even become hooked on computing.

Hard Disk Basics

PART

1

OUTLINE

1 A Hard Disk Primer

2 Choosing a Hard Disk:
   Self-Defense for Buyers

A Hard Disk Primer

This chapter introduces you to some hard disk basics. To understand how the hard disk operates, you first need to be familiar with some fundamentals of computer operation. In this chapter, you begin by exploring some essential computing concepts.

If that approach seems like a roundabout way of learning about disks, be patient. Learning about your hard disk is like building a house; putting in a basement before you build the house is much easier than adding a basement later. The concepts you learn in this chapter can give you a solid foundation for the chapters that follow.

After this crash course in computer operation, you learn the basics of how data is stored in a computer. You then take a look at the hard disk itself and how it works. Finally, you examine some of the different types of hard drives on the market.

Learning Some Computer Basics

You probably already know that a computer consists of a display monitor, a keyboard, and the system itself, sometimes referred to in slang terms as "the box." But many of you may not be aware of what goes on inside that box.

Although you don't need to be a computer expert to use a computer any more than you need to be a mechanic to drive a car, knowing what goes on inside the box can help you understand your hard disk better. And if you understand your hard disk better, you can use it more productively and efficiently. The following paragraphs describe the primary components of your computer system—the motherboard, the bus, and the microprocessor—so that you can get an idea of your computer's inner workings.

Examining the Motherboard

Inside your computer is a main circuit board called the *motherboard*. The motherboard houses the microprocessor, memory chips, and expansion slots for add-in cards sometimes known as daughtercards. Typically, hardware that you connect to your computer needs a card in order to communicate with the computer. The monitor generally has a video card, and the hard disk a controller card. (Exceptions exist. Some PCs have the graphics functions built directly into the motherboard, and as you learn later in this chapter, some hard drives have the controller built directly into the drive.)

Examining the Bus

The *bus* is the computer's basic communications infrastructure. It is the electronic highway that connects everything in the system to everything else. The size of the bus determines how much information the computer can process at one time, just as the size of a highway determines how much traffic it can carry.

A PC contains basically three types of buses: the control bus, the address bus, and the data bus. All three buses sometimes are jointly referred to as the *expansion bus*, the *input/output bus*, or the *I/O bus*.

The control bus is responsible for synchronizing the signals that flow between the microprocessor and the other system components. The address bus carries the source or destination addresses for data between the microprocessor and memory chips, and the data bus is responsible for transporting the data itself from one system component to another, for example, between the microprocessor and the hard drive.

The size of the address bus determines how much input/output the computer can address. The importance of the address bus is discussed in Chapter 8, "Using Memory To Speed Up Your Disk." The main concern in this chapter is the data bus. The size of the data bus determines how much data the microprocessor can send and receive at once. The wider the bus, the more information can be sent at one time. A microprocessor with a 16-bit data bus can send and receive twice as much information as a microprocessor with an 8-bit data bus.

Determining the amount of data that can be sent by a microprocessor can be confusing because internal and external data bus sizes can vary within the same microprocessing chip. The Intel 8088 chip is a good example. Although it can process 16 bits within the chip, it can send only 8 bits to and receive 8 bits from the rest of the system. For this reason, the

8088 chip is said to have an 8-bit data bus. Think of a 4-lane highway within a city that narrows to a 2-lane road at the city's limits.

Examining the Microprocessor

As mentioned previously, the *microprocessor* often is referred to as the computer's brain. In a computer, you have all these signals zipping around various buses, like impulses going through an electronic nervous system. The microprocessor processes all these signals, just as your brain interprets all the data coming in through your senses. The microprocessor coordinates all the computer's basic functions, from making the calculations required to run a program to coordinating the interplay between the monitor, keyboard, and disk drive. Data is processed and sent back and forth across the bus infrastructure. Although exceptions do exist in the form of Direct Memory Access, in which devices can bypass the microprocessor and go directly to memory, generally the microprocessor is in charge. And this "brain" is on a miniaturized integrated circuit, called a *chip*, that can fit on the tip of your finger.

A PC typically is referred to by its microprocessor size. When you see references to a 286 or 386 computer, or even to an AT or an XT, for example, the microprocessor is what's being referenced.

Microprocessing chips have different *clock speeds*. The clock speed, measured in MegaHertz (millions of cycles per second), is the operational speed based on the computer's internal clock. The higher the clock speed, the faster the computer, so a computer with a clock speed of 25 MHz is faster than the same type of microprocessor with a clock speed of 20 MHz. But you also have to consider the data bus size.

Although the same microprocessor type can come in different clock speeds, it always has the same size data bus. One 386SX PC may have a clock speed of 16 MHz and another a clock speed of 20 MHz, for example, but they both have a 16-bit data bus. Given that example, if you want more processing speed you should choose the PC with the faster clock speed. But if you have two PCs with the same clock speed, and one has a wider data bus, the one with the wider bus is faster because it can carry more data.

The Arithmetic Logic Unit (ALU)

The *Arithmetic Logic Unit* (ALU) is the component of the microprocessor that performs arithmetic and logical operations on data. These operations include adding, subtracting, dividing, and multiplying and also the conditional "If this, then that" types of processes.

The Central Processing Unit (CPU)

The *Central Processing Unit* (CPU) is the component of the microprocessor that is responsible for carrying out program instructions stored in memory and for managing the flow of information throughout the computer. The terms CPU and microprocessor sometimes are used interchangeably, although technically a CPU on a single chip is a microprocessor. (Intel's 286, 386, and 486 chips are all examples of microprocessors.)

The Intel Chip Family

Most of the microprocessors used in PCs are based on the Intel family of chips. (In case you're curious, Apple Macintosh computers use the Motorola family of chips.) The following paragraphs give you a quick overview of the Intel chip family, from least to most powerful (and least to most costly).

The *8088* and *8086*, each of which also is referred to as the XT, were included in the original PCs. Although you rarely see XT-class machines offered today, plenty of them are still out there. Both the 8088 and 8086 process 16 bits internally, but the 8088 has an 8-bit data bus, and the 8086 has a 16-bit data bus. The original PCs had clock speeds of 4.77 MHz. Compare that to the 10 MHz or higher clock speeds of more recent models.

The *80286* also is referred to as the 286 or the AT. Like the 8086, the 286 processes 16 bits at a time both internally and externally. What sets it apart from the 8086 is its higher clock speed, up to 20 MHz, and its capability to address more memory, which is discussed in more detail in Chapter 8, "Using Memory To Speed Up Your Disk."

The *80386SX* is a stripped-down version of the 80386 chip. The 80386SX processes 32 bits internally but has only a 16-bit data bus and a 24-bit address bus. This chip has the same built-in memory-management features as the 80386. Commonly considered the entry-level platform if you want to use such graphical environments as Windows, the 386SX has clock speeds of 16 and 25 MHz.

The *80386* also is referred to as the 386 or 386DX to differentiate it from the 386SX. The 386 offers full 32-bit processing internally and in its data bus and also has built-in hardware features that enable it to take advantage of extended memory. (For more information on extended memory, see Chapter 8, "Using Memory To Speed Up Your Disk.") Typical clock speeds are 25 and 33 MHz. Advanced Micro Devices (AMD) also offers a 40 MHz version of the 386 chip, but Intel does not have a version at that clock speed.

The *80486SX* chip is the same as the full-blown 486 but without the built-in math coprocessor. At the time of this writing, the 80486SX was available in 20 and 25 MHz clock speeds.

The *80486* also is called the 486 or the 486DX. Like the 386, it employs full 32-bit processing. Design improvements over the 386 include the addition of a built-in math coprocessor to speed up mathematic calculations, an 8K internal RAM cache to speed up memory access, and the addition of elements of RISC (Reduced Instruction Set Computing) architecture. With RISC, fewer clock cycles are needed to carry out instructions, which makes the chip faster—typically by 2 or 3 times—than a 386 chip with the same clock speed. To give you an idea of how far computers have come, the 80486 is 50 times faster than the 8088 chip.

At the time of this writing, Intel had announced technology that doubles the internal processing speeds of some 486 chips. DX2s, which are upgrade chips based on the 486DX chip, are expected to debut in two versions: 25 MHz/50 MHz and 33 MHz/66 MHz. Intel also plans to introduce a clock-doubling version of the 486SX chip called the overdrive chip.

Learning about Bits, Bytes, and Beyond

When discussing computers, you cannot escape learning about certain terms, and bits and bytes are foremost among them. Everything the computer does is based on binary math, which calculates everything in powers of two. Unlike the decimal math you're used to, which uses digits from 0 to 9, binary math uses only the digits 0 and 1. The smallest unit of computer storage is called the *bit* (short for binary digit). A bit has a value of 0 or 1, which indicates one of two voltage levels—on or off.

But a bit doesn't give the computer much to work with. Communicating with bits is like trying to write a novel with a 4-word vocabulary. The basic unit of computer storage is thus the *byte*, which consists of 8 bits. With 8 bits, you have 256 possible combinations of 0 and 1 (the result of 2 to the 8th power).

ASCII, pronounced "askey," stands for American Standard Code for Information Exchange. The character-coding system used by most computers, ASCII converts the various binary combinations into the characters and digits that people understand. One 8-bit combination represents the letter A, for example, another 8-bit combination represents the numeral 2, and so on. A byte, then, represents the amount of space required to store a single alphanumeric character.

Because the ASCII character set defines only 128 characters, the number of characters that can be represented by 7 bits, most computers use the ASCII extended character set, which uses all 8 bits and covers the entire alphabet plus special characters. (The 8th bit was left open for other uses. As a result, the extended ASCII character set varies; it's not a universally accepted standard like ASCII itself.)

The terms *kilobyte* (abbreviated either K or Kb) and *megabyte* (abbreviated as M, MB, or sometimes meg) also are widely used in terms of computer storage, for both memory and disk storage. You might, for example, have 2M of RAM or an 80M hard drive.

A kilobyte is roughly one thousand bytes (1,024 bytes to be exact, or 2 to the 10th power), and a megabyte is roughly one million bytes (literally 1,048,576 bytes, or 2 to the 20th power). A megabyte can store approximately one million characters. One million might seem like a lot, but it gets eaten up quickly. You see where it all goes when you get to Chapter 2, "Choosing a Hard Disk: Self-Defense for Buyers."

Exploring the History and Evolution of the Hard Disk

Although hard disks were in widespread use a quarter of a century ago, the computers that housed them happened to be mainframes— multiuser computers designed to meet the computing needs of large organizations. In fact, you still may hear hard drives referred to as "Winchester" drives, which is the nickname given to IBM's hard drives for mainframes.

When the IBM PC made its debut in 1981, it didn't even have a hard disk. Instead, it had a 5 1/4-inch floppy drive that used single-sided disks and also an interface for cassette tape storage! Not until the IBM XT appeared on the scene a year later were hard drives included. The IBM XT's whopping 10M drive was built by Shugart Technology, the first company to develop a hard disk drive for microcomputers. (Shugart since has evolved into Seagate Technology, one of today's leading manufacturers of hard disk drives.)

Hard drives of that era not only were limited in capacity, they also were slow. The XT's hard drive was rated at 80 milliseconds (thousandths of a second), compared to the 18 to 28 milliseconds found in many hard drives today. Improvements in the head mechanisms have played a part in this speed increase.

The technology used to store data on the disk platter's magnetic surface also has improved, so more data can be packed into the same amount (or less) of disk storage space. You might expect a 100M hard drive to take up 10 times as much room as a 10M hard drive, but it doesn't.

In the following sections of this chapter, you learn more about the modern-day counterparts to these early hard disks.

Comparing Data Storage Methods

Before you learn how a hard disk works its magic, take a look at two other computer storage methods. In the following paragraphs you learn about RAM (random-access memory) and floppy disk storage.

Comparing RAM to Magnetic Storage

RAM is a temporary storehouse for data. The amount of RAM a computer has determines how large a program it can run. The larger and more graphic a program is, the more RAM it needs. When you load a program, it's placed in RAM so that the microprocessor can access the program more quickly and easily. Whenever you work in a program, you work in RAM, and as you make changes, the changes are made in RAM.

But RAM consists of electronic impulses, so when you shut off your computer, everything in RAM is lost. That data has to go somewhere so that the CPU can find the information when it is needed again. For this reason, the computer needs some kind of permanent storage, such as a hard disk or floppy disk.

T I P

Because you always work with a program in RAM, you should save your work frequently (every few minutes). When you use a program's save command, the changes are stored to the disk rather than to RAM. In WordPerfect, for example, you save work to disk by pressing the F10 key. You can set up some programs to save work automatically at intervals you specify; then you don't have to worry about remembering to save.

Comparing Floppy Drives to Hard Drives

You may be wondering why you cannot just store the data on a floppy disk. After all, floppy disks are permanent, aren't they? The answer to that question is both yes and no. Floppy disks are permanent compared to RAM, but permanent is relative because floppies eventually wear out.

Floppy disks and drives also are susceptible to breakage, pollution, spillage, and other problems that hard disks aren't as prone to because the hard disk is sealed in its own case inside the computer.

Hard disks offer two other big advantages over floppies: greater storage capacity and faster speed. In terms of storage, floppies currently max out at 1.44M. Typical hard disks for individual users range from 40 to 120M storage capacity. Hard disks sharing resources on a local area network can store up to hundreds of times as much data as a floppy disk.

 NOTE Super-high-density floppies currently are under development, but they max out at 4M unformatted (before they have been prepared to work with DOS) and 2.88M after formatting. That capacity is still much less than the 40M widely considered the minimum for a hard disk.

Storage capacity is important because the days of single-disk programs are long gone. WordPerfect 5.1, for example, takes up 12 5 1/4-inch floppy disks or 6 3 1/2-inch floppy disks. You don't want to waste your time shoveling those floppies into and out of the drive when you're trying to finish the company newsletter. Better to have a hard drive and not worry about it.

Aside from the time you waste doing the floppy shuffle, you also save time with a hard disk just because of its processing speed. Hard drives are roughly 10 times faster than floppy drives. Both types of drives operate on essentially the same principle, however, and in the next section you learn the principle behind how the hard drive stores data.

Examining the Physical Structure of the Hard Disk

Floppy disks and hard disks store data on a magnetically treated surface. The storage surfaces, typically made of aluminum, are called *platters* in a hard disk system. Hard disks typically have two or three platters stacked like records on a turntable, less than an inch apart. Platters range from

3 1/2 to 5 1/4 inches in diameter in hard drives used on desktop PCs and are typically 1/8 inch thick. External hard drives may use 8-inch or 14-inch platters.

The technology used to treat the platters has improved over the years. In days gone by, platters were *coated* with ferric oxide (a fancy term for rust particles) and some kind of binding agent, which is the same process used for floppy disks. Today many platters are *plated* rather than coated. Plating applies pure metal, such as nickel, to the platter either by vaporizing it or using a technique called *sputtering*, in which the film is applied in a vacuum chamber. The process may be chemical, or the platters may be electroplated.

One way that plating differs from coating is that the plating process does not require a binding agent. The binding agent causes the oxide particles to be much farther apart on coated media than they are on plated media. The greater distance between particles, as well as the fact that oxide particles are larger than the metal particles used in plating, means that less data can be stored on the magnetic surface of coated media. Plated media can pack twice the amount of data per inch of surface.

Coated media also are roughly 10 times thicker than plated media, which is why plated media often are called *thin-film media*. The thinner coating enables faster flight of the read/write head over the platter's surface.

Tracks are concentric rings on each platter's surface that store data. Both sides of a platter have an identical number of tracks. The more tracks per platter, the greater the storage capacity of the disk. The outermost track on a disk is referred to as track 0, the next is track 1, and so on. Tracks are imprinted on the disk's surface when the hard drive is manufactured.

A vertical column of aligned tracks on a disk is known as a *cylinder* (see fig. 1.1). When several platters are stacked on top of one another in a hard disk, a cylinder consists of the tracks in a specific location on all the platters. Cylinders use the same numbering scheme as tracks. The outermost cylinder is cylinder 0, the next is cylinder 1, the next is cylinder 2, and so on. The layer of track 5s, for example, is known as cylinder 5.

Each track on the hard disk is divided further into sectors, which are designated during the *low-level* or *physical* format. A *sector* is a segment of the track that holds 512 bytes of data. (Some disk partitioning systems, however, change this number.) During the low-level format, any bad or unusable sectors are marked so that the operating system doesn't try to store data on them. When you buy a hard disk as part of a system, the low-level format already has been completed. If you purchase a hard disk, you may have to use a utility program to do this task yourself. But most of you will never have to perform a low-level format.

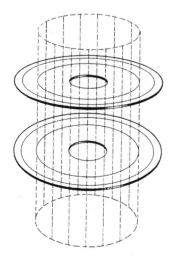

FIG. 1.1

A group of aligned tracks representing a cylinder.

The first few bytes of each sector contain the sector's identifying number, which is known as the *sector header*.

The number of sectors per track varies according to the drive's data-encoding method. Newer technologies can pack more sectors on a track. An ST-506 drive with MFM encoding, for example, typically has 17 sectors per track, a drive with RLL encoding has 24 to 26 sectors per track, and an ESDI drive typically has 35 sectors per track. Figure 1.2 shows a diagram of the relationship between tracks and sectors.

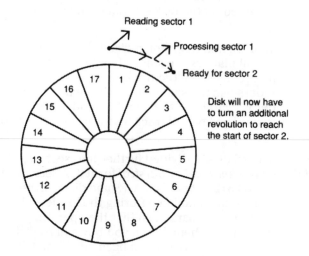

FIG. 1.2

Viewing the sectors on a disk.

Tracks, sectors, and cylinders all exist to help DOS find information on the hard disk. In the next section, you learn how the hard disk stores information.

Understanding How the Hard Disk Stores Data

When the computer is turned on, the platters are spinning constantly around a central spindle, like records on a jukebox. Floppy disks spin at 300 or 360 revolutions per minute (RPM) depending on the type of drive, but hard disk platters zip along at 3600 RPM, or 60 revolutions every second. (The newest hard disks spin at about 4000 RPM.)

Information gets to and from a platter by means of a *read/write head*, which passes over the spinning platter and either writes a bit of information to the surface or reads a bit of information from it. A hard disk usually has one read/write head for each platter side. Figure 1.3 shows a cutaway of the interior of a hard drive.

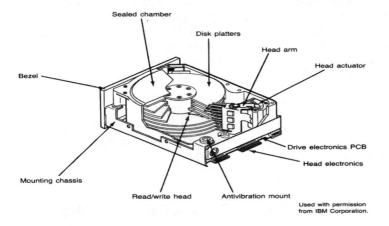

Sealed chamber

Disk platters

Head arm

Head actuator

Bezel

Drive electronics PCB

Head electronics

Mounting chassis

Read/write head   Antivibration mount

Used with permission
from IBM Corporation.

FIG. 1.3

The interior of a hard disk drive mechanism.

Note in the figure that the read/write heads are attached to an element called the head actuator. In the next section, you learn how this mechanism works.

Examining the Head Actuator

The *head actuator* controls the movement of the read/write heads. Because they are connected to a single mechanism, they move in tandem. When one read/write head is positioned over track 5, for example, all the platters' read/write heads are positioned over track 5 for their respective platter sides. The head actuator can be one of two types: a *stepper-motor actuator* (sometimes called an open-loop system) or a *voice-coil actuator* (sometimes called a closed-loop system).

Stepper-motor actuators, which are the same mechanisms found in floppy drives, derive their name from the fact that the motor moves a discrete step at a time, much like the movement of a watch hand on an analog watch. This type of head actuator rarely is found in newer hard drives.

Voice-coil actuators, in contrast, use magnetic force to move the read/write heads back and forth over the platters. Information to help the read/write heads find the proper area of the disk's surface is stored directly on the disk's surface, like a map, because the voice-coil read/write head isn't just clicking to a set position the way a stepper-motor read/write head does.

Typically up to twice as fast as stepper-motor actuators, voice-coil actuators are found in most of the hard drives built today. Besides speed, voice-coil actuators have another advantage over stepper-motor actuators: voice-coil actuators are less sensitive to temperature changes. Temperature changes sometimes can throw stepper-motor read/write heads off the track, because they're moving the same amount of steps even though the platter underneath them is expanding and contracting because of heating and cooling, thereby causing the data to shift. When this misalignment occurs, hard disk utilities are necessary to realign the data on the tracks.

Yet another advantage of voice-coil actuators is the fact that they offer automatic parking of the drive heads. When not in use, the read/write heads should be parked—kept on a data-free landing zone. You can use various software programs to keep the heads parked if your hard drive doesn't have a voice-coil actuator.

Understanding the Controller's Role

Although the head actuator is responsible for moving the read/write heads, the *disk-drive controller* is responsible for telling the heads which areas to read or write.

The drive controller also transfers data back and forth between the disk drive and the rest of the system and performs what's known as *data separation*, the translation process necessary to transform the stream of electronic signals generated by the magnetic surface to the digital 1s and 0s the computer can process.

Another responsibility of the controller is error detection and correction. When reading data from a segment of the disk, the controller also performs a *cyclic redundancy check* (CRC). Whenever data is written to the disk, DOS tacks some error-checking information to the end of the data before it is passed along to the controller. Then when the controller reads the data from the disk, the controller performs the same error check and compares its results to the results of the stored data. If the values don't match, DOS generates an error message, marks that sector (segment) as bad, stores the data somewhere else, and performs another check. (DOS's role is discussed in more depth in Chapter 3, "Understanding How DOS Works with the Hard Disk.")

In some hard drives, such as the ST-506/412 and ESDI drives, the controller is on a separate board; in other drives, such as the SCSI and IDE drives, it's built directly into the hard drive. For more information on these drive types, see "Examining Types of Hard Drives" in this chapter.

Reading from and Writing to Disk

Learning about disk reads and writes can give you some idea of how all the parts of a hard drive work together. A *write* occurs when you save something. You tell your word processor, for example, to save the article you just wrote for the company newsletter. DOS intercepts this request because part of DOS's job is taking all incoming requests from software programs. DOS then checks to see where space is available on the disk, because DOS also is responsible for keeping track of where data is located on the disk. DOS tells the BIOS (Basic Input/Output System) where the available space is. The BIOS, in turn, tells the disk-drive controller which space is available, and the controller tells the read/write head where to deposit the data.

A *read* is the same process in reverse. You tell your word processing program to load the article you wrote so that you can edit it. Your request is passed on to DOS. DOS looks up the location of your article, tells the disk-drive controller via the BIOS where to find the article and to deposit it in RAM so that you can work on it. This entire process happens in the blink of an eye, although DOS might have gone through a dozen steps to find the data.

Reads and writes are rather synchronized ballets when you stop to think about it. But here's the most impressive thing about the hard disk's read/write heads: unlike the read/write heads that work with floppy disks, the read/write heads on a hard disk don't touch the disk's surface. Instead, they float on a cushion of air created by the rapidly spinning platter. This air cushion is less than the width of a human hair. (Someone once explained it as the equivalent of a 747 cruising along at 800 miles per hour a foot or two above the ground.) And this design translates to less wear and tear on the hard disk.

You may be wondering how data crosses the gap, small as it is, between the read/write head and the platter's surface. Here is where the magnetic properties of the hard disk come into play. Remember, the platter's surface is treated with a magnetic substance. The read/write heads also are magnetic. The read/write head and platter come close enough together to influence each other's magnetic fields, making reads and writes possible.

Another question you may be asking is, "What exactly is the read/write head reading and writing?" The head isn't recording the sentences you type into your word processing program. Remember, computers don't speak English; they don't even speak programming languages, such as BASIC. Computers speak plain old binary language, in which everything is either a 1 or a 0, on or off. But how does that structure fit with magnetic fields, which generate electrically charged pulses?

When the read/write head passes over the disk in a read, the head's own magnetic field is not active. It simply picks up the electronic signals generated by the magnetic field on the disk surface and passes them back through the controller to RAM. In a write, the read/write head's magnet changes the magnetic pattern on the disk's surface to match the on-off pattern passed along from the computer's memory. This shift in polarity is known as a *flux change*. The smallest segment of the platter's surface that can hold one of these flux changes is known as a *magnetic domain*.

Watching Out for Head Crashes

You can see how the tiniest particle of dust would mess up this delicate balance. Not only would it cause a rough landing for the read/write head, but also the ensuing friction could scrape data right off the surface of the disk. To protect against that problem, hard disks are assembled in special clean rooms and sealed so that no particles can get into the hard-disk assembly.

Because of the dangers of dust, you should never take apart a hard disk. You can remove the sealed hard disk assembly and replace it, but don't open it up. The only exception, of course, is if it's already damaged and you just want to see what it looks like. A crashed disk looks kind of like what a CD would look like if you took after it with a fork.

The other danger to hard disks is from sudden jolts, which also can cause the read/write head to slam into the disk's surface. Such collisions are appropriately known as *head crashes*.

The results of a head crash can be much worse than the erasure of a file. When you erase a file—accidentally or not—you can get it back (see Chapter 12, "Raiders of the Lost Data"). When data has been scraped off the magnetic coating, you may as well kiss your data good-bye. But you can take some common-sense precautions to avoid head crashes. For more information, see Chapter 11, "Preventing Trouble."

Now that you have a feel for how hard drives work, you're ready to examine the different types of hard drives that are available. The following section introduces you to the ST-506/412, ESDI, SCSI, and IDE hard disk types.

Examining Types of Hard Drives

This section doesn't plumb the depths of the internal architectures of the various types of hard disks. As was mentioned in the introduction, the intention isn't to turn you into a hardware mechanic. You do see in this section, however, brief sketches about what makes each drive different. Knowing the IDE from the SCSI can help you become an informed shopper, something that is covered in more depth in the next chapter.

Comparing Device-Level and System-Level Interfaces

Before you get into the specifics of each hard disk type, you need to be aware that the types fall into two basic categories: device-level interfaces and system-level interfaces. In computerese, *interface* means a translator. An interface is any device or software that enables one component to communicate with another component. Computers are jam-packed with interfaces. The BIOS is DOS's interface for the system hardware. DOS is the interface for your word processing program. The disk-drive controller is the interface between the analog stream of magnetic information on the disk and the digital-speaking computer.

In a *device-level interface*, the controller acts as an intermediary, taking the raw data from the disk and decoding the data so that the microprocessor can understand it. The ST-506/412 and ESDI interfaces are device-level interfaces.

In a *system-level interface*, the data separation (decoding) takes place on the drive itself, and no intermediary controller card is necessary. The data is sent directly to the system in a form the microprocessor can understand. SCSI and IDE are system-level interfaces.

Examining the ST-506/412 Interface

The granddaddy of PC hard drive interfaces, the ST-506/412 interface was developed in about 1980 by Seagate Technologies. Its first implementation was in a drive called the ST-506, and a later implementation was the ST-412; hence the combined ST-506/412. The ST-506/412 interface quickly became the standard for hard drives, with such well-known disk manufacturers as Western Digital adopting its technology.

The ST-506/412, however, has the slowest data transfer rate of the four interfaces discussed in this chapter. The peak data transfer rate refers to how quickly the drive can get data back to you after you request it. The rate is often expressed in megabits (rather than megabytes) per second because of the interface's origin with the ST-506 drive. The ST-506 uses a *serial* interface, which means that it can transfer only one bit of data at a time rather than an entire byte (eight bits). (The data transfer rate also is sometimes measured in MegaHertz.)

The ST-506/412 interface uses two different types of data-encoding schemes: MFM (Modified Frequency Modulation) and RLL (Run Length Limited). The data-encoding scheme is the method used to translate data from digital information (1s and 0s) into magnetic patterns for storage on the disk.

MFM encoding, with a maximum data transfer rate of 5 megabits per second, was the first encoding scheme to be used on ST-506/412s. MFM encoding typically is used by floppy drives as well as many ST-506/412 hard drives. The data transfer rate was just about an even match for XT-class PCs, PCs that use the 8088 microprocessor, because the original microprocessor had a clock speed of 4.77 MHz. But 286-based PCs can have clock speeds of 16 MHz, and 386-based PCs can have clock speeds of up to 40 MHz. For this reason, the ST-506/412 is being replaced by other technologies. Although it still is widely used, given the installed base of PCs, the ST-506/412 basically is being phased out in favor of the IDE (Integrated Drive Electronics) interface.

RLL encoding packs 50 percent more data than MFM encoding on the same amount of disk surface. Drives that use RLL encoding are capable of transferring more data at once than MFM drives—7.5 megabits per second.

Advanced run-length-limited (ARLL) is a later, more refined version of the RLL standard. ARLL packs even more data on the disk than RLL and has an even faster data transfer rate (9 megabits per second).

NOTE   All the data transfer rates given in the previous paragraphs are theoretical rates. True transfer rates are much lower.

Examining the ESDI (Enhanced Small Device Interface)

The ESDI interface came along in 1983. It was developed by Maxtor Corporation in conjunction with other manufacturers for use in both hard drives and tape drives. (Tape drives are used to back up data when floppies aren't enough to do the job; for more information, see Chapter 10, "Understanding the Importance of Backing Up.")

Like the ST-506/412, the ESDI drive uses a serial interface, with only one bit transferred at a time. But ESDI stores more information on a disk and boasts a faster data transfer rate than the ST-506/412. The ESDI data transfer rate is typically 10 to 15 megabits per second, although it can go up to 24 megabits per second. Because of this faster data transfer rate, ESDI often is found on higher-capacity drives and systems with faster microprocessors. (XTs, for example, are most likely to have an ST-506/412 hard drive; systems with the faster 386 microprocessor are more likely to have ESDI hard drives.)

ESDI, like the ST-506/412 interface for smaller drives, is fading to a lesser extent in the high-capacity drive arena and is being replaced by SCSI (Small Computer Systems Interface) drives.

Examining the SCSI (Small Computer Systems Interface)

The concept of SCSI (pronounced "scuzzy") can be a little confusing because it doesn't refer just to hard drives. SCSI is a bus interface that eliminates the need for separate add-on cards for each device added.

Typically, when you add a hardware device to your PC, you have to add a card to the expansion bus so that your PC can communicate with the device. With SCSI, you don't have to. You simply install one card, called a *host adapter*, which can run simultaneously up to seven SCSI peripherals, such as hard disk drives, printers, and scanners.

The SCSI interface first gained popularity in the Apple Macintosh realm, because many Macintoshes don't have any expansion slots. Today, SCSI is becoming more widely used on the IBM side of the fence as well, because it's such a flexible interface.

SCSI hard drives offer several advantages over traditional hard disk technologies. They're very fast because they use a parallel data-transfer method rather than the serial method used by ESDI and ST-506/412. Data transfer rates for SCSI vary, ranging anywhere from 2 to 20 megabits per second. For this reason, many fast, high-end systems with large-capacity drives are turning to the SCSI interface.

SCSI drives are also smart. With the ESDI and ST-506/412, the controllers have to tell the drive mechanism not just where the data is but how to find it. The process is like taking a taxi and having to give the driver not only the address of your destination but directions on how to get there. In contrast, SCSI controllers just say "go to this address on the hard disk," and the drive finds it.

Examining the IDE (Integrated Drive Electronics) Interface

The IDE drive came about in the late 1980s, thanks in large part to Compaq. The IDE interface, also called the ATA (for AT bus Attachment) interface, is another up and comer in the world of hard disks. The IDE controller circuitry is housed directly in the drive.

The IDE controller can support two drives at once, which can be connected to an IDE socket built into the motherboard or to a host adapter card called a *paddleboard*.

IDE drives are rapidly gaining favor as a less expensive alternative to the controller card/drive combination. IDE drives are compact and use less power than other types of drives, so they rapidly gained favor on portables. But because they are less expensive, they have caught on with desktop models as well. In fact, IDE drives have nearly taken over the bulk of the PC market.

If you buy a garden-variety PC today, it probably will have an IDE hard drive. Higher-capacity drives of 600M and above are more likely to be ESDI or SCSI drives, but anything less than that is likely to be an IDE drive.

Some new computer motherboards have IDE connections built in, but those that don't can use the paddleboard. Some older technologies, however, may not be compatible. If you have an older machine, you may need to upgrade the BIOS if you want to add an IDE drive. Keep in mind that XTs do not work well with IDE drives.

Summary

In this chapter, you have learned about some basic PC components and terms as well as the main features of hard disks, how they work, and why they're important.

Hard disks offer large amounts of permanent storage, in contrast to both RAM, which is temporary, and floppy disks, which are limited in the amount they can store and also are less rugged than hard disks.

Hard disks store information on magnetically treated disks called platters. Information is written to and read from each rapidly spinning platter by means of a magnetic read/write head. Because the head has to come close enough to the disk's surface to detect or change its magnetic pattern without touching the surface, hard disks must be manufactured in special clean rooms and then sealed to protect the disk platters from dust and other particles.

DOS is responsible for knowing where information is stored on the hard disk. DOS tells the BIOS where the information is located. The BIOS, in turn, tells the disk controller where to find or deposit data, and the controller directs the read/write heads to the proper area of the disk and performs the magnetic-digital translation.

This chapter also has introduced you to the different types of hard drives from which you can choose. The ST-506/412 interface is the original interface that has since become a standard. Today, the ST-506/412 is found on smaller drives in older machines, although it has been replaced by the faster, more compact IDE drive on new machines. Large-capacity drives typically use the faster ESDI or SCSI interfaces instead. The IDE and SCSI drives have the disk controller functions built into the drive itself, thereby freeing up slots for use by other boards.

In the next chapter, you explore the hard disk in more depth, by examining performance factors and identifying some purchasing considerations.

Choosing a Hard Disk: Self-Defense for Buyers

I f you're like most people, the first hard disk you purchase will be part of a complete computer system, where many of the decisions already have been made for you. In this instance, your biggest concern is probably storage capacity, followed by processing speed.

When you decide to add a second drive or upgrade your old drive, you have more compatibility issues to consider. This chapter is intended to acquaint you with some of the terminology you may run into when you read ads or talk to salespeople during your search for a hard disk. That way, when the time comes to buy your system or hard drive, you can do so with confidence.

In this chapter, you also take a brief look at alternative storage technologies, such as hard disk cards, which are handy if you don't have room in your PC for a drive; removable hard disk cartridge systems, which are good for security or if you need to transport a large quantity of data; and optical technologies, which are used for reference or audit trails.

Deciding How Much Storage You Need

Determining your storage needs is probably your number one concern. The short answer to how much storage you need is *as much as you possibly can afford*. As far as conventional wisdom goes, definitions of what constitutes enough of anything in the computer industry seem to change almost weekly, and hard disks are no exception.

Although the 10M hard disk that came with the original IBM PC/XT seemed like more storage than anyone could ever want, these days 40M is considered an absolute minimum for a hard disk. You see 40M disks on many garden-variety 386SX-class machines and even on quite a few portables. On desktop models, 65M and 80M hard drives are becoming more common for everyday users, and 200M drives are reported to be doing well.

Quite frankly, you probably don't want to even consider accepting 40M for a desktop model unless you're certain that you will never want to do more than just word processing or keeping a small database. And not many users store only one application on the PC.

You might be surprised at how quickly that 40M gets gobbled up by programs. Take a look at a hypothetical small business that uses a 40M hard disk, and you can see exactly where the megabytes go.

T I P For the purposes of this example, the sample disk can hold 40M *after* formatting. When a disk is formatted to work with DOS, roughly 15 percent of the disk's space is taken up for the indexing information that helps DOS find data on the disk. When you see a disk advertised as 40M, find out whether it's 40M before or after formatting. If it's before formatting, you have only 34M left after formatting. And as you will see shortly, every megabyte counts!

Suppose that your business first purchases WordPerfect, which comes on twelve 5 1/4-inch or six 3 1/2-inch floppy disks. When you install all that information on your hard disk, 4.5M of disk space is consumed. Although WordPerfect has a fairly good spell-checker, suppose that you aren't overly comfortable with your written grammar. You decide that you want a product that checks your grammar and your writing style, because you want to make a good impression on your clients. You purchase Que Software's RightWriter for Windows. Kiss another megabyte of disk space good-bye.

Now your letters and reports are covered, but suppose that you also need a database to keep track of your clients. You want a fairly friendly product because you're buying only one computer, so you choose Borland's Paradox SE, which is designed for the first-time database buyer. Subtract another megabyte of disk space.

Suppose also that you need something to keep track of your expenses, so you decide to look at spreadsheets. Lotus 1-2-3, the top-selling spreadsheet, takes up 5M if you install the graphics features.

But you need one more thing. Because you want to produce promotional fliers and a quarterly newsletter for your clients, you need a desktop publishing program. You have heard a great deal about Microsoft Publisher, so you buy it. Publisher consumes 1.5M of storage space.

Oh, and you want to practice safe computing. You want to be prepared for any disaster, so you purchase the Norton Utilities (2.7M). But you also want to have fun, so you pick up a copy of the Far Side Calendar by Amaze!Inc (1.5M).

The PC you purchased already had DOS 5.0 and Windows 3.0 installed, so you started out with roughly a 10M deficit. The grand total of disk space consumed comes to 27.2M, and you haven't even created any files yet! You're likely to want other software programs, too, such as games or personal information managers. You have to remember that the graphics that make programs friendly also make them hungry for disk space.

You can understand why starting out with more than 40M is a good idea. Scrimp on everything else if you have to, but never scrimp on the amount of storage. Looking for the right hard disk is almost like buying a house. Do you honestly know anyone who has too much closet space?

Measuring Speed and Performance

Chapter 1, "A Hard Disk Primer," briefly explains the hard disk's structure, but making purchasing decisions requires a little more information. If you're concerned with the hard disk's speed, you need to know about the concepts discussed in the following paragraphs, including the data transfer rate, average access time, the mean time between failures, and track-to-track seek time. After reading about these different measures of a hard disk's performance, you can understand better what the ads are talking about, whether you're shopping for a PC, a replacement drive, or a second drive.

Checking the Data Transfer Rate

The *data transfer rate*, or the measurement of how quickly the hard drive can move data into RAM, is one measure of a hard disk's performance. One thing to keep in mind about the advertised data transfer rate is that it's the peak transfer rate, or best-case scenario. The true rate at which a hard disk system transfers data depends on other factors, such as the interleave (which is discussed in this chapter's section on "Understanding How the Interleave Affects Performance"), the disk controller, the bus speed, the CPU speed, and so on.

Understanding Average Access Time

Average access time, also called average seek time, is another indication of the hard drive's performance. This value is the performance measure you're most likely to see in an advertisement for a hard disk. Average access time is the average amount of time the read/write head takes to get to any random data on the disk. Because in one instance that data may be as close as the neighboring bit and in another may be on the farthest reaches of the platter, an average is taken.

T I P   Average access time is particularly important if you're doing a great deal of database work. Databases tend to have small chunks of information scattered throughout a disk, unlike such programs as spreadsheets that tend to work with larger, sequential chunks of data.

Average access time is measured in milliseconds, or thousandths of a second, typically abbreviated *ms* or *msec*. Most hard drives today have an average access time ranging between 18 and 28 milliseconds. (Practically all 100M and larger drives have average access times of under 20 milliseconds, so if you purchase a large drive you don't have to worry about the average access time.) If you have an older machine, a slower drive is acceptable because the microprocessor is also slower. If you purchase your drive as part of a new system, the drive more than likely has a fast IDE drive anyway.

NOTE   The average access times you see are typically for 20M partitions. Large drives are set up with small partitions before tests are performed. Times are slower if partitions are larger.

After finding the correct track, the read/write head still has to wait for the correct data to move into position beneath it. This waiting period is called *drive latency*. If you encounter this term in an ad or when talking to a salesperson, don't worry about that value; it isn't a measure of disk performance because it's the same for almost every drive. Because most drives spin at the same rate, most have the same drive latency (8.33 ms). Drive latency is also an average figure based on how long the drive takes to complete half a rotation.

Analyzing the Mean Time Between Failures (MTBF)

Another term sometimes used in advertisements is MTBF, which stands for *mean time between failures*. This term represents the average time before a hard drive can be expected to fail in some way and is thus an estimate of life expectancy.

MTBF ratings usually are expressed in tens of thousands of hours. Expect to see MTBF ratings somewhere between 15,000 and 30,000 hours, although some MTBF ratings go as high as 50,000 hours. MTBF is somewhat of a manufacturer's best guess as to how long the drive will last, so the rating doesn't mean a great deal in terms of concrete protection. Although you may feel better getting a drive with a longer MTBF rating, the warranty or guarantee that comes with the drive is much more important.

Measuring Track-to-Track Seek Time

Another measure of disk performance you may encounter in ads is *track-to-track seek time*. You don't see this term as often as the average access time and data transfer rate, however, which are the two measurements to which you need to pay more attention.

Unlike average access time, which measures how long the drive takes to find data located anywhere on the disk, track-to-track seek time measures how long the drive takes to go from one track to an adjacent track.

Typically, drives that use voice-coil actuators have a lower track-to-track seek time than drives that use stepper-motor actuators.

Understanding How the Interleave Affects Performance

The *interleave* is specified during the low-level format and refers to the way sectors are organized on the surface of a disk. Interleaves vary. In advertisements, interleaves are listed in the form of ratios, such as 1:1, 2:1, or 3:1. In a 1:1 interleave, the sectors are organized sequentially, or contiguously. Sector 2 is next to sector 1, sector 3 is next to sector 2, and so on. In a 2:1 interleave, every other sector is skipped. That is, you have sector 1, then another sector, then sector 2, then another sector, then sector 3, and so on, all the way around the disk. Figure 2.1 shows three interleave examples.

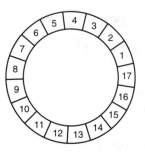

1:1 Interleave

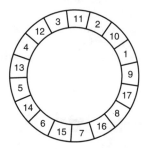

2:1 Interleave

FIG. 2.1

Comparing different
types of interleave.

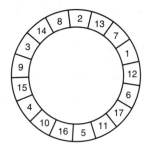

3:1 Interleave

The reasoning behind a 2:1 or higher interleave is to give slower hard
disks a fighting chance. Remember, you have this read/write head zipping along over the rapidly spinning disk surface, looking for the sectors
that contain the information the system needs. If the hard disk is slow, it
cannot handle a 1:1 interleave, because by the time the disk takes that
fraction of a second to save sector 1 and come back for sector 2, sector 2
already has gotten away from it, and the read/write head has to wait
until sector 2 passes by again. By staggering the sectors, you increase
the odds that the drive will catch sector 2 as it passes instead of having
to wait a full revolution.

Typically, the slower the machine, the higher the interleave. XT drives with interleave ratios of 5:1 or 6:1 weren't uncommon. The faster disks matched to faster microprocessors have faster interleaves. IDE and SCSI drives, for example, have 1:1 interleaves.

You shouldn't always assume that the machine you purchase has the best possible interleave for its setup. Fine-tuning the interleave can produce dramatic improvements in performance, as you find out in Chapter 9, "Exploring Hard Disk Fitness Programs." Some good software programs on the market can help you determine the best interleave for your machine.

T I P

Disk utility programs that are used to optimize the interleave by re-aligning the sectors (in effect, performing a safe low-level format) should not be used on IDE drives or SCSI drives, which are both known as translating drives. The reason is that low-level format programs attempt to take control of what they expect to be standard hardware, and both IDE and SCSI drives are hardware imposters. Both of them use nonstandard interfaces but pretend to be standard so that the computer can work with them.

IDE drives can "read" your system, determine what kind of setup it has, and then emulate that setup. SCSI drives are even more complex. They're sophisticated expansion buses in their own right, and, where DOS and the BIOS speak in clusters and sectors, SCSI speaks in blocks. Some elaborate translation has to take place among the three of them.

Although the utility programs warn you if you're trying to safe-format a translating drive, in the case of some older IDE drives, the programs don't even know that they're dealing with translating drives. A real mess can ensue, because an IDE drive probably has more tracks and sectors than the program thinks it has, and an SCSI drive doesn't have tracks or sectors at all.

Considering Disk Caches and Buffers

You may see some drives advertised as including disk caches; others are advertised as having buffers. Both disk caches and buffers are methods of using memory to enhance disk speed.

A *disk cache* is a portion of memory set aside to hold frequently requested information and thus speed up access to the hard disk. When the computer requests data from the hard disk, the controller checks the cache memory before checking the disk. If the cache doesn't contain the data the system is requesting (known as a "hit" in computer lingo), the controller proceeds to perform the slower disk access (known as a "miss"). Most of the drives that ship with 386 and 486 PCs include disk caches, with 32K and 64K caches common.

Two types of disk caches exist: software and hardware. Both types use memory to supplement disk storage, but software caches use the system's memory, whereas hardware caches (caching controllers) contain their own memory, freeing the system's memory for other tasks. Freeing up memory is important because memory is just as precious as disk storage. Disk storage gives you the elbow room to save a program, but memory gives you the elbow room to run it. You may think, then, that hardware caches are preferable. As always, however, trade-offs exist. Caching controllers free system memory, but then you cannot use their memory for anything else. They also cost a great deal more than software caches—anywhere from $500 to $2,000.

> **NOTE** Software and hardware caches are discussed in more depth in Chapter 8, "Using Memory To Speed Up Your Disk." They are mentioned in this chapter only because you may be confronted with these terms when you're shopping for a system or a replacement drive.

The terms cache and buffer sometimes are used interchangeably by salespeople and dealers. In the broadest sense, the two terms are synonymous. The bottom line is that both buffers and caches use memory for temporary storage, and getting data from memory always takes less time than getting data from a mechanical disk. But you should know that you're dealing with an intelligence spectrum here. Caches are smarter than buffers. Think of a *buffer* as simply a waiting room for data. All controllers contain buffers. In a read, a controller that employs a simple buffer reads the information that was requested and places it in the buffer until the CPU is ready to process the data.

> **NOTE** DOS also contains buffers, which are used to hold data that has been read from a disk. After performing a read, the controller passes its contents along to the DOS buffers, by means of the CPU in AT and above machines and by means of a special chip called the Direct Memory Access (DMA) chip in XT-class machines.

A *read-ahead buffer* takes the process a step further. A read-ahead buffer reads the requested data and also reads more neighboring data than is necessary until the buffer is filled, in hopes that the buffer will contain whatever the system asks for next. Not a lot of discrimination takes place here. Unlike the cache, the buffer doesn't consider whether the excess data has been requested once, twice, or never.

You may encounter the term *full-track buffer* as you scour the ads looking for the disk of your dreams. This type of buffer is one that is large enough to hold an entire track. During a read, the full-track buffer grabs the entire track containing the requested data. During a write, the buffer typically is emptied and the contents written to disk when the entire buffer is filled.

As you can see, buffers typically aren't too gifted. A cache, on the other hand, is like a great waitress—the kind who remembers from your last visit that you take your coffee black and magically appears with the pot the second you have emptied your cup. Caches work hard to anticipate what the system is going to ask for next. They discriminate in what they store. They hold information that recently has been requested, figuring that the system probably will ask for it again, and typically, the system does. Computers are creatures of habit; they often work with the same small chunk of data for several operations before they need another chunk of data. When the system requests a new piece of data, the cache dumps out its previous contents and stores the new data in the cache. If you plan to use programs that need data scattered all over the disk, such as database programs, a cache can be more helpful than a buffer.

Comparing Internal to External Drives

Yet another decision is choosing between an internal or an external drive. If you're purchasing a second or replacement drive and your computer doesn't have an available drive bay or expansion slot for a hard disk on a card, the answer is simple: you need an external drive.

External drives are easier to install because you don't have to open up the computer. They typically are more expensive, however, because you're paying for extras, such as a power supply. Internal drives use the computer's power supply; external drives have their own power supply.

Among internal drives, IDE drives are probably the easiest to install. Because the controller is inside the drive, you need only one cable rather than the two cables necessary with the ESDI or the ST-506/412 interface.

Looking at Price per Megabyte

If you are adding a second or replacement hard drive, you probably are especially sensitive to the drive's price, because you more than likely will purchase your first hard drive as part of a package deal. But price, of course, is always an issue.

The good news here is that the price per megabyte of hard disk storage is dropping. Even better news is that the larger the drive, the less the price per megabyte of storage. Current dealer prices at the time of this writing place 20M drives at around $129, or roughly $6.50 per megabyte; 40M drives in the $200 range ($5 per megabyte); and 80M IDE drives in the $300 range ($3.75 per megabyte). (This trend doesn't mean, however, that if you buy a large enough drive the manufacturer will owe you money.)

Finally, don't forget to ask about things like warranty and technical support. These concerns may seem too obvious to mention, but with computers you easily can get so caught up trying to follow the techie stuff that you forget about the common-sense angle—particularly if you're new at it.

Replacing Your Disk or Adding a Second Disk

Despite your best efforts at purchasing just the right disk for your needs, you probably will end up needing more storage at some point. Luckily, adding or replacing a disk is not difficult, but it does involve some special considerations. This section gives you some guidelines on what to think about, such as matching compatibility, data transfer rate, and form factor fit. For the lowdown on installation, you again may want to refer to Scott Mueller's *Upgrading and Repairing PCs*, 2nd Edition, published by Que Corporation.

Ensuring Compatibility among Components

When the time has come for you to replace your drive or add a second disk drive, you want to pay careful attention to the type of system, drive, and controller you currently have. Compatibility is a significant concern.

First, you need to make sure that the type of system you have supports the type of hard drive you want to add. Suppose that you want to add an IDE drive. If you have a newer computer, it may have a built-in IDE connection. If not, you need to purchase a host adapter card (sometimes called a *paddleboard*).

Then you want to make sure that your controller supports the drive. Some controllers can control two drives, so you might not have to purchase a controller for your second drive. ST-506/412, IDE, and ESDI controllers, for example, can work with two drives, although IDE drives can become picky about which one is the primary (master) drive.

You cannot, however, mix and match drives and controllers willy-nilly. ESDI drives have to work with ESDI controllers, for example. You cannot buy an ESDI drive and expect your old ST-506/412 MFM controller to work with it.

You also may encounter trouble if you try mixing and matching certain brands of IDE drives. IDEs aren't the standard interface that ESDI and ST-506/412 are, at least not yet, and different brands may not be compatible with each other. Your best bet may be to purchase all your drives from the same manufacturer.

Because of all the variables involved, don't hesitate to ask for help from a knowledgeable friend or a dealer. Installing the drive isn't as tricky as making sure that everything you have works with everything you want to add.

Remembering the BIOS

Another element to consider is the BIOS. If you purchase a new system, you don't have to worry about it. But if you want to upgrade from an older drive to a newer technology such as IDE, you need to make sure that your PC's BIOS is compatible with it.

As was discussed in Chapter 1, "A Hard Disk Primer," the BIOS is a set of basic operating system instructions that communicates directly with all hardware. Part of the information contained in the BIOS is a list of the hard disk types with which it can communicate. You need to be sure that your BIOS supports the type of drive you want to purchase. To be on the safe side, when you're shopping for a replacement hard disk, tell the dealer what type of BIOS your current system has. (When the system first boots up, the BIOS name appears in the upper-left corner of the screen. The message says something like ROM BIOS 1990, American Megatrends Inc. Make sure that it says ROM BIOS because a VGA BIOS also may flash on-screen.)

If the date of your BIOS doesn't appear when your PC boots up, you can find out how old the BIOS is by typing **debug** at the DOS prompt and pressing Enter. (If that command doesn't work, type **cd dos** at the prompt and press Enter to change to the DOS directory. Then retry the DEBUG command.) DEBUG is a DOS program that enables you to test executable files, or files that carry out instructions.

At the DEBUG prompt that appears (a hyphen), enter **D F000:F000**. A string of letters and numbers appears, with the BIOS date on the far right of the screen. To exit DEBUG, press Q at the hyphen prompt and then press Enter.

The age of the BIOS affects compatibility more than the kind of BIOS does. (Most BIOS come from Phoenix Technologies, Award Software, AMI, American Megatrends, or IBM.) Sometimes if you upgrade a machine that has an older BIOS to an IDE drive, for example, you get a Drive not ready error message.

You can check with your dealer or the company that manufactured your PC's motherboard to see whether a BIOS upgrade can help. You can upgrade your PC's BIOS for around $50—less than the cost of most software.

NOTE One of DOS's hidden files, IO.SYS, is the portion of DOS that handles input and output through *device drivers*—operating instructions that tell the computer how to communicate with hardware devices, such as hard drives, printers, and mice. IO.SYS sometimes is referred to as the DOS BIOS. Although this book at times refers to the BIOS as being the part of DOS that communicates with the hardware, you need to be aware that a difference exists between the ROM BIOS and the IO.SYS file. Both of them are needed to communicate with hardware. (IO.SYS is covered in more detail in Chapter 3, "Understanding How DOS Works with the Hard Disk.")

Matching the Data Transfer Rate to Your PC

When adding or replacing a disk, you also want to pay attention to the data transfer rate. When you're buying a hard disk as part of a system, the elements are usually well matched; the manufacturer takes care of it. When you're purchasing a separate drive, however, you need to be sure that the drive you're buying matches the system you have. You don't want to buy a 10 megabit-per-second ESDI drive for an XT, for example. The XT would have no hope of keeping up. If you put a fast drive on a slow machine, you don't get your money's worth out of the drive.

Considering the Form Factor Fit

Another element to consider when you purchase a second or replacement drive is the *form factor*, which is computerese for the drive's dimensions. Advertisements use phrases like "full height," "half height," and even "one-third height" in reference to drives. (The development of hard drives is an interesting phenomenon—drives are packing more data on each square inch of space, but they're shrinking, just as computers themselves are shrinking.)

Full-height drives are 3 1/4 inches high; half-height drives are 1 1/2 inches in height; and one-third height drives, which also are called low-profile drives, are 1 inch high. Both full-height and half-height drives commonly come in 5 1/4-inch and 3 1/2-inch diameters. Most 60M to 80M drives today come in the 3 1/2-inch form factor. (Even smaller 2 1/2-inch-diameter disk drives are becoming more common in portable computers, and some companies already are manufacturing 1.8-inch-diameter drives.)

You want to make sure that the drive you purchase can fit inside your system, in the *drive bay*. You sometimes can make a smaller drive fit in a larger bay; some 3 1/2-inch hard disks come in larger casings so that they fit in a 5 1/4-inch drive bay. You cannot, however, force a large hard drive into a drive bay that's too small for it.

You also need to make sure that the system even has an available drive bay. If you think that you will ever want a second internal hard drive (or a tape drive), make sure that the PC you purchase has more than one drive bay.

Considering Alternative Storage Technologies

Everything discussed so far in this chapter refers to nonremovable hard disk drives. Alternatives are available, however, including the hard disk on a card and the removable hard disk. A variety of optical storage technologies also is coming into play. The following sections discuss these alternative storage methods.

Using Hard Disk Cards

In a hard disk card, the disk drive is housed directly on the controller board. No cabling is required, which makes the hard disk card easier to install than a full-blown drive. The earliest hard disk cards, like the earliest hard disks, had 10M capacities. Today's models can store anywhere from 40 to 105M. If you have plenty of expansion slots but don't have an extra drive bay, a hard disk on a card can be a good choice. Street prices for hard disks on cards are comparable to separate drives; you may pay only slightly more for a disk on a card.

Although a hard disk card theoretically takes up only one expansion slot, hard disk card design varies enough that you may find two slots taken up. Not every PC is compatible with hard disk cards. Hard disk cards do not work, for example, with PCs that use Micro Channel Architecture. For this reason, check compatibility for your PC before you purchase a hard disk card.

Using Removable Hard Disks

Removable hard disks are removable cartridges that fit into specially designed drives. They're faster than floppy drives and hold more data, anywhere from 20 to 180M. The cartridges provide convenient backup and security (what can be more secure than physically removing your data?), which is discussed in more depth in Chapter 11, "Preventing Trouble," and Chapter 13, "Keeping Your Data Confidential."

One drawback to removable hard disks is price. They can run up to four times the cost of a fixed hard drive with the same capacity. Most of the people who purchase removable hard disks do so for security reasons.

Although other companies use Bernoulli technology to manufacture removable disks, Iomega Corporation's Bernoulli Box is probably the best known. The Bernoulli Box uses hard disk technology in reverse; the disk passes over the read/write head rather than the other way around.

In contrast to a regular hard disk, where a sudden impact causes the read/write head to crash into the disk's surface, the Bernoulli Box's disk falls away from the read/write head when a disturbance occurs. The design is based on the same principle that induces lift on an airplane's wings (known incidentally as the Bernoulli principle).

The Bernoulli Box uses a SCSI interface that requires the Iomega controller card or a standard SCSI adapter card. Either way, you need a free expansion slot.

Exploring Optical Technologies

Several new optical technologies also are rapidly gaining acceptance. They include CD-ROM drives, WORM drives, and magneto-optical, or rewritable optical, drives. These technologies currently are used to supplement magnetic storage, not replace it. Of the three technologies, CD-ROM is the least expensive and is the one you are most likely to purchase. CD-ROMs are used for reference materials, such as encyclopedias. Increasingly, the information they contain includes motion video and sound (called *multimedia*).

Where a hard drive translates changes in a magnetic field to binary 1s or 0s, optical technology uses laser beams to detect changes in the reflectivity of the disk's surface. The reflectivity is affected by pits burned into the disk's surface or by varying degrees of lightness and darkness, with the pits or darkened areas having a different binary value from the smooth or lighter surface areas.

CD-ROM

CD-ROM stands for Compact Disc Read-Only Memory. CD-ROM disks look just like their audio counterparts, but instead of storing music they store up to 550M of data on one disk. To give you some idea of how much information that is, the entire 21-volume *Grolier's Encyclopedia* fits comfortably on one CD-ROM disk.

CD-ROM technology isn't used to store data that you create. Instead, the CD-ROM primarily is used for publishing—housing large databases such as the *Grolier's Encyclopedia*. And CD-ROM drives rapidly are becoming more affordable. At the time of this writing, the Sony Laser Library CD-ROM system, shipped with six reference CDs, including *Compton's Family Encyclopedia* and *Microsoft Bookshelf*, has a suggested list price of $699. You can get a CD-ROM drive for less than $400.

CD-ROM drives are fairly easy to install. You install a card in one of the PC's expansion slots and install a software program, called a *device driver*, that enables the PC to communicate with the CD-ROM.

WORMs and Rewritable Technologies

WORM stands for Write Once Read Many. As the name implies, you can write data to a WORM drive only once; after that, it becomes a read-only medium. WORM drives typically are used where a permanent audit trail is necessary, such as the insurance industry or the medical profession. WORM drives start in the $2,000 to $3,000 range and typically are not purchased by individuals.

In magneto-optical or rewritable optical drives, the newest optical technology, the laser works in conjunction with a magnetic head to write to the disk. The disk surface has a special coating that can be magnetized only when heated. For a read, the laser reads information from the disk just as it does for a CD-ROM or WORM drive. Rewritable drives are the newest and most expensive optical technology. Not many are on the market yet, and they run upwards of $3,000 if you purchase them at a discount.

Looking at the Pros and Cons

Optical technology is not prone to head crashes because it uses beams of light rather than mechanical read/write heads. It also stores much more data in less space than magnetic hard disk technology can. And the transfer rate is generally about 150M per second.

The drawback is that optical technology, particularly CD-ROM technology, is considerably slower than hard disk technology. In 1990, half a second was an average wait time for a CD-ROM drive. That rate is a great deal slower than a hard disk, but on the other hand, it's a great deal faster than looking something up in a dictionary or driving to the nearest library.

Summary

This chapter has given you some guidelines to follow in your search for a hard disk. Whether you're purchasing a hard drive as part of a computer system or as a separate drive, the drive's capacity is probably the most important factor in your decision. Luckily, the price of storage per megabyte decreases as the size of the drive increases.

Another consideration is the drive's performance. You can study different measures of performance, such as the data transfer rate, the mean time between failures, average access time, and track-to-track seek time. The interleave, disk cache, and buffers also affect how quickly the drive can access data.

Probably the biggest consideration of all, however, has nothing to do with the specifications of the disk itself. Whether you purchase your disk drive as part of a system or as an upgrade, your biggest concern should be finding a dealer that you trust. You may prefer working with a local dealer, or you may know of a mail-order dealer with good service and support. Either way, if something goes wrong, you want to know that you have support for your problem.

If you're adding a second disk or a replacement disk, you want to watch for particular items, such as the form factor of the disk you want to add, the number of drive bays in your current system, the type of BIOS your computer uses, and whether the performance level of the drive you want to purchase is a good match for your system.

Alternative technologies also are available, including hard disk cards, removable hard disks, and optical technologies, such as CD-ROM drives, WORM drives, and rewritable or magneto-optical drives. At present, such technologies are used to supplement magnetic storage, not replace it.

This chapter concludes Part I. In Part II, you examine how DOS works with the hard disk and also look at how graphic operating environments, such as the DOS Shell and Microsoft Windows, are changing the way you manage your hard disk.

Operating System and Environment Basics

PART II

OUTLINE

3 Understanding How DOS
Works with the Hard Disk

4 Managing Your Hard Disk in
the Graphical Era

Understanding How DOS Works with the Hard Disk

So far, you have learned about types of hard disks, how they work, and things to watch for when purchasing one. You may have noticed that the subject of DOS kept cropping up in Chapters 1 and 2. Its role is a central and vital one. Without DOS, your computer would just sit there like an expensive, high-tech paperweight.

In this chapter, you begin by looking more closely at the role of the operating system. You examine the basic components of an operating system and learn about the major operating systems used today. Then you get down to brass tacks: how your hard disk is prepared to work with DOS, how to tell whether DOS is installed on your computer when you bring it home, and how to find out which version of DOS is installed on your computer.

Understanding the Role of the Operating System

The operating system is what makes everything work. Without an operating system, you would have to become fluent in machine (binary) language if you wanted to accomplish anything. That approach wouldn't quite give you the increase in productivity for which computers are famous. After all, a big part of the reason you use a computer is to speed up tedious tasks, not make them even more cumbersome.

The operating system helps you out by acting as part traffic cop and part translator. One aspect of the operating system's job is to translate your input, whether by keyboard, mouse, or even voice in some instances, and interpret it for the hardware so that the hardware knows how to respond. Without an operating system, the computer doesn't know or care whether the key you pressed means that it should display a letter, start printing something, or blank out the screen. Imagine that you're speaking English, and the computer is speaking Spanish. The operating system has to be fluent in both.

The traffic cop part comes in because you aren't the only one telling the computer to do something. The computer itself is a collection of hardware, with each piece assuming that it has the right of way. Something has to be responsible for regulating all the components of the computer so that the hard disk doesn't try to stash data in the piece of memory that the video screen is using to display your letter to Aunt Fay in Wichita. That responsible something is the operating system.

The operating system also frees your software programs from being even more bloated than they are now. Software programs are getting bigger all the time because they're becoming so graphics oriented. The pretty pictures and icons that computer users are coming to expect take a great deal of space. The situation would be worse, however, if each of your software programs had to include instructions for communicating with the hard disk and the display monitor. Operating systems manage the disk and display subsystems so that your spreadsheets and word processors don't have to.

Operating systems also perform housekeeping chores, such as managing files. How DOS handles those types of tasks is discussed in more detail in Chapter 5, "Keeping Files Organized," and Chapter 6, "Working with Directories on Your Hard Disk." DOS also enables you to create small programs of your own called *batch files*, which are covered in Chapter 7, "Using Batch Files and Macros."

Examining the Central Components of an Operating System

Although the names vary according to the operating system, all operating systems share common features. They all contain a basic input/output system, a kernel, a command interpreter, and utilities. This book uses DOS for most of the examples, but keep in mind that UNIX, OS/2, and the Mac System all have similar characteristics.

Just as DOS is the layer between your applications and the hardware, DOS itself is layered. The BIOS (Basic Input/Output System) communicates with the hardware, the kernel communicates with the BIOS, and the command interpreter communicates with the kernel. The design is somewhat of a high-tech version of a relay race, with one component of the operating system passing the electronic baton to the next component. The following paragraphs cover these components in more detail.

Examining the BIOS

The *Basic Input/Output System*, or *BIOS*, is a basic set of operating instructions contained on a chip that communicates directly with the hardware, as you learned in Chapter 1, "A Hard Disk Primer." But the BIOS also contains critical start-up functions. In effect, the BIOS gives the wake-up call to the rest of the system when you first turn on your computer. For more information, see this chapter's section on "The Boot Record."

Examining the Kernel

The *kernel* is the part of the operating system that is hidden from you, the user. These hidden, or system, files in DOS are called IO.SYS and MSDOS.SYS (or IBMDOS.COM and IBMBIO.COM in PC DOS). The kernel is responsible for such tasks as loading and running programs, managing memory, formatting disks, and handling the communications between your software applications and the hardware.

As the word "hidden" implies, you never see IO.SYS and MSDOS.SYS when you look in your directory listings unless you use special switches with the DOS ATTRIB command. (Displaying hidden files is discussed briefly in Chapter 6, "Working with Directories on Your Hard Disk.") If you stick with the ordinary directory listings, you cannot erase the system files accidentally because you cannot find them. The importance of the system files cannot be overestimated. Without these files, your system cannot boot up (start), and you cannot use your computer as anything more than a plant stand or a perch for your cat.

The kernel is DOS's central core. Previously you learned that without the operating system, your word processor and spreadsheet would have to contain their own commands for such tasks as sending output to the video display or to a floppy disk—or you would have to know how to write those commands yourself! The kernel is the part of DOS that handles these support tasks, which are managed by related groups of instructions called *service routines*.

Another service routine involves the DOS file-management system. You see a little later in this chapter that DOS has to create a map on the hard disk. This map is necessary in order for DOS to retrieve the data that's stored on the disk. (The tracks and sectors discussed in Chapter 1, "A Hard Disk Primer," are a beginning, but they aren't enough to help DOS find your letter to Aunt Fay, which you discover shortly.)

If that weren't enough, the kernel is also responsible for loading and running programs and managing memory. The kernel is the traffic cop component of the operating system, because it doesn't perform these tasks one at a time. The kernel loads a program, sends input to the display, and keeps an eye on memory usage all at the same time. You can see why the kernel is hidden from casual users who might damage it inadvertently. The kernel is kept safe and sound by its protector, the command interpreter.

Examining the Command Interpreter

In DOS, the *command interpreter* is known as COMMAND.COM. Acting as the translator between you and the DOS kernel, COMMAND.COM fetches the program or command you want and then passes it along to the kernel so that the kernel can do the work.

COMMAND.COM is simply the guardian of the gate to the inner workings of your PC, deciphering your requests, handling them itself if it contains them, or if necessary going to the disk to get them. The command interpreter also refuses your request if it's incorrect. If you type nonsense at the DOS prompt, COMMAND.COM gives you the message, Bad command or file name.

When you type something at the prompt, COMMAND.COM examines your keystrokes, looking for several criteria in a logical order.

The first thing COMMAND.COM does is check against its own list of roughly 40 commands, which are known as *internal commands*. All the commands you use to manage files and directories are examples of internal commands. For more information on specific directory- and file-management commands, see Chapter 6, "Working with Directories on Your Hard Disk."

If what you typed matches one of those internal commands, COMMAND.COM executes your command immediately, without having to search the hard disk. COMMAND.COM is one of the first things loaded into RAM when your computer boots up, and accessing RAM is much faster than accessing a disk.

If what you typed doesn't match COMMAND.COM's list of internal commands, the next thing the command interpreter does is go to the hard disk and search for any files ending in COM. These files are also DOS files, and they're called *external commands* (because they're external to COMMAND.COM). External commands also are known as *utilities*, which are covered in the next section, "Examining the Utilities."

If COMMAND.COM doesn't find any external command files either, it searches for files that end in EXE. The file that runs PKZIP, a data-compression program, for example, is called PKZIP.EXE. (Data compression is covered in Chapter 15, "Understanding Data Compression.")

Finally, if all else fails, COMMAND.COM looks for files that end in BAT. These are batch files, or miniprograms, that you can create by using DOS. (For more on batch files, see Chapter 7, "Using Batch Files and Macros.")

Finally, if what you typed doesn't meet any of these criteria, COMMAND.COM gives up and tells you that what you typed is a Bad command or file name. (Sometimes you see this message even after what you have typed is correct, but if you want to find out why COMMAND.COM is so recalcitrant, you have to read Chapter 6, "Working with Directories on Your Hard Disk.")

Examining the Utilities

The DOS utilities are aptly named, because they're as necessary to good hard disk management as electricity and heat are to maintaining your home. This built-in DOS tool kit includes several commands that help you manage your hard disk. The FDISK command is a necessary element in configuring (setting up) your hard disk. CHKDSK shows you the status of your disk—how large it is, how many bytes are used by files and directories, and so on—and also alerts you to the presence of problems in the file allocation table. FORMAT prepares hard and floppy disks for use with DOS.

These and other DOS utilities are covered throughout this book, so going into them here is unnecessary. For now, you need to know that the utilities perform a wide variety of useful hard disk housekeeping tasks.

Looking at Some Operating Systems

The focus of this book is on DOS because it is the undisputed leader of other operating systems in terms of popularity. But DOS is not the only operating system available. You also examine in the following paragraphs a few other operating systems, including OS/2, UNIX, and the Mac System.

Looking at DOS: Disk Operating System

DOS is used on more than 80 million PCs worldwide (called the installed base in computer marketing lingo). In this section, you learn more about this system and how it came to be. You review the history of DOS and then examine the changes made in the most recent version (5.0).

Having a Quick DOS History Lesson

Microsoft developed the MS-DOS version of DOS that is well known today. Contracting with IBM to create an operating system for IBM's personal computer, Microsoft purchased and developed the program and introduced it in 1981. IBM markets the system as PC DOS, but the two systems are nearly identical.

Other versions of DOS are in use, most notably Digital Research's DR DOS, which at the time of this writing was in its sixth version. DR DOS often is used on portable PCs. MS-DOS, however, is the most widely used DOS overall. When DOS is mentioned in this text with no other qualifiers, it means MS-DOS.

Here's a brief chronology of DOS versions, beginning with 1.0, which made its debut in August 1981:

Version	Change
1.0	Original version
1.25	Accommodates double-sided disks
2.0	Adds support for hard disks
3.0	Adds support for high-capacity floppy disks
3.1	Adds support for networks

Version	Change
3.2	Adds support for 3 1/2-inch floppy disk drives
3.3	Accommodates high-capacity 3 1/2-inch drives
4.0	Introduces the DOS Shell and supports larger partitions
5.0	Introduces the UNDELETE and UNFORMAT commands, improved memory management, improved hard disk management, and an improved Shell

 In this text of this book, DOS refers to DOS 5.0 unless stated otherwise.

Noting Changes in DOS 5.0

Version 5.0, which was released June 11, 1992, is the latest incarnation of DOS. DOS 5.0 introduced some major changes that influence how easily you can manage your computer's hard disk. One of the best is the addition of on-line help for both DOS commands and the Shell, DOS's graphic interface. (For more information on the Shell, which is the part of DOS with which you communicate, see Chapter 4, "Managing Your Hard Disk in the Graphical Era.")

The following paragraphs give you a brief look to get you familiar with some of the changes made in DOS 5.0.

This newest version of DOS offers improved disk drive support in several ways. Like DOS 4.01, Version 5.0 supports partitions (disk segments) larger than 32M. Unlike Version 4.01, however, the SHARE command no longer is required in order to take advantage of large partitions. (With DOS 4.01, the SHARE command was necessary because programs using old file access methods couldn't access the larger partitions.) With Version 5.0, you can establish partitions of up to 2 gigabytes.

DOS 5.0 supports more than two hard disk drives and more than two floppy drives per computer. It also has added support for the new high-density (2.8M) floppy disk drives. Another new addition is two disk utilities that formerly were available only in commercial products. UNDELETE enables you to retrieve accidentally deleted files. UNFORMAT enables you to retrieve files from a disk that was formatted accidentally. Both of these utilities are covered further in Chapter 12, "Raiders of the Lost Data."

DOSKEY is a TSR (terminate and stay resident) program that enables you to recall previous commands from a work session and edit them if necessary without having to retype them. With DOSKEY, you also can create macros. Chapter 7, "Using Batch Files and Macros," covers DOSKEY in more depth.

Finally, the DIR (directory) command has been improved substantially. For the first time, you can specify directory listings to be sorted by name, extension, date, and/or size. You also can search through multiple subdirectories with a single command, something that isn't possible in earlier versions.

Some of the other changes in DOS 5.0 enable you to create batch files more easily. Batch files are like miniature programs. They're files that contain more than one command, so you can execute several commands by typing only one. You can create a single batch file that carries out several functions. Turn to Chapter 7, "Using Batch Files and Macros," for an in-depth discussion of batch files.

T I P   Knowing which version of DOS you have is a good idea. You may try typing a command and get no or unexpected results, for example, and wonder what you're doing wrong. The problem may be that you have an older version of DOS, one that doesn't contain the command you're trying to get the system to perform.

If your computer is set to work with DOS, you see the prompt on your screen. You can find out which version of DOS you have by typing **ver** and pressing Enter at the prompt. The system responds by displaying the version number at the prompt, as in MS-DOS Version 5.0.

Looking at OS/2

OS/2, released on December 4, 1987, was supposed to be the next DOS. In fact, its name stands for Operating System 2, and it was developed jointly by Microsoft and IBM. These days, IBM is in charge of OS/2, with Microsoft focusing more of its energies on DOS, Windows (a graphics-based interface that is layered over DOS), and the company's yet-to-be-released next-generation operating system, NT (short for New Technology).

OS/2 has a built-in graphic interface called the Presentation Manager that is quite similar to the Windows interface and, like Windows, includes on-line help. These graphical interfaces feature pull-down menus and pointing devices called mice, which are covered in more depth in Chapter 4, "Managing Your Hard Disk in the Graphical Era."

A multitasking operating system, OS/2 enables you to have more than one program running simultaneously. And OS/2 doesn't have the 640K memory constraints DOS has (see Chapter 8, "Using Memory To Speed Up Your Disk"). OS/2 also features the High Performance File System (HPFS), which enables you to use file names up to 254 characters long (DOS's limit is 8) and supports multithreaded programs, which can be split into separate background tasks such as printing.

Unlike DOS, which was designed to work with the 8088 microprocessor, OS/2 was designed to work with the 286 microprocessor. OS/2 also was intended to run DOS programs as well as or better than Windows. But because OS/2 itself takes some memory that DOS needs in order to run applications, not all DOS applications can load. Add to those technical problems the on-again, off-again relationship between IBM and Microsoft, and you can see why OS/2 has had trouble gaining widespread acceptance.

OS/2 is a powerful operating system. A minimum of 4M of memory is recommended if you want to install OS/2 on a PC, and more is better. Compare that with the 640K recommended as a minimum and the 1M standard for machines that use DOS, and the 2M that is the recommended minimum for machines that use Windows.

In spite of its differences and its grand power, OS/2 uses many of the same commands used in DOS. If you are familiar with the way DOS commands work, then you will be comfortable working with OS/2. At the time of this writing, the release of Version 2.0 of OS/2 was expected to be imminent. This version is expected to take full advantage of the 32-bit architecture of the 386- and 486-class microprocessing chips.

Looking at UNIX

UNIX predated all the other operating systems currently used on PCs. It's a large, powerful operating system with more than 300 built-in utilities, compared to DOS's few dozen.

At the time of this writing, UNIX was the only 32-bit operating system available for PCs, but Version 2.0 of OS/2 may soon join it on the market. Operating systems that can process 32 bits of data at once are better able to keep up with the 32-bit microprocessors used in 386- and 486-class machines, and the advent of such powerful Intel-based machines has caused more people to consider UNIX as an alternative.

UNIX got its start in 1969 in AT&T's famed Bell Labs. It originally was developed for the DEC PDP-7 minicomputer. In the early 1970s, the programming code for UNIX was rewritten in the C programming language, which offered one big advantage: it made UNIX portable. (Portable is computer jargon for being able to run on any kind of platform, or computer type.) As a result, UNIX is used on more kinds of computers than any other operating system. It runs on everything from mainframes to minicomputers to portable PCs.

Perhaps the best-known use of UNIX is on scientific and engineering workstations for tasks such as computer-aided design (CAD). Workstations are computers that look like PCs on the outside but use chips with a different type of internal architecture. (Intel chips are CISC, or Complex Instruction Set Computing chips. Chips used in workstations are called RISC, for Reduced Instruction Set Computing. The two technologies are starting to blur; for example, Intel's 486 microprocessor contains elements of RISC design. And many workstations now are PCs.)

From the start, UNIX was designed as a multitasking, multiuser operating system, in contrast to DOS, which was designed for a single user performing one task at a time. UNIX contains built-in communications utilities that permit file transfer between PCs, such as a command that enables you to send electronic mail. Because it is a multiuser operating system, UNIX also is used often by businesses as an alternative to local area networks, which require a special operating system and add-in cards in order to share resources. Businesses using UNIX can have a powerful PC or workstation running the UNIX operating system with "dumb terminals"—machines with no internal processing power—sharing the host PC's resources.

Although UNIX's strongest footholds have been in the scientific workstation and multiuser environments, its growing acceptance by individual users is expected to continue throughout the decade.

 Keep in mind that several configurations of UNIX are available, and they are not 100 percent compatible.

Looking at the Mac System

Some people don't include the Macintosh operating system in their discussions of personal computers. Personal computers often are defined as machines that use the Intel family of microprocessors, and the Apple Macintosh uses the Motorola family of microprocessors.

But mentioning the Mac operating system, however briefly, is important. No one can deny the impact that the Macintosh with its easy-to-use graphical interface has had on the world of personal computing, as illustrated by the flurry of graphical user interfaces made available for all the other operating systems. The evidence speaks for itself. OS/2 features a graphical user interface, the Presentation Manager, built right into the operating system. UNIX and DOS have a host of graphical interfaces from which you can choose—Motif- and Open Look-based products for UNIX and the DOS Shell and what seems like a ton of third-party shells for DOS.

The difference between the Mac and the others is that the others all have command lines, a totally foreign concept to the Mac. From its inception, the Mac was promoted as "the computer for the rest of us." Just as the operating system shields you from the inner workings of the computer, the Mac shields you from the inner workings of the operating system.

One of the most radical things about the Mac is that you do not have to go through a maze of paths and directories after you create a file. (This difference may make more sense to you after you read Chapter 6, "Working with Directories on Your Hard Disk.") Instead of having to find and start a program to open a file, all you have to do is open the file—the program is "built into it" and starts automatically. After you read Chapter 4, "Managing Your Hard Disk in the Graphical Era," you will see that although the DOS Shell and Windows are friendly, they aren't *that* friendly.

The Mac's operating system is referred to simply by its version number, with the most recent version being System 7.

Preparing the Hard Disk To Work with DOS

Hard disks don't come out of the chute ready to accept your data. They have to be prepared to work with DOS, just as a highway needs to be adorned with road signs so that the people who drive on it can reach their destinations easily. Three basic processes have to take place before you can use a hard disk to save your programs and your data. Those processes are the low-level or physical format, the partitioning of the disk, and the high-level or logical format.

If you purchase your hard disk as part of a complete computer system, these tasks more than likely have been taken care of for you. To find out whether your system is ready to work with DOS, try starting the computer from the hard disk. If you have a 3 1/2-inch drive, first make sure that no floppy disks are in that drive. If you have a 5 1/4-inch floppy drive, open its door. The computer tries booting up from these drives before it tries the hard drive. If you have floppy disks in the drives, you get an error message. The only exception is if you have in the floppy drive what's called a bootable or system disk, which contains the information the computer needs to get started.

If your computer starts with no problem and displays the symbol C>, which is known as the prompt, then the system has been prepped and DOS has been installed. If the computer does not start, then it hasn't been prepped for DOS yet. In that case, read the following sections so that you can understand what needs to be done.

Don't worry; prepping a hard disk is easy and can even be fun. Half the fun is getting to indulge your rocket-science fantasies. When your friends ask what you did Saturday afternoon, you can say casually, "Oh, not much—I just partitioned and formatted my hard disk." You may gain their respect, but be forewarned: they probably will start asking you to program their VCRs.

Performing the Low-Level Format

As was mentioned briefly in Chapter 2, "Choosing a Hard Disk: Self-Defense for Buyers," the *low-level format* typically is performed at the factory if your hard drive comes as part of a complete system. If you purchase a separate hard drive, you may have to perform the low-level format yourself or get someone else to do it for you. If the disk you purchase hasn't already been formatted, it will include a program that you can use to low-level format the disk. (XT low-level format software usually is built into the controller card. For ATs, you need special software as well as DOS to perform the format.)

In the low-level format, the disk is imprinted physically with the information that serves as a road map for DOS. The low-level format divides the platter into tracks, cylinders, and sectors and establishes the drive's interleave (the way the sectors are organized).

Setting Up Disk Partitions

The next thing that has to take place before you can start working with your computer is the partitioning of the disk. Partitioning designates some or all of the disk for use by DOS. This section explains how to set up a basic partition. You can, however, set up partitions to act as logical drives, which look like separate disk drives to DOS. You also can have one partition set up for DOS and another partition set up for use by a different operating system, such as UNIX or OS/2. (OS/2 and DOS can share a partition, unless you're using the High Performance File System of OS/2.)

The following instructions assume that you're working with DOS 5.0 and that it hasn't been installed on your system yet. If DOS hasn't been installed yet, you can have the disk partitioned when you run the DOS SETUP program.

To get things started, insert the DOS Setup disk into your floppy drive; then type **setup** and press Enter at the prompt. Unless you tell it otherwise, the SETUP program creates one primary DOS partition that takes up the entire disk.

Two types of partitions exist: primary and extended. The *primary partition* is the one that contains the DOS kernel or system files (IO.SYS and MSDOS.SYS) and the command interpreter (COMMAND.COM). Other files can be on the partition, but these three files *must* be present. A primary partition is necessary in order to boot up from a hard disk.

The *extended partition*, which is optional, stores other files. Extended partitions are used to create logical drives, which are areas of the disk that act as separate drives. In fact, if you decide to create an extended partition, you have to divide it into logical drives.

Although setting up a partition during the DOS installation is the easiest approach, you do have an alternative. You can use the FDISK command to partition the disk. This command also enables you to display partition information so that you can see how your disk is set up. Follow these steps to create a primary partition:

1. After installing DOS, return to the DOS prompt, type **fdisk**, and press Enter. The FDISK Options window appears, as shown in figure 3.1.

2. Option 1, Create DOS Partition or Logical DOS Drive, is the option you use to set up your primary partition. Press 1 and Enter to select this option.

3. You then see another menu, which includes an option for creating a primary partition (option 1 again). Select this option and press Enter.

4. Another prompt appears, asking whether you want to use the maximum size for the primary partition and make it the active partition. Press Y to respond to this prompt. (The partition has to be active; otherwise, DOS cannot work with it.)

```
                    MS-DOS Version 5.00
                  Fixed Disk Setup Program
          (C)Copyright Microsoft Corp. 1983 - 1991

                      FDISK Options

Current fixed disk drive: 1

Choose one of the following:

1. Create DOS partition or Logical DOS Drive
2. Set active partition
3. Delete partition or Logical DOS Drive
4. Display partition information


Enter choice: [1]




Press Esc to exit FDISK
```

FIG. 3.1

The FDISK Options screen.

FDISK then creates a partition that takes up all the available space on the hard disk. If you have only one hard disk, DOS informs you that the system will restart and asks you to insert a DOS system disk (one that contains IO.SYS, MSDOS.SYS, and COMMAND.COM) and press any key.

T I P
If you want to create a smaller primary partition, press N to choose No when the prompt asks whether you want to make the partition the maximum size and make it the active partition (step 4). Then you must type **fdisk** and press Enter to get back to the FDISK Options screen. Select Option 2, Set Active Partition. (Only primary partitions can be active; if you try to make an extended partition the active partition, you get an error message.)

After you partition your disk, one of the first things you should do is use the MIRROR command to back up the partition information. Type **mirror/partn** and press Enter at the DOS prompt. The system asks you to insert a floppy drive so that MIRROR can create a file called PARTNSAV.FIL. Store the disk in a safe place so that you will have it if your partition table goes bad.

Performing the High-Level Format

Another type of formatting has to take place before you can start using your computer: the *high-level* or *logical format*. After you have partitioned the disk, you use DOS's FORMAT command to perform a high-level format on a hard disk, just as you use the command to format floppy disks. (If you prefer, you can have the disk automatically formatted during the SETUP process.)

The odds are that your disk has been logically formatted as well as partitioned if you purchased it as part of a system. If it hasn't, you can use this section to take you through the process.

To format the disk after you have partitioned it, simply type **format c: /s** and press Enter at the DOS prompt. (The /S switch tells DOS to format the hard disk as a system disk, which means that the system can start from it.)

FORMAT issues a warning, telling you that all data on the nonremovable disk drive C will be lost, and then asks whether you want to proceed with the format. Press Y to continue.

DOS keeps you posted as it formats the disk by reporting the percentage of the format completed. (Versions 4 and 5 tell you the percentage; earlier versions keep a running count of the number of heads and cylinders that have been processed.) The larger the disk drive, the longer the formatting process takes. After it's finished formatting the disk, DOS prompts you for a volume label. You can use up to 11 characters to label the disk.

In addition to the /S switch, you can use several other optional switches with the FORMAT command. Table 3.1 briefly describes these options.

Table 3.1 Using FORMAT Switches

Switch	Function
/?	Displays on-line help.
/B	Reserves space for the system but does not transfer.
/V:*label*	Specifies a volume label, which can be a maximum of 11 characters. If you omit the /V switch, DOS prompts you for a volume label after completing the format.
/Q	Deletes the FAT and root directory of a previously formatted disk but doesn't look for bad sectors.

continues

Table 3.1 Continued	
Switch	Function
/U	Performs an unconditional format that destroys all existing data on a disk and prevents a successful unformat process later. Microsoft recommends using the /U switch on drives that have had read and write errors.

The high-level format carries out several important tasks, including affixing address information for each sector and scanning the disk to make sure that all the sectors can hold data. If FORMAT finds some sectors that cannot hold data, the command marks those sectors as bad and makes them unavailable for use. After completing the format, the FORMAT command displays a report showing you how much space was formatted, how many bytes are used by the system files, and how many defective sectors (if any) were found. Don't be alarmed if you see that your disk has some defective sectors. A new hard disk with defective (bad) sectors is not unusual.

Most importantly, the high-level format creates three special areas reserved for use by DOS: the boot record, the file allocation table, and the root directory. In the following paragraphs, you take a look at each of these areas.

The Boot Record

The *boot record* contains critical information needed by DOS, such as the size of the file allocation table, the number of sectors per cluster, and the names of the two hidden system files, IO.SYS and MSDOS.SYS. (If more than one partition is on the disk, each partition has its own boot record, because the partitions are acting as separate disks. In that case, the disk also has a master boot record, which contains information on each of the partitions in addition to the information listed in the individual boot records.) The boot record resides on the first sector on the disk.

You may be wondering why the boot record is so important. The reason is that the system cannot get going without the information contained in the boot record. Consider the following puzzle: DOS is the operating system that controls the functions of your computer. But DOS is software, just as your word processing program is software, which means that DOS comes on floppy disks. In other words, DOS needs to be installed on your computer. But how are you supposed to install DOS, when you need DOS to install DOS? It's the electronic version of the chicken and egg question.

The way the computer industry gets around this problem is to put a tiny set of operating instructions—just enough to get the system warmed up—on ROM, the read-only memory. This set of instructions is stored on ROM during the high-level format because the contents of ROM are permanent. RAM (random-access memory), on the other hand, loses its contents when you shut off the computer.

Now, guess what's on ROM. Remember the BIOS, the Basic Input/Output System that communicates directly with the hard drive and other hardware? In addition to communicating with the hardware, the BIOS gets the computer up and running when you flip the switch to On. This process is called *booting up*, and it's borrowed from the phrase "pulling oneself up by the bootstraps." The BIOS contains just enough start-up information to perform the start-up tests, get the disk drive going, and find the boot record. The boot record contains the names of two hidden system files that the BIOS has to find and load into RAM during the booting-up process: IO.SYS and MSDOS.SYS, the DOS kernel. (On PC DOS, the IBM-specific version of DOS, the system files are called IBMBIO.COM and IBMDOS.COM.) After the BIOS finds IO.SYS and MSDOS.SYS, they are able to get COMMAND.COM, the command interpreter, up and running in turn.

Two types of boots exist: the cold boot and the warm boot. A *cold boot* is when you start from scratch. The computer is shut down, and you flip on the power switch. The BIOS immediately performs what's known as a POR, or *power-on reset*. The power-on reset clears RAM, the microprocessor, and the other circuitry, checking the memory chips, for example, to make sure that they're functioning properly.

The next step is the POST, or the *power-on self test*, in which the BIOS makes sure that everything in the computer is functioning normally. With some BIOS, you then see a memory countdown in the upper-left corner of the screen and the message Press ESC to bypass memory test. (The POST also is performed when you push the Reset button, if your computer has one. Using Reset is like flipping the power switch—everything starts from scratch.) If you press Esc, the BIOS skips the memory test and fetches the system files. If you don't press Esc, the BIOS continues its memory countdown until all the system memory has been accounted for. Then you see the message xxx kilobytes OK.

A *warm boot*, in contrast, is what you get when you press the Ctrl-Alt-Del key combination. In the warm boot, the POST is not performed.

Although oversimplified to some extent, that process essentially describes what happens. Your computer is warmed up and ready to work, but it cannot do so without the boot record that's set up when the disk is formatted.

NOTE Two other important files are involved at start-up. After COMMAND.COM is run, DOS looks for a CONFIG.SYS file and an AUTOEXEC.BAT file, both of which are files you can create. These files contain start-up instructions for hardware and file searches, respectively. CONFIG.SYS, for example, contains the instructions for working with a mouse if your system has one. AUTOEXEC.BAT tells DOS which directories to search when trying to locate files. For more information on using these two files, see Chapter 7, "Using Batch Files and Macros," and Chapter 8, "Using Memory To Speed Up Your Disk."

The File Allocation Table

The *file allocation table* (FAT), the second area created by the high-level format, follows the boot record on the disk. DOS uses the FAT as an index to keep track of all the files on the disk. Without the FAT, DOS would never be able to find a file on your hard disk. The FAT is so crucial that DOS keeps two copies of it on the disk so that a backup is available in case one is damaged.

The FAT tracks files by keeping an address for each cluster. A *cluster*, which consists of a group of sectors, is DOS's basic unit of measure for disk space. Because sectors are so small (512 bytes apiece), DOS uses clusters instead of sectors as a way of keeping its bookkeeping under control. Most hard disks use 4-sector clusters. Suppose that you have a file that takes up 4 clusters (a total of 16 sectors). DOS can keep track of the location of 4 clusters much more easily than it can 16 sectors. Using clusters also enables the FAT to take up less space on the disk. If you had to store a couple of hundred dollars in cash in your wallet, carrying 10 $20 bills is easier than keeping 200 singles on hand.

When you request access to a stored file, DOS checks the FAT to see which clusters contain the file. When you save a new file to the disk, DOS checks the FAT to see which clusters are available to store the file.

In addition to keeping track of which clusters are available and which contain files, the FAT also keeps track of which clusters contain damaged sectors and which ones are reserved for system use. The FAT tells DOS the following information about each cluster:

■ Whether the cluster is available

■ Whether the cluster is reserved for system use

■ Whether the cluster contains a damaged sector or sectors and should not be used to store data

■ Whether the cluster is being used by a file (The FAT record contains the number of the next cluster that is used by a file.)

■ Whether the cluster is the last cluster in use by a particular file

As the last two items indicate, the catch is that the FAT doesn't tell you which cluster indicates the beginning of the file. So how does DOS know where to start looking? How does it know that it's supposed to start with cluster 89 and not cluster 263? The FAT is almost like a list of home addresses with the street names omitted.

The answer to where a file begins is contained in the file's *directory entry*. Just as the FAT acts as an index for the location of all files on the disk, the file directory entry acts as an index for each separate file. Whenever a file is created, a directory entry for that file is created.

The directory entry contains the following information:

■ The file's name, which consists of up to eight characters

■ The file's extension, which consists of three characters (In the file REPORT.TXT, for example, REPORT is the file name, and TXT is the extension. For more information, see Chapter 5, "Keeping Files Organized.")

■ The file's size, expressed in bytes

■ The file's attributes, such as whether the file is a hidden file or a read-only file

■ The time the file was last saved to disk

■ The date the file was last saved to disk

■ The address of the allocation unit where the beginning of the file is stored

To find the file, DOS has to find the cluster or clusters that contain the file. If it's a small file, it may be in only one cluster. If it's a large file, it may take up several. The cluster address for the beginning of the file is what DOS uses to check the FAT. The FAT, in turn, keeps track of all the clusters that contain parts of the file.

Suppose that the directory entry shows that the file called MYFILE.TXT begins at cluster 8. DOS looks up cluster 8 in the FAT, which indicates that the next part of the file resides on cluster 27. When DOS checks cluster 27 in the FAT index, the FAT indicates that the file continues on cluster 15. Finally, when DOS checks cluster 15, the FAT indicates that the file ends there. This seemingly wild goose chase is critical because files eventually become scattered all over the disk. (File fragmentation and ways to overcome it are covered in depth in Chapter 9, "Exploring Hard Disk Fitness Programs.")

Now, to complete the picture, after DOS checks all that information in the FAT and finds out where the file resides, DOS passes the information on to the BIOS, because DOS never directly communicates with hardware. The BIOS keeps its own set of addresses and tells the controller where to send the read/write heads. When you think about all the different stops the data makes as it travels through your computer, the speed at which things happen is astonishing.

The Root Directory

The last element established by the logical format is the *root directory*. The sectors reserved for the root directory come right after the sectors reserved for both copies of the FAT. The root directory is the computer's main directory.

The root directory has a fixed size, typically 512 files, which also can include other directories called subdirectories. The root directory and subdirectories are discussed in more depth in Chapter 6, "Working with Directories on Your Hard Disk."

Summary

In this chapter, you learned that operating systems provide a vital link between your applications and the system hardware. If it weren't for the operating system, each of your software programs would have to contain instructions for communicating with the hardware.

The operating system also shields the user from the complexities of the system and handles basic but critical housekeeping functions, such as directory and file management.

Operating systems used in personal computers include DOS, OS/2, UNIX, and the Mac System. DOS is by far the most widely used operating system.

Before being able to work with DOS, a hard disk needs to be physically formatted, partitioned, and logically formatted. In this chapter, you learned how each of these steps prepares your disk. The physical format records tracks and sectors and also establishes the disk interleave. Partitioning sets up the disk partitions and prepares the disk for logical formatting, which creates the boot record, the file allocation table, and the root directory.

You also learned in this chapter how to find out whether the hard disk on your computer has been set up to work with DOS and how to find out which version of DOS you have.

In the next chapter, you explore hard disk management in a graphical interface.

Managing Your Hard Disk in the Graphical Era

The interfaces discussed so far in this book refer to methods of communication between hard drives and computers, such as the SCSI interface or the ST-506/412 interface. But another kind of interface called the *user interface* involves the way people communicate with computers and the way computers communicate back. DOS, in addition to translating between your software programs and the computer, also translates for you.

The world of user interfaces is changing. In this chapter, you look at how DOS-based computing is moving from what is called a character-based interface to a graphical user interface (GUI, pronounced "gooey").

This chapter also introduces you to GUI basics, because the computer you bring home more than likely will include a graphical user interface, whether in the form of the DOS Shell, Microsoft Windows, or both. Most of the focus in this chapter is on the DOS Shell, because even if your computer doesn't ship with Windows, it certainly will ship with DOS.

You also are introduced to the latest version (3.1) of Microsoft Windows, one of the hottest-selling software products of all time. When Version 3.0 of Windows came out in 1990, it sold a million copies in the first month.

And finally, you explore a couple of commercial DOS shells, which may interest those of you who either have older versions of DOS or want to know about alternatives to DOS and Windows.

NOTE In case you're wondering what all this information has to do with hard disk management, the answer is, "Plenty." The majority of hard disk management isn't glamorous. You don't spend the bulk of your time fine-tuning the interleave or re-formatting the drive alignment. Much of the hard disk management you perform consists simply of keeping the disk organized, and you handle a large portion of that by using DOS, Windows, or some other shell.

Looking at the Two Interfaces of DOS

Several years ago, figure 4.1 represented your only choice of DOS interface.

```
C:\
```

FIG. 4.1

An early DOS interface.

This simple interface is called the *command line* because it is where you type your commands, such as VER and FORMAT. Today, although you're still free to work from this simple command line, figure 4.2 shows you another choice.

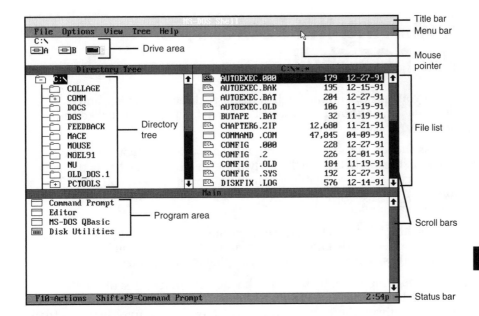

FIG. 4.2

A more expansive DOS interface.

What you're looking at in figure 4.2 is the improved Shell in DOS 5.0. When you install DOS, you can set it up so that it automatically starts the Shell. If you prefer not to use that option, you can call up the Shell by typing **dosshell** at the prompt and pressing Enter. (If you get the message Bad command or file name, type **cd dos** and press Enter to change to the DOS directory; then try typing **dosshell** and pressing Enter.)

In the following section, you learn more about the DOS Shell. Because the DOS Shell enables you to do so many things, the focus in this book is on tasks related to file, directory, and disk management. If you want to learn more about other Shell features, such as task swapping or creating program groups, use the tutorial included with the program and the DOS manual or try a book such as Que's *Using MS-DOS 5* or the Special Edition of *Que's MS-DOS 5 User's Guide.*

NOTE Keep in mind that the DOS Shell may give you some problems when you're working with certain software. If you launch Word 5.0 and press the Ctrl-F9 (Print Preview) key, for example, the print preview doesn't work if you used the DOS Shell to launch.

Exploring the Features of the DOS Shell

When you first call up the Shell, it displays directories, files, and a program list, as shown in figure 4.2. This default screen is called the *program/file list*.

Across the top of the screen is the *title bar*, which lets you know that you're in the MS-DOS Shell. Directly underneath the title bar is the *menu bar*, which lists the available menus: File, Options, View, and Help. The following paragraphs give you a brief tour of each of the menus accessed from the menu bar.

You use the *File* menu to perform your file-management tasks, such as creating, opening, deleting, copying, and moving files. You learn how to perform these tasks in Chapter 5, "Keeping Files Organized."

The *Options* menu enables you to change certain features of the DOS Shell, including the display colors and resolution. With this menu, you also can activate the Task Swapper, which enables you to run more than one program at a time. (If you activate the Task Swapper, an active task window also appears in the program area at the bottom of the screen.)

You use the *View* menu to change the look of the DOS Shell. The screen that you see when the DOS Shell first appears is called the *default screen*. In this chapter's section on "Changing the Look of the DOS Shell," you learn how to use the options from the View menu to change the look of this default Shell display.

The *Help* menu enables you to select an overall index of help topics. The help index also contains menus related to keyboard options, if you aren't using a mouse, and general commands and procedures for navigating the Shell. If you're new to the DOS Shell, you ought to select the Shell Basics option from the Help menu and browse through the items listed. Examining this list is a good way to familiarize yourself with the DOS Shell's capabilities.

You also can press the F1 key to pop up a Help window at any time as you explore the DOS Shell. The DOS Shell uses context-sensitive help, which means that the window that pops up is related to your current selection or action.

NOTE As you explore the Shell, you may notice that at times an additional menu item called Tree appears in the menu bar. You don't see this selection when the DOS Shell first comes up or when you have the program list active, but if the disk, directory, or file lists are active, Tree appears in the menu bar alongside File, Options, View, and Help. Tree gives you several options for viewing your disk's directory structure. You learn more about using the Tree menu in Chapter 6, "Working with Directories on Your Hard Disk."

In the next section, "Navigating the DOS Shell," you learn how to open all these menus from the DOS Shell screen.

Beneath the menu bar is the *drive area*, which shows all the available drives. To make a drive the active drive, you select it by either clicking its icon (the small on-screen graphic that depicts each drive) with the mouse pointer or pressing the Tab key until the drive area is highlighted and using the arrow keys to select the drive of your choice.

In case you aren't familiar with drive representations, the C drive is almost always the hard drive. If you have only one floppy drive, that's the A drive. If you have both 5 1/4-inch and 3 1/2-inch floppy drives, the 5 1/4-inch floppy drive is typically the A drive, and the 3 1/2-inch drive is the B drive. Some systems have two 5 1/4-inch drives as A and B drives.

T I P

The *directory tree*, on the left side of the screen beneath the drive area, displays the overall structure of directories and subdirectories on the selected disk drive (drive C in fig. 4.2). Having the directory structure on display is a big advantage. In Chapter 6, "Working with Directories on Your Hard Disk," you learn more about the nature of directories and why being able to see the structure makes navigation easier.

On the right side of the screen is the *file list*, which displays files for the selected directory, the highlighted directory in the directory tree.

The *program area* displays under the directory tree near the bottom of the screen. The Main program group is shown by default. (If you create any program groups, or categories, of your own by using commands in the File menu, these program groups also display in the program area.) The Main group lists two programs that you can run from the Shell: the Editor, which replaced EDLIN, the text editor found in older versions of DOS, and MS-DOS QBasic, a program known as a Basic interpreter that you can use to write and run your own programs in the Basic language.

The Main group also accesses the command prompt, which takes you out of the Shell and into the DOS command line, and the disk utilities. The disk utilities are the external commands discussed in Chapter 3, "Understanding How DOS Works with the Hard Disk," such as FORMAT, CHKDSK, and FDISK, among others.

NOTE   A note about the Editor is warranted here. If you're gun-shy of the Editor because you have heard all the nasty things about EDLIN, don't be. With EDLIN, if you made a mistake as you edited a file, you had to start all over. The editor had some cryptic aspects besides. But DOS's new Editor is great. It's as easy to work with as any word processor. You will want to use the Editor all the time when you start editing files.

At the bottom of the screen is the *status bar*, which displays shortcut keys, messages from the Shell, and the current time.

Navigating the DOS Shell

You will find that the DOS Shell, like other graphical user interfaces, is designed to work well with the *mouse* (although using a mouse is not required). The mouse is an input device that you move around on your desk in order to move the mouse pointer, a small on-screen rectangle, or that you click in order to choose options and buttons from the DOS Shell screen.

To open a menu, for example, you can move the mouse on your desk so that the mouse pointer on-screen moves onto the menu title and then click the mouse button. If you prefer using the keyboard or don't have a mouse yet, press the Alt or F10 key to access the menu bar; then press the arrow keys until you get to the menu title you want to access. (You know when you get there because the title becomes highlighted.) When the correct menu name is highlighted, press Enter to open the menu. Another keyboard menu-selection technique is available. You can just press the key that corresponds to the highlighted letter of the menu's name, such as F for the File menu. When you open a menu, using any one of these methods, a list of options or commands appears beneath the menu name. This list is called a *pull-down menu*.

> If you have never used a mouse before, don't be discouraged if getting the hang of steering it around and clicking where you want it to click takes you a little while. If you click and nothing happens, just try it again. Before long, you will be zipping around the screen like an expert.
>
> **T I P**

Other features of the DOS Shell screen include the scroll bars and the selection cursor.

The *scroll bars* appear to the right of each screen or window. If all the items can be displayed in a window at once, the scroll bar appears solid. When a list of items is so long that they cannot all be displayed in the window at once, the scroll bar has dark shading in it.

With a scroll bar, you move the hidden part of the screen into view by pressing the arrow keys or by using the mouse to click the up and down scroll arrows at the top and bottom of each scroll bar. You also can move the hidden part of the screen into view by clicking the scroll box, which indicates the position of the cursor relative to the list of display items. If you use this latter method, you need to click the left mouse button and continue to hold it down while you move (drag) the scroll box up or down.

The *selection cursor* marks the items that you select on-screen. When you select an item by using the arrow keys or the mouse, notice that the item becomes highlighted. A little arrow also appears to the left of the item. If you decide to make another area of the screen active, the arrow switches to a black triangle.

Suppose, for example, that you're using a VGA color screen, and you use the arrow keys or the mouse to select a file in the file list on the right of the screen. The file name appears highlighted in blue and has the little arrow. Then suppose that you decide to edit the file, so you make the program area at the bottom of the screen the active area and select the Editor. The Editor now appears highlighted in blue, and a little arrow appears to its left. The file you originally selected still is highlighted, but the highlight is black, and the black triangle appears to its left, which indicates that the item no longer is active.

Changing the Look of the DOS Shell

You don't have to look at the program/file list exactly as it appears by default. In this section, you learn how to use the View menu to change the look of the DOS Shell. The added bonus, of course, is that you find out how to work with a menu, which gives you a head start on Chapters 5 and 6, where you learn to work with directories and files.

Figure 4.3 shows the pull-down View menu. Remember that you can open this menu by clicking View with the mouse; by using Alt or F10, the arrow keys, and Enter; or by pressing the letter V.

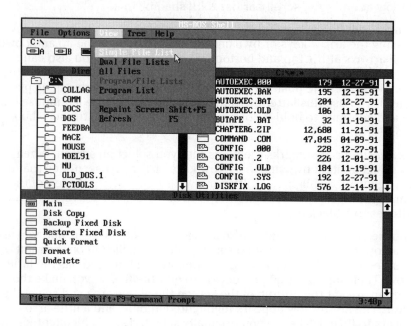

FIG. 4.3

The View menu.

Suppose that you don't want to see the program list at the bottom of the screen. If you simply want to show the selected directory and the list of files for that directory, you select Single File List from the menu. (Click it with the mouse or use the arrow keys to highlight it and then press Enter to select it.) The single file list version of the Shell screen is shown in figure 4.4.

One option you probably will use often is Dual File List. The dual file list screen enables you to show the contents of two directories at once, which comes in extremely handy when you want to copy files from one directory to another (or to another disk). For the display, you can select two directories from the hard drive or one from the hard drive and one from a floppy drive, as shown in figure 4.5.

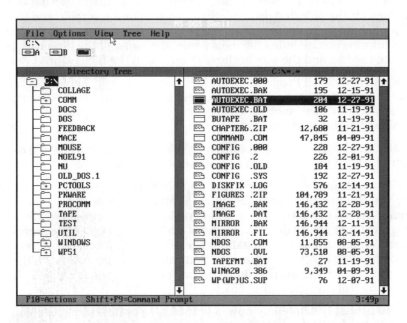

FIG. 4.4

Viewing the single file list.

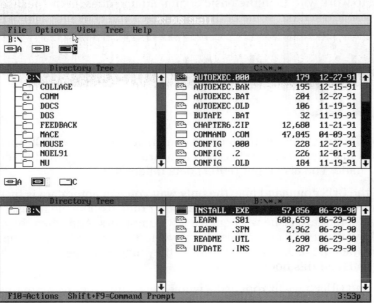

FIG. 4.5

Displaying a dual file list.

The dual file list is discussed in much more detail when you get to Chapter 5, "Keeping Files Organized."

The next option on the View menu, All Files, simply displays a list of all the files for the selected drive on the right side of the screen, and information about the selected file, directory, and disk is shown on the left. This information includes the file's name, the name of the directory containing the file, and the size of the disk on which the file is stored.

You also can select Program List, which, coincidentally enough, displays only the program list and no directories or files. If you create program groups of your own, such as word processing or games, they also are displayed in the program list.

Finally, the Program/File List option enables you to go back to the default display if you have used one of the other View options.

The last item in the View menu, the Repaint Screen option, probably isn't one you will use as often as the others. You can choose this option if you cannot get rid of a terminate and stay resident (TSR) program. TSRs are programs that are loaded into memory and that pop up a little screen when you press a key combination. Sometimes a TSR stays on-screen even after you exit the program, so you can make it go away with the Repaint Screen option. The shortcut for Repaint Screen is Shift-F5 (hold down the Shift key and press F5).

As you probably can tell by now, a graphical user interface gives you more to work with than the basic command line does. In the next section, you learn about some of the advantages you can enjoy with a GUI.

Looking at the Advantages of a GUI

The difference between the austere command line and the DOS Shell doesn't just stem from the screen's appearance, although that difference is dramatic. You also input (enter) data differently.

With the DOS command line, the only way you can enter data is by typing it from the keyboard. GUIs add another dimension—the mouse. Mice are now standard issue with quite a few computers. And when they aren't, you can pick up a mouse for anywhere from $15 to $200, depending on the type of mouse. Who knows, they may cost even less by the time you read this book.

Mice and GUIs have introduced a whole new approach to computing. Instead of typing a command, such as MD, at the prompt to create a new directory, you can point the mouse at the menu bar at the top of the screen, select File, pull down the File menu, and select Create Directory.

This point-and-click approach has four advantages. For one thing, zipping around with a mouse is much quicker than it sounds when you're trying to describe it.

The second advantage is not having to memorize a bunch of cryptic commands. You don't have to worry about getting the CD (Change Directory) command mixed up with the MD (Make Directory) command. As you learn in Chapter 6, "Working with Directories on Your Hard Disk," when you work from the command line, you have to know exactly where everything is located. Otherwise, you get the message Bad command or file name—even if the command or file name you typed is correct.

Which leads to the third advantage: GUIs eliminate the mistakes you can easily make when you type. You still will make mistakes; the subject is computers, after all, and often some little maddening glitches occur. But GUIs eliminate a particularly frustrating category of mistake.

GUIs also spare you from having to flip through your DOS manual. With a GUI, you have nothing to look up. If you know how to read, you can work with a GUI. (You still need to learn about things like directories and files, which you do in the chapters that follow. But you don't have the added burden of trying to remember all those commands.) If you do run into trouble, both the DOS Shell and Microsoft Windows have on-line help, and so do many commercial DOS shells, which are discussed later in this chapter (see "Looking at Commercial DOS Shells").

Exploring Microsoft Windows

Although it's sold as a separate software product, Microsoft Windows is increasingly standard issue with computers. At the time of this writing, the Software Publishers Association estimated that Windows had a worldwide installed base of 6 million. Windows really took off when Version 3 came out in 1990. The prior version, 2.0, had a less-than-friendly shell called the MS-DOS Executive Manager, but Version 3.0 was head and shoulders above 2.0. Version 3.1 is even more sleek, and the computer you bring home quite possibly will have Windows all loaded up and ready to go.

Version 3.1 has overcome an assumption contained in all earlier versions of Windows—namely, that everyone and their dog knows how to work a mouse and navigate their way through a maze of screens. The newest Windows contains two tutorials: one on basic mouse moves and one on using the mouse to resize, open, close, and move windows. It's a great improvement.

You can run the tutorials when you install Windows, or you can run them at any time simply by opening the Help menu at the top of the Program Manager screen and then selecting the Windows Tutorial option. The Program Manager is the main window shown in figure 4.6. As soon as you get into Windows, you are in the Program Manager window. (If you are at the C> prompt, you get into Windows by typing **cd windows**, pressing Enter, typing **win**, and pressing Enter again.) Like the DOS Shell, the Program Manager screen displays a title bar across the top with a menu bar directly beneath it. Identical icons for the Games group, the Accessories group, the Main group, and Applications (Windows and non-Windows) are displayed at the bottom of the Program Manager window.

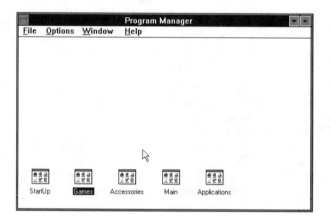

FIG. 4.6

The Program Manager window.

The following paragraphs give you a brief overview of each group of programs you access from the Program Manager window.

The *Games* group, which contains Solitaire and Minesweeper, is a great way to have fun while you learn Windows. Practically the first thing every Windows user learns to do is play Solitaire, which can be extremely addictive. (You can always tell your boss that you're practicing your hand-eye coordination.) At least try the game enough times to win. (Don't worry; your odds of winning Solitaire are much better than the odds of winning the Publishers' Clearinghouse Sweepstakes. But this version of Solitaire does have one bug: you cannot cheat.) The visual effects that appear when you win are worth the effort.

The *Accessories* group contains applications for simple word processing, drawing, and communications, plus other handy utilities such as a

calendar and a calculator. New additions to this group with Version 3.1
include the Object Packager, which enables you to create your own
icons that link actions to documents; the Media Player, which controls
CD-ROM drives, videodisc players, and animation and sound programs;
and the Sound Recorder, which enables you to play, record, and edit
sounds created by any of these devices or programs.

The *Main* group contains Windows system programs: the File Manager,
the Print Manager, the Control Panel (with which you can customize the
look of the Windows desktop, among other things), the Clipboard Viewer
(with which you can cut and paste data between applications), Windows
Setup, and the DOS prompt.

The *Applications* group (Windows and non-Windows) is set up based on
the contents of your hard disk. When you install Windows, it checks out
what's on your disk and assigns programs to the appropriate group.
(Windows applications, by the way, are ones that are designed specifically to take advantage of the Windows operating environment.)

Double-clicking (pressing the left mouse button twice in rapid succession) an icon loads the program or group of programs associated with it,
with the program or group appearing in a window. The screen for the
Main group of programs, for example, is displayed in figure 4.7. To select
a program from the Main window, just double-click its icon.

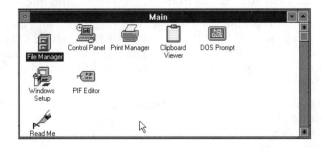

FIG. 4.7

The Main window.

In terms of hard disk management, if you find that you prefer working
with Windows over the DOS Shell, you will spend a great deal of time in
the File Manager. The specific commands for working with directories
and files are discussed in detail in Chapters 5 and 6. Just to give you a
little preview, however, the File Manager window is shown in figure 4.8,
with the DOS directory selected (highlighted) on the left and the files for
the DOS directory shown on the right. The File Manager is much improved in Windows 3.1.

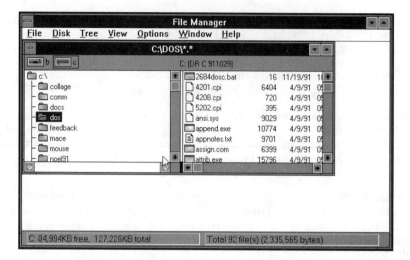

FIG. 4.8

The File Manager.

Looking at Commercial DOS Shells

DOS and Windows aren't the only games in town, if you want to take a graphical approach to managing your disk. Quite a few commercial shell programs can help you escape from the DOS command line.

The terms shell programs, file-management programs, and menu programs are all often used interchangeably. The idea behind DOS shells or file managers or whatever you want to call them is the same idea behind the DOS Shell: giving you an easier, more visually-oriented option than the DOS command line.

A few of the more widely known and used shell programs include XTree Gold, Central Point Software's PC Shell, which is part of PC Tools, Gazelle Systems' Q-DOS 3, Quarterdeck Office Systems' DESQview, and the Norton Commander.

In the following paragraphs, you take a brief look at Q-DOS 3 and DESQView to give you a feel for how these products look and function. This section isn't meant to act as a product review or to imply that these two products are the best. They're simply meant to represent available products. If you decide that you want to try something beyond the DOS Shell, you need to make up your own mind about what products are best for you.

Looking at Q-DOS 3

The main Q-DOS 3 screen, which you activate by typing **qd3** at the DOS prompt, is where you select commands for directory and file management. The command menu appears across the top of the screen. You can select one of these commands by using the arrow keys or the mouse to highlight the command or by typing the first letter of the command's name. (This particular type of menu often is called a Lotus-style command menu, because it's used by the popular Lotus 1-2-3 spreadsheet program.)

As each command is selected, a command description appears below the command menu, giving a brief explanation of the selected command along with directions on how to activate it. Directly beneath the command description is the path bar, which displays the name and path of the current directory. (The path tells you where you are in the disk's directory structure; you learn more about paths in Chapter 6, "Working with Directories on Your Hard Disk.")

The main part of the screen is divided into two parts: on the right, you see four columns of information about files for the selected directory. On the left, you see information about the selected directory, such as the total number of files, the total number of subdirectories, and which files are tagged. (Tagging is a method of selecting groups of files so that you don't have to work with them one at a time.)

The lower-left side of the Q-DOS 3 screen shows an index of the function keys you can use to select various operations, such as getting on-line help (F1) or exiting the program (F10).

Q-DOS 3 also enables you to view a map of the directory structure of your hard disk. To view this directory structure, select the word Directory from the command menu (use the arrow keys or the mouse or press D). The directory map displays all the directories of your hard disk in the form of a tree (similar to the Tree menu in the DOS Shell or the DOS TREE command, which are covered in Chapter 6, "Working with Directories on Your Hard Disk").

The Q-DOS 3 Directory Map screen contains several commands for working with directories, such as Make Dir and Rename. Notice that Q-DOS 3 also offers some "new" commands you may not have seen before, such as Prune and Graft. Pruning and grafting are similar to cutting and pasting in a word processing or desktop publishing program. You can use the Prune command to remove a subdirectory from a directory, and the Graft command to put that subdirectory in a different directory.

The current directory is displayed in a different color if you have a color monitor, or in reverse type if you have a monochrome monitor. To return back to the main screen after viewing or working in the directory tree, press Esc.

Looking at DESQview

The great thing about DESQview is that you can use it on any kind of PC, from an 8088 to a 486. If you have an 8088, which aces you out of Windows, DESQview is your ticket to the graphical era. But you should not think that DESQview is too old-fashioned. A 386-specific version of DESQview comes bundled with QEMM/386, Quarterdeck's sophisticated memory management software for the more powerful 386-based machines.

The DESQview window accesses the master list of commands. Open Window, Switch Windows, and Close Window are used respectively to start programs, switch between programs when multiple programs are active, and close programs.

Like Windows, when DESQview is installed, it scans the hard disk for popular applications and adds them to the Open Window menu. Selecting the Open Window option thus displays all known programs on the hard disk.

You use the main menu's Rearrange option to move, position, or resize current windows or freeze the program running in the window. With this option, you also can hide the current window by removing it from the screen without closing the program or put the window aside to a RAM disk or expanded memory, freeing up memory to run other programs.

The DOS Services menu is the list of DOS commands supported by DESQview. To access DOS Services, select Open Window from the DESQview main menu and then select DOS Services from the Open Window menu. The most often used commands, most of them pertaining to file management, are on the DOS Services menu. Less-used commands, including directory management and formatting commands, are on the DOS Services More menu.

The DOS services window appears in the left half of the screen, with the DOS Services menu on the right. When you select a command from the menu, the command is carried out in the DOS services window.

DESQview also includes the Auto Dialer, a communications software package that automatically dials a phone number from information listed in the current window. (You have to have a modem attached to your system in order for this feature to work.)

One of DESQview's most powerful features is called Learn. With Learn, you create macros—keystroke sequences that you record and play back with the press of a single key. Macros are discussed in more detail in Chapter 7, "Using Batch Files and Macros."

Deciding whether You Need a Third-Party Shell

This (admittedly brief) introduction to third-party shells may have left you wondering what the fuss is about. Q-DOS 3 enables you to view a directory tree structure, but so does Windows. DESQview enables you to select a DOS command from a menu instead of typing it out, but so does the DOS Shell.

In fairness, many of the third-party DOS shells that are used widely today gained their popularity before DOS 5.0 and Windows 3.0 came on the scene. When your visual choice was a dark screen with a stark C> prompt, and your only choice for copying a group of files was typing something like COPY C:\FILES\REPORT.* A:, these products provided welcome relief. Now that DOS itself contains many of the features that make file management easier (and more fun to look at), the benefits of third-party products are less obvious.

Your best bet is probably working with what you have before you embark on something new. If your computer has DOS 5.0, and it more than likely does, get to know the DOS Shell before you plunk down your hard-earned money on extra products.

DOS shells are following an evolutionary path that's quite familiar in the computer industry. In the days when word processors were bare-bones programs with which you could only create and save documents, for example, you had many third-party spell-checking programs from which to choose. The word processing programs of today are as sophisticated as they are huge. They do everything but make your morning coffee. Third-party spell checkers thus have either gone by the wayside or turned into grammar-checking products in an effort to stay one step ahead of the word processors.

Similarly, the DOS shells that survive in the next few years will have to offer features that you cannot get from the operating system itself. If you do end up purchasing a third-party DOS shell, it will be because the product offers you something that DOS does not, such as virus-checking capability. DOS shells may evolve to something entirely different from what they are now.

Summary

Graphical user interfaces are here to stay. In this chapter, you have learned about the DOS Shell, Microsoft Windows, and a variety of other third-party products that enable you to use pull-down menus and mice rather than the traditional DOS command line.

Regardless of the operating system interface you choose, odds are that you will not be using just the keyboard to manage your hard disk. Software programs are becoming increasingly graphical, and so are the environments you use to communicate with your computer.

This chapter concludes Part II. In Part III, you look at DOS's role in keeping your hard disk organized.

Organizing Your Disk with Files and Directories

PART

II

OUTLINE

5 Keeping Files Organized

6 Working with Directories on
Your Hard Disk

7 Using Batch Files and Macros

Keeping Files Organized

Now that your hard disk is all formatted to work with DOS, and you have directories set up to store information, you need something to put in those directories. Here is where files come in.

Every time you install software on your hard disk, you're installing the files the program needs in order to do its work. As soon as you start using that program, you begin creating files of your own as well.

Although keeping files organized may have a less glamorous ring to it than formatting or partitioning a disk, this area is where the lion's share of your disk-management skills comes into play. The key to an organized hard disk lies in these seemingly mundane housekeeping tasks. Hard disks that are cluttered and unorganized cause you to spend more time looking for your data than you spend working with it.

In this chapter, you learn how to use the DOS Shell to work with files. Procedures for using Windows and the DOS command line to organize your files also are given. You begin by finding out just what a file is and how to name it. You then learn about the different types of files—program, data, text, and others—and explore other attributes associated with files. And finally, you get into file management, learning how to display file lists and how to select, view, search for, copy, move, delete, and rename files.

What Is a File?

A *file* is DOS's basic unit of related information. Electronic files, like their paper counterparts, can hold just about anything and come in every size. One file may contain your letter to the editor of your local paper; another may contain your monthly food budget. Still a third file may contain the command that gets your word processing program to run. You look at what sets these files apart from each other in a following section, but first you need to know how file names work.

Using File Names and Extensions

In the world according to DOS, files, like people, have first names and last names. The first part of a file's name typically is called the *root name* or *base name* and is used to describe the file's contents. The last part of the file's name is called the *extension* and describes the file's function. The root name and extension are separated by a period, as in

basename.ext

You may have noticed that many of the file names you see in this book's examples and elsewhere are rather short. When you work with DOS, you're limited to eight letters for the root name and three letters for the extension. (Not all operating systems use this naming convention. OS/2, for example, enables you to use up to 256 characters in the file name!) Now you know why file names are sometimes so cryptic. The people who work with computers are not necessarily fond of secret codes, but the naming limits imposed by DOS do lead to creative abbreviations.

In addition to the limit on the number of characters you can use in a file name, you need to observe a few other conventions if you want to name your files wisely and well. These rules are described in the following list:

- File names may contain the letters A through Z and the numbers 1 through 9.

- The root name and extension must be separated by a period. You may name a file EXPENSE.DEC but not EXPENSEDEC.

- No spaces are allowed within root names or extensions. You may not call a file EX PENSE.DEC or EXPENSE.D C.

- You should not use COM or EXE as an extension, because they're used for program or command files.

- You may not use control characters such as ESC or DEL in a file name, but extended characters, such as Alt-255, are acceptable.

■ Every file within a directory must have a unique name, but files may have the same root name and different extensions (such as RE-SUME.1 and RESUME.2). And files in different directories may have the same name. You can, for example, keep a master file called SOURCES in your root directory and also files called SOURCES in a series of monthly directories containing sources specific to each month.

■ Root names are mandatory; extensions are optional. Thus, you may name a file either ACCOUNTS.REC or ACCOUNTS, but you may not name it .REC.

■ You may not use the following symbols in a file name, because they have special meaning to DOS:

+ = / [ ] " : ; , ? * \ | < >

■ You may, however, use the following symbols:

$ # @ ! ^ ( ) - { } ' ~ _ % &

(Why you would want to use these symbols is another question. File names are difficult enough to remember just with letters and numbers.)

T I P

Because DOS is so picky about the way you enter information (referred to as *syntax* in all the manuals), the best thing to do when you get the message Bad command or file name is reenter your data. You quite possibly may have accidentally entered a space or pressed the wrong key.

A letter to the editor might be called LETTER.DOC, the monthly food budget might be called JULY.WK3, and the file that runs the word processor might be called WP.EXE. The DOC extension usually indicates a document created using Microsoft Word, the WK3 extension indicates a file created in Lotus 1-2-3, and the EXE extension is used for files that run programs. Microsoft Word automatically tacks on the DOC extension when you create a document in that program. WordPerfect, in contrast, does not require an extension. You can call a file that contains a letter LETTER, LETTER.MAY, or MAY.LTR, creating your own extensions to classify documents.

Examining Types of Files

The letter to the editor and the monthly budget are files you create. The file that runs your word processor, on the other hand, was created by a programmer and is included in your word processing program when you purchase it.

You can split files into two types right off the bat: the ones you create and the ones someone else creates as part of your software programs. First, take a look at files that are included in your software programs.

Looking at Program Files

Files created by someone else often contain instructions to carry out tasks, such as running your word processing program. Such files are called *program* or *command files*.

You always can distinguish a program file from other types of files by looking at it. Because a program file is written in a binary code that only the computer understands, the file is unreadable to you. When you look at a program file, you see all kinds of symbols—everything from little grinning faces to what look like Egyptian ankh symbols.

T I P If you want to see what a program file looks like, change to the directory that contains a software program and use the TYPE command to display the program file. At the DOS prompt, type **type**, press the space bar, type the name of the file that runs your program, and press Enter. You need to type the full file name including its extension, which more than likely is EXE or COM. If you use WordPerfect, for example, type **type wp.exe** at the prompt. A screenful or more of true weirdness flashes by, and your computer starts beeping. Don't worry, though—it isn't harmful to your system.

Looking at Data Files and Text Files

The files you create can be subdivided into *data files* and *text files*. Although any file you create contains data, the term data file often is used to refer to files that contain special coding for individual programs. Such coding sometimes is referred to as *formatting*, not to be confused with disk formatting. Take word processing, for example. When you create a document, you more than likely will add special touches such as indented paragraphs or italics to emphasize a point. Each program uses its own specific set of encryption codes for such flourishes.

Text files also are referred to as *ASCII files*. ASCII, which stands for American Standard Code for Information Interchange is the *lingua franca* of computer programs. Although your Microsoft Word word processor doesn't speak WordPerfect, and vice-versa, for example, both of them speak ASCII. You therefore can exchange files with other users even if they don't use the same type of program you do.

Just as you can recognize a program file by its "unreadable" symbols, you also can distinguish a data file from a text file. The text file appears on your screen as plain text if you view it from the DOS command line; no fancy symbols appear. The data file is a cross between a text file and a program file. You see and can read your text, but you also see plenty of weird little formatting symbols.

Looking at Other File Types

You can find as many types of files as you can programs, and this text doesn't go into all of them. But the following paragraphs give you a brief introduction to some of the file types you will encounter in your hard disk adventures.

System files contain hardware information and sometimes are called *device drivers*. The Mouse Systems mouse, for example, comes with a driver called MSCMOUSE.SYS. DOS also contains system files, such as ANSI.SYS, which define functions including display graphics and cursor movement, and IO.SYS and MSDOS.SYS, the DOS kernel.

Batch files are files that contain a series of DOS commands executed one after the other as if you had typed them. You can identify a batch file by its extension, BAT. For more information, see Chapter 7, "Using Batch Files and Macros."

Graphics files are files that contain information needed to display graphics, such as menus, windows, and other display items. You usually can spot a graphics file by the extension TIF or PCX, although many others exist also.

Understanding Other File Attributes

A file has more than just a name. When you view a file in the DOS Shell file list or from the DOS command line, the size of the file, expressed in bytes, appears to the right of the file's name. (One byte is the amount of space needed to store a single alphanumeric character.)

To the right of the file's size, DOS displays the date and time the file was created or last modified. Modifying refers to changing the file's contents. If you simply copy or rename the file, the date and time don't change.

You can use the date, time, and size to help manage your files. Suppose that you change the name of a file, for example, and then have two files that contain the same information. Later you forget which file is which and whether you made any changes to either of the files. Looking at the date and size in the file list can help you determine which file is the most recent and whether the contents of both files are the same. You can distinguish between the files without having to read through them.

If you share your computer, keeping track of the date, time, and size of files also can help you determine whether someone else has been messing around with your files. If you come in on Monday and notice that a file's date has changed to Sunday, you know that someone else has been in your file. You then can take appropriate precautions if necessary.

Speaking of appropriate precautions—did you know that DOS can help you out? It contains a command called ATTRIB, which among other things enables you to designate a file as read-only to prevent its accidental deletion. (In DOS lingo, this process is called setting the file's read-only attribute or turning on the read-only flag.) If you share your computer with people whose love of tinkering outweighs their computer skills, you may want to remove the ATTRIB file after you have designated a file as read-only, to prevent someone else from removing the read-only flag.

Suppose that you have a file called COUNCIL in your PERSONAL directory. This file represents the text of your speech to the city council about proposed zoning changes affecting your neighborhood. To change this file to a read-only file, type the following command at the DOS command line and then press Enter:

ATTRIB + R C:\PERSONAL\COUNCIL

You have just indicated that you want to take the file named COUNCIL in the directory named PERSONAL and make that file a read-only file. (+R tells DOS to turn the read-only attribute on; -R tells DOS to turn the read-only attribute off.)

Archive is another possible file attribute, which you also set by using the ATTRIB command. The archive attribute is important for backing up files, which you learn more about in Chapter 10, "Understanding the Importance of Backing Up."

ATTRIB is a mixed blessing, however, thanks to DOS 5.0. Remember IO.SYS and MSDOS.SYS, the hidden files you learned about in Chapter 3? These files are so important that the system doesn't display them in a regular directory display listing, to decrease the odds of you accidentally damaging or deleting them. You can type **dir**, **dir/p**, or **dir/w**, but the files do not show up.

Thanks to DOS 5.0, you can display the hidden files by typing the following command at the DOS prompt and pressing Enter:

   DIR C:\ /A:H

Figure 5.1 shows a display of the hidden system files.

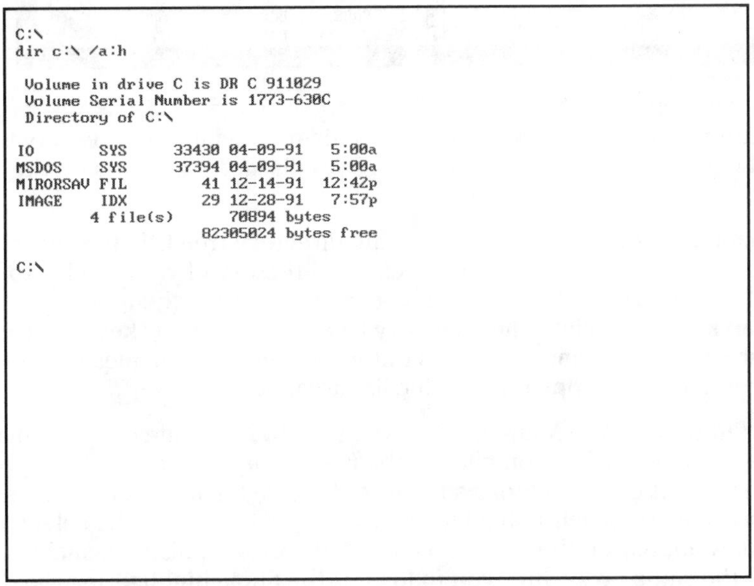

```
C:\
dir c:\ /a:h

 Volume in drive C is DR C 911029
 Volume Serial Number is 1773-630C
 Directory of C:\

IO      SYS     33430 04-09-91    5:00a
MSDOS   SYS     37394 04-09-91    5:00a
MIRORSAV FIL       41 12-14-91   12:42p
IMAGE   IDX        29 12-28-91    7:57p
       4 file(s)       70894 bytes
                    82305024 bytes free

C:\
```

FIG. 5.1

Displaying hidden files.

Displaying File Lists

As you learned in Chapter 4, you see a list of files on the right half of the screen as soon as you enter the DOS Shell (see fig. 5.2). The file list you see here depends on which directory is selected in the directory tree on the left. You can tell which directory is highlighted because its name appears in reverse video in the directory tree and also appears in the file list title bar.

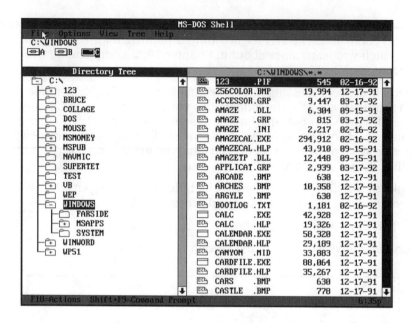

FIG. 5.2

Displaying the file list in the DOS Shell.

In figure 5.2, the WINDOWS directory is highlighted in the directory tree, and the list of files stored in the WINDOWS directory appears on the right.

To change the files on display, click the directory tree title bar to activate the directory tree and then click the directory of your choice to select it. (If you want to use the keyboard rather than the mouse, press the Tab key to highlight the directory tree, use the arrow keys to select the directory you want, and press Enter to select it.) The files for the selected directory appear in the file list area.

WINDOWS

The Windows 3.1 File Manager uses the same basic split-screen format as the DOS Shell. After you choose the File Manager from the Main program group, the screen looks similar to the DOS Shell screen with a directory tree on the left and a file list on the right. Files for the selected directory appear on the right. To change the files on display, simply follow the same procedure you follow for the Shell, highlighting the directory on your left to make the files for that directory appear on the right.

If you're working from the DOS command line, you use the DIR command to display the files contained in the current directory. Figure 5.3, for example, shows the files contained in the root directory—the list that appears if you type **dir** when the root directory is the current directory.

COMMAND

```
Volume in drive C is MS-DOS_5
Volume Serial Number is 184C-8130
Directory of C:\

DOS          <DIR>       02-12-92    4:09p
COMMAND  COM     47845 04-09-91    5:00a
WINA20   386      9349 04-09-91    5:00a
CONFIG   SYS       109 02-17-92    6:49p
TEST         <DIR>       03-16-92    7:23p
MOUSE        <DIR>       02-14-92    7:27p
WINDOWS      <DIR>       02-14-92    9:51p
AUTOEXEC BAT       163 03-03-92    8:43p
WP51         <DIR>       02-14-92   10:12p
SUPERTET     <DIR>       02-16-92    6:59p
WEP          <DIR>       02-16-92    7:10p
123          <DIR>       02-16-92    3:49p
MSMONEY      <DIR>       02-17-92    9:21p
WINWORD      <DIR>       02-18-92    9:09a
VB           <DIR>       02-19-92   11:17p
MSPUB        <DIR>       02-20-92    9:15p
NAVMIC       <DIR>       02-27-92    7:21p
MIRROR   FIL    141312 02-27-92    7:23p
COLLAGE      <DIR>       03-07-92    6:31p
Press any key to continue . . .
```

FIG. 5.3

Displaying the contents of the root directory.

A couple of options (called *switches*) make working with the DIR command easier. If you display files for a huge directory, for example, DOS just scrolls right through it until reaching the end. You're lucky if you can read a few of the entries near the end of the list; the rest of the entries speed by in a blur. To avoid that problem, you can type **dir /p**, which tells DOS to pause at the end of each screen so that you can look at your leisure. When you're ready to move on to the next screenful of entries, you simply press any key.

Another handy switch is /W. When you type **dir /w** at the prompt, DOS gives you a wide-angle view of all the files in a directory, displaying only the names and not the size, date, or time. Figure 5.4 shows the root directory displayed in a wide-angle view.

NOTE You can use several other switches with DIR. For more information, see Appendix A, the DOS command reference.

```
C:\>dir /w

 Volume in drive C is MS-DOS_5
 Volume Serial Number is 184C-8130
 Directory of C:\

[DOS]            COMMAND.COM      WINA20.386      CONFIG.SYS      [TEST]
[BRUCE]          [MOUSE]          [PKWARE]        [WINDOWS]       AUTOEXEC.BAT
[WP51]           [SUPERTET]       [WEP]           [123]           [MSMONEY]
[WINWORD]        [VB]             [MSPUB]         [NAVMIC]        MIRROR.FIL
[COLLAGE]
        21 file(s)       198778 bytes
                       53649408 bytes free

C:\>
```

Using Wild Cards When Working with Files

A *wild card* is a special character that stands for one or more other characters that may appear in the same place. Wild cards thus enable you to specify groups of files on the command line or in dialog boxes for copying, moving, and other file-management tasks. You can use a wild card in the base name or the extension—or both—of a file name specifier.

DOS accepts two wild cards: the question mark (?), which represents a single character, and the asterisk (*), which represents a whole group of characters. (Now you know why you cannot use those symbols in a file name.)

Wild cards can help you in a couple of ways. First, they enable you to act on whole groups of files at once. Second, wild cards are great when you're trying to find a file and cannot quite remember its name. Given that your computer can hold millions of bytes, or the equivalent of thousands of pages of information, the fact that you aren't on a first-name basis with all your files is no surprise.

You may have several drafts of your resume, for example, called RE-SUME.1, RESUME.2, and RESUME.3. Suppose that you don't remember which one is the most current one. You can type **resume.*** in the Search

For text box of the Search File dialog box to have DOS find all the resume files for you so that you can examine them to see which has the most current date. In this instance, you also can opt to use **resume.?** because the files differ by only one character. (For more information on finding files, see this chapter's section on "Searching for Files.")

Wild cards also are handy when you want to round up a group of files. Suppose that you're a graphic designer and need to send all your graphics files to a publisher. You don't want to have to copy them one at a time to a floppy disk. All your graphics files use the TIF extension, so you can type a single command—**copy *.tif**—to copy all the TIF files.

Selecting Files

Before you can take any action on a file, such as copying or deleting it, you have to *select* it. To select files in the DOS Shell, first be sure that the current directory contains the files you want to select. If not, select the appropriate directory by using the arrow keys to highlight it and pressing Enter to select it or by clicking the directory. (If this step doesn't work, double-check to be sure that the directory tree is activated (highlighted). To activate the directory tree, press the Tab key if you're using the keyboard, or click the directory tree menu bar with the mouse.) Next, select the file list area by clicking it with the mouse or pressing the Tab key.

In the following paragraphs, you learn how to select individual files, multiple files, or all files at the same time.

Selecting Individual Files

After you have selected the directory that contains the file you want to select and then have selected the file list area, you're ready to select the file itself. Scroll down the list, using the arrow keys or the mouse, until you reach the file. Click it with the mouse, or use the arrow keys to highlight the file and then press the space bar to select it.

When you select a file, DOS highlights (displays in reverse video) both the icon and the file name.

> If the name shows in reverse video but the icon doesn't, the file has not been selected. You may have forgotten to press the space bar.

T I P

T I P If you do not see icons next to your directories and files, you don't have the Shell set up for graphics mode. To select graphics mode, open the Options menu and select Display. Then choose the graphics mode of your choice. (You can choose from three text and five graphics modes.) The type you choose depends on your display adapter (video card). Not all support graphics, but all support text. If you're using VGA, you probably want 30- or 34-line medium resolution. The higher the resolution, the higher the number of lines, which means that the words and symbols appear smaller on-screen.

To select a file in Windows, click the file's icon with the mouse or use the arrow keys to highlight the file and then press Enter to select it.

Selecting Multiple Files

At some point, you may want to copy multiple files to a different directory. You may, for example, want to copy files to a directory for a new month or year or copy several files to a floppy disk to take to your PC at home. You may even want to delete a group of old files. The DOS Shell enables you to work with more than one file at a time.

If you want to select multiple files that are listed sequentially, click the name of the first file with the mouse. Then press the Shift key and hold it down while you move the mouse pointer to the last file you want to select and click that file. If you're using the keyboard, use the arrow keys to move to the first file you want to select, press Enter to select it, and hold the Shift key while you use the arrow and Enter keys to select the other files.

If you want to select multiple files that are not listed sequentially, press and hold down the Ctrl key while you click the name of each file you want to select. If you're using the keyboard, select the first file in the group by using the Enter key, then press the Shift key and the F8 key together. The word Add appears in the status bar at the bottom of the screen. Use the arrow keys to move to the other files you want to select, and press the space bar to select each of them. After you're finished, press Shift-F8 again to remove the word Add from the status bar.

Figure 5.5 shows a group of sequentially listed files selected on the DOS Shell screen. Figure 5.6 shows another group of selected files: ones that are not listed sequentially.

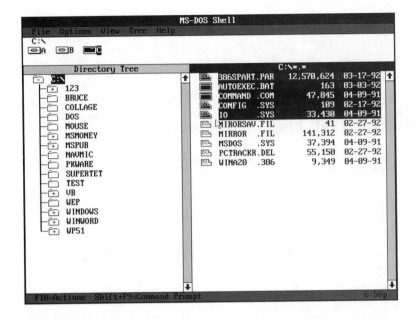

FIG. 5.5

Selecting more than
one file in sequence.

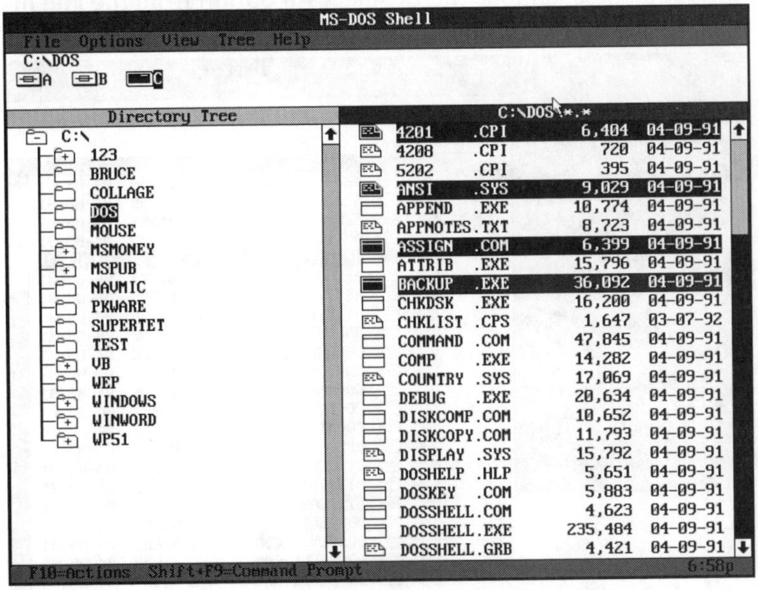

FIG. 5.6

Selecting a
nonsequential
group of files.

You use these same multiple-selection options to deselect groups of
files, which is handy if you make a mistake and select the wrong group.

WINDOWS

To select multiple files in Windows, go to the File Manager screen, select the directory you want, and then hold down the Ctrl key while clicking each individual file. If the files are in sequence, you can click the first file and then hold down the Shift key while you click the last file in the group.

Selecting All Files in a Directory

The DOS Shell offers a shortcut method for selecting all files in a directory. Follow these steps:

1. In the directory tree area, select the directory that contains the files you want to select.

2. Select the file list area.

3. Press the Ctrl-/ key combination or choose the Select All option from the File menu (see fig. 5.7).

The Shell displays all selected files for the current directory in reverse video, as shown in figure 5.8.

(To deselect all files, choose the Deselect All option from the File menu.)

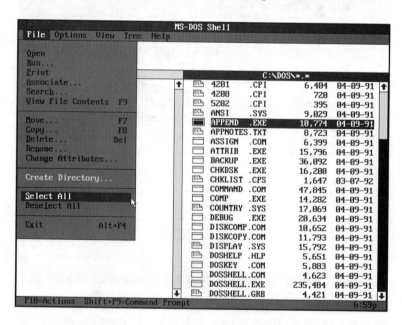

FIG. 5.7

Choosing the Select All option.

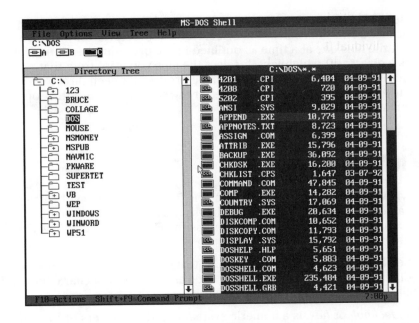

FIG. 5.8

Selecting all files in a directory, using the DOS Shell.

If you're using Windows, follow these steps to select all files in a directory:

1. Open the File menu from the File Manager menu bar.

2. Choose Select Files. A dialog box appears with the characters *.* displayed in the text entry box. Remember that this set of characters indicates that all the files in that directory will be selected. (If you want to select a single file, you simply type its name in the text entry box.)

3. Click Select or press Enter.

The command line works a little differently. When you work in the DOS Shell or in Windows, you select the files first and then choose the command to affect those files. On the command line, you specify the command before you select the files. You cannot, for example, just type *.* at the C> prompt to indicate that you want to select every file. You instead have to include the command that you want to act on every file—COPY *.* or DEL *.*, for example.

Selecting Files across Directories

You also can use the Shell to select files from more than one directory, a feature that comes in handy, for example, if you want to copy files from your word processing directory and spreadsheet directory to a floppy disk.

To select files from more than one directory, begin by opening the Options menu and then select the Select Across Directories option. You select the files one at a time as outlined in the preceding sections. You click a directory to highlight it, select the files you want from that directory's file list, and repeat the same process for each directory. Then you can manipulate all the files at the same time—use the Copy command to copy them, for example.

Viewing Files

To view a file in the DOS Shell, select the file from the file list by using the arrow keys or the mouse to highlight the file. (See the preceding section on "Selecting Files.") Then press the F9 key or select View File Contents from the File menu.

If the file you want to view is an ASCII (text) file, the Shell displays the ASCII file viewer. If the file contains code as well as ASCII characters, the Shell displays the hexadecimal viewer.

Hexadecimal, or *hex*, is a numeric system based on powers of 16. It includes the letters A through F as well as the numbers 0 through 9. Hex often is used by programmers because it's easier to work with than binary.

You can switch between the ASCII and hex viewers by pressing the F9 key. Figure 5.9 shows the DOS 5.0 README.TXT file as seen in the ASCII viewer, and figure 5.10 shows the README.TXT file in hex.

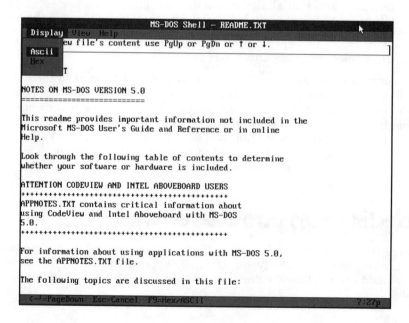

FIG. 5.9

Looking at a file in the ASCII viewer.

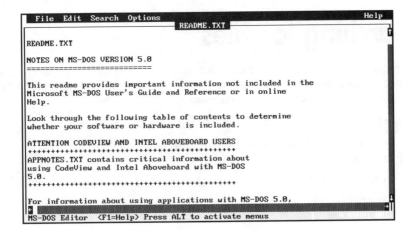

```
                    MS-DOS Shell - README.TXT
 Display  View  Help
       ew file's content use PgUp or PgDn or ↑ or ↓.
 Ascii
 Hex  ▸         20202020   20202020   20202020   20202020
                20202020   20202020   20202020   0D0A5245            ..RE
 000020         41444D45   2E545854   0D0A0D0A   4E4F5445   ADME.TXT....NOTE
 000030         53204F4E   204D532D   444F5320   56455253   S ON MS-DOS VERS
 000040         494F4E20   352E300D   0A3D3D3D   3D3D3D3D   ION 5.0..=======
 000050         3D3D3D3D   3D3D3D3D   3D3D3D3D   3D3D3D3D   ================
 000060         3D3D3D3D   0D0A0D0A   54686973   20726561   ====....This rea
 000070         646D6520   70726F76   69646573   20696D70   dme provides imp
 000080         6F727461   6E742069   6E666F72   6D617469   ortant informati
 000090         6F6E2069   6F742069   6E636C75   64656420   on not included
 0000A0         696E2074   68650D0A   4D696372   6F736F66   in the..Microsof
 0000B0         74204D53   2D444F53   20557365   72277320   t MS-DOS User's
 0000C0         47756964   6520616E   64205265   66657265   Guide and Refere
 0000D0         6E636520   6F722069   6E206F6E   6C696E65   nce or in online
 0000E0         0D0A4865   6C702E20   0D0A0D0A   4C6F6F6B   ..Help. ....Look
 0000F0         20746872   6F756768   20746865   20666F6C    through the fol
 000100         6C6F7769   6E672074   61626C65   206F6620   lowing table of
 000110         636F6E74   656E7473   20746F20   64657465   contents to dete
 000120         726D696E   650D0A77   68657468   65722079   rmine..whether y
 000130         6F757220   736F6674   77617265   206F7220   our software or
 000140         68617264   77617265   20697320   696E636C   hardware is incl
 000150         75646564   2E0D0A0D   0A415454   454E5449   uded.....ATTENTI
 000160         4F4E2043   4F444556   49455720   414E4420   ON CODEVIEW AND
 000170         494E5445   4C204142   4F564542   4F415244   INTEL ABOVEBOARD
 000180         20555345   52530D0A   2B2B2B2B   2B2B2B2B   USERS..++++++++
 ◄─┘=PageDown  Esc=Cancel  F9=Hex/ASCII                              7:24p
```

FIG. 5.10

Looking at a file in the hex viewer.

You also can view a selected ASCII file by simply double-clicking it in the file list. Instead of appearing in the ASCII viewer, the file appears in the DOS Editor, as shown in figure 5.11. The DOS Editor is similar to the ASCII viewer except that the Editor screen offers more options, such as editing or searching files.

```
   File   Edit   Search   Options                              Help
                              README.TXT                             ↑
 README.TXT

 NOTES ON MS-DOS VERSION 5.0
 ===========================

 This readme provides important information not included in the
 Microsoft MS-DOS User's Guide and Reference or in online
 Help.

 Look through the following table of contents to determine
 whether your software or hardware is included.

 ATTENTION CODEVIEW AND INTEL ABOVEBOARD USERS
 ++++++++++++++++++++++++++++++++++++++++++++++
 APPNOTES.TXT contains critical information about
 using CodeView and Intel Aboveboard with MS-DOS
 5.0.
 ++++++++++++++++++++++++++++++++++++++++++++++
                                                                     ↓
 For information about using applications with MS-DOS 5.0,
 ◄                                                              ►    ↨
 MS-DOS Editor   <F1=Help> Press ALT to activate menus
```

FIG. 5.11

Viewing a file in the DOS Editor.

Windows does not contain an equivalent to the View File Contents option. To view an ASCII file in Windows, simply select the file in the file list and double-click. This procedure works only with ASCII files. Windows does not contain an option for viewing hexadecimal files.

WINDOWS

As you learned previously in this chapter's section on "Looking at Program Files," the TYPE command is a fun way to see what a program file looks like. You also can use this command to view an ASCII file. At the DOS prompt, just type **type**, press the space bar, and type the file name. If the file you want to view isn't in the current directory, remember that you also must type the path, as in TYPE \WINDOWS\README.

The TYPE command has the same problem the DIR command has: if more than one screen of information is in the file, DOS races right through it until reaching the end. You can press the Pause key found on 101-key enhanced keyboards or the Ctrl-S key combination, but having lightning-quick reflexes doesn't hurt. The best way to get DOS to pause is to include the | MORE option after the file's name. (The | is the vertical bar character, which is Shift-\ on most computers.) Using this option causes the file to display one screen of information at a time. The message —more— appears at the bottom of the screen to indicate that more information is available. To scroll to the next screenful of information, simply press Enter.

Suppose that you want to look at the DOS 5.0 README.TXT file. You have two options. You can change to the DOS directory and type the following command:

TYPE README.TXT | MORE

Or you can issue the command from any directory by typing the following command:

TYPE \DOS\README.TXT | MORE

Searching for Files

No matter how well you organize your disk, the time will come when you cannot remember in which directory you have stored a file. Luckily, DOS has commands that make that task easier.

To use the DOS Shell to search for a file, follow these steps:

1. Select Search from the File menu. The Search File dialog box appears, as shown in figure 5.12.

2. In the Search For text box, type the name of the file you want to find.

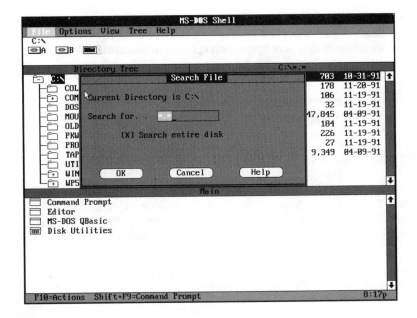

FIG. 5.12

The Search File dialog box.

NOTE When the Search File dialog first appears, *.* is in the Search For text box. As you may remember, *.* means that every file name and every extension are represented, so Search for: *.* tells DOS to search for all files. You need to type a file name or file specifier with wild cards to limit the search. You can search for all your 1-2-3 worksheet files, for example, by typing ***.wk3** in the Search For text box.

3. The Search File dialog box contains an option check box labeled Search Entire Disk. Unless you click this check box to unselect the option, DOS searches the entire disk for your file or files. If you want to limit your search to the selected directory only, click the Search Entire Disk box to remove the check mark.

4. Press Enter or click OK. The Search Results window appears with the file or files that meet your criteria. If your search doesn't turn up any files, the message No Files Match File Specifier appears. If you asked for a group of files, using wild cards, a list of the matching files appears.

WINDOWS

To search for a file in the Windows File Manager, select the directory you want for the initial search; then choose Search from the File menu. When the Search File dialog box appears, type the name of the file for which you want to search and click OK.

NOTE Although Windows does not contain a Search Entire Disk option, a check box labeled Search All Subdirectories is available. If you want the whole disk to be searched, make sure that you start your search at the root directory and select the Search All Subdirectories option.

COMMAND

To find files from the command line, use the /S switch with the DIR command. You can search for a specific file name or use wild cards. The /S switch tells DOS to search the current directory and all its subdirectories, so if you want to search the entire disk, issue the command with the root directory current.

If you want to use the DIR command to search for all your TIF files, for example, type **dir *.tif /s** at the prompt.

Copying Files

You probably will spend more time copying files than performing any other management chore. The DOS Shell gives you several options for copying files. You can copy single files from one disk to another or from one directory to another. You can use wild cards to copy entire groups of files. You even can change a file's name while you copy it. In the following sections, you learn how to use the File menu, the dual file list, and the mouse to copy files and also how to use Windows and the DOS command line for copying files.

Using the File Menu To Copy Files

To copy files by using the mouse and the File menu, follow these steps:

1. From the file list, select the file you want to copy.

2. From the File menu, click the Copy option. A Copy File dialog box appears, with the file you want to copy automatically entered in the From box.

> **T I P**
>
> If Copy doesn't appear as an option on the File menu, you don't have the file list highlighted. Highlight it by using the mouse or the Tab key.

3. In the To text entry box, enter the name of the destination directory or drive.

4. Click OK to copy the file.

To use the keyboard and the File menu to copy files, follow these steps:

1. Select the file or files you want to copy.

2. Select Copy from the File menu (or press the F8 key). The Copy File dialog box appears with the name of the selected file(s) in the From text entry box (see fig. 5.13).

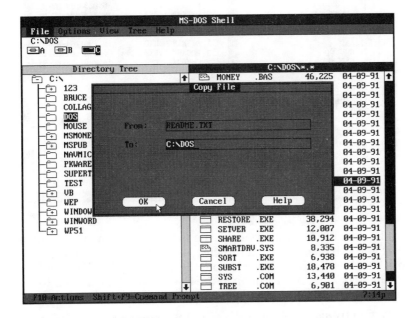

FIG. 5.13

Displaying the Copy File dialog box.

3. At the To text box, type the location of the destination drive or directory. (When the To box comes up, it always shows the source directory, so you have to type the destination directory.)

4. Press Enter or click OK. The files are copied to the new drive or directory but remain intact in the source directory as well.

Using the Dual File List To Copy Files

You may spend a great deal of time copying files to floppy disks. To copy a file to a different directory or drive, you can use the dual file list. First, select the Dual File List option from the View menu. (If you're going to copy a file to a directory on the same disk, you don't need to select Dual File List, but you can.) The dual file list displays two directory trees and file lists, as shown in figure 5.14.

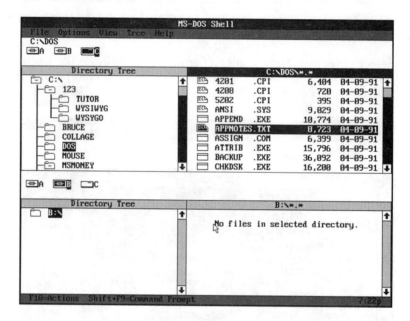

FIG. 5.14

Displaying the dual file list.

When the dual file list first appears, the top and bottom lists are identical. But you can change which directory trees appear. If you want to change the destination directory from the C drive to the B drive, for example, just click the B drive icon in the lower half of the screen to select that drive.

In figure 5.14, the files listed at the top of the screen are the files to be copied. The directory at the bottom of the screen, the destination disk, is empty.

To copy files by using the dual file list, follow these steps:

1. In the source file list, use the mouse to select the file or files you want to copy.

2. Hold down the Ctrl key and the left mouse button as you drag the files to the destination directory in the directory tree on the bottom half of the screen. If you have selected multiple files, they all drag at once.

The pointer changes from an arrow to a circle when you start dragging files with the mouse, as shown in figure 5.15. When the pointer reaches the destination directory tree, it turns into a file icon.

NOTE   If you're copying files to a different disk, you don't have to hold down the Ctrl key. If you're copying them to a directory on the same disk, however, you must hold down the Ctrl key; otherwise, the Shell moves the files instead of copying them.

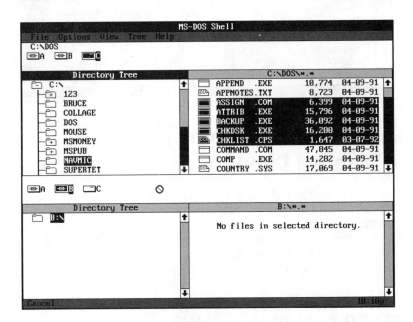

FIG. 5.15

Preparing to drag files with the mouse.

3. When you reach the destination directory, release the mouse button. A Confirm Mouse Operation box appears, as shown in figure 5.16.

4. Select Yes to copy the files.

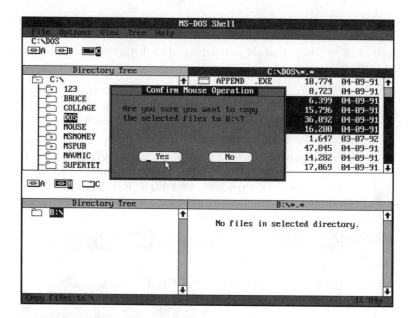

FIG. 5.16

The confirmation dialog box that appears when you copy files with the mouse.

Using the Mouse To Copy Files to a Different Directory

You don't have to use either the File menu or the dual file list to copy files if you're using a mouse. If you want to copy a file to a different directory on the same drive, you simply can select the file and use the mouse to drag it to the directory tree for the current drive, as shown in figure 5.17. The selected file appears as a document icon to the right of the selected destination directory.

Copying Files in Windows

Copying files in the Windows File Manager is similar to the DOS Shell operation. You select multiple files the same way, by pressing the Shift key as you click files. To use the File menu to copy files in Windows, follow these steps:

1. After selecting the file or files you want to copy, press F8 or choose Copy from the File menu.

2. In the To entry box of the dialog box that pops up, type the destination for the selected file or files (see fig. 5.18).

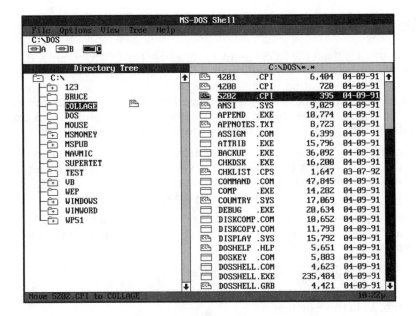

FIG. 5.17

Using the mouse to
drag a file to a new
directory.

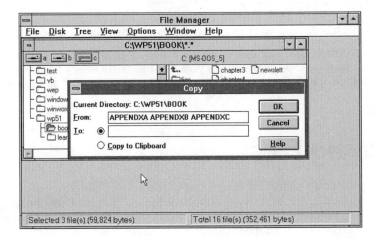

FIG. 5.18

Copying files with the
Windows File
Manager.

To use the mouse to copy files in Windows, hold down the left mouse
button, press and hold the Ctrl key, and drag the file's icon to a directory
icon or a minimized directory window on the same drive. (If you're
copying the file to a different drive, you do not need to hold down the
Ctrl key. Just drag the icon to a directory icon, drive icon, or minimized
window for the different drive.)

Using the DOS Command Line To Copy Files

COMMAND

To copy files from the DOS command line, use the COPY command. Specify first the location and name of the file from which you want to copy, then the location to which you want to copy. Suppose, for example, that you want to copy a file named REPORT from drive A to drive B. You type **copy a:report b:** at the prompt. In this example, the A drive is the *source drive* and the B drive is the *destination drive*.

If you're in the source or destination drive/directory when you copy, you don't have to specify that directory in your command. If you're in the A drive, for example, simply type **copy report b:** at the prompt, or if you're in the B drive, type the command **copy a:report**.

You also can rename a file while you copy it. If you want to change the name of the file from REPORT to ANNUALRP, for example, type this command:

COPY A:REPORT B:ANNUALRP

If you want to be sure that the copy process went well, add the /V switch, as in this command:

COPY A:REPORT B: /V

This switch tells DOS to verify that the copy was recorded properly.

Another option that can speed up your copying efforts is to use wild cards to specify groups of files. If you want to copy every file in the current directory to a floppy disk, for example, type **copy *.* a:** at the DOS prompt.

Moving Files

When you move a file, you take it out of the source directory and relocate it to a different directory. That process is different from copying a file, where you leave the original file intact in the source directory and create a copy of it in another directory or drive.

If you copy many files from one directory to another on your hard disk, you soon can see how space is being wasted with duplicate files. Moving the files is a better conservation tactic. You also may want to move files that you no longer need from a hard disk to a floppy disk.

Moving files in the DOS Shell is similar to copying them. You can use the Move option on the File menu or the mouse. To move files by using the File menu, follow these steps:

1. After selecting the file or files of your choice, press the F7 key or click the Move option in the File menu. The Move File dialog box appears, with the name of the selected file displayed in the From text entry box.

2. Type the name of the destination drive and/or directory. If you want to rename a file, include the new name after the directory name.

3. Click OK to move the files.

You also can use the mouse to drag selected file icons to a destination directory or drive.

To move files to a directory on the same disk, using the mouse, follow these steps:

1. After selecting the file or files you want to move, hold down the left mouse button and drag the files to the destination directory or drive icon.

2. Release the mouse button. A Confirm Mouse Operation dialog box appears and asks whether you're sure that you want to move the selected files.

3. Select Yes to move the files.

To move files to a directory on a different disk, using the mouse, follow these steps:

1. Select the file or files you want to move.

2. Hold down the Alt key while you press the left mouse button and drag the files to the destination directory or drive icon. If you don't hold down the Alt key, DOS thinks you want to copy the files.

3. Release the mouse button and the Alt key. A Confirm Mouse Operation dialog box appears and asks whether you're sure that you want to move the selected files.

4. Select Yes to move the files.

The Windows File Manager also contains a Move option in its File menu; you also can use the mouse to move files in Windows.

WINDOWS

To move a file or files in Windows by using the File menu, follow these steps:

1. Select the file or files you want to move.

2. Select Move from the File menu. A Move File dialog box appears with the source directory entered in the From box.

3. Type the destination directory and/or drive in the To box.

4. Select OK to move the files.

To move a file or files to a directory on the same drive by using the mouse in Windows, follow these steps:

1. Select the file or files you want to move.

2. Drag the file icons to the destination directory icon or minimized window.

3. Release the mouse button. A Confirm Mouse Operation box appears.

4. Select Yes.

To move a file or files to a directory on a different drive by using the mouse, follow these steps:

1. Select the file or files you want to move.

2. Hold down the Alt key while you drag the selected files to the destination directory. If you don't hold down the Alt key, Windows thinks you're copying the files.

3. Release the Alt key and left mouse button.

Deleting Files

When you no longer need a file, or after you have backed it up to a floppy or tape drive, you may want to delete the file to conserve space on your hard disk. To delete a file or files, using the DOS Shell, follow these steps:

1. Select the file or files you want to delete.

2. Choose Delete from the File menu or press the Del key. A Delete File Confirmation box appears. If you are deleting a single file, DOS displays its name and asks you to confirm the deletion. If you are deleting multiple files, all the names appear in a Delete box, and DOS asks you to confirm their deletion one at a time.

3. Press Enter or click the Yes button to delete the file or files.

T I P

The Options menu contains a Confirmation option that enables you to choose whether you want to confirm each deletion or skip that step. When you choose Confirmation, the window shown in figure 5.19 appears. Selecting the Confirm on Delete option is a good idea. If you don't, DOS simply deletes files without checking with you first. Taking that one last look to make sure that you aren't mistakenly deleting something important doesn't hurt.

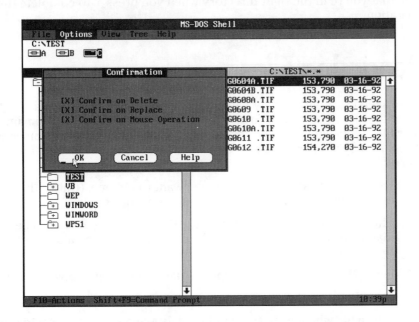

FIG. 5.19

Using the Confirmation option.

To delete a file in the Windows File Manager, follow these steps:

WINDOWS

1. Select the file or files you want to delete.

2. Select Delete from the File menu.

3. Type the name of the file you want to delete in the Delete window that appears.

4. Click OK. A Confirm File Delete dialog box appears, asking whether you want to delete the file.

5. Click Yes to delete the file.

To delete files from a directory by using the DOS command line, use the DEL (delete) or ERASE command. (They're interchangeable; many users choose to use DEL simply because it requires a bit less typing.) As with the other commands, you can use wild cards to delete groups of files or can specify the file name of a single file you want to delete. Suppose, for example, that you don't need your graphics files any more. Change to the directory that contains them and type **del *.tif** on the command line. To delete all files from a directory, type **del *.***. DOS warns you that all files will be deleted and asks for your confirmation. You want to be very sure that you're in the right directory when you press Y to complete this operation.

Renaming Files

If you keep track of things by date, you may want to rename files according to the month or year. You also may want to rename files if you name your files according to client, for example, and a client changes names or is replaced by a different client. To rename a file in the DOS Shell, follow these steps:

1. From the file list, select the file you want to rename. (Unlike the other commands, Rename is limited to one file at a time.)

2. Choose the Rename option from the File menu. The Rename File dialog box appears, displaying the file's current name along with a New Name box.

3. In the New Name text box, type the name you want to give the file.

4. Press Enter or click OK.

Renaming a file when using the Windows File Manager is identical to the DOS Shell approach. You select the file, select Rename from the File menu, and type the file's new name in the box.

Use the REN (RENAME) command to rename files from the DOS command line. Use this syntax:

    RENAME *oldname newname*

To rename JULY.ACT as AUGUST.ACT, for example, use this command:

    RENAME JULY.ACT AUGUST.ACT

If you want to move the file at the same time, type the paths, as in this example:

    RENAME C:\WP51\BOOK B:\FILES\CHAPTER6

This command renames the file named BOOK as CHAPTER6 and moves it from the WP51 subdirectory on drive C to the FILES subdirectory on drive B.

Summary

In this chapter, you have learned what a file is and how file names are organized. DOS file names consist of an eight-letter "first name" or root name and a three-letter "last name" or extension. The root name usually signifies the file's contents, and the extension typically indicates its function.

You also have learned how to display file lists and how to select individual files, multiple files, all files in a directory, and multiple files from more than one directory so that you can manipulate these files in a variety of ways. These ways include viewing, searching for, copying, moving, deleting, and renaming files—the meat and potatoes of disk management.

In Chapter 7, you learn about batch files, files that can streamline the way you work with your disk. You're heading from meat and potatoes to filet mignon, and you're sure to enjoy the uptown aspects of using DOS to organize your hard disk.

Working with Directories on Your Hard Disk

Understanding files is not enough if you want to do a good job managing the contents of your hard disk. Electronic files are no different from paper files in that you need some method of organizing them if you want to make the most productive use of your time. You wouldn't dream of tossing your paper files into a file cabinet at random; instead, you label manila folders and put related files into each of those folders. Can you imagine trying to do your taxes if your W-2s and expense information were jumbled together with your appliance owner's manuals, your car maintenance records, and your collection of Dave Barry articles? You would have to start slogging through that mass of paper in July to meet the April 15 deadline.

Here is where directories come in. In DOS, *directories* are the means by which you organize all the data you create on your computer. (Not every operating system uses this means of organization. The Macintosh, for example, takes the file cabinet metaphor all the way—you store your files in folders, which are represented on-screen by folder-style icons.)

The biggest thing to understand about directories is that they don't just magically appear. After DOS creates the root directory during the high-level format, the baton is passed to you—you're in charge.

T I P You typically don't have to worry about creating a directory for each of the software programs you install on your computer. Most of them create a directory for you. (Some are polite and ask your permission first; always say yes.) For the most part, you need to think about building directories for the work you create, your data files.

In this chapter, you learn some tips for developing a strategy for your directory system. No set rules exist for disk organization, but giving some thought to the way you do your day-to-day work is the best place to start.

This chapter also introduces you to the hierarchical directory system used by DOS. (DOS isn't alone in this regard; UNIX also uses this type of system.) You learn about concepts such as the path and the current directory.

You also are given step-by-step examples for working with directories. You learn how to create and name directories, make a directory the current directory, and expand and collapse the directory tree for easy viewing. Some examples assume that you're using the DOS 5.0 Shell, but procedures also are given for Windows 3.1 and the DOS command line.

Understanding basic directory concepts helps you in two ways. First, it helps you work more effectively because the time you would waste simply trying to locate your files is better spent on your work. Second, it cuts down on the time DOS wastes trying to find your files. DOS is methodical, which you discover shortly.

Viewing a Sample Directory

Although you're the master of your fate when it comes to creating directories, DOS doesn't abandon you completely. When you organize your paper files in manila folders, each folder doesn't automatically tell you how many files it contains, how large each file is, or when each file was created or changed. Your electronic directory, in contrast, gives you all that information and more.

Figure 6.1 shows you the contents of a sample directory, which you display by typing **dir** at the DOS command line. You learned how to use the DIR command to view files in Chapter 5, "Keeping Files Organized." Remember that when you use DIR, the contents of the current directory are displayed. You learn why that's important a little later in the chapter.

```
Volume in drive C is MS-DOS_5
Volume Serial Number is 184C-8130
Directory of C:\

DOS          <DIR>     02-12-92   4:09p
COMMAND  COM    47845 04-09-91   5:00a
WINA20   386     9349 04-09-91   5:00a
CONFIG   SYS      109 02-17-92   6:49p
TEST         <DIR>     03-16-92   7:23p
MOUSE        <DIR>     02-14-92   7:27p
WINDOWS      <DIR>     02-14-92   9:51p
AUTOEXEC BAT      163 03-03-92   8:43p
WP51         <DIR>     02-14-92  10:12p
SUPERTET     <DIR>     02-16-92   6:59p
WEP          <DIR>     02-16-92   7:10p
123          <DIR>     02-16-92   3:49p
MSMONEY      <DIR>     02-17-92   9:21p
WINWORD      <DIR>     02-18-92   9:09a
VB           <DIR>     02-19-92  11:17p
MSPUB        <DIR>     02-20-92   9:15p
NAVMIC       <DIR>     02-27-92   7:21p
MIRROR   FIL   141312 02-27-92   7:23p
COLLAGE      <DIR>     03-07-92   6:31p
Press any key to continue . . .
```

FIG. 6.1

Using DIR to display
the contents of a
sample directory.

The following paragraphs explain what the directory contains.

The *volume label* is the first line in the directory listing. This label is an optional identification that typically is assigned during the format.

The *volume serial number* is a number assigned automatically by DOS (Versions 4.0 and later). DOS uses this number to identify the disk.

Beneath the volume information, the following information appears for each file, from left to right: the file's name and extension, the size (expressed in bytes), and the date and time the file was created or modified.

Beneath the file information, the final directory listing tells you the total number of files the disk contains and how much free space is left on the disk (also measured in bytes).

Developing a Strategy

In the following sections, you learn the mechanics of creating, deleting, naming, and renaming directories as well as learn how to work with more than one directory at a time. Understanding how to perform all these tasks is important. But having a strategy for developing your directory system is equally critical.

First and foremost in your strategy should be this rule: Don't store files in your root directory. Your root directory should contain only other directories (subdirectories). If you store many files in the root directory, you will have a mess on your hands. Because of the way DOS is organized, it always searches the root directory first, unless you tell the system otherwise. If your root directory is cluttered with files, your programs take longer to load because DOS has to look through all the files in the root directory before finding your program instructions in their specific program directories.

Creating one directory called MYFILES to hold all your data files isn't the answer either. That method may work temporarily, but before long your directory gets out of control. You have too many files in one place and have such a long directory listing that you cannot find anything.

Before building your directory structure, you need to ask yourself these questions: What kinds of files are you storing? Word processing documents? Spreadsheets? Client databases? All of the above? Do your files change from month to month, week to week, or day to day?

The best place to start is to take a good look at how you do your work now. Look at the things you do over and over again. Look at the ways you tend to categorize things. If you're in a field that stresses monthly deadlines or reports, such as accounting, for example, you may want to organize your categories by month. You can have a PAYROLL directory, for example, containing files called PAYROLL.MAY, PAYROLL.JUN, and so on. At the end of the year you can create a new directory called PAYROLL.93 and store your 1993 payroll files there, using the same category the following year.

You may prefer to organize your directories by categories other than time. If you have a public relations or sales business, grouping your directories in terms of clients or projects, such as the SMITH.FND (Smith Foundation) or ELKSPRMO (Elks promotion), may be easier. If you share your computer with others in an office setting, organizing directories by person may be the best approach. You can have one directory for Nancy, another one for Sue, and another one for Bruce. Each one of those directories can contain subdirectories according to task. If Sue writes ads for the company and also edits the company newsletter, she can have one subdirectory called ADS and another one called NEWS.

You can get some good clues by looking at the patterns in your work now, whether you have been using a computer, paper, or both. You may even find certain categories that seem a little too big and might benefit from pruning. Suppose, for example, that you are in charge of a charitable organization and have an address list that has gotten out of control. You can subdivide such a list into previous ticket purchasers, current contributors, and volunteers.

Whatever you decide, the strategy you adopt has to feel comfortable for you as well as be able to help you find the files you need. Devising a plan does involve some work up front, but you can experiment until you find a method that works best for you.

Understanding How Directories Work

Subdividing your categories is where DOS's hierarchical directory structure comes in. In the next section, you learn how to take advantage of DOS's hierarchical design to fine-tune your disk's organization, how to navigate directory paths, and how to work with the current directory.

Understanding Hierarchical Directories

DOS organizes everything in a hierarchical fashion, which is a fancy way of saying that directories can contain other directories (called *subdirectories*), which in turn can contain even more directories. Think of those nesting-globe toys, where each globe contains a smaller globe, and you get the idea. This hierarchy stems from the *root directory*, which as you may remember is the hard disk's main directory created during the high-level format.

The structure often is depicted as an upside-down tree, with the root directory representing the root, of course, and the subdirectories representing branches. Figure 6.2 shows a sample DOS directory tree.

The hierarchical nature becomes more apparent when you look at the WP51, WINDOWS, and COMM directories. All of them contain subdirectories. WP51 and COMM each contain more than one branch (level) of subdirectories. COMM, for example, contains a subdirectory named FILES, which contains another subdirectory called GRAPHICS.

The DOS Shell window gives you a graphic depiction of this hierarchy in the directory tree on the left side of the screen (see fig. 6.3). The root directory is shown at the top of the tree, with its subdirectories and their subdirectories listed below the root directory. In this example, the WINDOWS directory is highlighted, and the files contained in the WINDOWS directory are shown on the right.

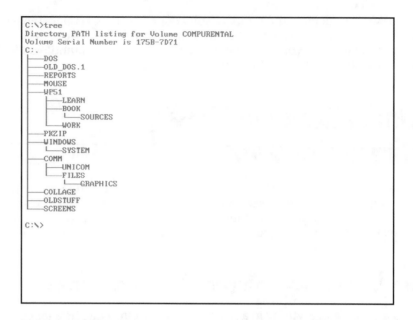

FIG. 6.2

Looking at a DOS
directory tree.

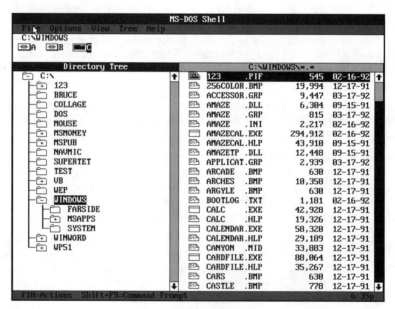

FIG. 6.3

Viewing the directory
tree in the DOS Shell.

You also can view your directory structure if you're using Windows (see fig. 6.4). Select the Main program group from the Program Manager window and then select the File Manager icon. What you see on-screen is similar to the DOS Shell.

WINDOWS

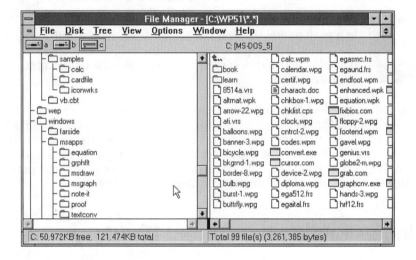

File Manager - [C:\WP51*.*]

File   Disk   Tree   View   Options   Window   Help

C: [MS-DOS_5]

```
        ┌─ samples              t..            calc.wpm         egasmc.frs
        ├─ calc                 book           calendar.wpg     egaund.frs
        ├─ cardfile             learn          certif.wpg       endfoot.wpm
        ├─ iconwrks             8514a.vrs      charactr.doc     enhanced.wpk
        └─ vb.cbt               altrnat.wpk    chkbox-1.wpg     equation.wpk
   ─ wep                        arrow-22.wpg   chklist.cps      fixbios.com
   ─ windows                    ati.vrs        clock.wpg        floppy-2.wpg
        ├─ farside              balloons.wpg   cntrct-2.wpg     footend.wpm
        ├─ msapps               banner-3.wpg   codes.wpm        gavel.wpg
            ├─ equation         bicycle.wpg    convert.exe      genius.vrs
            ├─ grphflt           bkgrnd-1.wpg   cursor.com       globe2-m.wpg
            ├─ msdraw           border-8.wpg   device-2.wpg     grab.com
            ├─ msgraph          bulb.wpg       diploma.wpg      graphcnv.exe
            ├─ note-it          burst-1.wpg    ega512.frs       hands-3.wpg
            ├─ proof            buttrfly.wpg   egaital.frs      hrf12.frs
            ├─ textconv
```

C: 50,972KB free, 121,474KB total   Total 99 file(s) (3,261,385 bytes)

FIG. 6.4

The directory tree in Microsoft Windows.

Notice that in all three figures, the root directory contains mostly subdirectories, with few files.

To view your directory tree from the DOS command line, type **tree** and press Enter at the prompt.

COMMAND

Don't worry about creating too many subdirectories because you can create as many subdirectories and levels of subdirectories as you want. But before you learn how to create directories, you need to understand the concepts of paths and current directories. Then you can save yourself from getting a lot of Bad command or file name messages and from creating subdirectories that end up in the wrong place.

Understanding Paths

Paths are closely related to the hierarchy established by DOS. A *path* specifies the precise location of a file within that hierarchy. Notice in figure 6.2 that the WP51 directory contains a subdirectory called BOOK.

Inside the BOOK subdirectory is a file called SOURCES. The path for that file is C:\WP51\BOOK\SOURCES, which means that the file named SOURCES resides in the directory named BOOK, which resides in the directory named WP51, which resides in the root directory, represented by the backslash symbol (\), which resides on the hard drive (C:).

 NOTE   In a path name, the first backslash after the hard drive (indicated by C:) is the root directory (C:\). The other backslashes simply serve to separate the file names and subdirectories.

The path is in effect the file's full address. The root directory is the state, the WP51 directory is the city, and the BOOK directory is the street address. You need all these components to find your file, just as you need the city and state as well as the street address when you send a letter. (Chapter 9 gives you shortcuts you can use to skip some of these path components. Turn to that chapter for more information.)

Understanding the Current Directory

If you don't specify a path for DOS, it always looks in the *current* (also called the *default*) directory for the file you want. (When you start up your computer, the default directory is the root directory.)

What's more, if DOS doesn't find the file you're asking for in the current directory, the system gives up. Here's a concrete (and classic) example. Suppose that you are in the DOS Shell and want to run WordPerfect. To do so, you need a file called WP.EXE. You select Run from the File menu and type **wp.exe** at the command prompt. Guess what happens? You get the message Bad command or file name. This error occurs because you are currently in the root directory rather than the WP51 directory, which contains the file WP.EXE. DOS cannot find the file in the current directory.

One option to surmount this problem is to specify the full path for the command. In the example, you can type **c:\wp51\wp.exe** on the command line, telling DOS to look in the WP51 directory for the file WP.EXE and execute that command.

Or you can change directories before you issue the command, making the directory that contains the command (WP51 in the example) the current directory. (See this chapter's section on "Changing the Prompt To Reflect the Current Directory.") A third option is described in Chapter 9, where you find out how to bypass those extra steps so that you can start your word processing program from any directory.

Here's another example, using the DOS command line. Suppose that you're looking at the C> prompt and want to start Lotus 1-2-3. Because you haven't learned how to bypass the extra steps yet, here are your two choices for starting 1-2-3:

- Specify the full path for the command. Because the command that starts Lotus, 123.EXE, is contained in the directory called 123, you need to type **\123\123** at the prompt. (You don't have to type the EXE extension.)

- Change the current directory to the Lotus 1-2-3 directory by typing **cd 123** and pressing Enter at the prompt. Then you can just type **123** to start the program.

Changing the Prompt
To Reflect the Current Directory

Normally, the DOS prompt shows only the drive name, such as C>, regardless of whether you're in the root directory, the WORD directory, or the 123 directory. One of the best things you can do, especially if you want to work in the DOS command line, is to change the prompt so that you always know which directory you're in. To change the prompt, you need to add a command to your AUTOEXEC.BAT file, a special file that is discussed fully in Chapter 7, "Using Batch Files and Macros." Don't worry, the process is easy. Follow these steps:

1. Find out whether your computer has an AUTOEXEC.BAT file. Go into the DOS Shell by typing **dosshell** and pressing Enter at the prompt; select File from the menu bar; and select Open from the pull-down menu. A dialog box appears, asking which file you want to open. Type **autoexec.bat** and press Enter. If you get the message Bad command or file name, type **cd c:\dos** and press Enter; then reenter the DOS Shell.

   If you have an AUTOEXEC.BAT file, the File Editor screen appears with the AUTOEXEC.BAT file displayed. If you don't have an AUTOEXEC.BAT file, a blank File Editor screen appears so that you can create one.

2. Type **prompt pg** in the file. (If you're typing in an existing AUTOEXEC.BAT file, type this line underneath any existing lines.)

3. Save the file by choosing Save from the File menu.

4. Reboot your computer by pressing the Ctrl-Alt-Del key combination. Your prompt should be C:\>, which lets you know that your current directory is the root directory.

Managing Your Directories

In this section, you learn all the ins and outs of working with directories. You find out how to navigate the directory structure, use absolute and relative paths, expand and collapse branches in the directory tree, create directories, rename directories, and remove directories.

Navigating the Directory Structure

Maneuvering your way around all the directories on your disk is one of the most important skills you can master. Luckily, that task is easy in the DOS Shell and in Windows. You simply click a directory in the directory tree to select that directory and make it the current or active directory. (You also can use the arrow keys to move the selection cursor to the directory name, and then press Enter.)

COMMAND

The job isn't quite so easy from the DOS command line, but the command CD or CHDIR (for Change Directory) helps. To make a different directory the current directory, type **cd**, press the space bar, type the directory's name, and then press Enter. That's all you need if the directory you want to make current is a subdirectory of the current directory. If you're in the root directory, for example, and want to make the WINDOWS directory the current directory, simply type **cd windows**.

If you're going the other direction in the hierarchy, however, you need the full path. Suppose that the BOOK subdirectory of the WP51 directory is the current directory, and you want to make WP51 the current directory. If you type **cd wp51**, you get the infamous Bad command or file name message. To get your command to work, you have to type **cd \wp51**, which tells DOS to begin searching for the specified directory at the root directory.

Using Absolute and Relative Paths

Absolute path and relative path are terms you may encounter in manuals or articles. In the preceding section, "Navigating the Directory Structure," you learned the difference between absolute and relative paths without even knowing it. The *absolute path* is the full path, from the root directory onward. The *relative path* is the path that begins with the current directory.

You may want to go over these concepts one more time, because if you're new to the world of directories, it can be difficult. Many newcomers encounter the Bad command or file name message because they aren't in the proper directory.

As outlined in the earlier examples, if you want to move from the current directory to its parent directory (the directory that contains the current directory) or any other outlying directory, you have to type the absolute path at the prompt. Hence, you cannot type **cd 123** to get to Lotus 1-2-3 from within the Microsoft Word directory if both directories are housed in the root directory. You have to type **cd \123**. And if you want to get to the BUDGET directory contained within the 123 directory, you have to type **cd \123\budget** to make BUDGET the current directory. In other words, you have to type the absolute path.

If you're moving to directories within the current directory, you don't have to go all the way to the root directory; simply start from the current directory. If you are in the 123 directory when you want to move to the BUDGET directory, for example, all you have to type at the prompt is **cd budget**—in other words, the relative path.

Moving from one directory to another by using the command line is different from working in the DOS Shell or Windows, where you simply point at the directory you want and click it to make it the active (current) directory. The trick in those graphic environments is to make sure that all the branches of the directory tree structure are visible. You learn how to do that in the following section.

Expanding and Collapsing Branches in the Directory Tree

At the DOS command line you're at a disadvantage. You can see the current directory if you set up your prompt, but you cannot see the rest of your directory structure unless you use the TREE command. And the TREE command only lets you look; you cannot move around or make any other changes while the tree structure is visible. In the DOS Shell and Windows, in contrast, you can make changes to the tree structure, but you have to learn how to bring up the view of the full directory tree. This section shows you how.

You can show more or fewer subdirectories in the directory tree of the DOS Shell screen. In the Shell menus, controlling the subdirectory display is referred to as *expanding and collapsing branches*. If you want to remove subdirectories, for example, you need to make sure that those subdirectory branches are displayed (expanded). (See this chapter's section on "Removing Directories" for more information.)

Figure 6.5 shows a portion of the directory tree for a root directory. Note that the directory names WINDOWS and WP51 have plus signs (+) preceding them. The plus signs indicate that the WP51 and WINDOWS directories are *expandable branches*—that is, they each contain subdirectories. The DOS Shell defaults to this view. If you want to see the subdirectory structure, you have to use the Tree menu option to expand branches.

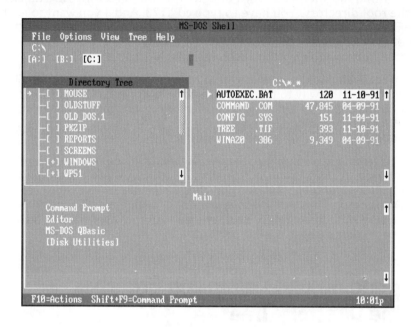

FIG. 6.5

Viewing a directory tree.

To see those subdirectories, select Tree from the menu bar at the top of the screen. Options in the Tree menu that appears include Expand Branch, which expands one level, or Expand All, which expands as many levels as you have. Figure 6.6, for example, shows the directory tree after Expand All has been selected. Notice that you can see both levels within the WP51 directory.

If you then use the Tree menu option to collapse branches, the DOS Shell goes back to the default view. No subdirectories appear, but the expandable directories have plus signs preceding them.

Windows follows a similar procedure for expanding and collapsing directory levels. The only difference in Windows is that Expandable Branches is an option on the Tree menu. You have to select this option if you want to see which directories contain subdirectories. In the DOS Shell, the expandable branches (directories) are shown automatically, indicated by the plus signs.

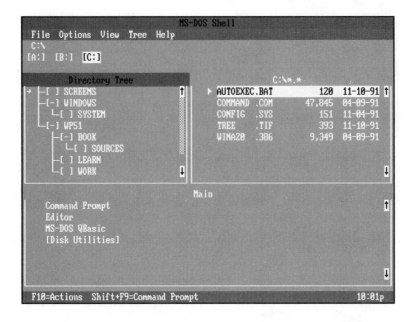

FIG. 6.6

Expanding all the
directory levels.

DOS contains a TREE command that you can use from the command line
to view the directory structure. If you use the /F switch with the command, you can see all the files contained within each directory. To use
this command, just type **tree /f** at the DOS prompt.

Creating Directories

Creating a directory in the DOS Shell is easy. You simply select Create
Directory from the File menu, and the dialog box shown in figure 6.7
appears.

Simply type the directory's name in the text entry box. If you want the
directory's path to start at the root directory, but you're currently in a
different directory, type a backslash (\) before the directory's name.
When you're finished, click OK or press Enter. The new directory appears in the directory tree on the left side of the screen.

To create a directory in Windows, follow these steps:

1. Open the File Manager's File menu.

2. Select Create Directory.

3. Type the name of the directory you want and the path if one exists.

4. Click OK.

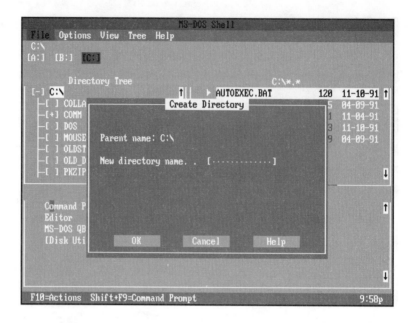

FIG. 6.7

Creating a directory in
the DOS Shell.

To create a directory from the DOS command line, type **md** or **mkdir**
(for Make Directory) at the prompt, press the space bar, type the name
of the directory you want to create (type the full path if you need it), and
press Enter. To create a subdirectory called FILES as a subset of the
current directory, for example, all you have to type is **md files**. If you
want the FILES subdirectory to reside in the root directory and you're
currently in some other directory, type **md \files**.

T I P

You know that DOS doesn't budge from the current directory when
looking for a file, unless you either specify a path or employ some
special tricks that you learn about in Chapter 9. Similarly, if you tell
DOS to create a subdirectory without specifying a path for it, DOS
always places the new subdirectory in the current directory. Always
double-check to see which directory you're in before you create a
new directory.

Renaming Directories

Sooner or later, you may want to rename a directory. Maybe your business expands, and you want to change the name of the REPORTS directory to CLIENTS. Or maybe you need to update your BUDGET.92 directory to BUDGET.93. To rename a directory in the DOS Shell, follow these steps:

1. Highlight the directory's name in the directory tree.

2. Open the File menu.

3. Select Rename. The Rename Directory dialog box appears as shown in figure 6.8.

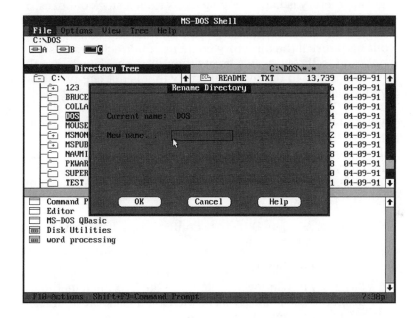

The Rename Directory dialog box.

4. Type the new name in the New Name text box.

5. Press Enter or click OK.

You follow a similar procedure when renaming a directory in Windows. Follow these steps:

WINDOWS

1. Open the File Manager's File menu.

2. Select Rename. A dialog box appears with the old name in the From text entry box.

138

3. Type the new name in the To text entry box.

4. Press Enter or click OK.

 DOS has a RENAME command, but it doesn't work with subdirectories; it works only with files. You therefore cannot rename directories from the DOS command line.

Removing Directories

Removing a directory is like removing a box from a stack of boxes. You cannot remove the bottom box from a stack; you have to remove the top boxes to get to the bottom. Similarly, you cannot remove a directory from your hard disk if the directory contains subdirectories. Also, you would not want to throw away a box without first checking to see that it was empty. If you try to remove a directory that is not empty, the system warns you, whether you're in the DOS Shell, in Windows, or at the DOS command line. You have to remove all the files contained in a directory before you can remove it. (To learn about removing files, see Chapter 5, "Keeping Files Organized.")

To use the DOS Shell to remove an empty directory, follow these steps:

1. In the directory tree, highlight the directory you want to remove.

2. Open the File menu.

3. Select Delete. A Delete Directory Confirmation dialog box appears, as shown in figure 6.9.

4. Click Yes or press Enter.

 Deleting a directory in Windows is similar to the DOS Shell method. Select Delete from the File Manager's File menu and click OK or press Enter when you see the confirmation dialog box.

 To remove an empty directory at the DOS command line, type **rd** or **rmdir** (for Remove Directory), press the space bar, type the directory's name, and press Enter.

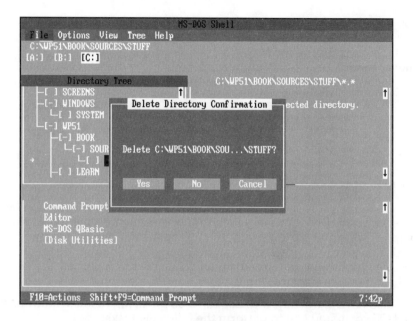

FIG. 6.9

The Delete Directory
Confirmation dialog
box.

DOS does not let you remove the current directory even if it's empty.
You have to go back one level to the parent directory. Suppose, for
example, that you're in the REPORT.JUN directory, which is a
subdirectory of BUDGET.92. To remove REPORT.JUN, you have to
change to BUDGET.92 (**cd \budget.92**) and then delete REPORT.JUN
(**rd report.jun**). If you try removing REPORT.JUN while you're in that
directory, you get the following message: Invalid path, not directory, or directory not empty.

T I P

Keeping Directories Organized

Creating, deleting, and renaming directories are some of the housekeeping tasks you can use to help you keep your hard disk well organized. If
you combine those technical skills with an overall strategy that helps
you organize your work, you will find that you and your hard disk are
both working at peak performance.

You don't, however, have to follow strict conventions. No right or wrong way exists—with the exception of not storing files in the root directory. Having a directory called MYSTUFF is fine as long as you don't mix the budget reports necessary for your job with letters to Aunt Fay, your copy of Super Tetris, and your Lotus program files.

Think carefully about the way you use your programs and the types of data you need to create, name your directories accordingly, and the time you spend with your computer will be rewarding rather than frustrating.

Summary

Directories are DOS's primary means of organizing information. In this chapter, you have learned about the hierarchical directory system of the hard disk, in which directories can be located within other directories. The chapter has given you some guidelines for developing strategies for building your directories.

You also have learned how to use the DOS Shell, Microsoft Windows, and the DOS command line to perform the following tasks:

- View the hierarchical structure of directories.
- Change the current directory.
- Expand and collapse branches of the directory tree.
- Create directories.
- Rename directories. (You cannot use the DOS command line for this task.)
- Remove directories.

Using Batch Files and Macros

In this chapter, you take a look at what batch files and macros are, why they are important, and some things to consider in deciding how to make the best use of them. You discover the many ways to create and maintain batch files and learn about some alternatives and supplements to batch programming. You also cover the use of macro programs—in particular, a new macro feature found in DOS 5.0: DOSKEY. If you don't have DOS 5.0, or if DOSKEY doesn't have the power you need, don't worry. Other alternatives are available, such as inexpensive commercially available macro programs that are covered briefly at the end of this chapter.

What Are Batch Files?

The computer term *batch* dates back to the days of punch card decks in which each card represented one command or data item in a process. Normally, two types of processes could run on a computer, on-line and batch. On-line was interactive processing, such as text editing or data entry, and batch was the sort of program that you would schedule to be run by people who operated the machines at the operators' convenience, typically overnight. Today's batch files are a descendant of these old processes and perform similarly, except that you also are the machine operator.

Think of any process that you perform in real life—making a cup of tea, mowing the grass, sharpening a pencil, washing your clothes, or going shopping at the store. Each one of these tasks requires you to complete a process or series of steps. A *batch file* is simply a process that can be performed in DOS with a series of steps. The batch file contains a series of DOS commands that are executed one after the other, as if you typed them.

Examining Batch File Structure

A typical real-life process list you might give someone is a shopping list, which might look something like this:

- Go to the bank and:
    Deposit check
    Withdraw $50

- Go to the drug store and buy:
    1 bottle of peroxide
    1 tube of toothpaste
    1 bottle of aspirin

- Go to the grocery store and buy:
    1 carton of milk
    1 loaf of bread

A batch file is like a shopping list that gives instructions to DOS to perform some tasks electronically. Quite often, you can use a PC and its applications without ever knowing that you are using batch files. In some cases, for example, batch files are created or modified by your application software.

The easiest way to learn about batch files is to take a look at one. Don't worry if you don't understand all the instructions in the following example. Everything will make more sense to you after you read on. The following batch file copies a group of files from the hard disk to a floppy disk:

```
DIR C:\BANK\*.*
ECHO Put the backup disk in drive
PAUSE
COPY C:\BANK\*.LST A:
PAUSE
BASICA MORTGAGE
```

In this example, the first instruction (DIR C:\BANK*.*) tells DOS to display a directory list of the BANK subdirectory. The ECHO command displays on-screen the message Put the backup disk in drive. The pause created by the PAUSE command gives you time to read the directory list and follow the reminder to insert a floppy disk in drive A. DOS then waits at the PAUSE line for you to press a key whenever you are ready. The command in the next line (COPY C:\BANK*.LST A:) tells DOS to copy all LST files from the BANK subdirectory onto the disk in drive A. The next PAUSE command causes DOS to wait for keyboard activity. The press of any key continues the batch process. BASICA MORTGAGE is just a sample of a typical program you might want to run after doing the batch file processing.

You can create a more sophisticated batch file to make provisions for those times when you don't put a disk in drive A or when an error occurs with the disk, such as the existence of a write-protect tab or lack of room on the disk.

> You can stop a batch file from executing. After it has started, the best method is to press the Ctrl-Break or Ctrl-C key combination. Otherwise, you have to resort to the more drastic methods of either pressing Ctrl-Alt-Del to reboot or turning the power off altogether. You may have to use this rather than Ctrl-Break if a program executed by your BAT file has disabled Ctrl-Break.

T I P

A batch file is a simple text file that contains mostly the same DOS commands that you might enter at the DOS prompt. But the file also contains some batch-processing controls, such as labels, loops, echo messages, parameters, and remarks, which are covered in more detail later in this chapter in the section on "Examining Commands and Features Specific to Batch Files."

Another special characteristic of a batch file is its name. So that DOS can recognize the file as something to interpret and execute, the batch file must have the extension BAT. You also must follow regular DOS naming conventions. For a review of those rules, see Chapter 5, "Keeping Files Organized."

Understanding Why You Should Use Batch Files

The most obvious reason to use a batch file is if you find that you frequently are typing the same sequence of DOS commands time after time. You can incorporate this repetitive sequence into a batch file. The PATH command, for example, tells DOS which path to follow to find a program. If DOS doesn't find your program on the path, you can use a batch file to point the way. Or you may want to shorten or change the name of a program. You can use the DOS RENAME command, but a batch file is better if you want to avoid confusion.

If you look at a BAT file, you notice that most of the commands can be typed at the DOS command line. In a BAT file, you may see DOS commands like COPY, DELETE, and MD or BAT-specific commands like IF, FOR, and ECHO.

Some introductory examples of BAT files you might want to write are a daily backup of your most important files, a list of 20 files that all need to be printed at the end of the day, or a list of 10 files that need to be deleted at the end of each day, as in the following example:

```
@ECHO OFF
DELETE TYLER.INF
DELETE KAOS.MMT
DELETE RTO.PUB
DELETE RANGE.LYT
DELETE FARMING.TXT
DELETE PURLEY.INF
DELETE WARREN.PUB
DELETE YOGI.BAR
DELETE FRODO.BAT
DELETE STUFF.WKS
```

Clearly, in this example, you simply can type the DELETE command for each of these files one at a time from the DOS prompt. But putting the commands in a BAT file is a much better approach if you have to repeat the commands many times, not only to save time but also to make sure that you don't accidentally delete another file by mistyping the name.

One special batch file that you can find on almost every PC is AUTOEXEC.BAT. Quite possibly you may not even be aware that one exists on your system, because some commercial programs modify or even create your AUTOEXEC.BAT for you when you install the programs on your hard disk.

NOTE If you don't have an AUTOEXEC.BAT file, it's about time you created one. You can create a BAT file in several ways. For more information on creating batch files, see this chapter's section on "Creating Batch Files." For more information on AUTOEXEC.BAT, see this chapter's section on "Understanding AUTOEXEC.BAT."

Another situation in which you might need to use a batch file is if a software manufacturer creates one for you. Often during a program's installation process, for example, you are asked some questions about where you want to load the software, what printer you're using, and what default settings you want to use. The installation program may create a batch file to contain all this information. This type of installation often enables you to change easily such things as the printer settings without having to reinstall the program. (You need to be careful about deleting batch files that you don't recognize. They may be more important than you think.)

Many other reasons exist for creating and maintaining your own batch files. As you learn in this chapter, they are relatively simple to create and extremely powerful. Ultimately, the deciding factor is how comfortable you feel working with batch files. But if you haven't tried them, you will never know.

Creating Batch Files

Often one of the first things that a newcomer to PCs asks is "How do I create a batch file?" This chapter covers enough of the basics to get you started, but keep in mind that you can do a great deal more with batch files. If you want more detailed information on batch files and batch programming, Que publishes a helpful quick reference entitled *Batch Files and Macros Quick Reference*.

The good news about creating batch files is that you can use any one of a number of methods. And you can rest assured that at least two options are available to you. In the following paragraphs, you learn how to create batch files by using COPY CON, EDLIN, EDIT, and other text editors.

Creating Batch Files with COPY CON

One of the most simple methods of creating a batch file is to use the COPY command with the CON for CONsole selected. The *console*, a throwback to the old days when teletype terminals were used, is a device name that refers to the keyboard and monitor. Whatever you type at the keyboard after you press Enter and before you press the end-of-file key (F6 or Ctrl-Z) is included in the file.

In the following example, you learn how to create a simple batch file, using the COPY CON method. Follow these steps:

1. At the DOS prompt, type **copy con**, press the space bar, and type the name of the batch file you want to create.

2. Type each of the command lines you want to include in the batch file.

For example, you might type the following lines:

COPY CON SIMPLE.BAT
DIR C:*. /W

3. Press Ctrl-Z.

If you make a mistake, simply start over—just press Ctrl-Z, F3 (Repeat Line), and Enter and then begin with the COPY CON command again.

Figure 7.1 shows how the screen looks after you press Ctrl-Z. All this batch file does is list the subdirectories on drive C's root directory. Just to prove that the file works, type **simple** at the DOS prompt to execute the batch file.

```
C:\>copy con simple.bat
DIR C:\*. /W
^Z

        1 file(s) copied
C:\>
```

FIG. 7.1

Creating a simple
batch file.

Figure 7.2 is more typical of the type of batch file you might want to create and use frequently. This file maintains backups of critical data. In this example, a weekly status report stored on a 1-2-3 spreadsheet consolidates and deletes all the weekly spreadsheets. which are a succession of files named with the days of the week and the extension WK1. To avoid disaster and to avoid having to type all those XCOPY commands one at a time, you can create this simple batch file to do it all. It even reminds you to insert the backup disk (PROMPT) and waits for you to put it in (PAUSE). All the ECHO OFF command does is tell DOS not to display the commands on-screen. This step doesn't affect the batch process but only makes it neater.

```
C:\>copy con c:lastweek.bat
echo off
prompt Put backup diskette in drive A:
pause
xcopy c:\123\mon*.wk1 a:\
xcopy c:\123\tue*.wk1 a:\
xcopy c:\123\wed*.wk1 a:\
xcopy c:\123\thu*.wk1 a:\
xcopy c:\123\fri*.wk1 a:\
^Z
    1 File(s) copied

C:\>
```

FIG. 7.2

Creating a batch file to perform maintenance tasks for you.

To create this file, type the following lines at the DOS prompt and then press Ctrl-Z:

COPY CON C:LASTWEEK.BAT
ECHO OFF
PROMPT Put backup disk in drive A:
PAUSE
XCOPY C:\123\MON*.WK1 A:
XCOPY C:\123\TUE*.WK1 A:
XCOPY C:\123\WED*.WK1 A:
XCOPY C:\123\THU*.WK1 A:
XCOPY C:\123\FRI*.WK1 A:

Creating Batch Files with EDLIN (DOS 2.X through 5.0)

EDLIN, which stands for LINe EDitor, is a primitive method of managing simple ASCII text files. Because of the possibility that it may be the only editor available to you, however, learning enough commands to enable you to create and maintain simple batch files is worth your while.

Often, you will be faced with the problem of needing to create or modify BAT files on a newly formatted hard disk with only DOS installed. If any version of DOS has been installed correctly, EDLIN almost always will be available. Keeping a copy of EDLIN on a bootable floppy disk for "emergency" situations may be helpful. The most likely situation is one in which you add a device driver (DEVICE=XXX.SYS) to your CONFIG.SYS file and it causes your system to hang. Having an editor on a bootable disk often can rescue you from this situation when your "regular" version of EDLIN is no longer available.

T I P   If you have DOS installed but don't have an AUTOEXEC.BAT file, chances are that you don't have a PATH set to your DOS subdirectory. In this situation, DOS cannot find EDLIN. If you seem to have problems getting EDLIN to run, type **path=c:\dos;c:** at the DOS prompt. (This command creates the path only temporarily. To retain the setting, you should include the PATH command in your AUTOEXEC.BAT file. For more information, see this chapter's section on "Knowing What To Include in AUTOEXEC.BAT.")

To use EDLIN to create a batch file, type **edlin**, press the space bar, type the name for your file (using the extension BAT), and press Enter at the DOS prompt. To create an AUTOEXEC.BAT file, for example, type the following command at the DOS prompt:

EDLIN AUTOEXEC.BAT

DOS then prompts you with the following message:

```
New file
*
```

Or if the file already exists, you see

```
End of input file
*
```

The asterisk (*) is EDLIN's prompt requesting instructions.

Table 7.1 lists some EDLIN commands that you will find useful as you're creating and modifying batch files.

Table 7.1 Using EDLIN Commands

Command/Key	Effect
L	Lists on-screen up to 23 lines of the file. The command *6,20L*, for example, lists lines 6 to 20.
I	Inserts new lines at a specified location. 5I, for example, inserts at line 5; I with no number begins inserting lines at the current line. Also known as *insert mode*.
Ctrl-C	After pressing I and inserting one or more lines, ends insert mode back to the * EDLIN prompt. You also can use Ctrl-Break.
D	Deletes the current line; 3-5-D deletes lines 3-5.

Command/Key	Effect
line #	Begins edit mode at the line number indicated. Typing 8, for example, puts you in edit mode at line 8.
E	Ends the EDLIN session, saves the file, and exits to the DOS prompt.
Q	Quits without saving the file.
F1	When you're editing a line, copies characters from old line one at a time.
F3	Copies the entire old line.
F6	Inserts a ^Z. Same as pressing Ctrl-Z. Also ends insert mode if you press Enter.
Del	Pulls back one character in the old line, thereby deleting the character.
Ins	Toggles between insert and overtype modes, inserting characters in the middle of a line.

NOTE   With DOS 5.0, the / (slash) key accesses help on and in EDLIN.

The best way to put all this information together and learn how to use EDLIN is to step through creating and editing a sample file. In the following paragraphs, you learn how to create a practical, important batch file: AUTOEXEC.BAT. (You learn more about AUTOEXEC.BAT later in this chapter, in "Understanding AUTOEXEC.BAT.")

To start up EDLIN and create or edit the AUTOEXEC.BAT file, type the following at the DOS prompt:

EDLIN AUTOEXEC.BAT

If you have not already created the file, you should see the following two lines on-screen:

```
New file
*
```

The asterisk (*) is prompting you for an EDLIN command. Because this file is new and empty, you need to start by inserting a new line. Press I and then Enter, and you should see the following new line on-screen:

```
1:*
```

This prompt shows you that you are positioned at line 1 and EDLIN is waiting for you to type something. Type the following command and press Enter:

@ECHO OFF

The next prompt, `2:*`, appears. EDLIN is telling you that it has accepted the input on line 1 and is now adding a new line, number 2. Repeat the same steps for the next two lines by entering the following commands:

PROMPT PG
PATH=C:\;C:\DOS

Now you should see a new prompt for the fourth line, `4:*`. To end the file, you can press Ctrl-C or F6 to add an end-of-file marker (^Z) on line 4. You then return to the EDLIN prompt:

```
    *
```

Simply press E and Enter to return to the DOS prompt. Congratulations, you have just created probably the most important BAT file on your hard drive.

Now suppose that you want to edit your AUTOEXEC.BAT and add a new subdirectory to the PATH statement (C:\BATCH). Type the same command at the DOS prompt:

EDLIN AUTOEXEC.BAT

Because the file already exists, you get a different message from the one you saw the first time:

```
End of input file
*
```

This message tells you that EDLIN has opened the AUTOEXEC.BAT file and has read the whole file successfully. To list the file so that you can see it on-screen, press L and Enter. Your file should look like this:

```
1: @ECHO OFF
2: PROMPT $P$G
3: PATH=C:\C:\DOS
*
```

To edit the PATH command, simply type the number of the line you want, in this case 3m and press Enter. The screen changes to look like this:

```
3:*PATH=C:\;C:\DOS
3:*
```

The current contents of line 3 are displayed. The asterisk (*) EDLIN prompt is requesting that you type a new entry. Whatever you type over-writes the current contents of line 3. Here is where the editing function keys come in. Press F3 to copy the existing line to the prompt line and then type the new addition to the end of the path (don't forget the semi-colon to separate the new PATH element from the rest):

```
;C:\BATCH
```

The screen looks like this:

```
3*PATH=C:\;C:\DOS
3*PATH=C:\;C:\DOS;C:\BATCH
```

Again, to save the file, press E and then enter.

> When you save a new version of a file you have just edited, DOS re-names the original file with a BAK extension just in case you change your mind and want to retrieve that old file.
>
> **T I P**

When you get back to the DOS prompt, type **dir autoexec.***. The directory should list two files: AUTOEXEC.BAT and AUTOEXEC.BAK. The BAK version is the old AUTOEXEC file that existed before you made your changes. If for any reason you want to revert to the old one, simply type the following at the DOS prompt:

ERASE AUTOEXEC.BAT
RENAME AUTOEXEC.BAK AUTOEXEC.BAT

Creating Batch Files with EDIT (DOS 5.0)

Starting with Version 5.0, Microsoft has included with DOS a full-screen editor called EDIT (see fig. 7.3). This editor was designed primarily as a program editor for people wanting to write BAT files but can handle any nonformatted ASCII text quite easily and also offers mouse support. Using the mouse helps in copying and moving blocks of text and enables you to jump quickly from place to place in the file. One important thing to note is that EDIT is in fact a QBASIC program and can take a little time (10 to 15 seconds) to load on some machines.

> **NOTE** Because the DOS 5.0 editor is written in QBASIC, it relies on the existence of the QBASIC interpreter QBASIC.EXE and its attendant help file QBASIC.HLP. In versions prior to DOS 5.0, a popular housekeeping tip to save a little disk space and reduce clutter for people with little or no use for BASIC was to remove any BASIC interpreters (BASIC.COM, BASICA.COM, GWBASIC.COM) and all files with the BAS extension from the DOS subdirectory.

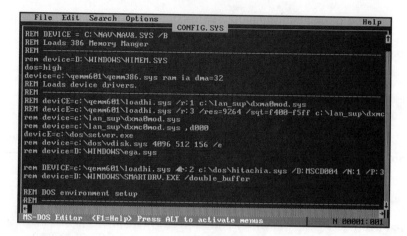

```
 File  Edit  Search  Options                                    Help
                              CONFIG.SYS
REM DEVICE = C:\NAV\NAV&.SYS /B
REM Loads 386 Memory Manger
REM
rem device=D:\WINDOWS\HIMEM.SYS
dos=high
device=c:\qemm601\qemm386.sys ram ia dma=32
REM Loads device drivers.
REM
REM deviCE=c:\qemm601\loadhi.sys /r:1 c:\lan_sup\dxma0mod.sys
REM deviCE=c:\qemm601\loadhi.sys /r:3 /res=9264 /sqt=f400-f5ff c:\lan_sup\dxmc
rem device=c:\lan_sup\dxma0mod.sys
rem device=c:\lan_sup\dxmc0mod.sys ,d000
deviCE=c:\dos\setver.exe
rem device=c:\dos\vdisk.sys 4096 512 156 /e
rem device=D:\WINDOWS\ega.sys

rem DEVICE=c:\qemm601\loadhi.sys /:2 c:\dos\hitachia.sys /D:MSCD004 /M:1 /P:3
rem device=D:\WINDOWS\SMARTDRV.EXE /double_buffer

REM DOS environment setup
REM
MS-DOS Editor  <F1=Help> Press ALT to activate menus          N 00001:001
```

FIG. 7.3

The DOS 5.0 EDIT program.

The DOS 5.0 EDIT program offers quite an extensive set of features that is covered more fully in the MS DOS 5 reference manual and the following Que books covering DOS: *Que's MS-DOS 5 User's Guide*, Special Edition, *Hands On MS-DOS 5*, and *Using PC DOS*, 3rd Edition.

Those of you who are WordStar users will recognize many of the EDIT commands. Some of the more popular Ctrl-key combinations are used for moving around within the file as you edit it.

Creating Batch Files with Other Text Editors

In addition to the DOS methods for creating batch files, you can use your word processor for the same purpose. The most important thing about using your word processor to create batch files is to ensure that the program can save files in straight ASCII format. In WordPerfect, for example, you need to use the Text In/Out (Ctrl-F5) option.

Another way to create batch files is to use a third-part text editor. Many commercial ASCII text editors are available, including BRIEF and KEDIT from Mansfield Software.

If you are using Windows, you can create batch files by using the Windows Notepad in the Accessories program group or a program called SYSEDIT.EXE, which you can find in the \WINDOWS\SYSTEM subdirectory. (In the Program Manager, press Alt, F, and R; type **sysedit**; and press Enter.) SYSEDIT automatically calls up a couple of the Windows Setup files, CONFIG.SYS and AUTOEXEC.BAT.

Finally, you have one more way to create batch files: using the DOSKEY history command. This method is covered in more detail later in this chapter in the section on "Creating Batch Files with DOSKEY."

Running Batch Files

Running a batch file doesn't involve much. If you type the file name of anything that has a BAT file extension, DOS attempts to execute the file whether it contains valid batch commands or not! The main points to remember are that you may have to ensure that you have a valid PATH set in order to find your BAT file and that the order of the subdirectories in the PATH statement is important if you want to have your BAT file executed rather than a DOS command or some other program. Batch files are executed last in order of precedence. Suppose, for example, that you have a program called TALK.EXE and then write a new batch file called TALK.BAT, putting it in the same directory as TALK.EXE. When you type **talk** at the DOS prompt, the TALK.EXE file is executed, and the TALK.BAT file is ignored.

Examining Commands and Features Specific to Batch Files

In addition to the normal set of DOS commands you can use in a batch file, an exclusive set of commands exists that you can use *only* from within a BAT file. Table 7.2 lists the commands and briefly describes what they do. For additional information on batch file programming, refer to your DOS manual and to other guides, such as Que's *Batch Files and Macros Quick Reference*.

Table 7.2 Special Batch-File Features

Feature	Function
%1, %2, %3	Parameters that can replace anything typed after the batch file name when you execute it. Up to nine replaceable parameters can be active.
%0	A special parameter that contains the drive, path, and file name of the BAT file.

continues

Table 7.2 Continued

Feature	Function
:	Indicates to DOS that the text following the colon is a label rather than a command. Often used with the GOTO command.
CALL	Enables one batch file to execute another batch file. When the called batch file terminates, control is handed back to the calling batch file at the CALL command's location.
ECHO	Used to display text and can be used to suppress messages (ECHO OFF).
FOR (IN,DO)	A complex command that is used to repeat a process by using variables. (See "Manipulating Parameters with FOR..IN..DO" in this chapter.)
GOTO	Used to branch to a label either directly or after a condition, such as one included in an IF statement, is met.
IF	Used to make decisions based on whether a statement is true or false. (See "Setting Conditions with IF" in this chapter.)
IF NOT	The reverse of IF. Used to find out whether two things don't compare or something doesn't exist.
PAUSE	Used to halt the batch process until a key is pressed. The message Press any key to continue... is displayed on-screen.
REM	Stands for remark and indicates that anything following the REM on the same line is not to be executed.
SHIFT	Used to shift the parameters down one position. With the three parameters %1, %2, and %3, for example, SHIFT causes %3 to become %2, %2 to become %1, and %1 to disappear. Useful if you want to have more than 10 parameters. (For more information, see the next section, "Using Parameters.")

Many other DOS commands can be used to enhance your BAT files. The most common option is the use of the command CLS (clear screen), which is useful to get rid of any screen messages left over from previous DOS commands or other BAT files. You can control screen colors, beeps, and other special features by using an externally loaded device driver called ANSI.SYS. (This feature is complex and beyond the scope of this book.)

The following paragraphs give you more information about how to use these commands in your batch files.

Using Parameters

Parameters are one way to pass information to a program or BAT file so that it can perform a function. In real life, you frequently see examples of parameters. A common one in England is a sign to the milkman that reads, "Please leave (blank) pints today." You have to fill in the (blank) with a number. That (blank) is a parameter, and the number that you replace the (blank) with is the parameter value.

You use parameters to modify part of the process of a BAT file after you have created it. Suppose, for example, that you have written the following BAT file to copy certain files from a subdirectory called TEST to a floppy disk:

```
CD \TEST1
COPY ENGINE1.DAT A:\
COPY FRAME1.DAT A:\
COPY TRANS1.DAT A:\
```

This file works fine until you find that you have to create another BAT file to perform some similar functions, such as

```
CD \TEST2
COPY ENGINE2.DAT A:\
COPY FRAME2.DAT A:\
COPY TRANS2.DAT A:\
```

Instead of creating all these similar BAT files, you can use just one and fit it with parameters, as in this example:

```
CD %1
COPY %2 A:\
COPY %3 A:\
COPY %4 A:\
```

Suppose that you call this new batch file TEST. You can type the following command from the DOS prompt to do the same work done by your first BAT file:

TEST TEST1 ENGINE1.DAT FRAME1.DAT TRANS1.DAT

Or, to execute the commands from the second BAT file, you can type this command:

TEST TEST2 ENGINE2.DAT FRAME2.DAT TRANS2.DAT

As you can see, anything you type after the name of the BAT file at the DOS prompt (TEST2, ENGINE2, and so on) temporarily replaces the corresponding parameter in the BAT file itself (%1, %2, and so on). The BAT file interprets the parameters in order, with %1 the first parameter (in this case the subdirectory), %2 the next, and so on up to a maximum of nine. (If you need access to more than nine parameters, you must use the SHIFT command, which is covered in this chapter's section on "Shifting Parameters with SHIFT.")

In this example, four parameters are used. If you enter only three parameters at the DOS prompt to execute the batch file, the last parameter is replaced with a blank. If you enter five parameters, the last one is ignored.

%0 is a special parameter that contains the name of the BAT file as it was executed. You usually use %0 in complex batch files for debugging or for special utilities that modify the batch file itself.

Parameters also are useful when you need to create a BAT file that executes an application that in turn loads a specific program. Suppose, for example, that you have a series of accounting programs—GL, AP, and AR for your general ledger, accounts payable, and accounts receivable—written in dBASE IV. You normally like to back up your database to floppy disks before running any of these programs, so you might create a BAT file like this one:

```
CD \DBASE
COPY ACCTS*.* A:
DBASE %1
```

Just for simplicity, suppose that you call this batch file DACCT.BAT. You can type **dacct gl** at the DOS prompt to copy the accounting data and then run dBASE with the GL program. Using the same BAT file, you can type **dacct ap** or **dacct ar** to perform the same backup and execute dBASE with the appropriate program. If you then add another dBASE accounting program called PAY, you simply can type **dacct pay** at the DOS prompt. (These sample programs are for dBASE IV, but the same rules apply to running almost any major software program.)

Controlling the Display with ECHO

One important feature of a BAT file is its capability to hide selectively from the user what is going on. Obviously, when you first set up a BAT file, you want to watch everything until you are satisfied that the file is working properly. But then you can turn off the file's display. If you are annoyed by seeing lots of gibberish when you boot up your machine, for example, you can tell the AUTOEXEC.BAT file not to show you every-thing. Take a look at your AUTOEXEC.BAT file. If you don't see @ECHO OFF as the first line in the BAT file, you might want to add that line. The @ symbol tells DOS not to display that one line, and the ECHO OFF tells DOS not to display on-screen any of the batch file's lines.

The ECHO command, on the other hand, displays text on-screen. You can use ECHO to send messages or instructions to anyone who uses the BAT file.

One useful way to use ECHO is to tell you where you are or what is about to happen in a BAT file when it is being executed. The following sample AUTOEXEC.BAT shows one use for ECHO:

```
@ECHO OFF
PROMPT $P$G
PATH=C:\;C:\DOS
ECHO ***WARNING ABOUT TO ERASE OLD FILES PRESS CTRL-C TO
ABORT***
PAUSE
DEL C:\WP51\*.OLD
```

This ECHO command displays a message warning you that you are about to take some drastic action unless you press Ctrl-C. You also can use ECHO to track down a problem in a BAT file. Simply put an ECHO state-ment before the suspected problem area to let you know that the ques-tionable part of the BAT file is being executed.

Adding Remarks with REM

REM in front of any line in a BAT file tells DOS not to process that line as a command. REM, which stands for REMark, is useful for commenting on the function of the BAT file without interfering in the file's operation. REM is also useful for temporarily disabling the operation of suspicious, erratic, or redundant parts of the BAT file. Take a look at this file, for example:

```
@ECHO OFF
REM None of these commands will work
REM DELETE *.*
REM FORMAT C:
REM PAUSE
REM This BAT file does absolutely nothing—thank goodness
```

Halting Processing with PAUSE

You use PAUSE to halt the operation of the BAT file temporarily. Whenever you insert a PAUSE command in a BAT file, DOS displays this message and waits for you to press a key before the rest of the file is processed:

```
Press any key to continue ...
```

You can use this command in conjunction with ECHO to tell the user to prepare something before the file executes, such as turn on the printer or insert a blank disk in drive A, as illustrated in the following example:

```
ECHO Put a blank disk in drive A:
PAUSE
COPY C:*.TXT A:
```

In this example, no files are copied until the user has pressed a key as prompted by the PAUSE command. The user thus has plenty of time to follow the ECHO instructions.

Setting Conditions with IF

IF is an interesting command because it enables you to insert a little more intelligence in a BAT file. The IF condition is used primarily to add flexibility to your BAT files, allowing them to adapt to a variety of conditions. The IF condition usually is used to compare information or check for the existence of a file within a BAT file.

Suppose, for example, that you have a BAT file that runs dBASE, but you need to make sure that a program name was entered as a parameter. You can use a file like this one:

```
@ECHO OFF
REM Program name for dBASE needed for this program to work
IF "%1"=="" GOTO NOGOOD
CD \DBASE
DBASE %1
GOTO ENDIT
:NOGOOD
ECHO No program name entered, try again
:ENDIT
```

In this example, the @ECHO OFF prevents each BAT file line from being repeated on-screen as it is executed. The REM line gives you a remark describing what the BAT file needs, in this case a parameter that is to be placed in %1. The IF condition looks at what's on either side of the ==

signs. If the two elements are the same (equal), the statement is true, so the file executes whatever is to the right of the IF statement, in this case the command GOTO NOGOOD. Thus if the parameter ("%1") is blank (""), DOS jumps down to the :NOGOOD line. Then DOS continues batch processing at that point. Because the colon (:) tells DOS that NOGOOD is just a label, DOS moves on to the ECHO line. The message No program name entered, try again displays on-screen, the second label (:ENDIT) is ignored, and the program terminates.

If the two elements on either side of the == signs are not equal, the IF statement is false, so DOS moves to the next line in the BAT file. In the example, if something is in %1 (in other words, a parameter was passed), DOS moves to the next line, a CD (Change Directory) command that changes to the DBASE subdirectory. Then DBASE %1 runs the DBASE program that was put in as the parameter %1. When that program is complete, the GOTO ENDIT command tells DOS to ignore everything until it reaches a label called ENDIT, which is in fact the end of the program.

Shifting Parameters with SHIFT

With the SHIFT command, you can shunt the parameters to lower numbers so that you can allow for a variable number of parameters. If %1, %2, and %3 are provided as parameters to a BAT file, for example, a SHIFT causes %1 to disappear, %2 to become %1, and %3 to become %2. With SHIFT and a single command line, you can add many parameters and perform the same batch process against each parameter.

IF NOT, the reverse of the IF command, is particularly useful for checking to see whether files exist and, if not, for doing something about it. You can use IF NOT in conjunction with SHIFT when you want to copy a series of files to a blank floppy disk, as in the following example:

```
@ECHO OFF
:BEGIN
IF "%1"=="" GOTO FINISH
ECHO Copying Acct file %1
IF NOT EXIST A:%1 COPY %1 A:
SHIFT
GOTO BEGIN
:FINISH
```

In this case, you can supply a large number of file names as parameters to the batch file. The IF NOT EXIST command checks to see whether the file already is stored on drive A. If not, the BAT file proceeds to copy the file. If the file is there, it simply is ignored. The SHIFT command shifts all the parameters down one number, and the loop returns to the BEGIN label. Each time the loop executes, a different file name is checked and copied. Eventually, no more parameters are there, so IF "%1" is equal to nothing, and the BAT file processing moves to the FINISH label and terminates.

Manipulating Parameters with FOR..IN..DO

The FOR..IN..DO series of commands is fairly complex and used to perform a series of parameter replacements in a single line. In a batch file, the generic form of the command is

FOR %%*variable* IN (*set*) DO *something*

 In addition to including this command in a batch file, you can type this command at the DOS prompt. If you do, type only one rather than two % symbols in front of the variable.

The easiest way to explain the command's function is by example. A simple one might be performing a multiple-drive DIR command, as in

FOR %%p IN (C:\ D:\ E:\) DO DIR %p

Here the FOR %%p IN replaces the variable %p with each of the items in parentheses in turn, each time performing any commands following the DO. You end up with a functional equivalent of these commands:

DIR C:\
DIR D:\
DIR E:\

You can use the FOR..IN..DO feature in many more sophisticated ways. For more complete information, refer to Que's *Batch Files and Macros Quick Reference* or your DOS 5.0 manual.

Examining Some Ways To Use Batch Files

Reasons for using batch files are numerous. In this section, you learn some of the ways that batch files can help you work efficiently and effectively. You learn how to use batch files to help organize your disk, perform housekeeping tasks, and create a menu system.

Using Batch Files To Help Organize Your Disk

After only a short time working on your hard disk, you may become bogged down trying to find programs, struggling with disk space, or simply not knowing what to type where. Intelligent use of batch files can help alleviate some of these problems.

One method is to keep a collection of batch files in a single subdirectory. Each batch file can be responsible for setting up an environment and running an application and maybe even cleaning up or making backup copies afterwards. Keeping all your BAT files in a single subdirectory is an effective way to keep track of programs on your hard disk. This approach also means that you can keep your basic PATH command short and simple because you can have each BAT file set up the PATH for the program or programs run by that file. More ambitious batch files can run entire menu systems to manage the hard disk.

The following shows a sample batch file that uses environment variables (variables stored by DOS) and the SET command to set up a special PATH for a program, run the program, and restore the old PATH after the program has completed.

The batch file consists of the following lines:

```
ECHO OFF
SET TEMP1=%path%
PATH=C:\;C:\DOS
CD \
DIR /w
PATH
PATH=%temp1%
PATH
```

The DOS SET command is a way to display or enter DOS environment variables. The environment is a special area that is set aside by DOS to enable programs and BAT files to pass messages and small pieces of information. Think of the SET command as rather like putting a sticky note on a bulletin board so that others can read it. Many manufacturers use the SET command to prepare a program for use by storing some critical information only available at run-time.

The %path% is an environment variable in which DOS keeps the text that is the current PATH. All you are doing with the SET command in line 2 is keeping %path% somewhere safe (TEMP1) so that you can change the PATH temporarily for a special application. Then the PATH command in line 3 sets the new path. The CD \ and DIR command in lines 4 and 5 merely are used as an example of a "special application." The PATH command in line 6 displays the current setting. This line is there to prove that you did change the path. Line 7 resets the path, using the environment variable %temp1%. With line 8 you verify that the PATH has returned to "normal."

Using Batch Files for Housekeeping Chores

You can use other batch files to perform special housekeeping tasks. You might, for example, want to create a file that stores backup copies of critical word processor files or spreadsheets on a floppy disk—just in case your hard disk crashes.

You also might want to create a special setup that enables you to run your programs with simple single-letter commands. W.BAT might load up your word processor, for example, and S.BAT might contain the commands to run your spreadsheet.

If you have more programs than disk space and your computer has enough memory to create a sizable RAM disk, you might consider using an archiving compression utility such as PKZIP in which to keep your programs and data. Then you can create a batch file to unzip everything to the RAM disk and run it from there. After you exit your program, you can use the same batch file to rezip anything that had changed or been added during the session. (You can find further coverage of using PKZIP in Chapter 9, "Exploring Hard Disk Fitness Programs.")

First, assuming that you have plenty of surplus RAM so that you can set up a RAM disk of 2M or more, you need to have the following line in your CONFIG.SYS file:

    DEVICE=RAMDRIVE.SYS 2048 /E

This line simply requests that DOS set up a RAM (aka virtual) disk using extended (/E option) memory of 2048K bytes or 2 megabytes in size.

The following file is an example CRIB.BAT file that archives (or zips) less popular applications. The RAM drive has been set up as D. The REM statements are simply there to explain what is happening as the BAT file proceeds.

```
REM CRIB.BAT File
REM Change default drive to the RAM drive D:
REM Now unpack the cribbage game
PKUNZIP C:\ZIPS\CRIBBAGE
REM Run the game
CRIB
REM Now clean up the RAM disk
DEL *.*
```

Using Batch Files To Create a Simple Menu System

One nice feature of the DOS Shell is the ability it gives you to execute programs directly from the DOS Shell screen. If you are working on a laptop or portable or do not have DOS 5.0, however, you do not have access to the DOS Shell. If you're in this situation, you can create an alternative: a pseudo full-screen application menu. To create this menu, you use a series of simple batch files.

Before you get started, identify the applications you want to run. Then create a small BAT file to execute each application. Store all these batch files in a single subdirectory named BATCH. Don't forget to include C:\BATCH as part of your PATH and set it up in your AUTOEXEC.BAT file. (See "Understanding AUTOEXEC.BAT" for more information.)

Suppose, for example, that you have four main applications: dBASE, WordPerfect, Lotus 1-2-3, and Norton Utilities. For simplicity's sake, you can create a batch file called D.BAT for dBASE, a file called W.BAT for WordPerfect, and so on. The D.BAT file might look something like this:

```
@ECHO OFF
CD \DBASE
DBASE
MENU
```

This file changes to the DBASE directory, executes the dBASE program, and, when returning from that, fires up the MENU program. MENU is a main menu batch file called MENU.BAT, which you also need to create. MENU.BAT simply clears the screen, prints a "splash screen," sets the prompt to invisible by using the $a argument, and waits for the user to type a letter corresponding to a BAT file. The MENU.BAT file might look like this:

```
@ECHO OFF
CLS
TYPE SPLASH.SCR
PROMPT $a
```

The "splash screen" (SPLASH.SCR) shows the menu options and might look something like the following:

```
Program Menu

Select a program by typing the FIRST letter and pressing
Enter

_ _ _ _ _ _ _ _ _ _ _ _ _ _ _ _ _ _ _ _ _
_ _ _ _ _ _ _ _ _

                (D)DBASE

                (W)WORDPERFECT

                (L)LOTUS 123

                (N)NORTON UTILITIES

                (Q)Quit this menu



        Enter D,W,L,N or Q.
```

Notice that the last item is a Quit option. You can create a special Quit batch file called Q.BAT to clear the screen and restore a more generally acceptable prompt:

```
@ECHO OFF
CLS
PROMPT $P$G
```

This approach is simplistic, but it is a straightforward and effective method of providing an application menu for yourself or for someone else. To add items to the menu, all you need to do is create additional BAT files and modify the splash screen.

Understanding AUTOEXEC.BAT

AUTOEXEC.BAT is clearly one of the most important files on your hard drive. AUTOEXEC.BAT is one of the few ways you have to change automatically the appearance and functionality of your DOS start-up. When you set up things like your PATH and environment variables in DOS, you lose that information every time you turn the machine off or reboot it. AUTOEXEC.BAT is one way to ensure consistency. Many useful functions can be performed by AUTOEXEC.BAT, such as installing terminate and stay resident (TSR) programs and setting environment variables.

AUTOEXEC.BAT is a special type of file because it is treated differently from other batch files. When your computer starts up DOS from a disk, three things happen. First, the computer loads part of DOS into memory by loading IO.SYS and MSDOS.SYS (or IBMDOS.COM and IBMBIO.COM in PC DOS) and running the program COMMAND.COM. This program in turn interprets the instructions contained in CONFIG.SYS, which configures your machine. After the system is set up, DOS looks to see whether a file called AUTOEXEC.BAT exists in the root directory; if so, DOS executes that file. If DOS does not find AUTOEXEC.BAT, you are prompted to enter the date and time.

> You may want to ensure that your ASCII file editor has a backup option or Save As selection. This feature enables you to keep backup copies of both your CONFIG.SYS and AUTOEXEC.BAT files. With EDLIN, prior versions are all changed to the BAK file extension. You may want to consider other meaningful file extensions for old CONFIG.SYS and AUTOEXEC.BAT files, naming them CONFIG.OLD and AUTOEXEC.OLD, for example.

T I P

Although most AUTOEXEC.BAT files contain only a few lines, making sure that you keep copies of your AUTOEXEC.BAT and CONFIG.SYS files on a bootable disk may be important as a safeguard against the erasure of the files in your root directory or some other catastrophe.

Knowing What To Include in AUTOEXEC.BAT

Many schools of thought exist on what should and should not be in your AUTOEXEC.BAT file. As you learned in Chapter 5, the minimum requirement is usually an AUTOEXEC.BAT containing these three lines:

```
ECHO OFF
PROMPT $P$G
PATH=C:\;C:\DOS
```

The PROMPT command changes your DOS prompt so that it always tells you the current directory. If you're in the WORD directory, for example, the prompt reads C>\WORD. This type of prompt enables you to navigate your disk more easily.

As for the PATH command, it makes sure that you can find DOS programs and anything else in the root (C:\) directory. When you type any command at the DOS prompt—DIR, CHKDSK, XCOPY, or even something odd like XYZZY—DOS first looks to see whether the command is one of DOS's internal commands. (Internal commands such as COPY, DIR, MD, and so on are made available at boot time.) Then DOS looks in the current directory and drive to see whether the command you typed at the prompt is there. Take XYZZY, for example. It isn't a DOS internal command, so if DOS finds a file called XYZZY.BAT, XYZZY.COM, or XYZZY.EXE in the current directory, that file is executed. If you don't have a PATH set, the search ends as soon as the current directory has been checked by DOS. If you do have a PATH set, such as *PATH=C:\;C:\DOS*, DOS first checks the current directory, then the C:\ directory, and finally the C:\DOS directory before giving up. (DOS searches the PATH from left to right for a command.)

Of course as you install new applications on your hard disk, the PATH command often needs to be enlarged. Each application's installation utility usually takes care of this adjustment. Notice that a semicolon separates each new subdirectory from the rest of the subdirectories in the PATH command.

Suppose, for example, that you want to add a BATCH subdirectory for any BAT files you create so that you can locate them easily and not clutter up the root directory. You change the PATH to read as follows:

    PATH=C:\;C:\DOS;C:\BATCH

You create a file called BACKUP.BAT and put it in the BATCH subdirectory. If you type **backup** at the DOS prompt with A:\ the current directory, DOS first checks to see whether BACKUP is an internal DOS command. If not, DOS then looks in the current directory (A:\). Presumably an executable BACKUP (.BAT, .COM, .EXE) file isn't found there, so DOS looks to see whether a PATH is set. DOS then looks to find BACKUP in the first PATH element (C:\). If BACKUP is not found there, DOS moves to the next (C:\DOS). It just so happens that DOS finds a file called BACKUP.EXE in that subdirectory and thus executes that file, totally ignoring the BACKUP.BAT you created.

This exercise simply underlines the need to take a little care in using the PATH command and also consider what you name your BAT files. Had you called it MYBACK.BAT, put it in the C:\BATCH subdirectory, and typed **myback** at the DOS prompt, DOS would have found the file. Or if you had changed the PATH command to *PATH=C:\;C:\BATCH;C:\DOS*, DOS would have found your BACKUP in the BATCH subdirectory before finding the program in the DOS subdirectory.

All PCs and compatibles from the PC/AT and up contain a real-time clock (backed up by battery). If you have an older machine, such as an

8088/PC/XT, DOS at start-up sets the time to 12:00 and the date to
01/01/80 before executing AUTOEXEC.BAT. On those machines, you may
have a real-time clock and a program that you need to run in order to
retrieve the date and time. To overcome the problem of old hardware,
you may want to add two additional lines—DATE and TIME—to your
AUTOEXEC.BAT file:

```
ECHO OFF
PROMPT $P$G
PATH=C:\;C:\DOS
DATE
TIME
```

You have learned the bare essentials for an operational AUTOEXEC.BAT,
but in real life, things rarely turn out to be so simple. Often you need to
add TSR (terminate and stay resident) programs such as mouse drivers,
macro programs, hard disk managers, and virus protection programs.
Luckily, almost all software packages come with an installation program
that adds these lines for you.

 Two applications may conflict in their use of AUTOEXEC.BAT
or CONFIG.SYS. You may find that you have incompatibilities
when using a setup specified by one installation method
and then significantly modified by a subsequent one. The
most common problem is "who's on first." Often, some
publishers *insist* on having their program as the first in an
AUTOEXEC.BAT. You have a problem if two of your programs
are battling for this position.

The order in which DOS searches the PATH for programs often can affect
your system's overall performance. In the next section, you learn how
to maximize your hard disk's performance by controlling the PATH
statement.

Knowing the Rules for a Fast Path

Often overlooked, the DOS PATH command is used primarily to give DOS
an alternative to the current directory when searching for the command
you type at the DOS prompt or the command you include in a batch file.

DOS follows a normal "pecking order" in its search for commands.
When you type a command, such as **pkzip**, at the DOS prompt, DOS first
checks its own internal table of commands (such as DIR, COPY, DEL, CD,
and so on). If the command isn't found there, DOS looks in the current
directory. With the PKZIP command, for example, DOS looks for

something called PKZIP.COM, PKZIP.EXE, or PKZIP.BAT. If the command isn't found in the current directory, DOS looks to its path, starting from left to right. If the path is PATH=C:\DOS;C:\;C:\UTIL, for example, DOS searches the C:\DOS subdirectory first, followed by the root directory (C:\) and finally C:\UTIL. If DOS doesn't find the command (PKZIP.BAT, PKZIP.COM, or PKZIP.EXE) in any of these directories, you see the message Bad command or file name.

When you set up your path, think about what files you plan to execute most often. If you use many DOS commands, for example, you might want C:\DOS as the first part of the path. If you have more than one hard disk on the path, put frequently accessed files on the faster drive and put that subdirectory early (towards the left) in the path. Try to avoid using deeply nested subdirectories, such as

C:\UTILS\HSKPG\GRAPHICS\DRIVERS\VIDEO\HIRES

Certainly avoid putting this complex a subdirectory in the PATH. If you do, you quickly will overrun that rare commodity: environment space, which is the part of RAM in which the PATH is stored when the computer is on. If you get the message Out of environment space, often an exceptionally long PATH statement is the culprit. To avoid this problem, you might want to consider creating a series of special path-setting batch files (such as the one outlined in fig. 7.4). You then can keep control over a series of complex path requirements.

One other trick is to arrange your start-up commands in the most efficient way. Put DOS commands that don't increase the size of the environment, such as CHKDSK, ECHO, and BREAK, at the beginning of AUTOEXEC.BAT. Then load your memory-resident (TSR) programs such as DOSKEY, making sure to include path names. (That approach is more efficient than letting the PATH command do it for you.) Finally, include all commands that enlarge the environment, such as PATH, PROMPT, and variables created with the SET command.

Many programs demand every ounce of the standard 640K that DOS sets aside for running programs (and itself). So if you are getting error messages suggesting that you don't have enough space available, you might want to take a look at your AUTOEXEC.BAT file. Anything that loads a TSR (terminate and stay resident) program in DOS can affect how much memory is left for programs to use, so you might fix the problem by removing the TSR itself or using the DOS 5.0 LOADHIGH command to keep TSRs out of the 640K area.

One final tip on squeezing out the last drop of memory is considering the order in which items are placed in AUTOEXEC.BAT. The environment includes as portions of your AUTOEXEC.BAT such commands as PATH and PROMPT and any environmental variables created with the SET command. TSR programs have a nasty habit of grabbing some memory and putting a copy of the DOS environment in it. By invoking the TSRs before any commands that increase the size of the environment, you can ensure that each TSR includes a smaller copy of the environment than if you had set up a large environment early on by putting PATH in AUTOEXEC.BAT first.

Here's a typical example of how a relatively efficient BAT file might look:

```
@ECHO OFF
BREAK ON
C:\DOS\DOSKEY F720=FORMAT B:/F:720
C:\DOS\DOSKEY BU=C:\UTILS\PKZIP -A A:BOOKBU C:\WP51\HDBOOK\*.TXT
C:\UTILS\VIRUSAFE
SET TEMP=D:\TEMP
PROMPT $P$G
PATH=D:\DOS;C:\;D:\BATCH;C:\UTILS;C:\WINDOWS;C:\WP51
```

Notice that the PATH is the last item in the file and that in this particular situation the D drive has a 9ms access speed whereas the C drive is 38ms, or four times slower. The most frequently used files are placed on the fast drive (D:\DOS and D:\BATCH). Also note that the TSRs (such as the DOSKEY commands) are loaded early followed by all the environment enlarging commands such as SET, PROMPT, and PATH.

Exploring Alternatives to Batch Programs

Some of the most effective alternatives or supplements to batch programs are DOS menu programs. Don't confuse menu systems with shell programs, as covered in Chapter 4, "Managing Your Hard Disk in the Graphical Era." DOS shells enable you to manage files while using a full screen. Menu programs enable you to execute programs and set up environments as you can with any batch process, but from a full screen menu rather than the DOS command line. In some respects, Microsoft Windows is a form of menu system that uses icons to represent the programs to be run.

Following the introduction of Microsoft Windows 3.0, graphical user interfaces have received a great deal of attention. Amidst all the media hype, people seem to forget the fact that many millions of machines are physically incapable of running Windows programs. As aging AT and XT hand-me-downs trickle into the hands of new PC users, the addition of a DOS-based menuing system can make those machines more immediately productive for beginners.

Many effective DOS-based menu systems are available. The following paragraphs give you a small sample of some of the more popular ones.

PreCursor (V.4.0) from the Aldridge Co. of Houston, Texas, is a hard disk menu system that enables you to build a customized series of menu screens from which you can select applications to run. Using PreCursor to control the applications is much easier than having to create batch programs from scratch. Options are available for allowing password protection of applications and logging information about the system usage. PreCursor is easy to use and maintain, which greatly simplifies hard disk operation for all levels of users. PreCursor is self-installing on the hard disk and also requires that the DOS TREE.COM file be stored in the root directory or that the DOS subdirectory be available in the DOS PATH.

Direct Access from Fifth Generation Systems of Baton Rouge, Louisiana, is an extensive program and batch file management system that organizes software programs into a user-defined menu. The most impressive feature is the automated setup and ease of use of the program.

Direct Access has a built-in database of well-known industry applications, recognizes almost 1,000 programs, and "knows" what is needed to run them. Typically, even experienced users would have to spend quite some time setting up such a system manually, using batch files and having to track down the appropriate subdirectories.

You can put up to 26 menu items on each screen and easily create multiple menus. A mouse is supported, and a usage tracking feature is even included that reports how often, when, and for how long programs were run. As a bonus, you can find additional features such as a virus detection program, password protection, and batch file processing.

Lazy Susan (V.4.1) is available from GETC Software, Inc. of Vancouver, British Columbia. Lazy Susan is a hard disk menuing system that features single-keystroke menu-item selection and multiple menu levels with up to 100 items per menu. Some of the major features include area-specific passwords and an effective audit trail that tells you who has used what program. Lazy Susan was designed to run batch files, DOS commands, and any generally executable program.

Automenu from Magee Enterprises, Inc., of Norcross, Georgia, is a budget priced, DOS menuing system that is provided as shareware. As with most utilities in this class, creating custom menus to access frequently used programs is a snap. From the menu, the system can execute any EXE and COM programs as well as batch files and internal DOS commands. Mouse support also is included. Automenu is robust and provides a level of password protection, file encryption, and screen blanking to avoid monitor burnout. You can use Automenu to create unlimited series of menu selections.

Literally dozens of effective menu programs are on the market. This chapter has focused on only a random sampling of some of the more popular ones. With the advent of the DOS Shell under DOS 5.0, Windows 3.0, DesqView and many other general purpose file management utilities, the humble DOS menu found in the plethora of third-party DOS menu packages that have appeared since 1982 will probably disappear on all but a few of the older PCs and some laptop machines.

Using DOSKEY

Available only in Version 5.0 of DOS and later versions, DOSKEY provides many options that enable you to reuse DOS commands easily by pressing single keys on the keyboard. In addition, you can store sequences of these commands, or macros, on disk for later use. The capability to store macros on disk makes them function more like batch files.

You already have looked at ways to use BAT files to customize DOS. DOSKEY is a different method that uses recorded keystrokes. In other words, you can type one or more DOS commands and use DOSKEY to create a list of each command typed at the DOS prompt. In the following sections you learn how to use DOSKEY commands, create DOSKEY macros, and create batch files with DOSKEY

Accessing DOSKEY Commands

Unlike batch files that are known to DOS, DOSKEY is an external program. To use it, you first must load it into memory. If you plan to use DOSKEY, you may want to include a DOSKEY line in your AUTOEXEC.BAT file. (For an example, see the batch file listed in this chapter's section on "Knowing the Rules for a Fast Path.")

After DOSKEY is loaded, it can keep track of between 20 and 40 commands, depending on the length of each command. These commands are stored in a revolving stack, and you can recover commands by using the up- and down-arrow (or PgUp and PgDn) keys to cycle through your old commands. After you have selected a previously entered command, you can edit it and reexecute it. Remember that you eventually run out of space for new commands, so DOSKEY at that point starts to overwrite the commands that were stored early on in the stack history.

DOSKEY includes numerous other features, many of which are summarized in table 7.3. You can use these commands anytime from the DOS prompt.

Table 7.3 DOSKEY Control Keys

Key	Effect
Selecting and moving the cursor	
Up arrow	Selects previous command
Down arrow	Selects next command
PgUp	Moves to top of stack
PgDn	Moves to end of stack
Editing a selected command	
Right arrow	Moves right one character
Ctrl-right arrow	Moves right one word
Left arrow	Moves left one character
Ctrl-left arrow	Moves left one word
Home	Moves to the beginning of the command
End	Moves to the end of the command
Esc	Erases the current line
General DOSKEY control	
F7	Lists all commands in the stack (including reference numbers)
F8	Searches for command that matches one or more characters you type
F9	Moves the "current" command pointer to selected number (from F7 list)
Alt-F7	Erases the whole stack
Alt-F10	Removes all macros from memory

Learning How To Create DOSKEY Macros

A *macro* is a short representation of one or many (usually complex) instructions. Consider, for example, a simplified real-life set of tasks you can call GETPAPER. What GETPAPER translates to is a series of events that results in getting a newspaper.

GETPAPER = GET IN CAR, DRIVE TO STORE, EXIT CAR, ENTER STORE,
SELECT PAPER, BUY PAPER, EXIT STORE, GET IN CAR,
DRIVE HOME, EXIT CAR

Some steps may be missing in this sequence, but you probably get
the picture. A DOSKEY macro represents a series of events just as
GETPAPER does, but the macros are designed to work on a computer
in a DOS environment.

To create a DOSKEY macro, the first step is to define the macro to
DOSKEY. To do so, simply type at the DOS prompt the command
doskey followed by a macro name, an equals sign, and some sort of
DOS command with replaceable parameters defined as $1, $2, and
so on through $9.

Trying a simple example can give you a better idea of how the process
works. In this example, you create a simple macro called DIRP for DIR
with pause. To set up DIRP, type the following at the DOS prompt:

DOSKEY DIRP=DIR /P

Here DOSKEY is being told to recognize the command DIRP, intercept it,
and substitute the real DOS command of DIR /P.

A slightly more complex DOSKEY macro is one to control the resolution
of the screen when ANSI.SYS (the DOS ANSI driver) has been loaded in
CONFIG.SYS. Call this macro RES and use a replacable parameter to
define 43- or 25-line mode:

DOSKEY RES=MODE CON LINES=$1

Here RES is being substituted with the MODE CON LINES=, and the $1 is
replaced with the parameter value, which is whatever you add as numbers to the right of RES. In this particular case, only one parameter is
allowed. If you type more than one, they are ignored. Suppose, for
example, that you type the following at the DOS prompt:

RES 43

DOSKEY substitutes MODE CON LINES=43.

You can add DOSKEY macros to any batch file, including
AUTOEXEC.BAT, or execute them at the command line. Creating a
DOSKEY macro is much faster than putting a batch file together, but you
still need to create a batch file in which to save the DOSKEY macros. If
you have only a few DOSKEY commands that you use often, the best
place to put them is in your AUTOEXEC.BAT file.

You might, for example, want to include these DOSKEY macro settings in
your AUTOEXEC.BAT file, with one DOSKEY command per line:

```
DOSKEY F720=FORMAT B: /F:720
DOSKEY BU=PKZIP -A A:BOOKBU C:\WP51\HDBOOK\*.TXT
DOSKEY BOOTD=FORMAT A:/S $T COPY C:\DOS\F*.* A: $T COPY
C:\DOS\SYS.* A:
```

The first line formats 720K floppy disks in your 1.44M drive B. The second line archives (zips) all the text files that make up the chapters of a book. And the third line creates a 1.2M boot disk and copies some critical DOS files to drive A.

After these DOSKEY macros are stored in memory, you can execute them by simply typing **f720**, **bu**, or **bootd** at the DOS prompt. You can add more commands manually to memory and can list whatever macros are in memory by issuing the DOSKEY command with the /M switch, as in **doskey /m**.

Creating Batch Files with DOSKEY

After reading the previous sections of this chapter, you already are familiar with several ways to create batch files. The history option (/H) in DOSKEY gives you another method.

Suppose, for example, that you need to copy a series of specific files to a floppy disk. First clear out the existing stack of commands by pressing Alt-F7; then proceed with your individual file copy operations from the DOS prompt. When you have finished performing the series of copies, type **doskey /h** and press Enter at the DOS prompt. You see on-screen the list of COPY commands just as you typed them. Now, type this command and then press Enter:

DOSKEY /H > MYCOPY.BAT

This command uses the > to tell DOS to redirect the list of commands to a file called MYCOPY.BAT rather than to the screen. You then need to edit this file, adding DOSKEY to the beginning of each line, and save the file as a BAT file so that you can execute it later. To execute all those commands, then, you just have to type the batch file name (MYCOPY, in this example) at the DOS prompt.

You can use a similar procedure to store your DOSKEY macros to a file so that you can reinstall them later. When you turn off your computer, all macros in memory are lost. If you want them back, you need to capture them to a file and reinstall them when you turn the PC on again. Use the DOSKEY /M option to list the macro definitions, as in

DOSKEY /M > MYMACS.SAV

Looking at Alternatives to DOSKEY Macros

If you don't have DOS 5.0, or if you want some additional macro capabilities, you may be interested in purchasing a stand-alone macro utility program. Keyboard macro programs were one of the first utilities to appear for the early PCs back in 1983. Like DOSKEY, the basic function for macro utilities such as RoseSoft's ProKey, Alpha Keyworks, and Borland's SuperKey is to record keystrokes as you type them, and then play them back later with the press of an Alt or Ctrl key. With all these programs, you can pause to insert a fixed or variable number of keystrokes—for example, a file name.

Unlike DOSKEY, these third-party macro utilities are designed to operate both within DOS and within programs that run under DOS. Most software companies now offer macro facilities within their own products, but a need still exists for products that can perform this type of function both in DOS and in many commercial software programs. Although not as prolific today, quite a few programs still are available, with many now offering additional features such as virus protection and screen savers. Several representative macro utilities are outlined in the following paragraphs.

Keyworks and *Keyworks Advanced* from Alpha Software Corp. of Burlington, Massachusetts, are both sophisticated, general purpose keyboard macro utilities. These utilities enable you to record keystrokes as you type them, and then play them back later with the press of a key, either Alt or Ctrl and another regular key. When recording keystrokes, you can modify Keyworks macros to let the user pause and insert a fixed or variable number of keystrokes or text, such as a file name, drive letter, or password.

Keyworks loads itself as a TSR (terminate and stay resident) program and has the capability to create a menu of your favorite macros. In addition, if you suddenly decide that you have just typed in a sequence you want to capture, Keyworks can back up and make a macro out of those keystrokes.

One notable achievement with Keyworks is its robustness (it doesn't hang up) and freedom of conflicts from other TSRs. If you don't want to become a programmer, you don't need all the conditional branching and looping that is available in Keyworks Advanced. For most people, the less expensive Keyworks 3.0 is perfectly adequate.

ProKey Plus from RoseSoft, Inc., of Bellevue, Washington, was among the first macro processing programs to become available for PCs. ProKey

Plus is a 67K TSR macro manager that readily can be unloaded from memory if needed. ProKey Plus offers cut and paste features, an event scheduler, and a history command to convert your last keystrokes into a macro. The menus themselves are in the popular Lotus style. The pop-up user prompts can include user-defined and annotated help messages.

SuperKey from Borland International, Inc., of Scotts Valley, California, has been available for many years, coming out shortly after ProKey Plus. The basic features are the same as for the Keyworks 3.0 utility, but SuperKey adds some extra features, including simple file encryption, passwords to lock out unauthorized users on an unattended keyboard, and a screen turn-off feature to protect your monitor from burnout or prying eyes. You can record macros on the fly (as you work) and save them to disk as a regular DOS file, and you can cut and paste any text-based screen information into anything that accepts keystrokes—editors, DOS, communication programs, and so on. One other added feature is the fact that SuperKey macros are compatible with RoseSoft's ProKey files.

Summary

In this chapter, you have learned about batch files and the significance of AUTOEXEC.BAT. You have learned about a number of ways to create and maintain DOS batch files by using COPY CON, EDIT, EDLIN, and other methods. You also have discovered some tips on how you can create efficient batch files and how they control programs on your hard disk. Menuing under DOS—both by creating your own and by using commercial packages—has been introduced.

This chapter also has introduced you to macros, in particular the DOSKEY macro program in DOS 5.0. In addition, you have at your disposal a series of basic reference tables and some alternative commercial program options to both batch files and DOSKEY macro programming.

In the next chapter, you learn about another important aspect of working with your hard disk: memory. Turn to that chapter to find out how you can speed up your hard disk operations by using memory wisely.

Fine-Tuning Your Hard Disk's Performance

8 Using Memory To Speed Up
Your Disk

9 Exploring Hard Disk Fitness
Programs

Using Memory To Speed Up Your Disk

Y ou need to understand an important fundamental about memory: memory doesn't do a thing to speed up your hard disk. Your disk keeps plodding along at its own 28-millisecond or 18-millisecond disk-access pace. What memory does is give the *illusion* of a faster hard disk. The different tips and tricks you can play with memory cause the system to look for data in memory before looking for data on the disk. And accessing memory of any kind is much faster than a mechanical disk access. Memory operates in nanoseconds, or billionths of a second, compared to the thousandths of a second involved in disk access.

Although it is one of the most vital aspects of your computer, memory also can be one of the most perplexing. This chapter offers some tips that can help you speed up your computer by using memory to supplement your hard disk. Before you get to that point, however, spend a little time going over some basic memory concepts so that you can better understand how these shortcuts work.

A brief review of memory may be helpful, if you missed mentions in earlier chapters or if you're finding memory as baffling as most people do on their first acquaintance. In contrast to disk storage, which acts as a repository for data and programs, memory is more of an electronic worksheet; it's where the program and data are stored while you're working with them.

When you start up a program or request a file, the data you need is placed in memory and is kept there while you work on the data. When you have finished working on a file and save it, the file then is saved to disk, and the next item you work on is loaded into memory. The memory that data is loaded into is called *RAM* (random-access memory).

RAM is different from ROM. When your computer shuts down, whether by accident or design, anything in RAM disappears. ROM (read-only memory) cannot make room for your data because it has information burned onto the memory chip. (Please note that this statement applies to basic, garden-variety ROM for desktop computers. Newer portable technologies are introducing ROM that can be changed.) For this reason, ROM contains the basic information your computer needs to get up and running. You don't want to have to go through a massive formatting process every time you want to tweak a spreadsheet.

 NOTE Unless otherwise indicated, in this chapter the general term "memory" is used to refer to random-access memory, or RAM.

Determining the Amounts and Kinds of Memory You Can Use

You learned in earlier chapters that RAM is the space your computer uses for the temporary storage of information, but RAM isn't the whole story. In order to understand how RAM works, you need to know how DOS finds the memory and also what kinds of memory are available. In the following paragraphs you learn about memory addresses, conventional memory, upper memory, expanded memory, and extended memory.

Understanding Addressable Memory

First, RAM needs to reside at an *address* in order for DOS to find the information RAM contains, just as the post office needs a street address in order to deliver your mail. Second, computers differ in the amount of address space they can use.

Just as your computer's magnetic hard disk is ordered into tracks and sectors so that finding information is easier, your computer's electronic storage cells are organized into addresses. Addressable memory is like unoccupied office space. RAM completes the address the way a tenant completes an office. Without an address, DOS wouldn't be able to find the information, and without usable RAM, the address wouldn't be able to store the information.

The amount of memory your computer can address is determined by the type of microprocessor it uses. The more powerful the microprocessor, the more memory the computer can address. Note, however, that just because a computer can address 16M of memory doesn't mean that the computer contains that much memory. Many 386SX computers, for example, ship with 1M of memory. 386DX computers often ship with 2M, and 486-class computers often are sold with 4M.

Figure 8.1 shows the amount of memory that can be addressed by various Intel microprocessors. You can see that a big difference exists between the addressable amount of memory and the amount of memory a computer contains. Think of addressable memory spaces as vacant lots; the amount of memory a computer contains is the number of houses built on those lots. You can see in the figure that the XT (8088/8086) is likely to have the least number of vacancies; it can address only 1M of memory and is likely to have at least 640K installed.

But 286-class and above PCs are in the situation XTs were in 10 years ago—that is, they have far more available addresses than they have memory to fill them. Basic entry-level 286 and 386SX PCs can address up to 16M of memory, while most of them ship with 1M. And 386/486 class PCs can address 4,096 megabytes of memory—roughly one to two thousand times more memory than most of these machines contain when you purchase them. You're far more likely to load 16M of memory on a computer you're using for a network server (a machine that stores files for many PCs) than on one you're using for your own programs. Still, knowing that the room is there is comforting when you want to add more memory.

Memory usage, however, isn't quite as cut and dried as assuming that an 8088-based machine can hold less memory than one with a 386 microprocessor. If you own an AT-class (286) machine, for example, you may be particularly chagrined if you purchase extended memory and find out that you cannot use it. Knowing the differences in the way each machine handles memory may save you from accidentally purchasing memory-management software or add-on memory chips that cannot be supported on your computer.

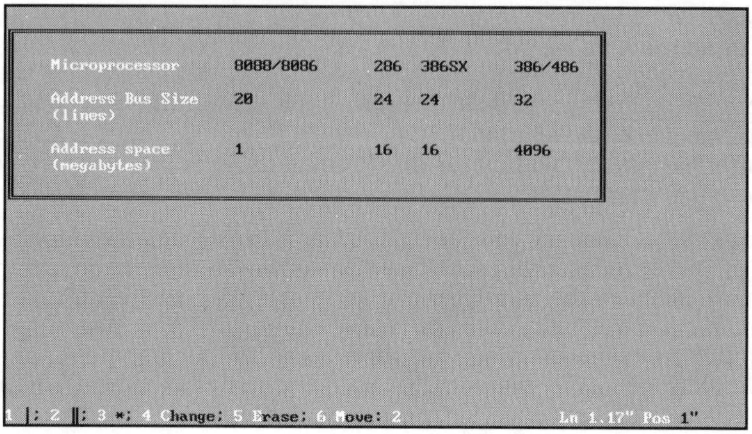

Microprocessor	8088/8086	286	386SX	386/486
Address Bus Size (lines)	20	24	24	32
Address space (megabytes)	1	16	16	4096

1 |; 2 ||; 3 *; 4 Change; 5 Erase; 6 Move: 2   Ln 1.17" Pos 1"

FIG. 8.1

Comparing memory capacity of various Intel microprocessors.

Using Conventional Memory

You may have noticed that computers with 8088- or 8086-based micro-processors can address only 1M of memory. Because DOS was designed for these XT-class machines, it also was designed to address only 1M of memory. Out of that 1M, the first 640K was set aside for running programs. That 640K commonly is referred to as conventional memory.

Unfortunately, although PCs are now capable of addressing up to 4 gigabytes of memory, DOS hasn't kept pace. The fact that your state-of-the-art 486 came loaded with 6M of RAM matters not one little bit to DOS. It's as if the post office delivers mail only as far as 1024K Memory Lane even though the neighborhood has grown to 4096K Memory Lane.

In fairness, although 640K seems like a mere pittance today, you have to remember that when this arrangement was set up more than 10 years ago, 640K seemed like more address space than anyone could ever use. Software programs of the day were not graphics-intensive and therefore were much smaller. The good news is that you can find ways around DOS's memory limitations—by purchasing expanded memory for older XT- and AT-class machines and by purchasing memory managers that take advantage of sophisticated 386- and 486-class extended memory.

Using Upper Memory

Although DOS can use only 640K to run a program, DOS recognizes addresses up to 1M. The remaining 384K originally was reserved for use by the video display screen, the ROM BIOS, and other hardware and system functions.

That area between 640K and 1M is referred to as *Upper Memory Blocks*, or *UMBs* (sometimes also called *high DOS*). UMBs provide loopholes in the form of unused address space, because the video display, BIOS, and other components leave a little wiggle room in that area. You can find out how upper memory is being used in your system by typing the following command at the DOS prompt:

MEM /C | MORE

DOS displays three columns of information about programs currently using system memory, including the largest available upper memory block.

 NOTE The upper memory area is not to be confused with the High Memory Area (HMA), which is the first 64K block (less 16 bytes) of memory beyond the 1M memory boundary. Note also that not all 1M machines have an HMA. To have an HMA, a PC must have at least 64K extended memory.

Using Expanded Memory

Expanded memory was designed as a way to get around the 1M addressable-memory limitation imposed by the DOS/XT collaboration. Expanded memory is the only kind of supplemental memory you can use on an XT. Because this type of memory has been around so long and because it works with all Intel-based computers, you can find software that works with expanded memory more easily than you can find programs that work purely with extended memory. You learn why that's important in the following section, "Using Extended Memory," when you learn how different machines use extended memory.

Expanded memory has no corresponding physical memory addresses. This realization leads to the obvious question: how does DOS find anything in expanded memory?

Here is where the real ingenuity—a slick engineering feat—comes in. Remember that if DOS were a post office, it would stop mail delivery at 1024K Memory Lane. But not all those addresses may be occupied. In this scenario, expanded memory is a subleasing arrangement. Expanded memory simply takes an unused chunk of conventional memory and borrows its address, in a neat sleight-of-hand maneuver called *bank switching*. Expanded memory managers "switch" the data they contain to an unused portion of conventional memory so that DOS can find the data. That portion of conventional memory serves as an electronic post office box for data that doesn't have an address of its own.

When you purchase expanded memory, you typically purchase a board and expanded memory software written to the LIM-EMS (Lotus-Intel-Microsoft Expanded Memory Specification), which dictates how it works with expanded memory. EMM (expanded memory manager) software written to the 3.2 LIM-EMS specification uses a 64K window within the upper memory blocks called a *page frame*. The page frame enables DOS to access up to four 16K pages of expanded memory at once.

EMM software written to the newer 4.0 LIM-EMS specification does not have the size or location limitations of the 3.2 software. This newer software can place page frames in conventional memory as well as in the upper memory blocks, and the size of the page can be up to 576K.

Purchasing an expanded memory board with expanded memory-management software, however, isn't enough to take advantage of unused addresses. The expanded memory manager that comes with your expanded memory board is simply a device driver—that is, it lets DOS know how to talk to the board. To tell DOS which data to route in and out of the page frame, you need special memory-management software, such as Quarterdeck's QRAM, or the memory managers built into DOS in the form of the EMM386.EXE device driver, which is explained in more detail in the subsequent section on "Examining DOS 5.0's Memory-Management Improvements."

If you have inherited an older PC with only 512K of conventional memory rather than the standard 640K, expanded memory uses these addresses as well, through a process called *backfilling*. Backfilling brings your PC up to the standard 640K.

Using Extended Memory

Extended memory is simply a linear extension of conventional memory. If the conventional and upper memory neighborhood stops at 1024K Memory Lane, the extended memory neighborhood starts at 1025K Memory Lane and extends out to 4096M (4 gigabytes).

No matter what you do, you cannot work with extended memory on an XT, because the XT's microprocessor can generate only 1M worth of physical addresses. But 286s, 386s, and 486s all are capable of using extended memory.

Just as expanded memory can pretend to be conventional memory, so can extended memory pretend to be expanded memory. That concept is important because expanded memory is compatible with more software programs. Most memory-management programs let extended memory mimic expanded memory.

But even here, things are not as straightforward as they seem. Architectural differences in the machines really come into play, and many 286 owners have been less than happy campers when the subject is extended memory. 386- and 486-based machines automatically enable extended memory to mimic expanded memory; this capability is built directly into the hardware. 286-based machines, alas, do not have this talent, unless they use special chip sets, such as Chips & Technologies NEAT chip set. Many a 286 owner has discovered with regret that the 2M of extended memory that came with the machine might as well be in Siberia for all the good it does. And if you want to use extended memory on an AT, you have to purchase an expanded memory board or All Computers' All Chargecard, even if that AT has 4M of extended memory on board.

That's the bad news. The good news is that memory-management programs that once required the purchase of third-party products are now making their way to DOS, and the money you save on software can go towards additional memory instead.

Examining DOS 5.0's Memory-Management Improvements

The latest version of DOS, 5.0, offers some improvements in the way it works with memory. First, you now can run DOS itself from the HMA, that first 64K chunk of extended memory beyond the 1M conventional limit. To do so, you use a device driver called HIMEM.SYS, which is DOS'S built-in extended memory manager.

Using HIMEM.SYS

All this information may sound complicated, but DOS 5.0 tries to make the process as painless as possible. If your system contains extended memory, the DOS Setup program typically installs DOS so that it automatically runs in the HMA.

You can tell whether DOS is running in HMA by looking at your CONFIG.SYS file. (Remember, CONFIG.SYS is a start-up file that contains configuration commands and enables you to customize DOS.) To look at your CONFIG.SYS file, type **type config.sys** at the prompt. (Depending on how your PC is set up, you may need to change to the DOS directory first by typing **cd dos** at the prompt.) Or you can use the Editor in the DOS Shell and type **config.sys** in the text entry box of the window that pops up.

Your CONFIG.SYS file should contain the following commands:

    DEVICE=HIMEM.SYS
    DOS=HIGH

The first command loads the HIMEM extended memory manager; the second command loads DOS into the HMA.

If you know that your system has extended memory and you're using DOS 5.0 but these commands don't appear, you may want to run the DOS Setup program or add these two lines to your CONFIG.SYS file by using the Editor in the DOS Shell or another text editor.

HIMEM.SYS also makes extended memory available to programs that use it according to the XMS (Extended Memory Specification), but as mentioned earlier you will find more programs that use expanded memory.

Using EMM386.EXE

DOS also contains a memory manager that enables your extended memory to mimic expanded memory. That memory manager is called EMM386.EXE.

NOTE EMM386, like other extended-to-expanded memory managers, works only with 386- and 486-based PCs because it relies on the hardware's capability to swap extended memory for expanded memory. You want to use EMM386 if your computer has only extended memory and you want to run programs that require expanded memory. If you don't have any such programs, you don't need to use this feature.

In addition to enabling extended memory to act like expanded memory, EMM386 gives you access to UMBs—the upper memory blocks between 640K and 1024K. You need to use some care, however, if you want to move device drivers and other memory-resident programs into the upper memory blocks. The process isn't automatic. You need to install the programs one at a time to make sure that they will work in the UMB area, and not all programs work there.

When you work with memory-resident programs (also called TSRs), you also will find that you must do things in a special order. Just as you have to remove the top box of a stack of boxes before you can remove the bottom box, you have to load certain TSRs before you can load others, and the last one you load must be the first one you unload. You may want to take Microsoft's word on this one: In the DOS 5.0 manual Microsoft recommends that the procedures used to move programs into the UMBs are technically complex and best left to advanced users.

If you want to learn more about this topic, the DOS 5.0 manual itself is rather comprehensive, or you may want to check out one of Que's publications, such as *Turbocharging MS-DOS*.

Now that you have learned several basic memory concepts, you are ready to look at some ways you can use memory to speed up your hard disk. The disk's true speed does not change, of course. But you can have DOS get memory from RAM rather than from the disk, making the disk *appear* faster.

Optimizing the Number of Buffers

One of the easiest things you can do to improve the speed of your system is to adjust the number of DOS buffers, the portions of memory that DOS sets aside to act as holding tanks for data when reading from or writing to a hard disk. (These DOS buffers are in addition to any caching capability contained in the controller or in special disk caching programs. For more on disk caching, see this chapter's section on "Working with Disk Caches." You also were introduced to buffers and caches in Chapter 2, "Choosing a Hard Disk: Self-Defense for Buyers.")

The trick in selecting the right number of buffers is finding a happy medium. You want enough buffers to improve performance but not so many that they rob your system of memory it could put to better use elsewhere.

The optimum number of buffers for your system depends on the size of your system's hard disk. According to Microsoft, the following are the optimum buffer sizes for hard disks of varying size:

Disk Size	Number of Buffers
Less than 40M	20
40 to 79M	30
80 to 119M	40
120M and above	50

To change the buffer size, simply change the number of buffers indicated in the BUFFERS line of your CONFIG.SYS file. Figure 8.2 shows what a plain CONFIG.SYS file looks like on a system that isn't using Windows.

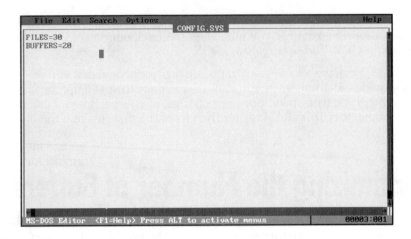

FIG. 8.2

A basic CONFIG.SYS file.

The FILES line refers to the number of files that can be open at once. BUFFERS refers to how much RAM is set aside for buffers, the units of memory that hold data temporarily. The typical default number for files is 20; the typical number of buffers varies, depending on the size of the disk.

The Editor found in the DOS Shell gives you an easy way to edit text files such as CONFIG.SYS. To edit CONFIG.SYS from the Editor, follow these steps:

1. Activate the DOS Shell by typing **dosshell** and pressing Enter at the prompt.

2. Select Editor from the program list at the bottom of the screen with the mouse, or activate that area of the screen by pressing the Alt key and use the arrow and Enter keys to highlight and select the Editor. (If you don't see the program list, select Program/File Lists from the View menu at the top of the screen.)

3. In the File To Edit dialog box that appears, type **config.sys** and click OK.

NOTE If you prefer to work from the DOS command line, just type **edit config.sys** at the prompt.

4. Position your cursor on the BUFFERS line and type the number of buffers you want to use in your system.

5. Select Save from the File menu to save the changes you made.

6. Reboot the computer to put the changes into effect.

Working with RAM Disks

Setting up a *RAM disk* (also called a *virtual drive* or *RAM drive*) is one popular way to use extended or expanded memory. A RAM disk is simply a portion of RAM that's set aside to mimic a hard disk. You store and retrieve files from the RAM disk just as you would from a hard disk.

If your computer is a 386 or 486, you don't need to bother with a RAM disk, but if you're using an XT or AT, you can notice a difference in performance when you're using a RAM disk with expanded memory, depending on the task.

DOS has its own RAM disk device driver, called RAMDRIVE.SYS. (In older DOS versions, it's called VDISK.SYS.)

> Because you're using RAM to impersonate a hard disk, any data contained in the RAM disk is lost if the power goes off before you have saved the data back to the hard disk. For that reason, the best approach is to save program files in the RAM disk, because they tend to be more stable than data files.
>
> **T I P**

The following sections explain how to create a RAM disk and how to copy files to that disk.

Creating a RAM Disk

Setting up a RAM disk is easy. All you need is DOS, Version 3.0 or later. To create a RAM disk, you simply add a line to your CONFIG.SYS file.

To open CONFIG.SYS for editing, follow steps 1 through 3 of the procedure given in the previous section on "Optimizing the Number of Buffers." Then add a DEVICE line (device driver) to CONFIG.SYS to let DOS know that you're setting up a RAM disk. Suppose, for example, that you want to add a 1M RAM disk to extended memory. Type the following line underneath the FILES and BUFFERS lines:

> **DEVICE=C:\DOS\RAMDRIVE.SYS 1024 128 64 /E**

 NOTE   In this example, the DOS directory is included in the path because normally you should set up a subdirectory for DOS on your computer. DOS is included in the path to help DOS find the RAM disk driver. If you don't have a subdirectory for DOS, leave that part (\DOS) out of the DEVICE line.

The first number after the path name, 1024 in this example, indicates the size of the RAM disk, which is 1024K or 1M. This number is not arbitrary. Although you can set up a 512K RAM disk just as easily, you do need to keep the computer's binary requirements in mind and use the appropriate multiples of two. You can use 64K, 256K, or 512K, for example, but not 391K or some other number that cannot be divided by 2.

The next two numbers, 128 and 64, refer respectively to the sector size, which sets up the size of each sector, and the entry size, which is the number of files or subdirectories you can have in the root directory of your RAM disk. The default value for sectors is 512, but you can use 128 or 256. The default value for entries is 64, but you can use anything from 2 to 1024.

Finally, the /E switch at the end of the DEVICE line notifies DOS that you want your RAM disk to use extended memory. If you want it to use expanded memory, use the /A switch instead. If your computer has extended memory, you may want to choose it for your RAM drive because fewer programs will compete with it. (More programs are designed to use expanded memory rather than extended memory.)

> **NOTE** If you use extended memory for your RAM drive, you must include in CONFIG.SYS a DEVICE command for DOS's HIMEM.SYS memory manager, and the RAMDRIVE command must come after the HIMEM.SYS command.

If you want to use conventional memory for your RAM disk, you don't need a switch, but using conventional memory for a RAM disk isn't a good idea. It's like draining half the fuel from your car's gas tank in order to have less drag weight. You might go faster, but you risk running out of gas. DOS needs most (or all) of that precious 640K to run programs, and faster access is moot if you don't have enough memory to run a program.

Figure 8.3 shows the modified CONFIG.SYS file with the RAMDRIVE.SYS file added.

You don't have to worry about what to call your RAM disk; DOS handles that task for you. If you have a hard drive, usually indicated by the letter C, DOS automatically assigns the letter D to your RAM disk. If you have a floppy drive only, usually indicated by A, DOS assigns the letter C to your RAM disk. (If you happen to add a hard drive later, DOS automatically makes the switch and reassigns the letter D to your RAM disk.)

After you have added the line to your CONFIG.SYS file and saved the file in the Editor by selecting Save from the File menu, you need to reboot the computer in order for the change to take effect. When you reboot the computer, try typing **d:** at the DOS prompt to make sure that the RAM disk works, or go into the DOS Shell and check to see whether the RAM drive's icon appears at the top of the screen with the other drive icons, as shown in figure 8.4.

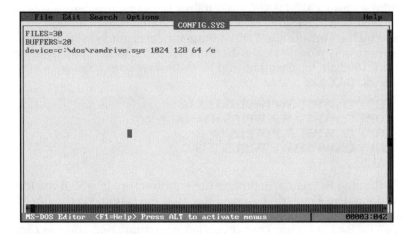

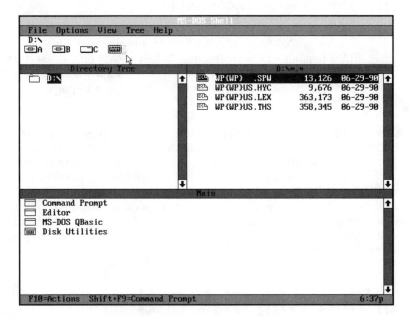

Copying Files to the RAM Disk

One of the most popular ways to use a RAM disk is to farm out to it portions of a large program such as a word processor. You can transfer files to your RAM disk every time you start the computer, but adding the program files to your AUTOEXEC.BAT file is much easier and faster. Then you have to do it only once. (For a review of AUTOEXEC.BAT, see Chapter 7, "Using Batch Files and Macros.")

To add the files to AUTOEXEC.BAT, follow the same procedure you used to edit the CONFIG.SYS file, calling up the file from the DOS Shell's Editor, adding the appropriate COPY command lines, and saving the file. If you want to add WordPerfect's dictionary, spell checker, and thesaurus to your RAM disk, for example, add the following lines to your AUTOEXEC.BAT file:

COPY C:\WP51\WP{WP}US.LEX D:
COPY C:\WP51\WP{WP}US.HYC D:
COPY C:\WP51\WP{WP}.SPW D:
COPY C:\WP51\WP{WP}US.THS D:
PAUSE

Notice that the full paths, including the subdirectory in which the files are contained, are included. Also notice that the last line is the PAUSE command. This command comes in handy if you want to see what AUTOEXEC.BAT is doing. Then if you left something out, you can notice it right away and correct the problem easily.

NOTE You're probably wondering how installing these files on a RAM disk affects performance. When a RAM disk is used on a 286-based computer, you can notice roughly a 25 percent performance increase when spell checking a 10-page document.

Another good use for a RAM disk is downloading compressed files from an on-line service, a service such as CompuServe or Prodigy that you access by using a modem over phone lines. (For more on data compression, see Chapter 15, "Understanding Data Compression.") Downloaded files typically are compressed into one large file, and decompressing them takes less time on a RAM disk than it does on a hard disk. Simply send the files you download to your RAM disk rather than to the hard disk. After you have decompressed the files, you can save them to your hard disk if you want.

Working with Disk Caches

Another option for using memory to speed up data access is the *disk cache*, a portion of memory that holds frequently accessed data. You then can avoid a call to the slower disk.

Disk caches often are confused with RAM disks, although the two are not the same thing. You copy entire files to a RAM disk, and the system reads and writes to RAM as though it were reading and writing to the hard disk. Disk caches, in contrast, are portions of memory that store small amounts of frequently used data so that the CPU can get to it more quickly.

Disk caches also often are confused with disk buffers, which are simply holding tanks for data. As was mentioned briefly in Chapter 2, "Choosing a Hard Disk: Self-Defense for Buyers," disk caches are more sophisticated than buffers. A disk cache determines which information has been accessed most frequently and holds that information. A buffer, on the other hand, may simply grab neighboring information regardless of whether it has been accessed recently.

> FASTOPEN is a DOS command that's somewhat of a pseudocache. It's not a full-fledged cache, but it does cache file names and locations, so if you open and close many files, FASTOPEN can be helpful. Keep in mind that FASTOPEN doesn't work with extended memory and should not be used from the Shell because your machine might lock up. You also might lose data if you use a disk-compaction program while you have FASTOPEN loaded. Quite frankly, if you're looking to DOS for any caching options, your best bet is just to stick with SMARTDRV.SYS, which is covered in the next section, "Using DOS and Windows Caches." (For more information on FASTOPEN, see Appendix A.)

T I P

Caching works because the microprocessor tends to keep working with the same small segment of memory for a while before needing another segment. A cache's efficiency is measured in *hits* and *misses*. If the cache contains the information the CPU needs, the access is known as a hit. If the cache doesn't contain the information, the access is known as a miss. Hit rates of 90 to 95 percent are considered excellent.

The success of a cache depends in part on the type of program used. Disk caches are most effective for programs such as databases that are disk-intensive, meaning that they spend a great deal of time reading from or writing to the hard disk. (To determine whether a program is using the disk frequently, look at the little red indicator light. If it's constantly flashing, the program is making many calls to the disk.)

Other factors that affect a disk cache's success are the cache's size and design. In the following sections, you compare the different caching options available to you.

Using DOS and Windows Caches

Microsoft Windows and DOS both include software disk caches called SMARTDrive. The DOS version of SMARTDrive requires that you add a DEVICE command to the CONFIG.SYS file, much as you would for a RAM disk; the Windows version of SMARTDrive installs itself as part of the Windows installation process. Another advantage to the Windows version is that it's designed specifically for Windows, unlike other software caches.

Whenever you use a cache, no matter whose it is, you should use only one. If you use Windows 3.1, you may want to stick with its improved version of SMARTDrive and not worry about setting up the DOS version. If you're using DOS 5.0 and Windows 3.0, however, Microsoft recommends using the DOS version of SMARTDrive.

To install a SMARTDrive disk cache in DOS 5.0, follow these steps:

1. Activate the DOS Shell by typing **dosshell** and pressing Enter at the prompt.

2. Select Editor from the program list at the bottom of the screen with the mouse, or activate that area of the screen by pressing the Alt key and use the arrow and Enter keys to highlight and select the Editor. (If you don't see the program list, select Program/File Lists from the View menu at the top of the screen.)

3. If the File To Edit dialog box appears, type **config.sys** and click OK.

4. Type a new DEVICE line to install the cache. The following example installs a 512K cache in extended memory:

       DEVICE = C:\DOS\SMARTDRV.SYS 512

   (You need to put this command after the HIMEM.SYS command. If your CONFIG.SYS file doesn't have a HIMEM command, insert the line DEVICE = C:\DOS\HIMEM.SYS before adding the SMARTDRV command.)

5. Select Save from the File menu to save your changes.

6. Reboot the computer to put the changes into effect.

 NOTE   You don't have to use switches to install a cache in extended memory, because SMARTDrive defaults to extended memory. If you want this cache to use expanded memory instead, however, you need to add an /A switch to the end of the DEVICE command.

How much cache do you need? Microsoft recommends not making the cache any smaller than 256K, because it wouldn't be large enough to be effective. On the other hand, you don't want to make your cache larger than 2048K because the performance gain isn't enough to justify using the extra memory.

Using Commercial Caches

A number of commercial caching programs also are available, such as VCache from Golden Bow Systems and Flash from Software Matters. Utility programs such as Central Point Software's PC Tools 7.1 and the Norton Utilities from Symantec also contain caching programs along with their other utilities.

 Whichever cache you decide on, you should use only one. Commercial products such as Super PC-Kwik's Disk Accelerator warn you to remove other caches before installing the new product.

Multisoft's Super PC-Kwik, a consistent award winner, is probably one of the best-known commercial disk-caching programs. You can purchase Super PC-Kwik separately or as part of PC-Kwik PowerPak, which contains a RAM disk, a print spooler, and keyboard and screen accelerators. Super PC-Kwik uses an easy-to-follow installation format. Figure 8.5 shows the PC-Kwik cache indicator for Windows.

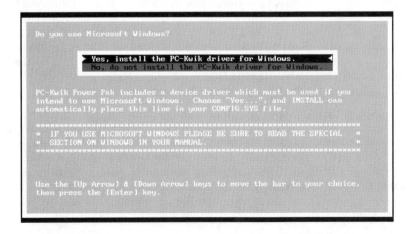

FIG. 8.5

The PC-Kwik cache indicator for Windows.

Super PC-Kwik's Disk Accelerator disk cache can use conventional, extended, or expanded memory. The cache also lends memory to other PowerPak utilities and programs as needed and even includes a pop-up measurement program that shows you how many disk accesses you're saving by using the disk cache. When you press a hot key, a box appears showing the number of logical transfers (cache hits), physical transfers (disk accesses), and transfers saved. (You can use this option only when the monitor is in text mode. If the DOS Shell or some other program is in graphics mode, the feature doesn't work. You can, however, call up the file SUPERWIN.EXE from the Windows File Manager to display cache activity while Windows is active.)

A related feature is the cache hit indicator, which appears as a flashing asterisk in the upper-right corner of the screen whenever the cache is accessed (much as the hard disk light flashes when the disk is accessed). This option also requires that the monitor be in text mode.

Using Hardware Caches

Caching disk controllers, or *hardware caches*, are a more expensive caching option. Caching controllers range anywhere from several hundred to a couple of thousand dollars and typically are used on large-capacity drives. Manufacturers of caching controllers include Perceptive Solutions, Distributed Processing Technology, and CompuAdd. Compaq and Zenith are also building caching controllers into their latest PCs.

Hardware caching controllers are easier on system memory than software options are, because the hardware versions contain their own RAM and don't diminish the system's RAM. You then are less likely to run into the conflicts that can arise when you're trying to get different software programs to "play nice" with memory. The downside is that the memory used by the caching controller isn't available for any other use by the system. Another disadvantage is that controllers have to deal with bus traffic; software caches don't because they consist of system RAM.

A less expensive hardware option is the *track buffering controller*, which costs up to ten times less than full-blown caching controllers and works in conjunction with caching software. Aside from the cost advantage, these cards enable the memory to be used for other purposes when not needed by the hard disk, because they work with system memory instead of housing memory on the board. Track buffering controllers are less sophisticated than caching controllers because track buffering controllers simply grab an entire track when a sector is requested.

Caching controllers vary in design. Some have what are known as *read-ahead caches*, which are more sophisticated and typically larger than track buffers. Instead of simply grabbing the track that contains a sector, they may store several tracks as sectors from each request, thus increasing the odds that DOS will request a sector already contained in the cache. Read-ahead caches are better for data that's scattered all over a disk.

What you have read so far concerns data that's read from the disk, but cache design also affects how quickly data is written to the disk. *Write-through caches* are ones that instantly forward any and all writes to the hard disk. *Delayed-write* or *write-back caches*, in contrast, pass the write to disk at a later time. Exactly how much later depends on the cache design. Some write-back caches don't pass writes along to the disk until they're full; others wait for a certain period of inactivity.

Although write-back caches are faster, the slight danger always exists that something can happen to wipe out the contents of the cache memory before your writes get passed back to the hard disk. If that disaster happens, you're out of luck.

The caching option that is right for you depends on your comfort level and your checkbook balance. You may find that you can get by quite nicely with the caching capabilities built into DOS or Windows. If you have money to spare and are interested in getting the most performance out of your hard disk, you may look to the more expensive hardware options. Built-in caching hardware is also handy if you don't want to fool around with making sure that one program's caching capabilities don't step on another program's toes in the memory department.

Summary

In this chapter, you have learned the differences in conventional, upper, expanded, and extended memory. Conventional memory is the amount of memory that DOS can use to run a program, typically from 0 to 640K. Upper memory is the remaining memory beyond the 640K mark and up to the 1M limit imposed by DOS. Expanded memory is memory that does not contain corresponding physical addresses but borrows unused addresses from DOS's conventional limits. Extended memory is a linear extension of physically addressable memory beyond DOS's 1M limit.

You also have learned in this chapter about the differences between RAM disks, which are portions of RAM set aside to mimic a hard disk, and disk caches, which are portions of memory used to store the most recently and frequently used data from the disk. You have explored many of the software and hardware caching options on the market and have examined the built-in caching options available in DOS and Windows.

In the next chapter, "Exploring Hard Disk Fitness Programs," you find out about more ways to fine-tune your disk's performance.

9

CHAPTER

Exploring Hard Disk Fitness Programs

Ask any health specialist about the human body, and the usual recommendation is that a good diet, periodic medical checkups, and regular exercise can prolong active life. The same is true for hard disk drives, which can thrive on a balanced "diet" of organizing subdirectories, periodically backing up, and regular restructuring.

In Chapter 6, "Working with Directories on Your Hard Disk," you learn how to organize the directory structure to improve your disk's efficiency. In Chapter 8, "Using Memory To Speed Up Your Disk," you look at ways of using memory to speed up the performance of the hard disk. In this chapter, you focus on another way to provide some additional performance: tuning the physical layout of the hard drive in addition to planning and maintaining control of the subdirectory structure.

You can tune your hard disk when you first buy and install it, using whatever formatting options come with your disk. If you already have low-level formatted your hard disk, you may have noticed that the process usually enables you to change certain performance parameters such as the interleave and sector size. For many first-time hard disk owners, these numbers can be relatively meaningless. The tendency is to accept whatever the defaults are. In many cases, however, these defaults may not be the optimum. Or the optimum layout may change depending on the mix of applications.

In this chapter, you learn how to take control of such factors as fragmented files and inefficient interleaves. And you learn about a variety of commercial products that provide ways to tune your hard drive to achieve its optimum performance.

What Is Disk Optimization?

From a literal standpoint, optimization of any system is a method of improving performance by varying some of the controlling pieces. Take, for example, a traditional vintage automobile engine. A mechanic might vary the flow of fuel and air to the carburetor and adjust the timing for maximum power output (manual optimization). Many modern engines use fuel injection and can adjust the timing themselves by the use of a small on-board computer (automatic optimization).

Manual optimization of a hard disk may involve several things: using a stopwatch to see how long some programs take to run, adjusting some parameters such as BUFFERS and FILES in the CONFIG.SYS file, creating all your subdirectories before loading any files onto them, or reducing the number of directory tree levels.

Automatic optimization of the hard disk involves the use of a utility that varies several control parameters and performs some testing on the hard disk itself. This type of utility provides you with the test results along with a recommendation of which set of parameters to use. Most optimization utilities change the parameters for you and then walk you through the installation and formatting. These utilities normally provide a way to perform optimization with all data "in place." But a word of warning is warranted here: backing up your disk prior to performing any optimization on your hard disk is a good idea. (See Chapter 10, "Understanding the Importance of Backing Up.")

T I P   The more recently developed hard drives, such as IDE drives, do not allow some of the low-level modifications because the drives are specially preformatted at the factory. In most cases, you should not force a utility to low-level format any IDE drive because you may end up having to send it back to the factory for recalibration and formatting. All the other optimization techniques apply, however, because IDE drives suffer from many of the same problems that any other hard disks running DOS experience.

Successful optimization depends on the type of drive you use and the type of applications you need to run. Whatever your final decision about how to optimize your disk, optimization sometimes can appear to be a moving target as the needs of applications change. Ultimately, the level of optimization may depend on how much money you are willing to spend on utilities to help you optimize and how much time you are able to devote to working on performance improvement. Finally, the law of diminishing returns kicks in, and you cannot optimize the disk much further. At that point, you need to look into more drastic and expensive options, such as adding caching disk controllers or replacing the drive altogether.

Understanding Why Disks Need Optimizing

Many hard disk owners think that if they buy the biggest, fastest drive available, they will never need to mess around with tuning performance or space management. Usually within two years, the drive is full, and the owner is complaining about slow response time.

Ultimately, even today's fastest hard drive will need optimizing eventually, simply because as newer software and operating environments come along, they always seem to need more resources, especially disk space and speed. Take, for example, a computer necessity like DOS. Version 1.0 could fit on a 320K floppy disk and didn't even know what a hard drive was, but version 5.0 needs 2.8M of disk space to store everything. On an unoptimized 6 MHz IBM PC/AT, the DOS 5.0 full-screen editor can take 25 seconds to load.

If you're a typical PC user, you probably don't think too much about performance before loading up the hard disk with data and applications. Typically, performance doesn't become an issue until you fire up an application and it seems to take an incredible amount of time—more than 30 seconds—to run or load. A few prime application environments appear to be the most noticeable from a performance standpoint. These are typically Windows applications, CAD/CAM programs, large databases, and even some of the more demanding games packages.

Structuring your subdirectories as outlined in Chapter 6, "Working with Directories on Your Hard Disk," and using BUFFERS in the CONFIG.SYS file and adding caches or FASTOPEN as outlined in Chapter 8, "Using Memory To Speed Up Your Disk," all can help you improve performance. Ideally, you should set up your hard disk for optimal speed when you first install the drive. Then you can forestall many performance difficulties for some time to come. You also can run an optimization utility regularly, which may alleviate many of the performance difficulties.

Whatever method you choose, a certain amount of planning and analysis is required as well as a basic understanding of what is going on in the hard drive when you change these parameters.

Dealing with Fragmentation

As the name implies, *fragmentation* is the breaking up of large items into a series of smaller chunks in order to fit them into available space. If you were able to arrange those large items one after another, you might not have to break them up. Fragmentation of a disk is caused by the method that DOS uses to allocate disk space for files, which involves breaking up files to fit into available spaces. Disk defragmentation is the reconstitution of the broken-up pieces of data into single files and arranging them in order with no extra space in between.

Understanding How Disks Become Fragmented

Disks become fragmented because of DOS's incapability to manage hard disk space intelligently. Despite major improvements in DOS in other areas, the allocation of disk space hasn't changed much in the operating system's 10 or so years of life.

If you were simply to write all your files to the hard disk once and never delete or overwrite a file from that point on, you would never have fragmentation on the hard disk. Obviously, that scenario is an impossible one, but it does highlight the root causes of fragmentation: deleting, adding, and overwriting files.

Sometimes you might not be aware that files are being created and deleted all the time by the programs you run. Windows 3.0, for example, creates and destroys temporary swap files. Another program may save its environment in a temporary file to disk when shelling out to DOS; then upon exiting DOS and reentering that program, the environment is restored from the temporary file and deleted.

Although you do not need to understand exactly how DOS manages file space allocation, having a grasp of the type of operations involved is useful so that you can gauge how badly fragmented your hard disk is and how it may impact your applications. The best way to illustrate fragmentation is to outline a theoretical hard disk environment.

Figures 9.1, 9.2, and 9.3 present a simplified set of illustrations explaining how disks become fragmented. In Chapter 3, "Understanding How DOS Works with the Hard Disk," you learned about the file allocation table (the FAT) and how it relates to directory entries. In figure 9.1, a file called FILE1 is stored to an "empty" hard disk. The directory entry for FILE1 points to the first "available" cluster, which is cluster 1. DOS has calculated how many clusters are needed to store the file—in this case, five for FILE1. DOS then "chains" together the entries in the FAT. When DOS is asked to read this file again, it goes to the directory entry, which points to the starting FAT number (in this case 1). DOS reads cluster 1 in the FAT and notes the next entry in the chain, number 2 in this example, then 3, then 4, then 5, which is marked as the last in the chain (EOF). Then DOS simply reads the corresponding clusters (the contents of the file) associated with the FAT numbers.

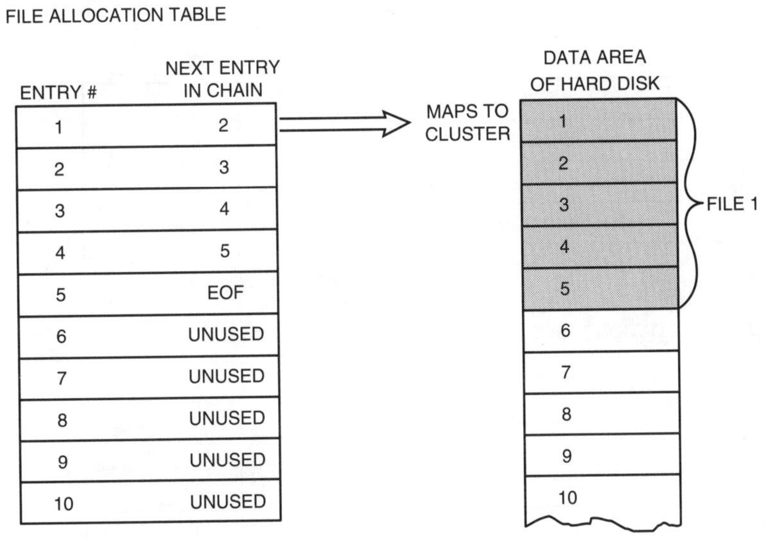

FILE ALLOCATION TABLE

ENTRY #	NEXT ENTRY IN CHAIN
1	2
2	3
3	4
4	5
5	EOF
6	UNUSED
7	UNUSED
8	UNUSED
9	UNUSED
10	UNUSED

MAPS TO CLUSTER

DATA AREA OF HARD DISK

| 1 |
| 2 |
| 3 | FILE 1
| 4 |
| 5 |
| 6 |
| 7 |
| 8 |
| 9 |
| 10 |

FIG. 9.1

FILE1 stored to disk.

Suppose that the next thing DOS is asked to do is store another file, FILE2. This one is much smaller and needs only two clusters to hold the data. This time DOS searches the FAT for the first available entry, which happens to be cluster 6. DOS grabs cluster 6 and saves the number of the next cluster in the chain, which happens to be 7 (also the last in the chain). After FILE2 has been stored, the disk arrangement looks like figure 9.2.

Finally, suppose that DOS is asked to rewrite FILE1. The only problem is that someone added information to FILE1, making it bigger, and two more clusters are needed to store it. DOS searches the hard disk for the next available FAT entry, which is cluster 8 in this example. DOS changes the "last cluster" designation of entry number 5 and instead indicates the next cluster in the chain (8), which points to the next entry (9), which also is marked as the last entry in the chain belonging to the now larger FILE1 (see fig. 9.3).

FILE ALLOCATION TABLE

ENTRY #	NEXT ENTRY IN CHAIN
1	2
2	3
3	4
4	5
5	EOF
6	7
7	EOF
8	UNUSED
9	UNUSED
10	UNUSED

DATA AREA OF HARD DISK

CLUSTER

1	
2	
3	FILE 1
4	
5	
6	FILE 2
7	
8	
9	
10	

FIG. 9.2

FILE2 stored to disk.

FILE ALLOCATION TABLE

ENTRY #	NEXT CLUSTER
1	2
2	3
3	4
4	5
5	8
6	7
7	EOF
8	9
9	EOF
10	UNUSED

DATA AREA OF HARD DISK

1	
2	
3	FILE 1
4	
5	
6	FILE 2
7	
8	FILE 1 CON'T
9	
10	

FIG. 9.3

The larger FILE1 becomes fragmented.

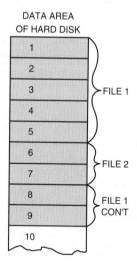

Although this example is a simplistic and not totally accurate (for all versions of DOS) depiction of what happens when disk space is allocated, it should give you an idea as to what fragmentation is all about. Consider also what would happen if FILE2 were deleted. You would have a "hole" in the middle of the FAT entries for FILE1. Now multiply this situation a thousandfold, and you get an inkling of how mixed up the disk becomes over time. With little bits of file scattered all over the disk, when your program requests access, the drive head jumps all over the place picking up the file's data. In fact, one way to tell that your drive is becoming fragmented is if it becomes louder (a lot of disk "chattering") when you haven't even added much data.

Looking at How Defragmentation Works

You can purchase utilities to help you defragment your disk. Later in the chapter, you learn about some specific programs you can use. They basically all work the same way, with only a few exceptions and special features.

The basic function of a defragmentation utility is to move file data and its corresponding FAT entries around to make all the files contiguous. Watching a defragmenting utility such as Symantec/Norton's Speed Disk in action is quite fascinating. Figure 9.4, for example, shows a gross simplification of the typical results of defragmentation.

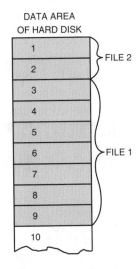

FILE ALLOCATION TABLE

ENTRY #	NEXT CLUSTER
1	2
2	EOF
3	4
4	5
5	6
6	7
7	8
8	9
9	EOF
10	UNUSED

DATA AREA
OF HARD DISK

1
2
3
4
5
6
7
8
9
10

FILE 2

FILE 1

FIG. 9.4

The results of defragmentation.

In this example, FILE1 is read into memory and then written to a temporary area (FAT entries in the 10+ region) on the disk (for safety reasons in case of power loss). The directory entry now points to this area, and its old FAT entries are deallocated. (FAT is used to keep track of added portions of disk by allocation; removing entries in the FAT "deallocates" the portion of the disk.) Then FILE2 is read into memory and written to the beginning of the disk—FAT entries 1 and 2. FILE1 hasn't been forgotten; it is read into memory from its temporary location and placed in the next available contiguous slot, in this case FAT entries 3 through 9. The directory record for FILE1 is changed from the temporary area to point to FAT entry number 3. Finally, the temporary area used to hold FILE1 is deallocated.

Although this example is limited in scope, the basic operation is similar for most of the defragmentation utilities, which include Norton's Speed Disk, Gazelle's Optune, and FastTrax. Some of these utilities optimize the location of subdirectories and may even enable you to specify selected files to be more optimized than others—perhaps because you use them more frequently.

Understanding Why Defragmentation Is Important

Aside from the obvious performance improvement, you enjoy some other beneficial side effects when you defragment your hard disk. If you maintain the disk in a relatively defragmented state, you may increase the life expectancy of the drive itself simply because of the reduced wear and tear. This benefit arises even despite the fact that the hard drive is subjected to quite a bit of heavy use during the defragmentation process itself. And from a "noise pollution" standpoint, a fragmented drive can sound significantly louder than one that's been recently defragmented.

Understanding How the Interleave Affects Performance

You learned about interleaves in Chapter 2, "Choosing a Hard Disk: Self-Defense for Buyers." Just to recap, the interleave is there to give your system time to process the data read from and written to the disk. Typically, XT- and AT-class (8088 and 80286) machines using older ST-506 technology require an interleave of 6:1 for an XT and 3:1 for an AT, which can be adjusted to 2:1. An interleave of 1:1 is required for most 386+ systems. Most newer IDE drives have a 1:1 interleave also, which in reality means no interleave at all. If you move a hard drive from a slower machine to a faster one or vice versa, the existing hard drive interleave setting is quite possibly not optimal. And the default interleave may not even be the best one when you bring the hard drive home, depending on your applications.

Look at an example that illustrates how different interleaves affect performance. Your hard disk spins rather fast at 3600 RPM, and the hard drive control circuitry has to read or write information on each sector as it whizzes by the head. The hard drive circuitry talks to the hard disk controller in the PC, and ultimately a program that is running on the PC gets access to the data, as shown in the diagram in figure 9.5.

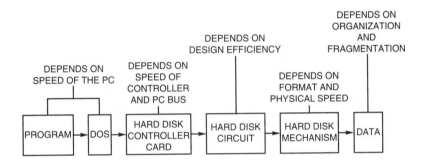

FIG. 9.5

Performance obstacles between your program and its data.

As you can see, many obstacles arise between your program and its data—any one of which can be a weak link. In this chapter, you are focusing on the latter end of the chain, in particular with the interleaving that affects the physical composition of the hard drive. The interleave setting also depends on the speed of the PC, which changes the rate at which the data can be moved to and from the controller and ultimately the hard drive itself.

Figure 9.6 represents two disks, one with an interleave of 1:1, the other with an interleave of 2:1. A piece of data is read by the hard drive from sector 1 as it spins by. This data usually is stored in a local buffer, which is cleared out and transferred to the PC and ultimately the program that needs the data. Assuming that this drive has some fast circuitry, it's all ready to read sector 2 just as it spins by and then on around the disk. This drive seems efficient with a 1:1 interleave.

But suppose that the PC is slow and cannot handle data as fast as the drive can send it. The PC tells the drive to "hang on a bit, I need to work on this data before I can read your buffer." Because the drive's buffer is full, it cannot read any more sectors for now. Then comes a signal from the PC, "OK, you can send me some more now." The hard disk was going to read sector 3, but while waiting for the slow PC, sector 3 whizzed by and sector 4 is now under the head. The hard drive needs to wait for the disk to spin an entire revolution until sector 3 can be read. This example illustrates a poor interleave factor. The drive was fast enough, but the environment in which it was being used wasn't.

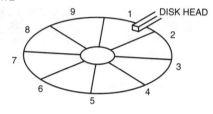

FIG. 9.6

Examining disk
interleaves.

Now consider this same scenario with a 2:1 interleave. The drive reads sector 1, ignores sector 6, and then reads sector 2. The PC tells the drive to wait while it processes the data. The drive doesn't care, because all that is under the head at the moment is sector 7, which isn't needed. Then the PC tells the drive to send some more, and guess what? Sector 3 is under the head. This scenario illustrates optimal interleaving.

Several commercial products are available to monitor the performance of the hard drive and estimate an optimal interleave.

Examining Some Disk-Fitness Utilities

Many commercial programs are available that help you improve your hard disk's performance. In the following paragraphs, you learn about a representative group of these utilities: Compress and DiskFix in PC Tools, Speed Disk and Calibrate in Norton Utilities, FastTrax, Optune, and SpinRite.

> With any optimization program, a good practice is to remove from memory any resident programs that can interfere with the optimization process. Try defragmenting a test floppy disk first if you need to keep any resident utilities or caching that might cause a conflict. Also, you should not run any of the utilities discussed in this chapter under Windows or within a multitasking environment.

T I P

Using PC Tools Compress

Compress corrects file fragmentation and moves all free disk space to the end of the disk to reduce the risk of further fragmentation as you add more files. Moving directories and selected files to the beginning of the disk enables faster access because the disk head does not have to move far to get there.

Compress gives you a great deal of control over the placement of files during optimization, enabling you to lock them in place or specially arrange files within directories. You select the organizational method for directories and files when you configure the program. The "standard" method places directories at the beginning of the disk in the order you specify. (If you don't specify any order, the directories are placed in the order in which they are listed in the DOS PATH.) A "file-placement" method places specified files immediately following the directories at the beginning of the disk, with COM and EXE files put in front. A "directories first" method moves the directories to the front of the disk and then puts all the files in each directory together. This option usually maximizes performance by putting applications and their respective data in close proximity.

Compress's user configuration enables you to select from various optimization techniques. These options are described in the following paragraphs.

The *Optimize Directories* option simply moves directories to the front of the disk, displacing any nondirectories. Because no defragmentation is performed, Optimize Directories is a fast procedure that can be of great performance benefit.

The *Optimize Free Space* option pushes all used data space to the front of the disk. The time required to complete the operation can vary dramatically, depending on the fragmentation and amount of the free space, but does not defragment files on the drive. This option can be useful if you expect to load some big files to your hard disk, because they will be loaded contiguously without fragmentation. You also might want to run this option after you have installed Microsoft Windows, because Windows can create some huge swap files.

The *Unfragment Files* option defragments all files but does not move the free space to the end of the drive. Any new large files thus tend to be fragmented immediately.

The *Full Optimization* option defragments the files and optimizes the free space. In addition, the files and directories are arranged to whatever options you set. This option is relatively slow and is best performed just before you go to lunch!

The *Full Optimization with Clear* option is the same as Full Optimization but also wipes any unused clusters that contain data, thus reducing the risk that erased files can be undeleted. This technique is a useful security measure if you have had any erased sensitive files on your drive.

Compress also offers a comprehensive map of the disk fragmentation, analyzes the disk for you, and recommends how the disk should be compressed and whether you need to run the PC Tools repair utility DiskFix. (Diskfix has an additional option to revitalize a disk, which is discussed in the next section.)

Analyzing the disk before defragmenting is a good idea. The resulting analysis helps you decide how to proceed with the optimization.

Compress works on all types of drives with the exception of Novell servers, networked drives, and OS/2 disks. As with most defragmentation utilities, removing any resident programs from memory is a good practice. Disk caching programs also are best removed or at least used with caution. These types of systems do not have standard DOS structure and cannot be optimized the same way.

Using the Revitalize Option in PC Tools DiskFix

DiskFix is aimed primarily at evaluating the state of a drive and repairing any errors or potential problems encountered during its operation. The repair functions of DiskFix are covered later in Chapter 12, "Raiders of the Lost Data." In this section, you learn about the Revitalize option, which checks the timing on a drive, determines the physical characteristics of the drive, and makes recommendations for optimizing low-level options such as the interleave.

First, DiskFix checks for defects or anomalies in the drive that can interfere with the revitalization process. Having done that, DiskFix then checks a series of disk timings. *Random-seek timing*, more commonly known as disk access time, moves the head all over the drive and times the response. *Full-stroke timing* is the time taken to move the head from the beginning to the end of the disk. *Track-to-track timing* is the time taken to step between tracks.

DiskFix next reports a series of technical statistics about the drive, including the spindle speed in RPM, sector angle, bits per track, data encoding type, hard disk BIOS, current interleave, track transfer revolutions, and maximum data rate.

After analyzing the current status of your drive, DiskFix can make a recommendation. By this point, DiskFix also knows whether the drive can be low-level formatted and the interleave modified if needed. DiskFix is aware of the low-level formatting restrictions on IDE and other newer technology drives that are already optimized at the factory for the best performance. If your drive can be optimized by changing the interleave, a graph showing the various options and their expected performance improvement is displayed. Assuming that your drive can be non-destructively low-level formatted, you then can select an interleave and enable DiskFix to proceed with the operation.

Using the Norton Utilities Speeddisk Command

The Norton Utilities Speeddisk command is Symantec's hard disk optimization utility, which defragments files and arranges the data on the disk in what the program considers to be the most efficient manner. As with PC Tools Compress, you have several optimization options for processing the disk, defragmenting files, consolidating free space, and putting directories at the beginning of the disk. You can select some or all of these options. Speeddisk automatically uses the PATH statement to determine the primary sort order for the directories.

The first process that Speeddisk performs is an analysis of the current status of the hard disk with a recommendation as to how to proceed. A map representing the used space on the disk is displayed to support this recommendation. Speeddisk even provides a comprehensive file fragmentation report on each individual file.

With Speeddisk, you can select the method of optimization (Full, Unfragment Files Only, Unfragment Free Space, Optimize Directories, and Sort Files) and the order of directories/files, indicate immovable files (such as copy-protected programs), and verify any data that is moved around.

Calibrate is another Norton utility that helps to improve hard disk performance by modifying the interleave if needed. Calibrate also refreshes the data on the hard disk by performing a low-level format.

Using the Norton Utilities Calibrate Command

The Norton Utilities Calibrate command can optimize the speed of your drive by adjusting the interleave factor with data in place. Calibrate improves the integrity of data on the drive by testing every byte on the hard disk and marks any clusters found to contain a suspect byte as bad. Any such marked clusters are skipped over by any program that writes out a file to disk.

Calibrate operates by performing a nondestructive low-level format of the hard drive. The procedure is relatively safe because if a power loss occurs, Calibrate resumes and restores the disk to its previous state. System integrity, seek testing, data encoding, and the interleave are all tested and reported on. Figure 9.7 illustrates Calibrate's interleave recommendation for a sample hard disk.

FIG. 9.7

Norton Calibrate's interleave report.

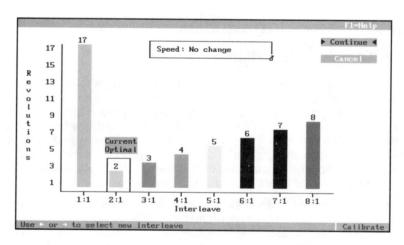

For this analyzed disk, Calibrate indicates that the optimum interleave is 2:1. At that interleave, the fewest number of revolutions (in this case 2) is required to select an entire track's worth of data. Like PC Tools DiskFix, Calibrate shows the 1:1 interleave as being very inefficient because 17 revolutions are needed to read the entire track.

 NOTE As was mentioned earlier in this chapter, most hard disk utility programs like Calibrate are unable to perform this type of modification to certain types of drives, such as IDE drives.

Using FastTrax

FastTrax comes in a package that contains two primary modules: MakeTrax and FastTrax. MakeTrax is a setup utility that you can run before running FastTrax. FastTrax is a utility that evaluates the structure and location of files on your hard disk. Having done that, the utility defragments and optionally moves files and directories and much more, depending on how you configure the program.

The first step of the analysis is a fragmentation map, as illustrated in figure 9.8.

```
FastTrax V4.03     (C) Copyright 1986-1991 Mark Elfield     All Rights Reserved

Drive C Fragmentation Map; each symbol represents 34,816 bytes (17 clusters)

h######bhhhhhh#ooo######oo##o####oo###ooo#############ooooo######hhoo##
##ho#########ooo##oo#########o##hoo###hhh#####oooo##oooo##!############
#o####################ooooooooo##########oooo#############o############!#
####oo#############oooooooooooooo####o##ooooo####o##ooo###ooo#########oo
ooooo#############ooooo#####!--------o------------!ooooooooooooooooooooo
o#####o####o###o###ooooo#-----------------------------------------------
---------------------------------------------------------------------------
--------b------------------------------------------------------------------
-----------------------------------------------------------------------b---
-------------------------------h---

o means OPTIMIZED,     # means CONSECUTIVE (spans one extra disk cylinder),
! means FRAGMENTED,   h means HELD,   - means FREE,  b means BAD CLUSTER

     There are 404 user names (387 files and 17 directories).
  99.2% are contiguous (70.5% are optimized, 28.7% are consecutive).
   0.8% are fragmented.  There are 32 deleted directory entries.

            Do you want to continue (Y/N)?  Y
```

FIG. 9.8

The fragmentation map produced by the FastTrax utility.

After FastTrax performs its initial analysis, you are given a choice of optimization types. The default is to optimize all files. Alternatively you can optimize only fragmented files or simply move the directories to the front of the disk. A clear option clears out data from deleted files and directories.

If you use the MakeTrax utility before using FastTrax, you also can build a list of customized optimization settings, which FastTrax uses to optimize the disk. You then can maintain your frequently used files on the fastest part of the disk and push any files you declare as "low" priority to the far end of the disk. A portion of the MakeTrax file placement selection is illustrated in figure 9.9.

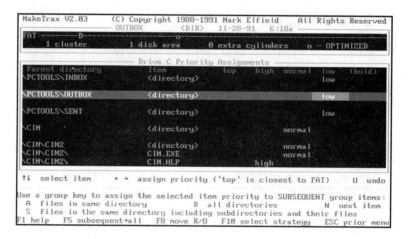

Unlike many disk optimizers, FastTrax is highly tunable and can even relocate the disk space so that the minimum number of cylinders are used. This technique reduces the number of track-to-track seeks needed when accessing a file.

After completing the optimization procedure, FastTrax provides a summary of whatever changes were made. Figure 9.10 shows an example of FastTrax's final analysis.

```
FastTrax V4.03    (C) Copyright 1986-1991 Mark Elfield    All Rights Reserved

Phase 1:  Removing 32 deleted directory entries on drive C.
          2,048 bytes reclaimed (1 cluster).  Your drive has:

          31,768,576 bytes total disk space
              75,776 bytes in 4 hidden files
              38,912 bytes in 17 directories
          13,125,632 bytes in 387 user files

Phase 2:  Determining the new organization...
          ...................

Phase 3:  Reorganizing drive C, Data Verify is ON, press SPACE to abort.

          13,066,240 total bytes to move (6,380 clusters)
                   0 remaining bytes to move; elapsed time is 8:18
          (average transfer rate is 1,574,245 bytes/minute)

Phase 4:  Completing all deferred disk writes...

          Do you want to see the new organization (Y/N)?  Y
```

FIG. 9.10

Viewing the FastTrax
summary.

Unlike most of the other utilities described in this chapter, FastTrax is
somewhat less polished. You get no fancy graphs or animated screens.
Yet FastTrax offers you more hands-on control over the optimization
process itself. You also can run FastTrax in a batch operation mode
using a series of optional parameters. Another advantage is its size.
FastTrax is one of the smaller sets of optimization utilities available,
fitting on a single 360K floppy disk.

Using Gazelle's Optune

Optune from Gazelle Systems is a fast set of optimization routines that
provide what appears to be rapidly becoming the basic standard set
of optimization facilities: directory/file DOS restructure, file defragmentation, and interleave optimization. One point to note is that the
Optune set of utilities is extremely small. At 137K for all files, Optune
easily fits on a 360K disk. This small size also helps Optune perform optimization tasks significantly faster than competing products.

Interleave optimization enables you to modify the low-level format of
your hard disk as outlined previously in this chapter. Figure 9.11 illustrates the results of an Optune analysis of the optimum interleave for
a drive. In this case, the suggested interleave is 2:1.

```
┌─ OPTune 1.3 ──────────────────── Tune-Disk ──────────────── by GAZELLE ─┐
│ ┌──────────────────────────────────────────────────────────────────┐ │
│ │ ┌──────────── HARD DISK DRIVE PARAMETERS ──────────────┐          │ │
│ │ │ DOS drive designation:                     [C]       │          │ │
│ │ │                                                      │          │ │
│ │ │             Interleave tests completed!              │          │ │
│ │ │         Press any key to return to the main menu     │          │ │
│ │ │                                                      │          │ │
│ │ │    Optimum interleave:                  →[2:1]←      │          │ │
│ │ │    Current interleave:                   [2:1]       │          │ │
│ │ └──────────────────────────────────────────────────────┘          │ │
│ └──────────────────────────────────────────────────────────────────┘ │
│ ┌──────────────────────────────┬──────────────────────────────────┐ │
│ │ INTERLEAVE    DELAY INDEX     │ INTERLEAVE      DELAY INDEX       │ │
│ │    1:1            349         │    9:1              176           │ │
│ │    2:1             41         │   10:1              195           │ │
│ │    3:1             60         │   11:1              215           │ │
│ │    4:1             79         │   12:1              233           │ │
│ │    5:1             99         │   13:1              253           │ │
│ │    6:1            118         │   14:1              273           │ │
│ │    7:1            137         │   15:1              291           │ │
│ │    8:1            156         │   16:1              311           │ │
│ └──────────────────────────────┴──────────────────────────────────┘ │
└──────────────────────────────────────────────────────────────────────┘
```

FIG. 9.11

Using's Optune to determine the optimum interleave.

Optune also offers its own version of DOS's CHKDSK command. Check-Disk offers the same functions in that it verifies the FAT structure and corrects cross-linked files and the like. Typically, Optune's Check-Disk works several times faster than the DOS CHKDSK command and works on DOS 2.0 and later versions.

Verify and/or Fix Disk, another option offered by Optune, provides a complete scan of the disk media and marks any suspect areas on the disk. If any data is found in the suspect area, Optune attempts to move the data and mark that area to be avoided by DOS.

Optune's claim is that most other optimization utilities spend much of their time (up to 40 percent) updating the FAT (file allocation table) and directory entries. This approach is considered a dangerous practice because the longer you spend digging in the FAT or other sensitive areas on the disk, the greater the risk that power loss or other catastrophic failure can cause physical data loss.

Overall, Optune is extremely fast and is ideal for those older machines that just don't have the horsepower to support a series of sophisticated data screens, statistics, and menu options. As mentioned previously, however, do not run Optune under Windows or within a multitasking environment. In addition, try to avoid using Optune on an active network or when running a software disk cache.

Using SpinRite II

SpinRite II Version 2.0 from Gibson Research is possibly the ultimate in hard disk testing and optimization. SpinRite II, which claims to be able to "test anything that spins," features an easy-to-use, menu-driven, comprehensive hard disk analysis and a support utility that covers a wide range of drive types at a low level, including ESDI, SCSI, IDE, and Plus/Quantum derivatives such as the Hardcard series.

SpinRite II is a utility that maximizes performance, prevents potential data-loss problems, and prolongs the life of hard disks. More specifically, the program reads and repairs most damaged, unreadable, or uncorrectable data before it can interfere with hard disk operation. SpinRite also checks the hard disk and controller compatibility, determines the best sector interleave (which improves the exchange of data in and out of the hard disk), and examines the surface of the drive itself (the surface on which the data is stored). Like PC Tools and Norton Utilities, SpinRite II also renews and restores the low-level format of the hard disk. The program performs these functions without damaging any of the data already stored on the drive.

Because it does not destroy any data, SpinRite II is intended to give your hard drive a type of tune-up needed to keep it running at peak performance and to avoid any potential future problems. Gibson Research recommends that you always make a backup copy of your hard disk before you use any hard disk utility for the first time. (The old adage of "It's always better to be safe than sorry" comes up frequently when using any of these hard disk fitness utilities.)

Before running SpinRite II or any other hard disk optimization utility, you need to understand that you must not use the program from within any multitasking program, such as Microsoft Windows, Desqview, or Taskview. Because SpinRite II may relocate data to a more efficient place on the hard disk, the program must have complete use of DOS.

Running a DOS CHKDSK command on the hard disk before using Spin-Rite II's low-level format feature is a good idea. You then are alerted to any serious drive problems that may already exist. You should not run SpinRite II if CHKDSK does not verify the health of the drive, normally indicated by a warning about lost chains and clusters. Another consideration is the TSR (terminate and stay resident) program, which is loaded into memory when the system boots up. Run SpinRite II only on a machine free of any TSR programs. (You can avoid them by simply booting the system from a separate floppy disk rather than from the hard drive. Simple and complete directions for making such a disk with the necessary CONFIG.SYS and AUTOEXEC.BAT files are included in the SpinRite II manual.)

Figure 9.12 shows the SpinRite II main menu and its six primary operations. Table 9.1 describes these menu options.

```
+++++++++++++++++++++++++++++++++++++++++

+     Select Desired Operation     +

+++++++++++++++++++++++++++++++++++++++++

+  1. Quick Surface Scan         +

+  2. Begin SpinRite Analysis    +

+  3. Alter SpinRite's Operation +

+  4. Print Full Operation Summary +

+  5. Display SpinRite Information +

+  6. Terminate SpinRite Now      +

+++++++++++++++++++++++++++++++++++++++++



++++++++++++++++++++++++++++++++ Info ++++++++++++++++++++++++++++++++++++

+  From time to time, it's a good idea to do a quick scan of the hard disk  +

+  to detect evolving correctable errors before they become uncorrectable!  +

++++++++++++++++++++++++++++++++++++++++++++++++++++++++++++++++++++++++++++



Select by number or use 218   and Enter +                    Press ESC to exit
```

FIG. 9.12

The SpinRite II main
menu.

Table 9.1 Using SpinRite's Menu Options

Option	Function
Quick Surface Scan	Performs a rapid, read-only scan of the entire disk surface. Detects correctable and uncorrectable read data errors, areas with format problems, and sectors and tracks currently marked as bad.
Begin SpinRite Analysis	Performs system diagnostics, measures drive performance, checks drive/controller compatibility, optimizes the sector interleave to improve data exchange, and nondestructively low-level formats and eliminates any surface defects on the drive.

Option	Function
Alter SpinRite's Operation	Enables you to customize the program's operation in different ways.
Print Full Operation Summary	Generates a printed report of the findings of SpinRite II's latest operation.
Display SpinRite Information	Displays a product summary and support information.
Terminate SpinRite Now	Exits the program.

You can terminate SpinRite II at any time, even while in mid-operation, with little fear of losing data integrity. You can halt operation in order to run another program or turn the system off altogether, allowing for those nasty electrical power blackout/brownouts. When you restart SpinRite II, it prompts you with a menu that resumes the operation from where it was interrupted.

NOTE Choosing Quick Surface Scan or Begin SpinRite Analysis may bring up a menu that asks you to specify on which partition of the hard drive to perform the function. Partitions are simply the different divisions of the hard drive, which you may set up as the C drive, D drive, and so on. For more information about partitions, see Chapter 3, "Understanding How DOS Works with the Hard Disk."

SpinRite II, during any operation, displays a Time Monitor time-of-day clock that continually estimates the current operation's time of completion. Some operations, such as a quick surface scan, take only a few minutes; operations such as low-level formats can take several hours to complete. You also can use a screen blanker. If you press B, SpinRite II replaces the normal screen with a floating box stating that the computer is not idle and is performing hard disk analysis. This screen also displays the percentage of the operation completed.

As SpinRite II performs its low-level format, the program also performs *pattern testing.* In this process, SpinRite II scrubs the entire disk surface with several gigabytes of worst-case data patterns. (You determine the depth of this scrubbing and can choose from Minimal Pattern Testing Depth, Average Pattern Testing Depth, and Extremely Thorough Pattern Testing Depth.) You can choose to bypass the entire pattern test, which greatly increases the speed of the low-level format. You should bypass only after the disk has been scrubbed at least once with the deepest degree of pattern testing.

When performing a quick surface scan or a low-level format, SpinRite II creates a detailed log of its findings. You can view this log as it is being created by pressing the space bar. Each press of the space bar rotates you through three different screens, and pressing the arrow keys enables you to scroll through the contents of each screen.

Gibson Research advises that you never forget to park the hard drive's heads before turning off the computer. Especially with older types of hard drives, powering up a system that hasn't been parked can damage a hard drive's data. Included on the SpinRite II disk is a program called PARK.COM, which quickly and correctly parks the heads of a hard drive. After you park the heads, the system is not locked up. By pressing any key on the keyboard, you can recall the DOS prompt and make the system usable again. Many of the hard drives sold today are self-parking. If you know that you have a self-parking drive, PARK.COM is not necessary, but unlike some parking utilities, it does not damage your disk if you use it inadvertently.

Because SpinRite II is completely menu driven, it is not complicated to use. And the manual that accompanies the program covers all aspects of operation in a concise, clear manner. With these easy instructions, you can have the program up and running with little effort.

Summary

In this chapter, you have looked at what optimization is all about. You have examined the pitfalls and benefits and looked at a large number of the available utilities that support performance improvement, including Norton, PC Tools, Spinrite II, Optune, and FastTrax, and some good old DOS-supported options.

One underlying theme that needs to be reiterated here is the importance of backing up your hard disk prior to attempting to perform these types of optimization on your drives. Another critical warning is to remember to remove any caching software and as many TSR programs as you can prior to running any optimization procedure.

In this next chapter, you begin Part IV, which focuses on helping you keep your hard disk secure. Chapter 10 introduces you to the importance of backing up your disk.

Keeping Your Hard Disk Secure

10 Understanding the
    Importance of Backing Up

11 Preventing Trouble

12 Raiders of the Lost Data

13 Keeping Your Data
    Confidential

14 Immunizing Your PC against
    Viruses

15 Understanding Data
    Compression

Understanding the Importance of Backing Up

Notice that this chapter is titled "Understanding the Importance of Backing Up" rather than something like "How To Make Backups of Your Files." The choice of title is intended to let you know that making regular backups of your data is the most critical element of hard disk management. Having a hard drive with the ideal interleave or the fastest transfer rate on the block is not essential, but protecting your data is. You can always replace a hard drive or a software program; you cannot always replace the hundreds of hours of work you poured into a project.

The more comfortable you get with something, such as working on your computer, the more likely you are to become complacent. Learning how to use computers is much like learning to drive a car. When you take driver's ed, you're conscientious. You signal every turn 100 yards in advance and keep your hands positioned at ten o'clock and two o'clock on the wheel. As you grow in confidence, you learn that even if you hold your steering wheel with one hand, the car doesn't veer instantly into the nearest telephone pole.

Computers are similar. You're afraid to make a false move in the beginning because you're terrified that you will blow up the machine. As you gain confidence, you realize that your computer isn't going to explode if you take a shot at redesigning the C> prompt. You may go so far as daring to install new software from the original floppy disks instead of creating working copies. You may even take or leave some of the advice that's in this book.

But whatever you do and wherever you decide to take shortcuts, don't make backing up your precious data one of them. The importance of backing up your data cannot be overemphasized. The more important a file is to you, the more likely it will be the one file on the sector of the hard disk that crashes. And if all the data for a critical project resides only on the hard disk, the hard disk will pick the night before deadline to go belly up.

If you think this gloomy warning sounds like Mom telling you to eat your vegetables, heed a real-life example before you disregard the message. In the time taken to write this book, the two coauthors lost a battery, a hard drive, and a floppy drive. You have to expect these things to happen. But here's the worst part: After a group of files were copied to the recently resurrected floppy drive, the same files were destroyed (not deleted, destroyed—you learn about that in Chapter 13, "Keeping Your Data Confidential") from the hard drive. After all, four sets of copies on floppies had been made. Unfortunately, all the files on all four copies were so trashed that the disks couldn't even be reformatted. But fortunately, all the hard drive's information also had been backed up to the computer's internal tape drive, which hadn't yet been erased.

If you think this series of incidents is a fluke, consider a former colleague who had the hard disk on her new computer crash a couple of days after she brought it home—while she was working on a project with a deadline that hovered somewhere between imminent and yesterday.

These dire tales are not intended to frighten you away from computing—99 times out of 100, everything works just fine. But no one can afford that hundredth time. After all, you use your computer to do productive work, not play Solitaire in Windows (well, at least most of the time).

T I P   Here's another reason to back up your data. In the following chapters, you learn about ways to recover your data when your disk crashes or is otherwise damaged. But these methods all depend to some degree on how well you backed up your disk. The more recently you have backed up either your data or information about the disk itself, the better chance you have at recovery success.

Because backing up is such a crucial element of successful computing, you have quite a few options. In this chapter, you start by exploring some of the alternatives DOS gives you, ranging from commands that work well with small amounts of data to commands that are designed to back up entire drives.

Some good commercial backup programs are on the market as well. These products can schedule backups automatically so that you don't have to worry about it. You look at FastBack Plus from Fifth Generation, Back-It 4 from Gazelle Systems, Norton Backup in the Norton Utilities, and Central Point Backup in PC Tools. Although other fine products are available, these products are ones you're most likely to encounter; they also have good reputations.

Next you look at some of your hardware choices. You may be able to get by just fine working with floppies (if you make sure that the disks work!) for small amounts of data. If you have too much information to store comfortably on floppies, however, or you want the next line of defense, you will want to consider tape drives.

T I P

You don't necessarily have to back up program files such as your word processing program or your desktop publishing program. Their contents remain stable, and if something happens, you have the original program floppy disks. Most vendors recommend, however, that you make "working copies" of the programs and use those copies for installation. That way, if something happens to damage the floppy, the original disks are still safe.

What you *must* back up are the reports and layouts you create, because they are subject to constant change. Carrying all the changes in your head isn't possible unless you have a photographic memory.

If you have configured your programs a certain way, however, and you don't want to have to re-create all your settings, backing up your programs, too, is well worth your while.

Deciding Where To Keep Your Backups

No matter what backup method you choose, don't back files up to a different directory on the hard disk or to a different partition on the disk (a partition, or logical drive, is a portion of the disk that acts like a separate disk). Although that approach may work if you end up with just a damaged sector, if the entire disk fails, you're out of luck. Always back up to floppy disks, tape drives, or a portable hard disk, not a partition on the same hard disk.

Some people recommend keeping your backup data offsite. You have to make that choice, but either way you don't want the data in or near the computer. The computer may be damaged by a natural event such as a fire or may be stolen. If you keep your backup information on floppies that are located near the computer, they may be stolen or damaged as well. If taking these kinds of precautions seems a little excessive, ask yourself if having a life insurance policy seems excessive. You hope you never have to use it, but if you need it, you will be glad it's there.

Deciding How Often You Should Back Up

The frequency of your backups depends on how often your data changes. Most people who work with computers should perform a weekly backup at the least. If you spend a great deal of time creating or modifying data, a daily backup is better. Those of you who work on LANs (local-area networks, systems of connected PCs) are lucky; the network administrator worries about backups for you. But those of you working on stand-alone machines have to be your own data security administrators.

People who are responsible for networks typically perform some kind of incremental or differential backup every day, which means that they back up only files that have changed since the last backup, and perform a full backup once a week. Doing the same with your own data isn't a bad idea.

Think about the type of work you do and how often it changes; then ask yourself how much trouble re-creating a day's or week's worth of work would be. If the thought of re-creating a day's worth of work makes you uncomfortable, you need to back up your data every day. (If you're working on something that's changing rapidly in a short period of time, such as a long report or a big database, you may even want to copy your work to a floppy hourly.)

Backing Up with DOS

DOS itself contains some commands that you may find useful for backing up your data. In the following paragraphs you briefly review the COPY command, which can be useful for backing up small amounts of data, and also explore the XCOPY, BACKUP, and RESTORE commands, which were designed specifically for backing up and restoring larger amounts of data.

The approach in this chapter is a little different from that of earlier chapters, where more of the emphasis was on using the DOS Shell. XCOPY, BACKUP, and RESTORE don't have equivalent commands in the DOS Shell, so the focus here is on the DOS command line. Although you can create directories and copy files by using the Shell, it doesn't have a command at present that combines directory and file management the way XCOPY does.

Examining COPY and Its Shortcomings

If you have to worry only about hourly or daily changes in one file, or you have a few files at most to back up, you might be able to get by just fine with the COPY command. But don't count on it for large amounts of data. It's too clunky.

Suppose that you have a directory called FREELANCE in your hard drive's root directory. FREELANCE has two subdirectories, EXPENSES and CONTACTS. You want to copy everything in FREELANCE and each of its subdirectories to a floppy disk. But you also want to set up the same directory structure on the floppy.

COPY gives you one measly shortcut for getting the data from drive C to drive A: you can copy all the files within a directory by using the *.* wild-card file specification. That's all. To set up a directory structure, you have to do the directory shuffle. First, you have to create the EXPENSES and CONTACTS directories for drive A. Then you have to work with the source directories one at a time.

If you're in the FREELANCE directory, for example, you have to type **cd expenses** to make the EXPENSES directory the current directory and then type **copy *.* a:\expenses**. Or you can remain in the FREELANCE directory and type the following:

COPY C:\FREELANCE\EXPENSES *.* A:\EXPENSES

(Remember, you have to type that whole string because if the directory you're copying from isn't your current directory, you have to include its full path.)

Now you get to repeat the entire process with the CONTACTS directory.

Working with XCOPY

Wouldn't it be nice if you could just copy everything, directory structure and all, in one fell swoop? Well, you can. You can use XCOPY, which was introduced with Version 3.2 of DOS.

To handle the copy operation described in the preceding section, for example, you can use the following XCOPY command:

XCOPY \FREELANCE A:\FREELANCE /S

This command enables you to copy the entire contents of a directory, including its two subdirectories, to a corresponding directory structure on a different disk. DOS asks you the following question:

```
Does FREELANCE specify a file name or directory name on
the target (F=File, D=Directory)?
```

Because you want to re-create the exact directory structure on drive A, you press D, which lets DOS know that it should copy the directory structure to the target disk (A). The /S switch tells DOS to copy all the files from the source directory and all its subdirectories (everything contained within FREELANCE, EXPENSES, and CONTACTS on drive C).

And XCOPY has even more tricks up its sleeve. Suppose that the FREELANCE directory had some empty subdirectories in it. You can copy these subdirectories as well, by using the /E switch. If the FREELANCE directory also contained empty subdirectories, for example, the command should appear as follows:

XCOPY \FREELANCE A:\FREELANCE /S /E

What if you want to pick and choose the files you copy? With COPY, the process is something of an all-or-nothing proposition. You can copy single files, or you can copy them wholesale. The * and ? wild cards narrow things down a little, but they let you work only with groups of files that have some aspect of their names in common. Because COPY pays attention only to the file's name and extension, that's all the fine-tuning the command can do.

XCOPY has you covered there, as well. You can add the /P switch, which stands for Prompt. DOS then pauses with each file and asks whether you want that file copied.

XCOPY has still another advantage over COPY. Suppose that you want to copy every file from the EXPENSES subdirectory to the floppy disk. You're not worried about having a destination subdirectory for this example; you just want the data to go on the floppy. That's a job COPY can handle; you simply type **copy *.* a:** from within the EXPENSES subdirectory. But here's the catch: what does COPY do if the floppy disk

doesn't have enough room for all the files? Nothing. You get the message
`Insufficient Disk Space, # files copied.` You can insert a new
floppy disk, but you don't know which files to start copying unless you
look at the contents of the floppy disk you just filled. Then you probably
have to copy the rest of them manually (or you can highlight them in the
Shell and copy them as a group).

XCOPY has a better way. You can use it with the /M switch, which resets
the file's archive attribute bit as the file is copied. (The archive attribute
bit is the one that indicates whether the file has been changed or modified.) If the target disk fills up, all you have to do is pop in a new disk,
use XCOPY with the /M switch again, and press Enter. XCOPY automatically picks up where it left off, starting with the files that haven't had
their archive attribute reset yet.

 You need to be aware of one other detail. Before you can
have XCOPY reset the archive attribute, you need to let
XCOPY know which files have their archive attribute set. To
set archive attributes for files in the current directory and all
its subdirectories, type the following at the DOS prompt:

ATTRIB +A *.* /S

If you want to copy everything in the root directory, including all
subdirectories and even empty subdirectories, and let XCOPY know
where to start copying again if the target disk fills up, type this command:

XCOPY \ A:/S/E/M

Table 10.1 gives you a complete list of the switches you can use with
XCOPY, with a brief explanation of each.

Table 10.1 Using XCOPY Switches

Switch	Function
/?	Displays on-screen help
/A	Copies only files that have their archive bits set
/D:MM-DD-YY	Copies only the files that have been created or changed after the specified date
/E	Copies empty subdirectories (must be used with the /S switch)
/M	Copies files that have their attribute bits set but clears the attribute as it copies each file

continues

Table 10.1 Continued	
Switch	**Function**
/P	Prompts for confirmation before copying each file
/S	Copies subdirectories and creates a tree on the destination disk if necessary
/V	Verifies that each copy is performed correctly
/W	Tells XCOPY to wait for a signal from you (Press any key) before copying any files

In summary, XCOPY is a good way to back up some or all of your hard disk if you don't own one of the commercial backup utility programs. XCOPY is better than COPY because it can handle entire directory structures and also can be configured to copy only those files that have changed.

XCOPY also compares favorably with BACKUP and RESTORE, which are discussed in the next section, because XCOPY creates ready-to-use file and directory structures.

Many people who bring work home use XCOPY to keep data synchronized between the computer they use at work and the one they use at home.

T I P   Beginning with DOS 5.0, XCOPY no longer copies hidden or system files. If you want to copy hidden or system files, you need to use the ATTRIB command to change their attributes. The ATTRIB command is covered in more depth in Appendix A.

Working with BACKUP and RESTORE

Just as XCOPY can handle more data than COPY, BACKUP and RESTORE can handle more than XCOPY. XCOPY, for all its virtues, isn't designed to handle the contents of an entire hard disk. XCOPY, for example, cannot split monster files between destination disks. If you need to back up graphics files or other files that are too large to fit on one floppy, or you want to back up the entire contents of your 40M hard disk and don't have a commercial backup program, you need to call on the special services of BACKUP and RESTORE.

DOS 5.0 RESTORE can work with all old versions of DOS, but be careful when mixing old versions of BACKUP and RESTORE. The BACKUP and RESTORE commands are designed to work in tandem. Unlike XCOPY, BACKUP uses a special file format that compresses the data it backs up so that the data takes less space. RESTORE decompresses the data when restoring the file, which means that if you use BACKUP to create a backup file, you have to use RESTORE to bring that file back to a usable condition.

You need to be sure that you have plenty of blank floppy disks on hand before you back up the contents of your hard drive. You can calculate how many disks you need by running CHKDSK. Look at the number of bytes taken up by user files (see table 10.2). Suppose, for example, that the number is 18,493,440 bytes (roughly 19 megabytes).

Table 10.2 Number of Floppy Disks Needed for a Backup

Bytes To Back Up	Diskette Capacity			
	360K	720K	1.2M	1.44M
10M	29	15	9	8
20M	59	29	18	15
30M	83	44	27	22
40M	116	58	35	29
70M	200	100	60	50

Now you can divide that number by the capacity of the floppy disks you are using. To determine the capacity of the disks expressed in bytes, run a CHKDSK on the floppy disk. A 3 1/2-inch, 1.44M disk has 1,457,664 bytes of total disk space. When you divide 18,493,440 by 1,457,664, you get 12.687039, which tells you that you need 13 1.44M disks to back up this particular hard disk.

The general syntax (format) for the BACKUP command is

    BACKUP *srcedrive:path\filename.ext destdrive: /switches*

If the floppy disks aren't formatted yet, and you are using a version of DOS later than 3.2, you can add the /F switch to the BACKUP command. This switch tells BACKUP to format disks during the backup operation. Be sure to add the switch in advance, however, because once the backup operation has started, you cannot interrupt it to format disks.

T I P If for your backup disks you decide to use floppy disks that already have data on them, make sure that it's data you can live without, because BACKUP erases the existing data while creating the backup files.

Suppose that you want to back up everything on your hard disk to drive A. Type this command:

BACKUP C:\ A:/S

If you guessed that the /S switch backs up the contents of subdirectories as well as the root directory, you're right. It's just like the /S switch used by XCOPY. You don't have to use archive switches as you do with XCOPY, because BACKUP automatically resets each file's archive bit as it goes.

As your disks fill up, BACKUP prompts you to insert new ones and continues where it left off. The command can split large files between disks. Every time you insert a disk during the backup process, BACKUP tells you that it's backing up to *diskette number such-and-such*. Watch for that message; it makes labeling your disks easier. And having the disks labeled with the correct numbers is essential for the RESTORE process.

The general syntax for RESTORE looks like this:

RESTORE *srcedrive: destdrive:path\filename.ext /switches*

To restore all the files you backed up from the hard disk, type this command:

RESTORE A: C:*.*/S

This command copies files from the backup disks in drive A back to the hard drive and re-creates the original subdirectories. DOS prompts you to insert your backup disks by number.

T I P You have to make sure that you're working from compatible versions of DOS when you use BACKUP and RESTORE. You cannot use an old version of the RESTORE command (Version 3.2 and earlier) to restore files that were backed up using Version 3.3 or later. If you upgrade to a new version of DOS, backing up your hard drive with the new version of BACKUP is a good idea. You also should test to make sure that you can restore what you backed up.

BACKUP and RESTORE have several switches that enable you to customize the commands. Table 10.3 lists the switches for BACKUP, and table 10.4 lists the switches for RESTORE.

Table 10.3 Using BACKUP Switches

Switch	Function
/A	Adds new files to a backup disk without erasing existing files.
/S	Keeps the subdirectory structure intact.
/M	Backs up files that have changed since the last backup.
/D	Backs up files by date. Format is /D:*mm-dd-yy* or /D:*mm/dd/yy*.
/T	Adds a time specification to the date switch. Format is /T:*hh:mm:ss*.
/F	Formats the backup disk before backing up data. New with DOS 4.0.
/L	Creates a log (inventory) of the files copied to the backup disk. New with DOS 3.3.

Table 10.4 Using RESTORE Switches

Switch	Function
/S	Restores files to original subdirectory structure.
/P	Prompts you before restoring a file that has changed since the last backup.
/B	Restores all files that were changed on or before a specified date. Format is /B:*mm-dd-yy* or /B:*mm/dd/yy*.
/A	Restores all files that were changed on or after a specified date. Format is /A:*mm-dd-yy* or /A:*mm/dd/yy*.
/M	Compares backup files to those on the hard disk and restores only the files that have been changed or erased since the last backup.
/N	Restores files that aren't on the hard drive.
/E	Restores files that were changed before a specified time in the following format: /E:*hh:mm:ss*.
/L	Restores files that were changed after a specified time in the following format: /L:*hh:mm:ss*.

Although BACKUP and RESTORE are your DOS methods of choice for an entire hard disk's worth of information, you also can use them to work with specific directories, subdirectories, or files.

BACKUP and RESTORE are no doubt handy, but if you decide that you want more speed and power in your backups, or you want to have automatic backups without having to write batch files, check into commercial products, such as the ones covered in the next section.

Using Commercial Backup Programs

Because they typically bypass normal read/write operations and use the DMA (Direct Memory Access) channel instead, commercial products are faster than DOS at performing backups. These programs also offer the advantages of working with user-friendly pull-down menus and on-line help.

More importantly, these products were designed specifically for backing up your precious data and include more sophisticated features for managing your backups. They typically create report files, for example, that contain information related to the backup. The programs typically enable you to fine-tune the data compression method they use. They also take the work out of scheduling automatic timed backups, where in DOS you need to be skilled enough to create your own batch files.

This section doesn't go into a comprehensive overview of each product. Instead, the following paragraphs try to give you a feel for what it's like to use each of these products to perform a basic backup.

 NOTE   One note of caution is warranted here. These products, like the DOS BACKUP and RESTORE commands, should not be mixed and matched among different versions. Gazelle warns you, for example, that Back-It 4 cannot restore data that was backed up by an earlier version of Back-It.

Using FastBack Plus

To install FastBack Plus, offered by Fifth Generation Systems, you insert the working copy you have made of the program disk and type **install** at the prompt. (Remember first to make the drive from which you're installing the program the current drive.) If you're using a monochrome monitor, you type **install -m** at the prompt.

The rest of the installation is automatic; the program asks whether you want it to change your CONFIG.SYS and AUTOEXEC.BAT files and whether you want to set up automatic timed backups, using the FastBack Plus Scheduler. The program also asks whether you will be using it with Microsoft Windows.

As part of the installation procedure, FastBack Plus performs a check of your PC's DMA structure. You need a blank floppy disk when you install FastBack Plus because it uses that disk as part of its hardware testing procedure and also performs a test backup and verification of the directory it creates (\FASTBACK is the default). The floppy disk must be of the highest capacity the drive can handle; in other words, if you have a 1.44M capacity drive, you need to use a 1.44M disk, not a 720K disk.

After you have installed FastBack Plus, you change to the FASTBACK directory and type **fb** to start the program. The FastBack Express menu appears, as shown in figure 10.1.

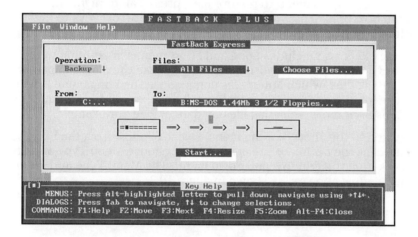

FIG. 10.1

The FastBack Express menu.

The Express menu is designed to let beginners start making backups easily and quickly. To back up your entire hard disk, simply select Start, because All Files is the default setting.

As FastBack Plus performs the backup, a Backup Progress window appears (see fig. 10.2). This window displays information on the status of the backup operation, including the elapsed time, the number of files and bytes being backed up, and the percentage of the backup that is complete.

From the Express menu, you also can choose to perform incremental backups and selective backups. An *incremental backup* backs up only the information that has changed since the last backup. One popular backup method is to perform an incremental backup daily, with a full backup (a backup of all files regardless of whether they have changed) once a week. A *selective backup* backs up only files you choose.

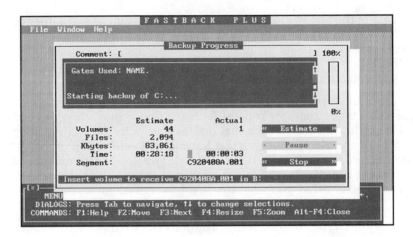

FIG. 10.2

The Backup Progress window.

To use the Express menu to restore files, press Tab to highlight the Operation box, press Enter to open the list, use the arrow keys to highlight Restore, and press Enter.

FastBack Plus also includes Long and Short menus in addition to the Express menu. With the Short menu, you can use the macro capabilities of FastBack Plus, which automates commands. The Long menu is what you use for more advanced operations. It enables you to customize your backups even more, selecting files by date or size, for example.

To switch to the Short or Long menu, select Window from the Express menu (click the option or press Alt-W) and choose Menu Type and Preferences from the Window pull-down menu. The Menu Type and Preferences window appears, as shown in figure 10.3.

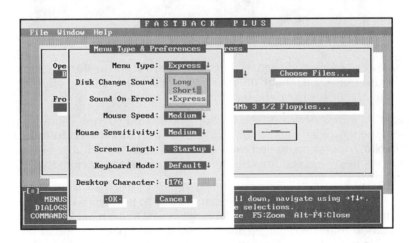

FIG. 10.3

The Menu Type and Preferences window in FastBack Plus.

Using Back-It 4

Like FastBack Plus, Back-It 4 from Gazelle Systems supports a mouse. Back-It 4 also supports some tape drives, which are discussed later in this chapter in the section on "Making Tape Backups."

Installation, as for most of these products, is nearly automatic; you just type **bksetup** at the A> or B> prompt and then press Enter. The program prompts you for the letter of the drive on which you want to install the program and then automatically creates a subdirectory for you (the default subdirectory name is BACKIT4).

As with FastBack Plus, if you think that you want to use automatically scheduled backups, the easiest way is to let the program add a scheduling command to your AUTOEXEC.BAT file during the installation process. Back-It 4's scheduling command is called BKSCHED.

Type **bk4** at the DOS prompt to open Back-It 4's main menu, which is shown in figure 10.4. When you select Backup from this menu, a Backup menu appears. You have two choices for backing up: Backup Manager, which is used to set up and run frequently repeated backups, and Direct Backup, which is used for onetime custom backups or to define and perform a full backup of your hard disk. Backup Manager is shown in figure 10.5

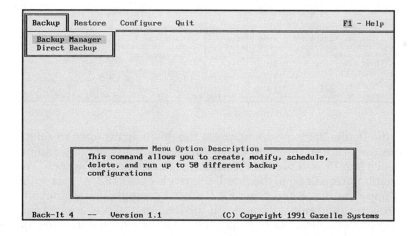

FIG. 10.4

The Back-It 4 main menu.

If you want to perform a full backup of your hard disk to floppy disks, for example, you type **bk4** at the DOS prompt, select Backup from the main menu, and then select Direct Backup, which brings up the Define Backup screen shown in figure 10.6.

```
Backup   Edit   Schedule   Add   Delete                  F1 - Help

    Name                Description              Last Full    Last Mod

FULL  C:          Full backup of C:             ---------    ---------
MODIFIED C:       Modified backup of C:         ---------    ---------
                                                ---------    ---------
                                                ---------    ---------
                                                ---------    ---------
                                                ---------    ---------
                                                ---------    ---------
                                                ---------    ---------
                                                ---------    ---------
                                                ---------    ---------
                                                      Schedule

                                                Start backup at:   N/A

                                                   Timeout (min):      0

                                                Su Mo Tu We Th Fr Sa
                                                      M  M  M
   Back-It 4                  Backup Manager              by Gazelle
```

FIG. 10.5

The Backup Manager.

```
   F1 - Help      F2 - Backup      F5 - Restore defaults    F9 - Estimate

                                    Name

 Name: FULL  C:              Description: Full backup of C:

                                   Source

 Backup From:

                                 Destination

 Backup To: FLOPPIES - A:(1.2→1.2)

        File Selections                        Parameters

 Modified only?:        no            Verification:       Normal
 Include filespecs:     (see window)  Compression:        Super
 Exclude filespecs:     (see window)  Error correction:   Normal
 Start date range:      Jan  1, 1980  Archive flag:       Reset
 Last date range:       Dec 31, 2099  Overwrite:          no
                                      Force Estimate:     YES

   Back-It 4                  Define Backup               by Gazelle
```

FIG. 10.6

The Define Backup
screen.

From the Define Backup screen, press the down arrow once to select Source, press Enter, highlight C: if it isn't already highlighted, and press the space bar. Press Enter to return to the Define Backup screen. The Destination box will be highlighted. If it reads FLOPPIES A:, place the first floppy in drive A and press F2. Back-It 4 prompts you when you need to insert additional floppies. (If the Destination box doesn't show the correct configuration, highlight the FLOPPIES: option to bring up the Destination for the Backup window, use the arrow keys and space bar to select and edit the destination, and press Enter to return to the Define Backup screen.)

Back-It 4's Backup Manager enables you to set up frequently repeated backups once and save and schedule them for later use. These pre-defined backups are called *presets*. You can add, delete, or edit up to 50 preset backups. After you have a preset defined, you can perform the backup by simply typing **bk4** followed by the preset's name at the prompt.

Back-It 4 comes with two presets included. FULL backs up all files on drive C, and MODIFIED backs up all the files on drive C that have been created or changed since the last backup. The Backup Manager's Preset Display screen, which appears the first time you select the Backup Manager, is shown in figure 10.7. If you create additional timed backups, they also appear on this screen.

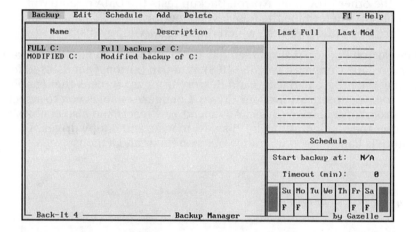

FIG. 10.7

The Preset Display screen.

You can specify the day and time to run each preset. You may, for example, want to run an incremental backup everyday at 6 p.m. and a full backup every Friday at 8 p.m.

To use Back-It 4 to retrieve data, you select Restore from the main menu and then select the Direct-Restore-from-Backup-Set option from the Restore menu. After you have specified the source device containing the files to be restored, you select the appropriate options from the Restore Options screen. When everything is set the way you want it, you press F2 to begin the restore operation. Back-It 4 displays a Restore Progress screen that keeps you apprised of how the backup operation is going.

Using Norton Backup

Norton Backup includes Windows and non-Windows versions, with documentation for each. As with the other programs, installation is easy; you just type **install** to get off and running. After the program is installed, a configuration screen appears that asks whether you want to operate Norton Backup at the Preset, Basic, or Advanced level. (Basic is the default.) In this screen, you also configure mouse, video, and floppy drive settings. If you're using a mouse, you just click an item to select it. If you're using the keyboard, you use the Tab key to move among fields, the arrow keys to move within fields, and the space bar (*not* the Enter key) to make selections.

Like the other programs, Norton Backup tests the DMA circuitry of your computer to determine the best level of performance. The program also performs a confidence test, which requires two floppy disks.

The Norton Backup main screen has three push-button modes: Backup, Restore, and Configure (see fig. 10.8). A fourth button, Quit, is used for exiting the program. Backup and Restore bring up screens that enable you to back up or restore your drives. Configure enables you to select the program skill level (Basic, Advanced, or Preset) and also enables you to reset the configurations for display, mouse, and floppy drives. This feature is handy if you upgrade your system or add a mouse.

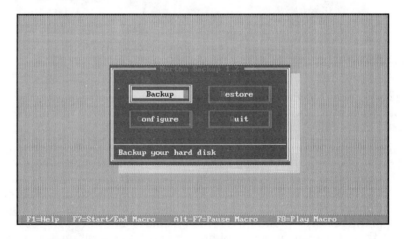

FIG. 10.8

The Norton Backup main screen.

The type of screen you see when you select Backup depends on the user level you selected. If you selected Basic, the Norton Basic Backup screen appears. From that screen, you select the drive from which you want to back up and the drive to which you want to back up.

The next step is choosing the backup type. Norton Backup offers five kinds of backups: full, incremental, differential, full copy, and incremental copy.

Full backs up all selected files and marks them as backed up.

Incremental backs up only the files that have been created or changed since the last full backup. Use this method if you access many different files every day. If you think that you will want to save all the versions of your files, keep different sets of floppy disks for each incremental backup. (If you use the same set of disks, you replace the older files with each backup.)

Differential backs up selected files that have changed since the last full or incremental backup but doesn't mark them as backed up. Symantec recommends using this option if you use the same few files every day.

Full Copy copies all the selected files without marking them as backed up. Use this option if you're transferring work between a computer in your office and one at home. This option is similar in theory to the DOS COPY command, but you have to use Norton Backup to read these files.

Incremental Copy copies all the files that have changed since the last copy and doesn't mark them as backed up. It's like using Full Copy except that you're copying only the files that have changed.

After you choose the type of backup you want, you choose other options, including whether you want to compare the backup data to the data on the hard disk, compress the data, or have Norton Backup prompt you before it overwrites any disks. You also can use the Backup Options window to tell the program whether you want it to beep when it's finished.

The next step involves choosing the Select Files button to access the file selection screen, which is where you choose the files you want to back up. You may select entire directories or specific files.

As with the other programs, after you start the backup procedure, Norton Backup displays a screen that gives you a running progress report.

Like Back-It 4, Norton Backup enables you to preset backup configurations for backups that you plan to use more than once. You don't have to stick to DOS naming conventions with your setup files. Norton Backup gives you a 24-character leeway, so you can call your scheduled Friday full backup FRIDAY FULL BACKUP if you want.

To set up automatic backups, you need to use the Advanced level of Norton Backup. You can change from the Basic to the Advanced level by selecting Configure from the Norton Backup main screen and changing the Program Level setting to Advanced. Figure 10.9 displays the Configure menu with the Program Level selection window set to Advanced.

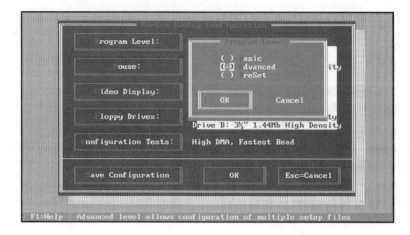

FIG. 10.9

Setting the program
level to Advanced.

To perform a basic restore operation, using Norton Backup, you select
Restore from the main menu and then select the drive from which you
want to restore.

Your next step is choosing the catalog to use in restoring. The *catalog* is
the record-keeping file created by Norton Backup every time it backs
something up. Catalogs are stored in the Norton Backup directory and
on the last disk of a backup set. They have file names such as
CC00221A.INC, which indicates that the file holds an incremental backup
performed on February 21, 1990. (If it were a full backup, it would have
the extension FUL.) After you select a catalog, you load it from the Select
Catalog menu, and you're brought back to the Basic Restore screen.

The rest of the process is similar to the process you use for a basic
backup. When you select the Options button from the Restore screen,
you can choose options from the Restore Options pop-up window, such
as telling the program to verify the data that's restored (see fig. 10.10).

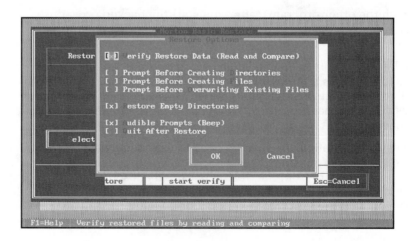

FIG. 10.10

The Restore Options
window.

After you have chosen the options you want, close the Restore Options window and choose Select Files from the Basic Restore screen. After you have selected the files you want to restore, choose OK to return to the Basic Restore screen, which now indicates the number of files you have chosen. Click the Start Restore button on the Basic Restore screen, and the system prompts you to insert the proper disks.

Using Central Point Backup

Unlike the other programs discussed in this chapter, which are sold as separate products, Central Point Backup (called PC Backup in earlier versions) from Central Point Software is included in PC Tools, a collection of all-purpose disk and file-management utilities that is discussed throughout this book. (This section assumes that you have PC Tools 7.1 installed on your computer.)

To use Central Point Backup, type **cpbackup** at the DOS prompt and press Enter. The first time you run the program, you see a welcome screen that asks you to configure the program to your computer. This screen asks whether you have a tape drive attached to the computer. If you indicate that you do, the program scans the system for any supported tape drives. (You may be asked for configuration information about your tape drive.)

The screens that follow ask you to select the type of floppy drives in use by your computer and the types of floppy disks you plan to use for your backups. Central Point Backup also includes a backup confidence test, which is optional but highly recommended. The confidence test sets the highest speed setting that your computer can handle for reliable backups. The Backup Confidence Test window appears as part of the first-time configuration.

After the program is configured, you type **cpbackup** and press Enter whenever you want to perform a backup. Central Point Backup offers three experience levels: Beginner, Intermediate, and Advanced.

The Express interface is the default interface; it requires approximately 470K of free memory. If you don't have that much memory available, the Classic interface appears when you initiate your backup. The Classic interface isn't as graphics oriented as the Express interface and so requires less memory.

When you select Backup from the Express main menu, the Express window appears. This window offers a one-stop approach. You select the source and target drives as well as options for verification, scheduling, and the method of backup (full or incremental). When you have selected the options you want to use, click the Start Backup button (or press S) to start the backup.

To restore files, type **cpbackup** again at the DOS prompt; this time select Restore from the main menu. If the drives highlighted in the Restore From and Restore To boxes are not the ones you want, select those options and choose the correct drives. Choose Retrieve History to get the report file (the program prompts you to insert the last disk or requested tape from the backup). Then choose Start Restore.

Central Point Software also enables you to create setup files for automatic timed backups. As with the other programs, this option is available only at the advanced user level, which you can select from the Configure menu.

All the commercial products mentioned in the previous sections have proved their reliability. Quite frankly, you may not even need one of these products; you may be able to get by just fine using floppy disks. Of the four products mentioned, FastBack Plus has been around the longest. Norton Backup is the new kid on the block but has the sterling Norton reputation behind it. Gazelle's Back-It 4 and Central Point Backup also have respectable followings; many people use these products to back up their valuable business data. You may want to shop around and see what your friends and associates are using, but rest assured that you will not get burned by any of these products.

Making Tape Backups

Earlier in this chapter, you learned that 13 1.44M floppy disks are needed to back up 19M worth of data. If you want to back up 40M, you're looking at 28 floppies. With an 80M or 100M hard drive, the process gets even more cumbersome. If you're facing having to back up onto more than a few disks, you should give some serious consideration to using a tape drive for your backups. It takes up much less room than dozens of disks do (especially if it's internal), and the money you spend on disks to back up a 100M or 130M drive would make a worthy contribution toward the cost of your tape drive.

Tape drives come in a wide variety, just as hard drives do. You can install an internal tape backup in your computer just as you install a hard drive, by fitting it into one of the system's drive bays, or you can purchase an external tape backup drive. (As with hard drives, you need to be sure that the internal tape drive you want fits inside the system's drive bay.)

Two types of tape drives are used at present: *helical scan drives* and *QIC (quarter-inch cartridge) drives*. Helical scan technology is found on 8mm (millimeter) drives and the newer 4mm DAT (Digital Audio Tape) drives. Standard 8mm cartridges typically hold 2.2 or 2.3 gigabytes; standard 4mm DAT cartridges hold 1.3 gigabytes.

Helical scan drives are more commonly used to back up network file servers; individual users are more likely to purchase QIC tape drives.

Helical scanning drives are an offshoot of VCR technology. They can pack more data on a tape than a QIC drive, because the rapidly spinning tape head records data at a diagonal angle to the surface of the tape. QIC drives, in contrast, record the data longitudinally, or along the entire length of the tape. A QIC drive reads or writes the entire length of one track and then reverses direction and makes its way back the entire length of the next track.

QIC tape drives are slower than helical scan technologies, which is more of a concern for networks backing up gigabytes of data than it is for those of you backing up 40 to 250M. After all, you don't save data to tape because you want to use the tape for everyday data access. It's there as an emergency backup safeguard.

QIC tape cartridges come in all kinds of capacities, which are expressed in an array of numbers just as the capability of an Intel microprocessor is expressed in numbers. Two of the better known are the DC2000 cartridges and the DC600 cartridges. DC2000 cartridges typically hold from 40 to 150M of data. DC600 cartridges format to 60M.

QIC drives also are numbered. QIC-40 drives, for example, have a capacity of 40M, and QIC-80 drives can accommodate 80M.

Where tape drives differ from hard drives and other peripherals, such as printers, is that tape drives usually include the software that you need to use for the backup and restoration process. The software determines how well the backup system will work, so be sure to take that component into account when you shop for a tape drive.

Software considerations include user friendliness. If you cannot figure out how to work with the drive, you will not use it the way you should. Other considerations include the program's capability to verify that the data on the tape matches the data on the hard drive.

Products such as Gazelle's Back-It 4 and PC Tools' Central Point Backup also support tape drives, so you may want to shop for a drive that can work with one of these third-party products.

And remember that backing up data is only half the process; be sure to try restoring data when you test the product. More than one horror story has been relayed about people who never tested the system's capability to restore data and found out the hard way that it didn't work. An industry saying claims that backups are done at leisure but restores are done in a panic, so you want to test your product's restore capabilities before a crisis strikes.

Summary

In this chapter, you have learned that the best thing you can do in terms of hard disk management, not to mention your peace of mind, is to make regular backups of your data.

You can use DOS's COPY, XCOPY, and BACKUP and RESTORE commands to work with everything from a single file to an entire hard disk. If you want more sophistication and ease of use than DOS can provide, you may want to consider one of the commercial backup products on the market. Similarly, if you need to back up more than a few floppy disks worth of data, you may want to consider a tape drive.

Chapter 11 gives you some more helpful information on keeping your hard disk secure: you learn how to *prevent* trouble from happening in the first place.

Preventing Trouble

C hapter 1 covered the basics on how a hard drive works, the components of a typical drive, and the interfaces. This chapter introduces
some of the factors affecting the physical operation of the hard drive and
ways to check periodically on your hard drive's condition. The first part
of this chapter focuses on a "keep fit" approach to enable you to coax
the maximum performance and life from your hard drive. Later on, you
take a look at some hard disk diagnostic/repair features found in utility
programs, such as Symantec's Norton Utilities and Central Point's PC
Tools.

Ensuring a Healthy Environment
for Your Hard Disk

Only a few of the components that make the drive work are mechanical,
but these parts are of a high precision. Minor disturbances often can
cause disk failure. And even under ideal conditions, these components
are subjected to a fair amount of stress and wear.

Figure 11.1 puts the whole thing in perspective. If you think of the hard
disk surface as the ground, and the read/write head as a Boeing 747,
then a hard disk in use compares to the 747 flying at 3,000 MPH, 5 feet
from the ground! On the same scale, a dust particle would be the size of
a Volkswagen Beetle, and a human hair would be about as big as a train!

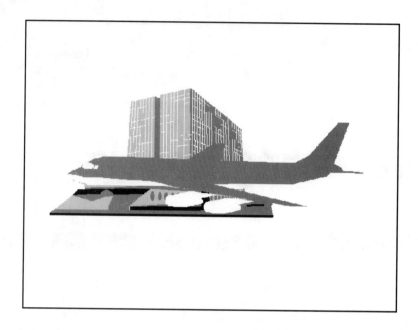

FIG. 11.1

Visualizing hard drive reality.

Many of the drives in the early '90s started adding extra circuitry to sense potential threats to the drive's existence and to take compensatory steps. Today, you might see specifications from a hard disk manufacturer claiming that its latest drive has an MTBF of 40,000. As you learned previously, MTBF stands for *mean time before failure* and is measured in hours. By a rough calculation, 40,000 hours is about 4 1/2 years. Obviously, hard disk manufacturers aren't going to test drives for 4 1/2 years, so this figure is an estimate based on accelerated stress testing and computer projection. The *mean* part of MTBF relates to an average over the potential life of the drive. Ironically the ranges fall between 1 day and 9 years.

Examining Factors That Cause Trouble

You can take many steps to give your drive every chance to survive well past its MTBF. Some of the primary causes of catastrophic drive failure include: heat, nonparked heads (in older machines), vibration, impact, power fluctuations, and spurious magnetic fields.

Heat

Heat is the enemy of almost all electronic and mechanical components. For your hard drive, heat can be a problem if the PC power supply fan has failed. In this situation, all components in the PC are at risk, so you need to turn the machine off quickly. A rapid increase in heat also might occur if you completely enclose the PC system unit in a box or poorly ventilated cabinet.

Excessive heat can cause uneven expansion and even evaporation of drive lubricants. Avoid rapid changes in temperature whenever possible. Don't leave your PC sitting in a frozen car overnight, bring the computer into a warm house, and turn it on. The sudden uneven expansion of hard disk components can cause a crash. The solution here is to bring in the PC and let it get to room temperature—typically, 30 minutes is a good waiting period.

Nonparked Heads

Head parking is a throwback to the early 1980s and possibly earlier. Older style hard drives had no mechanism for automatically parking the head, so each manufacturer provided a program to park the heads for you. A head parking program moved the read/write head and dropped it on a specific unused or physically protected area of the disk. You need to heed a word of warning about some hard disk parking programs: they aren't interchangeable among drives. Some programs can conflict with some types of drives (especially the self-parking ones). Avoid using on your drive a head parking program designed for another type of drive. In some cases, not parking the heads may be better than using an alien parking program. A self-parking program designed for one drive may tell another drive to drop the heads in the middle of the platter, causing a crash.

As a rule, drives that date from the late 1980s onward have some kind of self-parking mechanism built in.

Vibration

The obvious sources of vibration are machinery such as air conditioning, constant engine noise such as found on a ship, and close proximity to any kind of constant, loud mechanical equipment.

Vibration, although not always obvious, can cause serious drive problems even if the machine is turned off. This problem occurs especially in older drives, where the disk heads may not have been parked. Also, because each hard drive has a tiny resonance, a complementary vibration might seriously resonate in the hard disk and cause severe damage.

One solution to this problem is to buy an industrial-strength shock-mounted PC. Of course, the chances are that it will be relatively expensive. Another solution is to buy a relatively inexpensive foam rubber pad to place under the affected PC, hopefully isolating some or all of the harmful vibrations.

Impact

Impact is one of the most common underlying causes for hard disk failure. Generally, the precision components in a hard drive do not take too kindly to being hit violently. In some cases, "violently" may be picking up a running system and dropping it only an inch or two. The worst possible time of all to hit a hard drive is when you're powering it down. In this situation, the heads aren't fully retracted (if it's self-parking) and are dangling around with no power holding them up. A sharp jolt sends them crashing into the still-spinning hard disk platters, usually with catastrophic results.

Most manufacturers of drives list a shock rating measured in Gs, the standard amount of gravitational force. The higher the shock rating, the more impact the drive can sustain without permanent damage. Usually, drive manufacturers give two G ratings, one for a running drive and one for a powered-off drive.

Dropping an object from only a few inches can easily impart 30 Gs, which is enough to destroy a drive from an older IBM AT-style machine. Even older XT-class hard disk drives generally cannot survive an impact of 20 Gs or less. Many of the more recent designs have shock ratings between 70 Gs and 110 Gs.

Reducing impact problems is similar to reducing the threat of vibration. Shock mounting with a foam pad may help reduce the effects of a nearby impact but obviously not a direct hit. In these situations, the only way to prevent damage is to use a specially designed "ruggedized" computer in which every sensitive component (especially the hard drive) is heavily shock mounted.

Power Fluctuations

Turning a PC rapidly off and on can seriously damage most of its components, with the hard drive at the top of the list. When the power is turned on and off repeatedly, the hard drive is rapidly speeding up and slowing down, which causes severe stress on the drive mechanism, and voltage spikes from the power supply place some stress on the electronic components on the controller.

Dirty power in the domestic supply also can be a serious threat to the health of your hard disk (dirty power is power that surges and changes frequency or has other signals mixed in). For this reason, purchasing a spike and surge suppressor is a good investment if your area is prone to these problems.

Ultimately, the best solution to unavoidable power fluctuations is the uninterruptible power supply, which is a box that recognizes when power is lost. This supply uses internal large batteries and a device called an inverter to create a temporary 110V (or 240V) supply for up to 20 to 30 minutes. You thus have time to save your work and shut down your PC.

Magnetic Fields

Magnetic fields surround us all the time, some of them weak, some strong, and some strong enough to affect data on your hard disk. Some potential culprits include the following:

> X-ray machines in an airport or hospital
> MRI scanners in a hospital (some airports)
> Electric motors in subway trains
> Electric pencil sharpeners
> Older electric fans sitting on your PC
> Electricity generators

Basically, any high-powered electric motor, X-ray, or magnets can cause damage to the data. Generally, this type of damage is not permanent. You usually can recover from the problem by reformatting the disk. (And if you have read Chapter 10, "Understanding the Importance of Backing Up," you know all about backing up your data.)

Deciding Whether To Leave Your Machine Running or Turn It Off

This question is a longstanding bone of contention, with learned proponents on both sides of the argument. Although the item in question is the whole PC (and both sides agree that turning off the screen when not in use is a good idea), the safety of the hard drive is the concern behind making this decision. This book does not attempt to pass judgment but merely relays the arguments.

Those who say that you should leave your machine running claim that to do so ensures that all the powered safety mechanisms are operational at all times. Every time you power a machine on, it is under a great deal of stress. This stress applies not only to the electrical components but also more significantly to the mechanical ones such as the hard drive. The most likely time for system failure is during power up, so by keeping the system powered up, you can remove this factor. A typical PC system unit, if left on, consumes only about as much power as a couple of household electric light bulbs.

On the other side of the coin, others say that powering off your machine is best because heat is the greatest threat to component life. A constantly running hard drive can break down the lubricant with excessive heat. Also, a powered-down hard drive can withstand more of an impact, and a powered-up machine is prone to getting hit by power surges, blackouts, and brownouts. Although rapidly powering a machine on and off is bad practice, normal power operation should not cause undue problems. And a continually running machine uses more electricity, a precious resource.

The ultimate decision is yours.

Protecting Your Data from Yourself

How many times have you told yourself, "I wish I hadn't done that"? Accidentally erasing or overwriting something you wanted to keep can be a great source of frustration. But you can take some simple steps to avoid these kinds of accidents. You can change a file's attributes and make it read-only, hidden, or both.

Making Files Read-Only

One of the simplest ways DOS enables you to protect data is by making a file read-only. When you decide that a file is too valuable to lose, and you are not going to be changing it frequently, you need to consider making it read-only. DOS 5.0 provides the ATTRIB command to be used at the DOS prompt for this purpose.

To turn read-only on for a single file, type the following command at the DOS prompt and then press Enter:

ATTRIB +R *filename.ext*

(Substitute the file name for *filename.ext*.) Then if you attempt to erase this file by using DEL or to change it by using EDLIN or some other editor, you get the message `Access denied` from DOS. To make the file editable again, type this command and press Enter:

ATTRIB -R *filename.ext*

You also can use wild cards to specify more than one file. Suppose that you want to make all the batch files in the current directory read-only to protect them. Issue the following command at the DOS prompt:

ATTRIB +R *.BAT

Just typing in ATTRIB by itself (without the +R or -R) shows you which files are already set to read-only. Issuing the command C:\ATTRIB *.BAT, for example, might produce a list like this:

```
A        C:\OWP.BAT
A        C:\HS.BAT
A        C:\SQ4.BAT
A    R   C:\AUTOEXEC.BAT
A    R   C:\MF.BAT
A        C:\BKBAK.BAT
A        C:\TEST1.BAT
```

In this case, the R flag indicates that the AUTOEXEC.BAT and MF.BAT files are protected from accidental erasure or modification. (The A flag indicates that the archive bit is set. This bit is turned off when a DOS backup is performed.)

Hiding Files

Another way to protect your files is to make them *hidden*. Hidden files do not show up in a directory listing when you execute a DIR command. From the protection standpoint, when you try to delete a hidden file with the DELETE command, you get a `File not found` message rather than an `Access denied` message.

Hiding a file is nearly identical to making a file read-only. You simply change the flag. To hide a file, use this format:

ATTRIB +H *filename.ext*

To unhide the file, you use this command:

ATTRIB -H *filename.ext*

The problem with this method is that you sometimes can forget that a file even exists. You may want to check periodically for the existence of hidden files. You can look at a list of hidden files in a couple of ways. One way is to use the ATTRIB command on its own and look for the H flag, just as you check for read-only files (see the preceding sections on

"Making Files Read-Only"). The other method is to issue a DIR command, using the selected attribute. To produce a directory containing the hidden files only, type

DIR *.* /A:H

The /A:H tells DOS to list only those files that have the attribute of hidden.

> **NOTE** If you really want to protect a file, you can make it read-only and then hide it from view.

If you are using DOS 5.0, you can list all files, including hidden ones, using the DOS Shell program. You first must select Options from the main menu and then File Display Options from the Options menu to display the File Display Options dialog box shown in figure 11.2. Then you select the Display Hidden/System Files option.

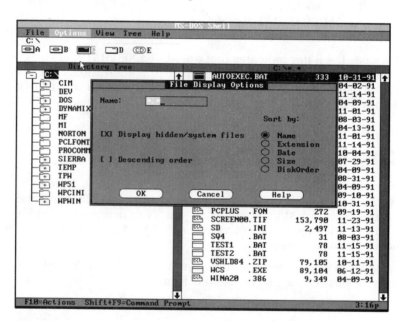

FIG. 11.2

Using the DOS Shell to display attributes of files.

To have the DOS Shell let you know at a glance what each file's attributes are, you need to select either Show Information or Change Attributes, as outlined in the next section.

Using the DOS Shell To Display and Change Attributes

The DOS Shell in Version 5.0 enables you to modify the file attributes of one or more files. To do so, follow these steps:

1. Select the file or files whose attributes you want to modify (click the file name or press the arrow keys to reach it and then press the space bar). If you need to select multiple files, hold down the Shift key as you select file names.

2. Open the File menu and choose the Change Attributes option. The Change Attributes dialog box appears, as shown in figure 11.3. From this dialog box, you can toggle the file attributes of the selected files by clicking an attribute with the mouse or by using the arrow keys to move to the attribute and pressing the space bar to change the setting.

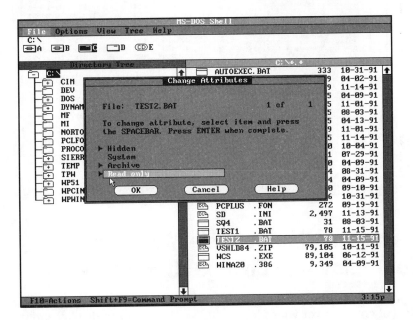

FIG. 11.3

Changing file attributes by using the DOS Shell.

T I P

If you need to find out what the current attribute settings are, select only a single file before selecting Change Attributes. Then the Change Attributes dialog box shows the current attribute settings for the selected file.

You have one other way to display (but not change) the file attributes in the DOS Shell. Follow these steps:

1. Select a single file.

2. Open the Options menu and select the Show Information option. The Show Information dialog box appears, as shown in figure 11.4. This dialog box displays a great deal of information about the file, the directory, and the drive itself. Note that the second item of information, Attr, tells you the file's attributes. In figure 11.4, the selected file is hidden (h), and the archive attribute is set (a).

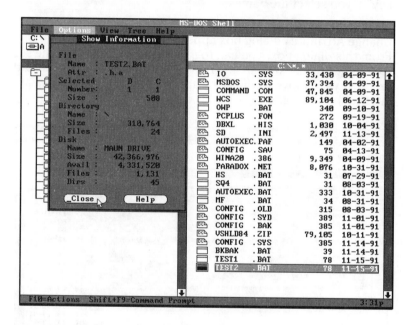

FIG. 11.4

Displaying file attributes by using the DOS Shell.

Using the Windows File Manager To Display and Change Attributes

If you use Windows 3.0 or greater, the File Manager gives you a great deal of control over your files, including the ability to display and modify the file attributes. Select the file whose attributes you want to display or modify, open the File menu, and select Change Attributes to display the Change Attributes dialog box. Note that the file attributes are listed along with the date, time, and size of the file.

To change the attributes from this screen, you simply click the check boxes of the attributes you want to set.

 NOTE Windows 3.1 has a slightly different selection under the File menu. Instead of selecting Change Attributes, you select Properties and use the check boxes to set/unset each file's attributes.

Performing Hard Disk Checkups with Disk Analyzers

Most people visit their doctor regularly for a checkup just in case a change in their physiology might indicate a health problem. In medicine, early detection often means much easier and less painful remedies. Your doctor also may tell you to exercise, eat the right kind of food, avoid too much sun, and not smoke.

From a hard disk's standpoint, your doctor is absolutely right. You already have learned how to avoid the bad habits and rough life that can damage a hard disk. Now you take a look at what's needed for a regular checkup and some defensive measures you can take. Several hard disk diagnostic utilities are available in the marketplace. You even have a way to provide a limited number of these functions by using CHKDSK, which is part of DOS 5.0.

Using the CHKDSK Command

CHKDSK has been available in all versions of MS DOS from 1.0 to 5.0 and will be no doubt in future versions. Each new version of CHKDSK, however, adds another small feature. Even Digital Research's DR DOS has a CHKDSK version of its own. This DOS external command checks the file allocation table (FAT) against the spaces (called clusters) on the disk claiming to have a file associated with them. CHKDSK reports on space it finds that apparently is not associated with a FAT entry and also provides other pertinent drive and memory information. Performing a CHKDSK on your drive gives you results similar to the following:

```
Volume MAUN DRIVE  created 07-06-1991 2:15a
Volume Serial Number is 3E1D-09D3
Errors found, F parameter not specified
Corrections will not be written to disk
```

```
   96 lost allocation units found in 2 chains
  196608 bytes disk space would be freed
42366976 bytes total disk space
   75776 bytes in 3 hidden files
  108544 bytes in 44 directories
37826560 bytes in 1130 user files
 4159488 bytes available on disk
    2048 bytes in each allocation unit
   20687 total allocation units on disk
    2031 available allocation units on disk
  655360 total bytes memory
  488224 bytes free
```

If you include the /F option at the end of your CHKDSK command, DOS recovers the lost allocation units (also referred to as clusters in some versions of DOS) and associates each chain of clusters with a file name. DOS creates (or fixes) a file for each chain, calling the first file FILE0001.CHK, the second FILE0002.CHK, and so on. If you mysteriously lose some files and cannot undelete them or they end up with a file length of 0, you might want to use the /F option with CHKDSK.

The bad news is that you may not be able to do much with the files DOS forms (FILE0001.CHK and so on). Programs and binary files generally don't work if parts of the files, particularly the beginning parts, are missing. Many word processor files and ASCII text files are among the most likely to be recovered successfully with CHKDSK, because you can tell what the original file came from and thereby its importance by using an editor and reading the text. Chapter 12, "Raiders of the Lost Data," gives you information about recovering files by using DOS commands and commercial utilities.

Periodically using CHKDSK can give you some indication of current or forthcoming problems. The good news on the sample CHKDSK report given previously, for example, is that it discovered no bad sectors, which means that the disk is unflawed. A large number of bad sectors (greater than 5 percent) or ones that start to show up increasingly on a previously clean drive can indicate a potential problem.

You can perform a more comprehensive disk diagnosis by using commercial packages, as outlined in the next sections of this chapter.

Using the Norton Utilities

The Norton Utilities published by Symantec is one of many commercial packages that offer a hard disk diagnosis feature. In the Norton Utilities, this feature is called NDD or Norton Disk Doctor. Running a utility like

NDD periodically on your hard disk is an excellent preventive measure. Using NDD is simplicity itself. All you do is type **ndd** and press Enter from the DOS prompt (and the C:\NORTON directory), and you get a screen like the one in figure 11.5.

As you can see in figure 11.5, starting the NDD program doesn't involve much work. You even have a way to undo anything that happened in the previous session.

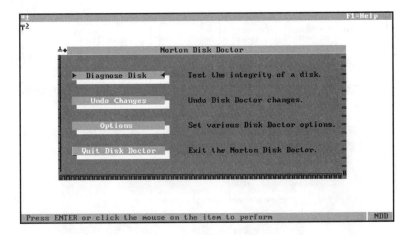

FIG. 11.5

The Norton Disk Doctor (NDD) initial selection screen.

After starting up the disk diagnosis, you will notice an ongoing progress report that checks off each step in the process. The process itself is thorough, going through the partition table, the boot record, the FAT, and the directory and file structure. The most interesting step is during the Disk Test process, where the allocated and unallocated space is illustrated graphically (see fig. 11.6).

During these processes, if any errors are found, NDD tries to fix the problem—as long as you have enabled the "repair" option. (This option is given before you start NDD. In other words, you know that the disk needs repairs before you start NDD. Otherwise, you are just checking, and NDD notices the problem and gives you the option.) When suspect areas of the disk are discovered, NDD attempts to read the data and, if successful, moves it to a safe location and marks the defective areas as bad. Any sectors marked as bad are not used by DOS to store data. Lost chains are not bad areas of the disk but are simply pieces of lost data that are not associated with any particular file. NDD attempts to reconstruct the lost chains into as complete a file as possible. Finally, having completed the diagnosis successfully, NDD provides a report such as the one in figure 11.7.

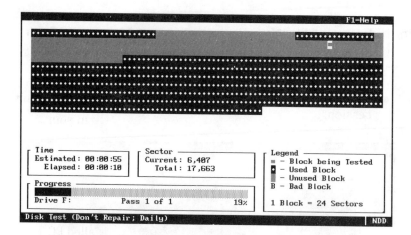

FIG. 11.6

The Norton Disk Doctor (NDD) Disk Test screen.

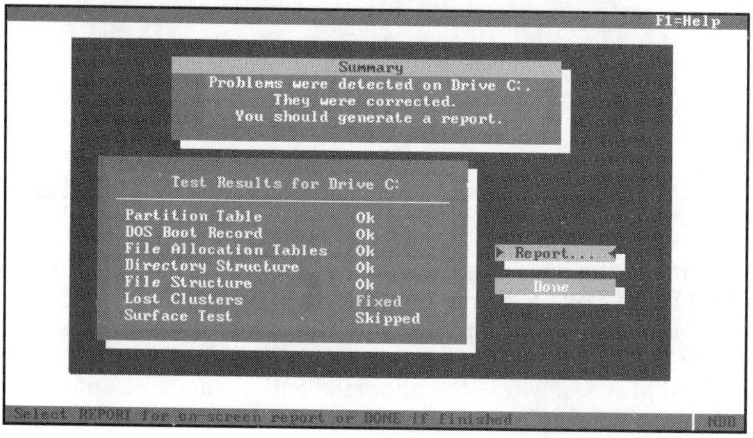

FIG. 11.7

Norton Disk Doctor (NDD) summary report.

In figure 11.7, you can see that some lost chains and allocation units were recovered by NDD successfully. The disk passed all the other tests.

Another Norton utility is Image, a utility that takes a snapshot of the system (or bootable) area of your hard drive and saves it to a file. You can place the Image command in AUTOEXEC.BAT when you install Norton Utilities or add the command later by editing AUTOEXEC.BAT.

In Chapter 3, "Understanding How DOS Works with the Hard Disk," you learned the importance of the boot record, the file allocation table, and the root directory. Image maintains a copy of these areas in a file called IMAGE.DAT. As an added safety feature, Image makes a backup copy of your previous IMAGE.DAT file in a file called IMAGE.BAK. If you accidentally reformat your hard disk, you can use a utility called UnFormat, which uses IMAGE.DAT to rebuild your lost hard disk environment. Ideally you should put Image in your AUTOEXEC.BAT file to ensure that the command is performed at least once per PC session.

Using PC Tools

Central Point Software provides a collection of utilities called PC Tools. One of the features of PC Tools is a utility called DiskFix, which when used in conjunction with another program called Mirror offers a high degree of disk protection.

Repair Drive, the first available DiskFix option, performs a diagnosis and prompts you for permission to repair any problems it finds. When used regularly, DiskFix scans the disk drive for defects and can locate and lock out potential problem areas before DOS can. As with Norton Disk Doctor, if a corrupted part of the disk is discovered, DiskFix attempts to read and relocate the data as best it can.

As in NDD, lost clusters can be recovered into files, and lost directories can even be rebuilt. You also can ignore lost clusters selectively or, if you determine that they are of no use, can even delete them to free up some disk space. The most comprehensive diagnosis is performed by the Surface Scan feature.

DiskFix offers many other features, such as optimization, encryption, and virus protection, which are covered more extensively in Chapters 9, 13, and 14. After DiskFix has performed a diagnosis and possible repair, it can produce a report of its findings. The following is a sample report produced after DiskFix is run on a hard drive and discovers a lost chain error:

```
            PC Tools DISKFIX
               Version 7
     Status Report for logical drive C:
            11/24/91 20:36:21

    _ _ _ _ _ _ _ _ _ _ _ _ _ _ _ _ _

62,234,624 - bytes total disk space
29,532,160 - bytes in 583 files and 20 directories
32,702,464 - bytes available on disk
       512 - bytes in each sector
         1 - sector in DOS Boot record
        31 - sectors in each FAT (1 copies)
        32 - sectors in root directory (512 entries)
   121,616 - sectors in logical disk
       F8h - media descriptor
    16 bit - File Allocation Tables
     8,192 - bytes in each allocation unit (cluster)
        16 - sectors in each allocation unit (cluster)
     7,597 - total allocation units for data storage
Logical Drive C: is accessed as bios disk 80Hex with:
        17 - sectors in each track
         5 - tracks in each cylinder (number of read/write
                  heads)
       732 - cylinders on drive
```

```
    AREAS TESTED AND RESULTS:
  PARTITION AND BOOT INFORMATION

  _ _ _ _ _ _ _ _ _ _ _ _ _ _ _ _ _ _

Partition & Boot Information:        No errors were found



      FILE ALLOCATION TABLES

  _ _ _ _ _ _ _ _ _ _ _ _ _ _ _ _ _ _

Media descriptors:                   No errors were found
FAT validity checks:                 No errors were found



      DIRECTORY STRUCTURE

  _ _ _ _ _ _ _ _ _ _ _ _ _ _ _ _ _ _

Cross Linked Files:                  No errors were found
Directory Structure and File System: No errors were found
Lost Cluster Chains:                 DISKFIX repaired errors
                                                      found.

     Converted Lost Cluster Chain
C:\PCT00000.FIX with

at 339 into a file named:
8192 bytes (1 clusters)
```

Mirror, not to be confused with DOS 5.0's MIRROR command, is another PC Tools utility. Similar in function to Norton's Image, Mirror is a housekeeping routine that should be run daily and is best included in the AUTOEXEC.BAT. Mirror saves a copy of the boot record, the file allocation table, and the root directory. Optionally, you can use a floppy disk to store this information along with the partition table and CMOS settings. The latter two items are often the toughest to find when you need to recover your hard disk.

PC Tools Data Monitor is a TSR (terminate-and-stay resident program) that offers a form of security umbrella for hard disk users. One of the most important elements is the Write Protection feature, which enables you to select files that you do not want overwritten or erased. The file protection can vary from just the system files to a series of files and directories or even the entire disk, including floppy drives. You can track file deletions for later recovery by using a feature called the Delete Sentry. Other features include a screen blanker, a disk light, and password protection on directories. Password protection is covered in more detail in Chapter 13, "Keeping Your Data Confidential."

Using the MIRROR Command in DOS 5.0

A new feature that first appeared in DOS 5.0 is an UNDELETE command that can attempt to recover a deleted file. This command is covered in more detail in Chapter 12, "Raiders of the Lost Data," but is mentioned here because a major feature of UNDELETE relates to the MIRROR command. MIRROR provides the mechanism to track deleted files—in particular, it creates a file called PCTRACKR.DEL. When running MIRROR, you can specify the number of deletions that can be tracked, up to 999 deleted files. If you want to track up to 100 deleted files on drive C, for example, you use the command in this form:

MIRROR /TC-100

The /T tells the command to track deleted files, the C is for drive C, and the 100 is the number of deleted files to track. Note that you must include a hyphen between the drive letter and the number of deleted files to be tracked.

Summary

In this chapter, you have learned that simply by avoiding some of the harmful situations such as heat, shock, vibration, and power surges you can give your hard drive every chance to survive at least to its MTBF (mean time before failure). You have looked at ways to keep a check on the physical status of your hard drive and some diagnosis utility programs such as Norton Disk Doctor and PC Tools DiskFix. DOS offers some limited diagnosis through its CHKDSK utility and in Version 5.0, a data "safety net," the MIRROR command.

One final note is that hard disk drives do not last forever. Planning for the day when you turn on your machine and get the dreaded message Not ready reading drive C is a good idea. In this chapter, you have learned some guidelines that you can use to evaluate the current state of your hard drive. If you notice that you are losing clusters continually, you either have a virus (see Chapter 14) or need to think about buying a new drive.

In Chapter 12, "Raiders of the Lost Data," you turn to another facet of hard disk security: recovering data that is already lost.

Raiders of the Lost Data

The things you have learned about the file allocation table and related concepts in Chapter 3, "Understanding How DOS Works with the Hard Disk," are going to pay off in this chapter, because here you learn ways to recover lost data, and the FAT and other hard disk elements play a big part.

Few things can make you feel as sick as discovering that you have deleted a file you didn't intend to delete. One of these "things" is finding out that you accidentally formatted (erased) your hard disk when you thought you were formatting a floppy disk. According to the Law of Computer Averages, the likelihood of such an occurrence is in direct proportion to the closeness of your impending deadline.

Luckily, you can recover from both accidents. One of the best improvements to DOS 5.0 is the addition of data-recovery features. UNFORMAT, UNDELETE, and MIRROR give you capabilities for recovering data that weren't available in earlier versions of DOS.

Although the primary emphasis in this chapter is on working with DOS 5.0, the text deviates from previous chapters, where the primary focus was on the DOS Shell. Unlike other commands, the DOS data-recovery commands are used from the DOS command line, otherwise known as the DOS prompt. Nor are any Windows procedures included in this chapter, because Windows does not have similar commands.

You do, however, look at some third-party products in this chapter. Some of the best-known disk-management and utility products, such as PC Tools and the Norton Utilities, include data-recovery features as an integral part of their repertoire, and some of those features are discussed in this chapter.

All these products have undelete and unformat capabilities (in fact, DOS's UNDELETE, UNERASE, and MIRROR commands were licensed from Central Point Software, the makers of PC Tools). Because the process of undeleting or unerasing a file is similar no matter which product you use, in this chapter the DOS commands serve as a representative example of this process. But you do learn about the capability of these third-party programs to repair damage to DOS's structural areas: the FAT, the boot record, and the partition table.

Understanding Why Lost Data Isn't Really Lost

Recovering deleted or erased files may seem like a contradiction in terms, not to mention downright impossible. But contrary to what you might think, when you erase or delete a file, you don't erase the contents of the file. The contents remain intact until you overwrite them—that is, until you save another file at the location occupied by the first file.

To understand why deleted files can be recovered, you need to review and further explore some of the concepts you learned in Chapter 3. You may remember that one of the first things DOS does in a logical format is set up the file allocation table (FAT). The FAT is the lookup table DOS uses to keep track of each file's location on the hard disk. DOS does so by means of clusters (also called file allocation units). A cluster is DOS's basic unit of allocation for disk space. Clusters consist of contiguous sectors, typically four sectors per cluster in a hard disk. DOS uses clusters instead of sectors because they're larger and therefore easier to work with.

Here is where the complicated part comes in. You cannot just say that file X is located at cluster Y. As you learned in Chapter 9, "Exploring Hard Disk Fitness Programs," files may be larger than an individual cluster can hold, and the next contiguous cluster may be taken up by another file. Files also are constantly erased, replaced, or enlarged. The end result is that portions of a file may be scattered at random throughout the disk. This phenomenon is known as *fragmenting*.

To find all those fragments, DOS uses a method called *chaining*, where the FAT entry of each cluster points to the location of the next cluster. So when looking up cluster 4 in the FAT, DOS sees the number 12, which means that the file is continued on cluster 12.

Here are possible entries in the FAT:

- The end of the cluster contains the location of the start of the next cluster for a given file.

- The cluster is the last cluster in the file.

- The cluster is available.

- The cluster is not available because it's reserved for use by DOS.

- The cluster is not available because it's faulty.

Here's the catch: The FAT tells DOS where the next cluster is located but doesn't tell DOS where the first cluster for that file is located. To use the preceding example, DOS can tell when it looks at cluster 4 that it is supposed to look at cluster 12 next. But how does DOS know that it's supposed to start at cluster 4?

The FAT gives no clue as to where the file begins. That information is stored in the file's directory entry. You may remember from Chapter 3 that the directory entry holds the file's name, size, and attributes. But there's more to the file's name than meets the eye. Just as the FAT indicates a cluster's status, so does the file's name indicate a file's status.

The first character in a file's name field mimics the FAT entry. The first character may just be the first letter of the existing file, may indicate that the file is used by DOS, may indicate that the directory space is available, or may indicate that a file has been erased.

When you erase a file, DOS simply marks the first byte of the file's name with a marker to indicate that the file has been erased and then clears the file's FAT entries. Rather than go through and erase the file, DOS simply indicates that the space is available for use by other files, just as you probably don't erase used cassette tapes before you record over them.

If you were to save another file at this point, DOS might overwrite your old file, because the clusters for the erased file appear to be available. Then the original file or portions of it really are lost. For this reason, acting as quickly as possible in an emergency is important. If you don't save any new files, you don't overwrite the files you deleted, and you easily can recover the entire file or files.

Understanding Why Unformatting Is Possible

The accidental format happens to practically everyone sooner or later. You're sitting at your computer, your mind elsewhere, performing what you think is a routine format of a floppy disk. You notice, too late, that you have just formatted your hard disk. Your stomach drops to somewhere in the vicinity of your shoelaces. (The moment feels a lot like that high-school rite-of-passage accident with Dad's car.)

The reason you hear so many horror stories about accidental formats is because formatting a disk is a simple process. In earlier versions of DOS, the process was *too* simple. All you had to do was type **format** and press Enter at the prompt to format the current drive. DOS contains checks and balances now that make the accidental format a little tougher to manage.

Suppose that your current drive is the hard drive, and you want to format a floppy disk in drive A. You have two choices: switch to drive A by typing **a:** at the prompt, or stay in the current drive and type **format a:** at the prompt. If you type **format** without specifying a drive, you get the message Required parameter missing. But mistakes still can happen. If your mind is elsewhere, you easily can type **format c:** when you mean to type **format a:**.

Unformatting a disk is possible for the same reasons undeleting a file is possible. When performing the logical format, DOS sets up the root directory and the FAT. If you're making the disk bootable by typing **format /s** (for system), DOS also sets up the system files that you learned about in Chapter 3, "Understanding How DOS Works with the Hard Disk." If any data is on the disk when you format, the data is untouched, just as the contents of a file are untouched when you delete a file. (The one exception is if you use the FORMAT command with the /U [for unconditional] switch, which does destroy all the data on the disk. Use this switch with great caution.)

Although no data on the disk is destroyed, the formatting process wipes the slate clean in terms of bookkeeping by creating a new FAT and new root directory. Although all the data is intact, DOS now has no idea of how to find it. Suppose that the post office suddenly lost complete track of where everyone lived. They're all still at the same addresses, but the mail carriers no longer know how to get to them.

To unformat the disk, DOS has to use a backup map to replace the one that was lost. This feature is what data-recovery programs have in common: they employ utilities that create a backup map of the disk's vital structures. When an accidental format takes place, a companion utility re-creates the structures from the backup map. In DOS 5.0, the mapping program is called MIRROR; the utility that re-creates your disk structure is called UNFORMAT.

Examining the MIRROR Command

MIRROR is a new DOS command that works in conjunction with both UNDELETE and UNFORMAT. MIRROR creates an *image file*, sometimes called a *snapshot*, of the disk's vital structures: the partition table, the FAT, and the root directory. This image file, which is called MIRROR.FIL, is used by UNFORMAT to re-create the disk structure in case of an accidental format or disk crash.

Because having the most current structural information is so crucial, you need to keep MIRROR.FIL as up-to-date as possible. One of the best and easiest ways to do so is to keep the MIRROR command in the AUTOEXEC.BAT file so that MIRROR.FIL is updated whenever you start the machine. (For a review of the AUTOEXEC.BAT file, see Chapter 7, "Using Batch Files and Macros.")

MIRROR also includes a TSR (terminate and stay resident) program that tracks all deleted files. Microsoft recommends that you use MIRROR's deletion-tracking file; it's more reliable than the DOS directory listing of deleted files.

To activate PCTRACKR.DEL, the MIRROR file that keeps track of all file deletions, use the /T (tracking) switch with the MIRROR command. If you want to keep track of all file deletions on your hard disk, for example, type the following command and press Enter at the DOS prompt:

MIRROR /TC

The C after the switch specifies the hard drive.

(Remember, if you want this command loaded into memory each time you start the computer, add it to the AUTOEXEC.BAT file.)

You can specify multiple drives if you prefer. Suppose that your system has a hard drive and both 5 1/4-inch and 3 1/2-inch floppy drives. To track deletions on all of them, type this command at the prompt:

MIRROR /TC /TA /TB

Using DOS's UNDELETE Command

The UNDELETE command is new to Version 5.0 of DOS. You can use UNDELETE with MIRROR or as a stand-alone utility.

TIP Although you can execute the UNDELETE command from the DOS Shell, doing so probably isn't a good idea. The reason is simple: If you run the UNDELETE file from the Shell, the first thing DOS does is save the contents of RAM to a disk file. The disk file DOS creates may overwrite the data you're trying to recover. If you're in the DOS Shell when you realize that you need to recover a file, your best bet is to exit the DOS Shell before you use the UNDELETE command.

To use UNDELETE for a single file, simply type **undelete** followed by the file's name and extension (and path if necessary) at the DOS prompt. To restore a file called PICNIC.DOC in the BUDGET subdirectory, for example, type the following at the prompt and press Enter:

UNDELETE C:\BUDGET\PICNIC.DOC

You also can use wild cards with UNDELETE. To restore all files in the BUDGET subdirectory, for example, type

UNDELETE C:\BUDGET\ *

TIP Use the UNDELETE command as soon as you notice that you have deleted a file. Waiting increases the odds that the file will be overwritten.

UNDELETE contains several switches that enable you to perform varying tasks. Typing **undelete /?** at the prompt displays all your options, as shown in figure 12.1.

Using the /DT switch tells UNDELETE to recover only the files that are listed in the deletion-tracking file created by MIRROR. When you use the /DT switch, you are prompted for confirmation of each file undeletion. If the deletion-tracking file is not installed, the command does not proceed.

The /LIST switch shows you all the deleted files available for recovery but does not recover any of them. Files that are only partially recoverable are marked with an asterisk (*) to the left of the file name; files that cannot be recovered are marked with two asterisks (**).

```
C:\
undelete /?
Restores files which have been deleted.

UNDELETE [[drive:][path]][filename] [/LIST | /ALL] [/DT | /DOS]

  /LIST  Lists the deleted files available to be recovered.
  /ALL   Undeletes all specified files without prompting.
  /DT    Uses only the deletion-tracking file.
  /DOS   Uses only the MS-DOS directory.

MIRROR, UNDELETE, and UNFORMAT Copyright (C) 1987-1991 Central Point Software,
Inc.

C:\
```

FIG. 12.1

Viewing your
UNDELETE options.

T I P

If the list of available deleted files is longer than one page, use the
Ctrl-S key combination to pause the display. To resume scrolling,
press any key.

The /DOS switch tells DOS not to look for the deletion-tracking file and to
look for files in the DOS directory instead. Like the /DT switch, the /DOS
switch prompts you for confirmation.

The /ALL switch recovers deleted files without prompting you for confirmation. If you have installed the deletion-tracking file, DOS checks that
file first. If the deletion-tracking file is not present, UNDELETE searches
the DOS directory, substituting the # symbol for the missing letter of the
file's name.

If you do not specify a switch but simply type **undelete** at the prompt,
DOS searches the deletion-tracking file first. If the deletion-tracking file is
not installed, DOS searches the directory listing.

Using UNDELETE with MIRROR

Figure 12.2 shows some sample results of using UNDELETE with
MIRROR's deletion-tracking file.

The UNDELETE message lists the name of the specified file. In the example in figure 12.2, because a file name isn't specified, UNDELETE displays all available deleted files in the WordPerfect directory.

```
Directory: C:\WP51
File Specifications: *.*

    Deletion-tracking file contains     5 deleted files.
    Of those,     5 files have all clusters available,
                  0 files have some clusters available,
                  0 files have no clusters available.

    MS-DOS directory contains     7 deleted files.
    Of those,     2 files may be recovered.

Using the deletion-tracking file.

     WP}WP{    SPC     4096 12-11-91  9:10p  ...A  Deleted: 12-11-91   9:11p
All of the clusters for this file are available. Undelete (Y/N)?n

     WP{WP}    BK1     9935 12-11-91  8:55p  ...A  Deleted: 12-11-91   9:10p
All of the clusters for this file are available. Undelete (Y/N)?n

     WP}WP{    SPC     4096 12-11-91  7:55p  ...A  Deleted: 12-11-91   9:10p
All of the clusters for this file are available. Undelete (Y/N)?n

     WP{WP}    BK1     8774 12-11-91  8:25p  ...A  Deleted: 12-11-91   8:55p
All of the clusters for this file are available. Undelete (Y/N)?
```

FIG. 12.2

Using UNDELETE with MIRROR.

NOTE   If you have created and deleted several different versions of a file with the same name, UNDELETE lists all of them. Typically, you want to restore the most recent version and discard the others, unless you need portions of each draft.

The message also indicates which files are completely restorable (have all clusters available), which are partially restorable (have some clusters available), and which are not restorable (have no clusters available).

To recover a deleted file, simply press Y at the `Undelete (Y/N)?` prompt for that file. You then see the following message:

    `File successfully undeleted.`

If you have used another utility such as Norton's WipeInfo to delete the actual file (remember, DOS just deletes the record of that file from the address until something else is written over the file), DOS is not able to retrieve the file. In that case, you get a `No entries found` message.

If you have created another file by the same name, UNDELETE displays the following message:

    `The filename already exists. Enter a different filename.`
    `Press "F5" to bypass this file.`

To recover the file, simply type a new name for it.

Using UNDELETE without MIRROR

If you don't have the deletion-tracking file installed when you accidentally delete a file, use the /DOS switch with UNDELETE. The procedure you follow is similar to the procedure you use when the deletion-tracking file is installed, with a couple of exceptions.

First, when you see the list of files on-screen, notice that the first letter of each file name is missing, as shown in figure 12.3.

```
C:\WP51
undelete /dos

Directory: C:\WP51
File Specifications: *.*

    Deletion-tracking file contains    5 deleted files.
    Of those,    0 files have all clusters available,
                 0 files have some clusters available,
                 5 files have no clusters available.

    MS-DOS directory contains    5 deleted files.
    Of those,    2 files may be recovered.

Using the MS-DOS directory.

    ?P}WP{   CHK       0 12-15-91  9:15p  ...A Undelete (Y/N)?n

    ?P}WP{   TV1       0 12-15-91  9:15p  ...A Undelete (Y/N)?n

    ?P}WP{   BV1       0 12-15-91  9:15p  ...A Undelete (Y/N)?n

    ?P}WP{   SPC    4096 12-15-91  9:15p  ...A Undelete (Y/N)?
```

FIG. 12.3

Using UNDELETE without MIRROR.

Because you're using the directory instead of the deleted file list prepared by MIRROR, remember that DOS changes the first letter of a file name to indicate that it has been deleted.

Because DOS doesn't know what the first character of the file name is anymore, you are prompted to enter it after you press Y at the Undelete (Y/N)? prompt. Type the beginning letter of the file's name at the prompt (you do not need to press Enter). DOS then recovers the file and displays the same message it uses with the deletion-tracking method:

    File successfully undeleted.

Recovering from an Accidental Format with UNFORMAT

Whereas in days gone by, you were up a creek if you didn't have PC Tools or the Norton Utilities handy, now you can turn to DOS to bail you out if you accidentally format your disk. Version 5.0 contains its own utility called UNFORMAT.

You can use UNFORMAT in one of two different ways: to re-cover from an accidental format, as explained in this section, or to rebuild damaged partition structures, as discussed in this chapter's subsequent section on "Recovering Damaged DOS Structures." (You also may need UNFORMAT if you have problems with the DOS RECOVER command.)

UNFORMAT is simple to use. You just type the command followed by the name of the drive you want to unformat. If you find that you accidentally formatted your C drive, for example, type this command and press Enter at the prompt:

UNFORMAT C:

As with UNDELETE, you will have the best luck with UNFORMAT if you use it immediately after formatting.

T I P   UNFORMAT doesn't work on disks that have been formatted with older versions of DOS. You can use UNFORMAT only on a disk that's been formatted with DOS 5.0 without the /U switch.

UNFORMAT, like UNDELETE, contains several switches, which you can call up by typing **unformat /?** or **help unformat** and pressing Enter at the prompt, as shown in figure 12.4.

```
C:\
unformat /?
Restores a disk erased by the FORMAT command or restructured by the RECOVER
command.

UNFORMAT drive: [/J]
UNFORMAT drive: [/U] [/L] [/TEST] [/P]
UNFORMAT /PARTN [/L]

  drive:   Specifies the drive to unformat.
  /J       Verifies that the mirror files agree with the system information
           on the disk.
  /U       Unformats without using MIRROR files.
  /L       Lists all file and directory names found, or, when used with the
           /PARTN switch, displays current partition tables.
  /TEST    Displays information but does not write changes to disk.
  /P       Sends output messages to printer connected to LPT1.
  /PARTN   Restores disk partition tables.

MIRROR, UNDELETE, and UNFORMAT Copyright (C) 1987-1991 Central Point Software,
Inc.

C:\
```

FIG. 12.4

Viewing your
UNFORMAT options.

The /J switch is used to verify that the information recovered by MIRROR accurately reflects the most current disk information.

The /L switch is somewhat analogous to UNDELETE's list switch; it lists the file and directory names found in a formatted disk.

The /P switch sends all output to a printer.

The /TEST switch, as the name implies, provides a test run; it lets you know whether UNFORMAT will be able to unformat a disk successfully.

The /U switch is what you use to unformat a disk if you didn't have the MIRROR image file installed.

The /PARTN switch is used to rebuild a damaged hard disk partition table. For more information on that process, see this chapter's section on "Repairing Damaged DOS Structures."

Using UNFORMAT with MIRROR

As with UNDELETE, you're better off using UNFORMAT in conjunction with MIRROR. Suppose that you have MIRROR installed in your AUTOEXEC.BAT file and you just accidentally formatted your hard disk. Now what?

First, take a deep breath. Don't panic. Be thankful that you're working with DOS 5.0 and not DOS 2.0. Then type **unformat c:** at the prompt and press Enter. (Unlike most of the other commands, you don't want to try this command for practice. Don't use UNFORMAT unless you absolutely have to. If you want to try it, use it on a floppy disk.) The following warning message appears:

```
Restores the system area of your disk with
the image file created by MIRROR

WARNING!              WARNING!
This should be used ONLY to recover from the inadvertent
use of the DOS FORMAT command or the DOS RECOVER command.
Any other use of UNFORMAT may cause you to lose data!
Files modified since the last use of MIRROR may be lost.
```

After that rather sobering message, UNFORMAT lets you know the last two times (the time, month, day, and year) MIRROR was used. MIRROR is a cautious animal; whenever the MIRROR file (MIRROR.FIL) is updated, MIRROR saves the previous MIRROR.FIL file as MIRROR.BAK.

To compare the contents of MIRROR.FIL to the FAT and root directory, press the letter L as indicated by the prompt. To compare MIRROR.BAK instead, press P at the prompt.

After you enter your response, the computer beeps again, and the following message is displayed:

```
The MIRROR image file has been validated.
Are you SURE you want to update the SYSTEM area
of your drive c (Y/N)?
```

If you press N, you're returned to the system prompt. If you press Y, UNFORMAT takes the FAT, root directory, and boot record that have been stored in MIRROR.FIL or MIRROR.BAK and writes them to the hard disk's system area. Everything on the drive is restored except any files that may have been changed or added since the last time you ran the MIRROR program.

Verifying MIRROR Information

After you install MIRROR, you can use UNFORMAT to verify that the MIRROR image file accurately reflects the disk's system structures by typing **unformat a: /j** and pressing Enter at the DOS prompt. You get almost the same message you get when you're running UNFORMAT for real. Figure 12.5 shows the message that appeared when UNFORMAT was tried on a floppy disk in drive A.

```
Insert disk to rebuild in drive A:
and press ENTER when ready.

Restores the system area of your disk by using the image file created
by the MIRROR command.

     WARNING !!          WARNING !!

This command should be used only to recover from the inadvertent use of
the FORMAT command or the RECOVER command.  Any other use of the UNFORMAT
command may cause you to lose data!  Files modified since the MIRROR image
file was created may be lost.

Searching disk for MIRROR image.

Just checking this time.  No changes written to disk.

Bad sector being bypassed.

Bad sector being bypassed.

Bad sector being bypassed.
```

FIG. 12.5

Verifying the contents
of MIRROR.

Because you are only verifying the MIRROR image, note that the message Just checking this time is included in the display. This message assures you that nothing will be written to the disk.

As in the case of a real UNFORMAT procedure, the next thing UNFORMAT does is tell you the last two times the MIRROR files were updated. Press the letter L if you want to compare MIRROR.FIL to the current disk structure; press P if you want to compare MIRROR.BAK instead.

If the contents of the MIRROR file you selected match the disk's FAT and root directory, UNFORMAT notifies you by displaying the following message:

```
The SYSTEM area of drive c has been verified to agree
with the image file.
```

If they don't match, UNFORMAT tells you that the system file does not agree with the image file. If you get this message, files have been changed or added since MIRROR was used last. Perhaps, for example, you ran it first thing in the morning and have been hard at work on a spreadsheet all day. If you use UNFORMAT at this point, you will lose those files.

Using UNFORMAT without MIRROR

What if you accidentally format a hard disk that didn't have MIRROR installed? Even though the process that uses MIRROR takes less time and, more importantly, is less risky, you still might be able to restore most of the data.

To unformat a hard disk without MIRROR, type the following command and press Enter at the DOS prompt:

UNFORMAT C: /U

You also can use the optional /P, /L, and /TEST switches for printer output, a list of available files and directories, and a simulated UNFORMAT, respectively. (The test UNFORMAT tells you which files you will be able to recover.)

When you unformat a hard disk without the benefit of MIRROR, you see the following message:

```
CAUTION ! !

This attempts to recover all files lost after a
FORMAT, assuming you've NOT been using MIRROR. This
method cannot guarantee complete recovery of your
files.

The search-phase is safe: nothing is altered on the
disk.

You'll be prompted again before changes are written to
the disk.
```

```
Using drive c:

Are you SURE you want to do this?
If so, type in 'Y'; anything else cancels.
```

After you press Y, UNFORMAT keeps you apprised of its actions. You see on-screen messages telling you how many root entries, files, and subdirectories the command has found. After UNFORMAT finishes its search, it lists the found subdirectories and gives them all a new name, SUBDIR.xxx because FORMAT wipes out directory names at the root-directory level.

Next you get another warning that lets you know that UNFORMAT is going to make changes to the disk. You are asked whether you're sure that you want to continue. If you are, press Y at the prompt.

One small problem: UNFORMAT doesn't know what to do with fragmented files. It asks whether you want those file portions to be truncated (recovered) or deleted. When DOS prompts you, press T to recover the file fragments or D to delete them.

Repairing Damaged DOS Structures

You can recover erased files. You can even recover from formats. But what happens if, perish the thought, the structural underpinnings themselves become damaged? This section examines the worst-case scenario, where either the disk itself, or the structures that serve as road maps, are damaged.

If the partition table for your hard disk is damaged, for example, DOS cannot read any information from the disk. You get the scary Invalid drive specification message. If you have used the DOS MIRROR program to back up your partition table, you can use MIRROR to get into the disk and restore the partition table. (For more information, see "Using MIRROR To Recover Partition Information.")

The first thing to remember is that you have options. The other thing to remember is that your options depend on making backups of the disk structure itself as well as the data stored on it.

Knowing Which Error Messages Indicate Disk Trouble

In addition to the Invalid drive specification message, which indicates damage to the partition table, the following messages also may indicate hard disk trouble:

```
Read/write errors.
Bad or missing command interpreter.
Disk boot failure.
Error loading operating system.
General failure.
Disk Error reading Drive C:
Non-system disk or disk error.
Sector not found.
General failure.
File allocation table bad.
```

If you see one of these messages, which indicate *run-time errors*, you need to resort to a data-recovery method. For more information, see this chapter's subsequent section on "Performing CPR for Structural Damage."

Looking for FAT Trouble

You need to take a second to look at FAT symptoms because you may run into some of them as you're using either DOS or a data-recovery program. Symptoms include FAT error messages, inaccessible files or data, cross-linked files, and orphaned clusters.

Cross-linked files are two or more files that claim the same FAT entry. The DOS CHKDSK command lets you know if cross-linked files are present but cannot do anything about them.

Orphaned (or lost) clusters are ones that have been cut off from their original file. Although the FAT marks these clusters as being in use, they are not allocated to any file in the directory system; they exist in a kind of electronic limbo.

To see whether your FAT is acting up, run the DOS CHKDSK command (covered in Chapter 11, "Preventing Trouble"). When you run CHKDSK, it reports the presence of orphaned clusters but doesn't do anything about them. If you add the /F switch (fix) to CHKDSK, it renames these clusters and puts them in the root directory.

Performing CPR for Structural Damage

Products like the Norton Utilities or PC Tools can bail you out if you encounter any of these nasty messages. In fact, as indicated in Chapter 11, they may even be able to help you *prevent* such messages.

Aside from having utilities that perform preventive medicine by analyzing and repairing the disk's FAT, boot record, and directory structure, these programs give you the Disk Doctor (Norton Utilities) and DiskFix (PC Tools), all of which can be used for hard disk CPR.

You should put one of these utilities into action as soon as you detect trouble in the disk, but you might not know that you have a problem until suddenly the machine won't boot up (start), and you receive one of the nasty messages mentioned previously.

If your computer will not boot, you need to start the system from a bootable floppy disk, one that has the DOS system files on it, and then use the utility of your choice to repair the damage.

T   I   P   If you bring any of these products home in a panic because you're trying to recover data, do NOT attempt to install the products on the hard drive. The act of installing them overwrites the data you're trying to recover. Instead, run them from their floppy disks. DiskFix has a reminder on the installation screen that tells you not to go through with the installation process if you're trying to restore data, and the Norton Utilities has a clearly labeled emergency floppy for such purposes.

The following sections serve as introductions to each product. They are not intended to serve as comparisons or comprehensive product reviews, nor are they intended to serve as endorsements. Other disk-utility packages are on the market; but these two are widely known and as such can serve as examples of how data-recovery utilities work. They check the following areas of the hard disk: the boot sector, the FAT and FAT backup copy, the directories, and the media surface. They also check for cross-linked files and orphaned clusters.

Using PC Tools DiskFix

DiskFix is the disk analysis and repair component of the PC Tools comprehensive disk-management package. DiskFix uses an easy-to-follow menu format, which enables you to choose from a list of on-screen options.

The Repair a Disk option is what you use when the machine will not boot up. You also use this option to remedy lost clusters and cross-linked files.

Surface Scan is what you use when you have read/write errors. This option removes damaged sectors from use and moves data from those sectors to a safe location when necessary.

You can opt to receive a printed report of the scan or have the report saved to a file in the system. A sample log report is shown in figure 12.6.

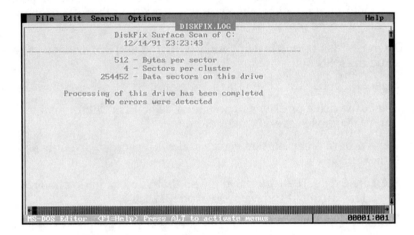

FIG. 12.6

Viewing the DiskFix log report.

If Repair a Disk and Surface Scan have not been able to repair damage to a file, use the Revitalize a Disk option. You also use this option when you have read or write errors in the disk's FAT or root directory or when you notice an increasing number of read/write errors.

Revitalize a Disk performs what's known as a safe low-level format, which affects the surface of the disk. (You also can use this option to optimize the interleave.)

T I P   Many newer disk technologies, IDE in particular, use technology that does not permit low-level formatting. DiskFix warns you if you try performing a low-level format on such a drive and does not let you continue with the process.

Finally, the Undo a DiskFix Repair option enables you to restore a drive to the condition it was in before DiskFix made any repairs. To be able to use this option, you must save the original information during the repair process.

Using the Norton Disk Doctor

If you have the Norton Utilities, you can get into the Norton Disk Doctor from the menu that appears when you type **norton** at the DOS prompt, or you can just type **ndd** at the prompt.

The Diagnose Disk option is what you use to find and repair damage to DOS structures. Six steps are involved:

1. Select Diagnose Disk from the main menu.

2. Select the drive or drives to be tested. (The Disk Doctor enables you to diagnose several drives at once.)

3. If the program encounters errors, follow the screen prompts as indicated.

4. If errors exist, create an UnDo file so that you can undo changes if they don't turn out the way you expected.

5. Test the disk surface for physical defects. (This step is optional.)

6. Generate and print a copy of test results. (This step is also optional but highly recommended.)

After the Norton Disk Doctor checks the DOS structures, it performs an optional surface test of the disk.

You can tell NDD to go over the surface of the disk more than once. Testing once is usually sufficient, but some errors don't show up the first time. You also can set the test to perform a quick scan, a slower scan, or an automatic weekly scan (the Auto Weekly option, which performs an automatic test every Friday). You can set the test to diagnose the disk without taking any action, to inform you before it makes a repair, or to make all repairs automatically.

When the tests are finished, a Summary screen appears, as shown in figure 12.7. Selecting the Report button from this screen gives you the option of viewing an on-screen report or having a report output to a printer.

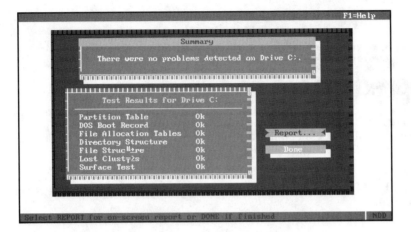

FIG. 12.7

Viewing the NDD Summary screen.

Using MIRROR To Recover Partition Information

DOS doesn't offer the disk repair capabilities of the data utility programs outlined in the previous sections, at least not in the current version. But you can use DOS's MIRROR program to get out of a jam if something happens to your disk's partition table—that is, if you used MIRROR to back up the partition table in the first place.

If you cannot get your computer to boot up from the hard disk, you may have to start the system from a bootable floppy. (Remember, a bootable floppy is one that has the DOS system files on it. If you haven't created a backup system disk, use the original DOS Install disk.) To boot from a floppy, just turn off the computer, insert the bootable floppy, and turn the computer on again. The DOS prompt should appear.

After you have the DOS prompt up and running, you need to install the DOS Startup disk, because that has the UNFORMAT file on it. Insert the Startup disk and type **unformat /partn** and press Enter at the prompt.

UNFORMAT then tells you to insert the disk containing the file PARTNSAV.FIL and enter the name of that disk drive. (This process assumes that you backed up your partition tables as part of your disaster recovery plan.)

MIRROR then rebuilds the partition table from the information on the floppy disk. After the process is complete, MIRROR asks you to place a bootable disk in drive A and press Enter to reboot your computer. Now you can use the UNFORMAT command to restore the FAT, the boot record, and the root directory.

Repairing Damaged Spreadsheet and Text Files

You may want to note that the Norton Utilities and PC Tools contain utilities designed especially to repair damaged dBASE files. The PC Tools and Norton Utilities programs are both called File Fix.

The Norton Utilities and PC Tools utilities also can recover damaged Lotus 1-2-3 files; in addition, the PC Tools utility can recover Lotus Symphony files.

Deciding Whether To Use the DOS RECOVER Command

The RECOVER command enables you to recover data from a file that either has bad sectors or is in a disk with a damaged directory. At the DOS prompt, you type **recover**; press the space bar; type the file's name, extension, and path if necessary; and press Enter.

 NOTE   According to Microsoft's DOS 5.0 manual, RECOVER, unlike other DOS commands, does not work with wild cards (* and ?). The word on the grapevine, however, is that you *can* use wild cards within the file name.

Microsoft recommends using the RECOVER command only as a last resort. Although you can use RECOVER on either a specific file or a drive, most people recommend that if you're going to try it at all, use it only on specific files. Do not attempt to use it on a drive because the command will turn the disk's contents into a garbled mess.

The Norton Utilities goes so far as to advocate that you remove RECOVER from your hard disk. The Norton Utilities data-recovery documentation even includes specific instructions designed to help you undo the mess created by using RECOVER on more than one file.

If you get into that kind of structural trouble on your disk, the best approach is probably to use a product with a good track record, such as Norton or PC Tools.

Summary

In this chapter, you have learned why deleted files don't disappear, what happens during a format, and messages that warn you of impending hard disk trouble.

You also have learned about ways to get out of trouble in the event of an accidental deletion or format. You have learned how to use DOS commands and various data-recovery utilities when DOS isn't enough to do the job.

What you learned in this chapter will help you understand why simply deleting a file isn't enough if you're concerned about confidentiality. To keep your data truly confidential, you need to remove the data, not simply delete DOS's record of it. The next chapter shares ways to keep your data truly secure.

Keeping Your Data Confidential

As the title of this chapter suggests, here you are going to learn about protecting your information from others. The range of protection you need varies depending on the apparent value of your data, the legal requirements for its safety, and quite often the integrity of the environment where the computer is kept.

In some parts of the world, you still never need to lock the door to your house. The same small number of places exist from a computer standpoint. Unfortunately, in the majority of cases, however, you have an element of risk.

The most basic method of protection is to lock your office door, or if you don't have an office, lock your computer. (Most of the PCs built in the last five years or so have had keyboard and system locks installed.) Beyond these physical means, you can use a number of methods to minimize the risk without having to go out and spend any money. Such methods involve using floppies and other removable media, taking care with passwords, and practicing some basic security procedures. You take a look at some of these techniques in this chapter.

One aspect to be aware of is that although a moderate amount of computer data "snooping" goes on, some of the reported hype is produced by the very data protection software publishers that want to sell you their latest anti-snooping or data-protection packages. Although computers are a soft target for would-be industrial spies, a significant amount of information still is leaked by word of mouth, electronic mail, and the contents of your wastepaper basket. But the threat is real in many cases, and numerous packages of varying cost can combat that threat. You learn about some of these programs in this chapter.

Examining Your Basic Security Options

In the following paragraphs, you examine some of the simplest and often the most effective methods of protecting data from unwanted access or meddling—assuming that you have security concerns that go beyond locking your office door.

Using Floppies

Keeping all your data on floppy disks and locking them up in a safe when not in use is one relatively foolproof way of protecting data. In fact this method is recommended in the more sensitive government research departments at Lawrence Livermore Laboratories in California. The major problem with this approach is that floppy disk access is slow, often five to ten times slower than a hard disk drive. In addition, the current highest 3 1/2-inch floppy disk capacity that is readily available is 1.44M, which may be too small for some large database files. The next proposed standard that is supported by MS DOS 5.0 is 2.88M, but this capacity is not generally available at the time of this writing because the media and drives are still relatively expensive.

Relying on backing up data to floppy disks and then erasing the original hard disk data is not a good idea. As you learned in Chapter 12, "Raiders of the Lost Data," erased data often can be recovered unless a data-wiping utility is used.

A final method of protection is to save all data on a floppy disk and keep the data with you. Your data certainly remains safe from prying eyes, and this approach has an interesting side effect in that you have created an off-site backup inadvertently. If your workplace burns to the ground, at least you still have the critical data with you on a floppy. But this method does have one flaw: if your home burns to the ground, so does your data. You can surmount this problem if you make two copies to keep in separate places, effectively doubling the risk of interception.

Fireproof safes are a good option for both locking up your disks and keeping them safe in the event of a fire. One important point to note is that you should store floppy disks only in a fireproof safe specifically designed for disks and not one designed for paper. General-purpose fireproof safes are designed to keep the heat level to just below the flash point of paper; floppy disks can survive only less than half of that temperature.

Using Removable Hard Disks

Removable hard drives are more expensive than floppies but have a much greater capacity and offer a higher performance than the lowly floppy. Although the storage capacity of a floppy disk is limited from 1.44M to as little as 360K on some older machines, removable hard drives run from 20M to about 100M.

The cost of the removable drive and a housing often cost 50 percent more than their fixed counterparts, but the removable portions of the drive are usually less expensive. Some removable hard drives such as the Plus Passport are self-contained modules that incorporate both the drive and some electronics. Others, such as the Bernoulli, offer a removable cartridge containing just the magnetic media and a case. Whatever you choose, the removable portion can be safely locked away from would-be snoopers.

You also should consider the stand-alone external drive. This drive usually is connected to the PC by a cable. By simply disconnecting the cable, you can remove the drive and place it somewhere secure. This kind of external drive tends to be lower in cost and offers a higher performance.

If you choose removable media, consider that because the media is fairly transportable, it also can be easily stolen. The ideal situation in which these types of drives should be used is in an area of constant vigilance or security. When you are not using the data, you should return the media for safe storage if your office cannot be secured.

Understanding Why Erasing and Deleting Files Isn't Enough

You may think that the obvious way to stop unauthorized people from accessing your data on a hard drive is to copy the data to a floppy disk, lock up that floppy, and delete the copy on the hard drive, right? Wrong! Remember that you learned in Chapter 12, "Raiders of the Lost Data," that when deleting a file, DOS only frees up the index to that disk space, indicating that the space is available to be used when new space is requested by another program.

Figure 13.1 reviews for you what happens when a file is deleted. In the normal, nondeleted file, the directory entry points to the starting cluster in the FAT (file allocation table). Each FAT entry corresponds to a piece of occupied disk space that contains the data for the file. A FAT entry usually points to another FAT entry that corresponds to the next piece of the file, or indicates that the entry is the last piece in the chain of clusters making up the file.

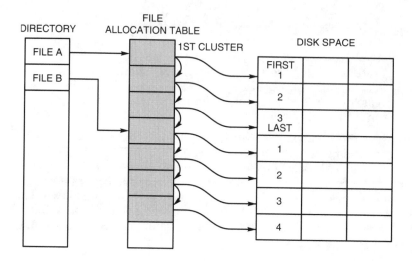

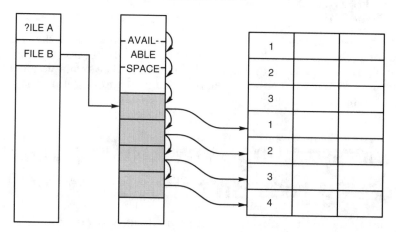

FIG. 13.1

Understanding what happens when a file is deleted.

When the file is deleted, the directory entry file name has its first letter changed to a question mark (?), and the FAT entries indicate that they are free. The data, however, is still intact in the disk space area. The FAT entries still contain the file's chain information until they are reused by another program. To undelete this file, all you need is a program to change the directory entry back by substituting the question mark with a regular character and reallocating the available FAT entries to that file. DOS 5.0 offers an undelete facility, which does just that with intact files.

Even several years after a file has been deleted and the space reused, recovering fragments of the file is still possible. To rebuild partial files, Norton Utilities UnErase offers a way to fish through the disk and extract useful pieces of ex-files and reconstruct them into something vaguely resembling the original. A skillful hacker might be able to recover enough to be able to understand the document, which raises a potential serious security problem.

In the next section, you learn how to remove permanently such deleted information from your disk.

Wiping Data from the Disk

Several programs enable you to wipe data from the disk so that the data is not recoverable. Two of the most prominent include Norton Utilities WipeInfo command and PC Tools Wipe.

Using Norton's WipeInfo

WipeInfo is a combined replacement in Versions 5.0 and 6.0 for the older Norton Utilities 4.5 versions of WipeDisk and WipeFile. WipeInfo permanently erases files and disk space by completely overwriting the deleted disk area or files. As described in the previous paragraphs, a deleted file is not deleted because the data still can be found. If you have high security risk information and need to erase it permanently, you need to write physically over the area where the file resided. This process is called *wiping*. If you have to replace a hard drive, you may want to wipe the entire drive.

To make matters a little more complicated, getting at the data on the drive may still be possible after a single wipe. Traces of the old data may remain "underneath" the wiping process (see fig. 13.2).

This problem normally occurs because the drive heads don't always line up precisely. In this situation, someone with sophisticated equipment could read the small "missed" band of data after the wiping process had been performed. The way to combat this problem is to perform multiple wipes. The U.S. Department of Defense has developed such a multiple-wiping standard for wiping sensitive material from disks. This standard is referred to as DOD 5220.22M.

You can use WipeInfo on the entire drive, on selected files or their "slack areas," or just on unused areas of the disk. You have quite a bit of control over this process in that you can select the value of the characters that overwrite the "wiped" areas or files and the number of times the file or disk should be wiped.

DISK SURFACE BEFORE WIPE

DATA 1	DATA 2	DATA 3	DATA 4

FIG. 13.2

Leaving traces of data after wiping the disk.

AFTER WIPE

WIPED	WIPED	WIPED	WIPED
DATA 1	DATA 2	DATA 3	DATA 4

 READ/WRITE DISK HEAD

You can select a file or set of files by using wild cards. If you want to select all files in the subdirectory, for example, you use the *.* specification. You also can select entire subdirectory trees by using the Include Subdirs option, which wipes files under each subdirectory. And you even can wipe hidden and read-only files.

The Wiping Method option enables you to select what you want to do to a file. Delete Files is the same as a plain old DOS delete, except of course you can include subdirectories. The Wipe Unused File Slack Only option simply wipes the area that is reserved for the file but has no data on it.

After you have selected files and a wiping method, you can opt to confirm a wipe on every file or simply let every one get wiped without interruption. Even with the wipe confirmation turned on, you can change the action on the rest of the file wipes by selecting the Auto option, which proceeds to wipe all the remaining files in your selection set. An emergency stop button enables you to cancel any remaining wipes.

Wiping a drive is useful if you pass your computer to someone else to whom you do not want to give access to your data or programs. Or perhaps you need to send a computer back to the leaseholder after your lease has expired. WipeInfo offers a selection screen for an entire drive. Each drive is listed, and you can select whether to wipe the entire drive or merely any unused space. The unused space can be comprised of leftover areas of deleted files or residual data areas left over from the last time the drive was formatted.

Figure 13.3 shows the configuration screen for WipeInfo. On this screen, you set up the level of data obliteration required on either a file or a drive. If you select Fast Wipe, a single-pass wipe is performed, using a single character (of value 0 to 255). This method is usually enough to foil most would-be data spies. You can perform the wipe several times to ensure complete erasure—even though anyone needing to get to the original data after even a single wipe would need access to some sophisticated and expensive equipment. The Government Wipe option is far more sophisticated and is derived from a scientific study on how data is retained magnetically on a disk and how best to scramble the recording particles. The likelihood of anyone recovering data after a Government Wipe operation is zero, or as near to zero as anyone can measurably get.

As with most of the Norton Utilities, you can execute WipeInfo from the DOS command prompt or from within a batch file.

NOTE Norton Utilities 6.0 offers the capability to password-protect access to some or all of its utilities. In some situations, leaving Norton Utilities unprotected in an unsecured environment is like leaving a loaded weapon lying around. Some unscrupulous person might use it against you.

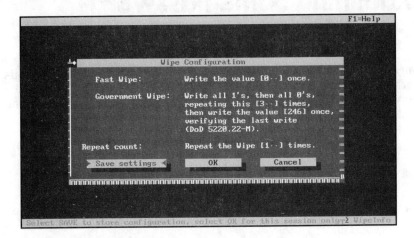

FIG. 13.3

The WipeInfo configuration screen.

Using PC Tools Wipe

Like the Norton Utilities WipeInfo command, PC Tools Wipe protects confidentiality by completely destroying traces of data for both existing and deleted files. After a file has been wiped, it cannot be recovered.

The list of features for PC Tools Wipe is nearly identical to that for the WipeInfo utility. The same Department of Defense standards of data destruction are followed. The file options in PC Tools Wipe are quite extensive. You can confirm each file wipe; include subdirectories, hidden files, and read-only files; and wipe only modified files, only unmodified files, or both. Instead of wiping files, you can choose to clear only unused file space or just to delete files. You even can specify dates and times before or after which files should be wiped.

After completing a series of wipes, PC Tools Wipe produces a summary screen to confirm any action taken.

As with most PC Tools utilities, you can use Wipe from the DOS command line and thereby also in batch files. The following command, for example, wipes an entire floppy disk in drive A:

WIPE A: /DISK

All the options available in the File Options screen also can be set at the DOS command prompt or in a batch file.

Examining Some Password Dos and Don'ts

Many software packages offer security options to protect against unauthorized use, usually with the help of a password. The most likely place you will encounter a password is when you're using an external communications service such as CompuServe, MCI Mail, or Dow Jones.

You need to follow some basic rules when selecting and using a password. Here are some of the more common principles:

- Never write a password down.

- Avoid at all costs telling someone your password.

- If you do, change the password immediately.

- Change your password regularly—monthly, for example.

- Do not use the same password on many services and packages.

- Do not use obvious passwords such as

    Your name
    Your telephone number
    Your wife's name—in fact, the name of anyone in the family,
    The name of anyone with whom you are associated
    Your street address
    Your company name
    Your favorite football team
    Your favorite color
    Anything else that someone who knows you could figure out

■ Do not use the same password more than once, just changing the month number (martin1, martin2, and so on).

■ Avoid putting passwords into automatic logon macros and scripts.

■ Try to use passwords of at least four characters, preferably more.

■ If you are provided with a default password, change it immediately.

■ If you feel that your password has been compromised, change it immediately.

Although you may think this list is lengthy, some companies and government agencies apply even stricter guidelines than these. Some of the less obvious rules are worth expanding upon. Why, for example, would you not use the same password on several systems? The answer is simple. A "security" person on one system can get hold of your password and then have access to your other systems. What's wrong with telling your password to someone you trust? The answer is that it's *your* password, and even a close friend might not protect your interests as closely as you do, knowingly or not. He or she might write the password down or mention it inadvertently within earshot of an unscrupulous person.

Exploring Some Data-Protection Programs

Many of the popular utility programs on the market today provide data-protection capabilities. In the following sections, you learn about such features included in PC Tools, Norton Utilities, and Fifth Generation Systems. You also learn about another powerful disk-protection program called Watchdog.

Using Security Options in PC Tools

PC Tools 7.1 offers a couple of security options in addition to Wipe: PC Secure and Data Monitor. As with the Wipe utilities, you can set the encryption methods selectively to U.S. government standards such as DES. If you use PC Tools outside the U.S. and require protection, a different encryption algorithm is available. In the following paragraphs, you learn the ins and outs of PC Secure and Data Monitor.

Using PC Secure

PC Secure keeps any selected files or programs secure by encrypting and compressing them. You can achieve further levels of security by encrypting the file or files keyed to a particular password. If you have a substantial security requirement, selecting an effective password is important to provide maximum levels of protection.

You can encrypt and decrypt files easily from the PC Secure file selection screen. The first time you start up PC Secure, you are asked for a master password. You *must* remember this password, also referred to as a key. Individual files may be encrypted with different passwords, and if you forget any of them, you can use your master password to decrypt those files.

Other options enable you to select the level of encryption. Full DES is the most secure, followed by Quick Encryption, which uses a shortened form of DES, and finally Compression. You can use PC Secure's password option with any of these methods. You also can use one password to encrypt all files, hide or make the encrypted files read-only, and delete the original, unencrypted files.

You can use the program with the same functionality from the command line. This capability enables you to use PC Secure from within a batch file. The following command typed at the DOS prompt or placed in a batch file, for example, encrypts all TXT files in the current directory by using the Quick Encryption method and applying the key (password) QUETEST:

    PCSECURE /Q /KQUETEST *.TXT

Many command-line switches (options) are available with PCSECURE. Each switch must be preceded by a slash (/) or hyphen (-) character. You can place switches individually, as in the following examples:

    PCSECURE /Q /P /S *.DOC
    PCSECURE -Q -P -S *.DOC

Or you can place the switches in a string with one switch indicator, as in these examples:

    PCSECURE /QPS *.DOC
    PCSECURE -QPS *.DOC

Table 13.1 gives you a list of the available control switches for PCSECURE.

Table 13.1 Using Switches with PCSECURE

Switch (/ or -)	Effect
/K*nnnnn*	Tells PCSECURE that *nnnnn* is your password key and that anything else is assumed to be a file specification, with the exception of other switches.
/C	Turns off compression during encryption (default is on).
/G	Sets the security level to the U.S. government (DOD) standards.
/M	Enables multiple encryption. You can, for example, use this switch to require two people's password keys to access a file. Otherwise, you can encrypt a file only once.
/S	Turns on silent mode, which suppresses all messages other than errors during encryption/decryption.
/? or /H	Gives command-line help for PCSECURE switches.
/VIDEO	Gives help on the mouse and video parameters.
/D	Decrypts specified files that are listed after the switch.
/F	Performs full DES encryption on specified files. Available only in U.S. versions.
/Q	Performs a quick encryption on specified files. Available only in U.S. versions.
/E	Encrypts the specified files by using a non-DES method. Available only in international versions.
/P	Forces a prompt for a password key.

Using Data Monitor

Data Monitor is a memory-resident utility that includes a set of options to prevent data loss and protect data from illegal access or modification. Some of the main features offered by Data Monitor include a Screen Blanker, which shuts off the display after a specified amount of inactivity. A user-defined hot-key selection can be used to invoke the blank screen immediately. In addition, you can add a password for full protection. You then have to type the correct password to restart the application.

Data Monitor also includes a Directory Lock utility that encrypts files in a selected directory so that they cannot be read by anyone who doesn't know the password. In order for locked directories to be accessed, the Directory Lock utility must be loaded. When you attempt to access a locked directory, you are prompted for a password. After you have entered the correct password, you have full access to the files.

Another important piece of Data Monitor is the Write Protection utility, which prevents selected files from being deleted or overwritten. You can specify certain file types, such as EXE or COM files, as write protected. You even can protect the entire drive, including both hard and floppy disks. If an attempt is made to violate the write protection, a dialog box appears, asking whether you want to continue the operation, cancel it, or disable the write protection until further notice.

Using Security Options in Norton Utilities

The Norton Utilities include Disk Monitor, which features disk-protection capabilities, and Diskreet, which protects your file contents. In the following sections, you learn a little more about these helpful utilities.

Using Disk Monitor

Disk Monitor offers three features: Disk Protect, Disk Park, and Disk Light. Disk Monitor is similar in function to the Data Monitor utility in PC Tools except that the screen-blanking facility is found in another Norton utility: Diskreet. Although the primary focus in this chapter is on Disk Protect, the Disk Park and Disk Light options are covered briefly also.

The Disk Park option moves the drive heads to a "safe" landing zone on the disk. Most modern drives park themselves automatically when powered-down. In most cases, parking a self-parking drive is safe, but if you know for sure that your drive parks itself, you should let the drive do it and not use any parking programs.

The Disk Light option flashes the drive letter in the top right corner of the screen whenever that drive is accessed. This feature is more useful for network drives or if you have a drive not connected to a drive light.

Disk Protect provides protection against any selected writes to your drives. You can protect system areas, files, and even entire disks from being written to. This protection guards against deletions, formatting, overwrites, and writes to specific areas or files on the disk. As a side effect, this feature also protects against many virus attacks, which often attach themselves to EXE and COM files.

When protecting files, Disk Protect can selectively prevent writes on groups of files including EXE, COM, OVL, BIN, and SYS files. In addition, you can specify exceptions to these file types by adding your extensions to the list. You also can use wild cards. The extension WK*, for example, protects all Lotus and Quattro spreadsheets from being overwritten without your permission. After you have configured Disk Protect to cover a series of files and drives, you can turn on the protection from the DOS command line by typing this command:

DISKMON /PROTECT+

You can put this command in a batch file—perhaps your AUTOEXEC.BAT to run the command at start-up. The one area in which Disk Protect cannot put up a dialog box is in a graphical environment. The protection of files still works, but if you are working in a graphics environment when you attempt to write to a protected file, you don't see a screen telling you so. Instead, the computer just beeps at you. If you know that working on the file is acceptable (even though you cannot see the file name), you can press D to disable disk protection and let writes occur.

You may need to turn off Disk Protect before running a particular program if you know that the program is going to change (legitimately) a protected file. To turn off protection, simply type the following command at the DOS command line and press Enter:

DISKMON /PROTECT-

On the selection screen for Disk Protect, the file types are listed for write protection; the exceptions list (the blank list on the right side of the screen) contains a list of any particular files you may want to waive from protection. If you use a file transfer product such as LapLink 3.0, for example, which modifies the LL3.EXE file whenever any options are changed, you may want to except LL3.EXE from write protection. Another popular exception is CONFIG.SYS, because it is the only SYS file that is not a device driver and is changed frequently.

Using Diskreet

Diskreet protects files so that they cannot be accessed without the correct password. To accomplish this feat, Diskreet uses encryption based on the password you select. This function is fairly similar to that of the PC Secure utility described earlier in this chapter.

Unlike PC Secure, Diskreet offers a facility to create a "virtual drive" by creating a hidden protected file and encrypting any data going to it. This protected file appears to DOS as another drive and is called an NDisk. When Diskreet is loaded as a TSR, it lies to DOS, telling DOS that it has one or more extra drives. Any files written to that "disk" are encrypted, using a password. The first attempt to access the drive requires the correct password to be entered. All subsequent accesses then are just like accessing any drive, but under the covers Diskreet is encrypting and decrypting files going to and coming from the NDisk. With another Diskreet option, you can enable NDisks at boot time or when referenced. Again, the correct password is required.

As with most of these utilities, you can select the encryption methods with Diskreet. Also, as an NDisk grows, shrinks, or is deleted, Diskreet can wipe any surplus space formerly used by the NDisk.

NDisks can be closed by timing out, which means that if you walk away from your system, the NDisks close themselves after a period of inactivity. They then require a password to be activated again. You also can set up a hot-key selection to close all NDisks. One other useful option is the ability to provide an audit trail of NDisk activity.

You may not want to create an NDisk to encrypt a file. Instead, you can use the File Selection menu. You then have several choices for encrypting selected files, such as hiding the encrypted files, deleting the originals, or wiping the originals. You can use an individual password on each file or can elect to use a global password for all files.

Overall, Norton Utilities 6.0 and PC Tools 7.1 offer an almost identical set of data-protection methods. One way to decide which is best for you is to compare how your needs stack up against the features outlined in this chapter. The next couple of utilities, DiskLock and Watchdog, are aimed purely at disk and data protection.

Using Fifth Generation Systems' DiskLock

DiskLock offers a level of security a step higher than that offered by PC Tools and Norton Utilities. Two stages of protection are offered. The first is the *lock*, which prohibits unauthorized access to your hard drive even when the system is booted from a floppy drive. Lock requires that the correct password be entered to access the hard drive.

For extra protection, you can *encrypt* some or all of the data on the drive. Two password levels are allowed, a primary and a secondary. The secondary access is useful, for example, if you share your computer with another person to whom you want to give access only to the unencrypted areas of the disk. The primary password gives you access to the encrypted areas of the disk as well as the DiskLock Configuration menu. DiskLock also creates a log of any attempts to enter the wrong password.

An unattended lock is provided to lock the system after a period of inactivity. And you can use a user-defined hot-key combination to lock your system instantly. This feature is ideal for anyone who frequently has to leave while the computer is still running and doesn't want others to access it.

DiskLock protects access to the drive by making it appear to the DOS FDISK command as a non-DOS disk and adds a loader to the bootable part of the hard disk itself. Thus, even if someone were to boot from a floppy, the DiskLocked drive would not be accessible. Because of the way DiskLock installs itself, backing up your drive before installation is vitally important. If the installation is interrupted by a power outage or other disruption, your hard drive may very well be rendered unreadable by any utility and require reformatting.

The only other disastrous situation is if you forget your primary password. You always can reset the secondary password if you forget the first one. Review the section on passwords earlier in this chapter for more guidance in choosing the right password for you.

Figure 13.4 shows the DiskLock Configuration menu with options to encrypt or lock files and directories, lock logical drives, set the auto lock delay time, and configure an instant system lock hot key.

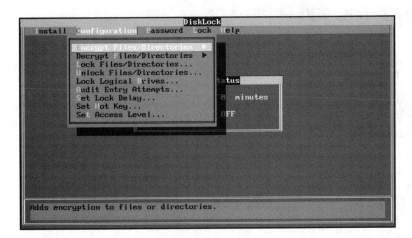

FIG. 13.4

The DiskLock
Configuration menu.

Using Watchdog

Watchdog is a sophisticated data security system for the PC that from a protection standpoint leaves no stone unturned. This product was the first PC-based security program to be endorsed by the National Computer Center of the U.S. Department of Defense.

Watchdog's menu system is an added organizational tool bonus. With the menu system, you can see which directories are secure and have easier access to them—if you are an authorized user. The administrator can use the menu system to specify access restrictions and user permissions.

Watchdog offers one of the most complete security systems available in the PC marketplace. Along with the hardware component, Watchdog Armor, Watchdog makes illegal access to the PC and its data a virtual impossibility. Watchdog products are available for multiple computer types from the PC to an IBM mainframe.

The features in Watchdog are extensive. The following paragraphs give you a summary of the scope of this system.

Restricting and Controlling Access

To monitor and prevent unauthorized access to your system, you can set it up so that an ID and password are requested. You even can modify or increase the level of protection by requiring long passwords. You also can set passwords to expire after a specified period.

Protecting Data and Files

You can control individual subdirectory access by restriction based on user ID. File access privileges can be controlled for each ID within a subdirectory. You also can restrict permissions for Execute, Read, Write, Create, and Delete based on ID. DES data encryption is available as an additional deterrent and is completely transparent to an authorized user.

Protecting Resources

With Watchdog, you even can protect the use of attached devices and system resources. Your options include requiring permission to use the DOS operating system commands, the floppy drives, and printer and communication ports.

Protecting against Boots and Formats

Accidental formatting of the hard disk is protected as is any attempt to thwart the system by interrupting the boot process. Watchdog Armor is an optional board that you can use with the Watchdog software to control system booting from a floppy disk. Armor requires that you boot from the hard drive only under the watchful eye of the Watchdog software. Armor also has a "tamper-proof" clock to ensure that time and date stamps are authentic. This protection is needed to ensure that aging processes such as password expiration are not fooled by the changing of the system or the CMOS clock. DES is provided at the hardware level in ROM on the board. This feature totally removes the possibility of tampering, at least from a software standard.

Protecting Old Memory and Files

Often some or all of a previous user's program is still in system memory when the next user comes along. Watchdog modifies the memory after use, making it unreadable by another user. You can have deleted files filled with zeros to ensure that they cannot be unerased.

Protecting against Viruses

Watchdog provides a series of protection systems similar in nature to the products outlined in Chapter 14, "Immunizing Your PC against Viruses." Alteration of any DOS or system file, including the hidden files and boot record, is restricted. AUTOEXEC.BAT and CONFIG.SYS files also are given a high degree of protection.

Keeping an Audit Trail

All transactions performed on the PC are recorded, including general use, system administration, and any attempts to violate system security. The audit trail lists the user ID, project ID (if any), subdirectory, program executed, date, and time. If you are the system administrator, you may want to add comments and such to the reports. You can modify and access them easily because they are in a standard dBASE database format.

Using Systems with Built-in Protection

Many recent offerings from PC manufacturers support the use of a password prior to the boot process. The password is often in an encrypted state and is stored in the battery-backed memory area referred to as CMOS. The system does not start until you type the correct password.

These systems are difficult to defeat, but keep in mind that forgetting the password can mean disaster. The usual method of getting around the password requires unlocking the system case and disconnecting the battery for up to 15 minutes or so to let the CMOS lose its information. Unfortunately, this method also causes you to lose a great deal of information, including the date, time, memory size, and hard disk configuration.

In the following paragraphs you learn about several PC systems that offer built-in security measures.

Examining Compaq's Security Features

One of the most comprehensive power-on protection systems has been provided by Compaq. Compaq Computer Corp's Deskpro 286N and 386N microcomputers were some of the first workstations to provide comprehensive built-in security features. This feature makes them ideal for areas requiring a variable degree of protection such as in a network or an open campus environment. Compaq offers both software- and hardware-controlled security features enabling users to make a choice as to the level of protection required. The most obvious security option on any computer is the case lock, which usually locks the keyboard as well. This feature prevents anyone from removing, adding, or exchanging expansion boards.

Compaq implemented several levels of protection. One powerful security feature provides the ability to disable the ROM-resident SETUP utility so that users cannot modify the system SETUP. This protection works with or without the Compaq installation and configuration disk. To protect the system further, you can disable floppy disk writes. Data then cannot be removed from the computer to a floppy, preventing anyone from stealing sensitive data. In addition, an option is available that disables the ability to boot from a floppy. This feature effectively foils the popular method for defeating a hard disk protection system.

Compaq did not use a keyboard lock with the case lock. Instead, you may want to implement another option, the keyboard password, to ensure that the integrity of the system remains intact. To set the keyboard password, you can use up to seven characters and select something called a Quicklock key sequence. The Quicklock sequence enables you to lock the keyboard in the middle of an application. Any typing on the keyboard does not affect the system until the user enters the correct password. Typically the Quicklock sequence starts with Alt-Ctrl and the letter of your choice.

A power-on password protection system also is provided. A password can be required any time the system is started up and the POST (Power On Self Test) utility is executed but before any disks have been read. You can select this option by using a switch on the motherboard. Without the correct password, a user cannot even access the ROM-resident SETUP or boot the system from the setup and configuration disk. This password is stored in the CMOS area, which is backed up by battery.

Because the computer is totally unusable if the password is not entered, Compaq gives you the ability to disable this feature in an emergency. If you forget the password, you can unlock the case and disable the power-on password check. If you want to enable it again, you need to go into SETUP to do so.

Examining AST Research's Security Options

AST Research Inc. offers a range of computers called the Bravo family, which includes i386 and i486 systems. The type of protection is a chassis lock and a POST/CMOS lock password system similar to that of the Compaq. In AST's case, if you forget your password, you have to unlock the case. Then you can reset it by disconnecting the CMOS battery from the system board.

Examining IBM's Security Options

Starting with the IBM PS/2 series, a CMOS battery-backed password-protection feature was added to all mainstream IBM desktop PCs and above. This feature is basically a POST-type protection similar to Compaq's and can be reset if you remove the CMOS backup battery and wait 15 minutes.

Exploring Other Hardware Options

Several hardware systems are available to improve security on your system. One particularly interesting offering is from Alarmcard in Bellevue, Washington. This product is a card-based security device that at first sounds more like a car intruder alarm because it includes motion sensors. When these sensors are triggered, the PC locks up, and an alarm is sounded. A password is required to restart the system. The password is user-defined and is stored in battery-backed memory.

One simple system to prevent anyone from booting your system from the floppy drive is the LamaLock Security System from Lama Systems, Inc. of Austin, Texas. This deterrent simply provides a floppy drive lock for drive A. The lock works on 5 1/4-inch and 3 1/2-inch disk formats and on either a PC or Mac with or without the floppy disk in the drive. The basic intent of this device is to prevent floppy disk loss and unauthorized floppy insertion. In addition to the physical lock package, the program also includes something referred to as Authorized Personnel Only software, which provides simple password security during the boot-up process and while the system is in use.

Zenith/Bull has produced a secure SupersPort laptop that uses an intelligent card reader to authorize access to the system. The laptop was developed to conform to Canadian government security standards. The modified SupersPort laptop also offers an encryption device. Each user of the system has an individual smart card and has to run that card through the reader, which then allocates system resources depending on the user's rights and privileges.

Thunderbyte from Trend Micro Devices Inc. is a small PC card that attaches between the hard disk controller and drive by cables. When in place, Thunderbyte monitors all writes to the disk. When an anomaly is detected, such as a program messing with DOS interrupts or writing to the disk using direct calls to the BIOS, an alert is provided for the user. This method of protection is an excellent deterrent to virus attacks. A password feature also is included. Passwords are stored on the Thunderbyte card itself. This design effectively bars even attempts to start the system from a bootable floppy disk in drive A. The only way that you can defeat this system is by physically removing the card and correctly replacing the drive cables.

One interesting utility is aimed at protecting access to laptops. LapGuard is offered by a company called Personal Computer Card of Lakeland, Florida. What LapGuard does is require the user to insert a floppy KeyDisk and then enter an access code number before being allowed to boot the portable. The most intriguing aspect of this product is that it greets unauthorized users with a barking sound. For emergencies, LapGuard does include an emergency access disk in case the KeyDisk is lost or the access code is forgotten. No doubt this system also could protect standard desktop computers.

Summary

In this chapter, you have learned about many ways to protect your system against unauthorized access. By far, the most reliable method is still an effective physical lock, but in a modern office environment this protection is not always possible. In some instances, a significant degree of precaution is mandated by government or company regulations.

You have looked at both PC Tools and Norton Utilities from the file/disk protection/encryption standpoint and also have examined two of the more protective and bomb-proofing of the disk locking utilities, DiskLock and Watchdog. With the addition of cards or other internal/external hardware, the system becomes even more secure.

The bottom line to protection revolves around your particular need to secure your data from others. Sometimes the effort required to protect the system simply doesn't warrant itself in marginally insecure areas. Often security threat paranoia can spread through an office like wildfire, and you end up spending considerable time, money, and effort protecting a system. If the threat is real and the potential loss great enough, however, you have plenty of ways to achieve an (almost) totally secure PC environment.

In the next chapter, you learn about another way to protect your data—preventing virus attacks.

Immunizing Your PC against Viruses

I n earlier chapters, you looked at ways to avoid the *accidental* loss of
data on your hard disk. In this chapter, you look at the kinds of programs that make *deliberate* attempts to destroy your data. This phenomenon mostly falls into the category of computer viruses. You also take a
look at some preventive measures as well as some commercial programs
that can help you clean up an infected system. Viruses have become a
real threat to the integrity of your data and have provided a ready market for the plethora of programs ready to do battle with these invaders
of your system.

Examining Threats to Your System

Viruses are only one way to get a destructive program covertly into your
system. Several general categories of programs with malicious intent
exist, some of which are much simpler yet no less deadly than viruses.
These categories usually are referred to as Trojan horses, bombs, and
worms.

Trojan horse is a generic term describing a malicious program purposely
hidden inside a seemingly harmless larger program. Trojan horses tend
to do things you don't expect them to do. The term comes from a his-
toric battle where the long besieged city of Troy was offered a large
wooden horse as a gift. Unknown to the defenders of Troy, the horse
contained soldiers whose orders were to open the gates under cover of

darkness. Unwittingly, the Trojans accepted the gift in good faith, and the rest is history. Trojan horses have been around ever since. During the second world war, Q Ships appeared to be unarmed merchant ships to enemy submarines. To preserve precious torpedoes, a submarine would surface in order to sink a seemingly unarmed merchant with deck guns. To the sub crew's surprise, panels fell away from the Q Ship to reveal heavy armaments, and the submarine quickly became the victim.

A Trojan horse of some sort is usually the carrier of a virus. Just as in the original Trojan horse, the carrier is an offering that you definitely want to try out and run on your computer. In most cases, the virus "hitches a ride" on an otherwise normal program.

Worms, which have been found on computer systems since the early 1960s, are programs that often can duplicate themselves but don't infect other programs. Some worms use a great deal of system resources to clog up your hard disk space or memory gradually. By their nature, worms often are introduced through exploiting bugs or "trap-door" features in a program. Worms are most frequently found on networks.

Bombs are a less subtle type of worm but tend to do their damage more instantaneously. A bomb might expand to use all memory or might disable a disk drive by creating a huge file or marking every unused sector as bad. Memory bombs usually happen only when you execute the bomb program. They don't attach themselves or reproduce the way viruses do. ANSI bombs are special character sequences that affect your system only if you have the ANSI device driver loaded from your CONFIG.SYS. Typically, the ANSI bomb affects the screen or the keyboard.

Bombs and worms were popular destructive pranks during the early days of PCs and are rarely encountered now. Of all the potential threats to your system, the virus is still the most prolific and dangerous.

What Is a Virus?

A virus is a program just like any other, but unlike most, its sole purpose in life is to infect other programs, usually to affect performance or function or simply just to get itself noticed. You even may encounter "do-nothing" viruses, many of which were intended only as testing utilities for anti-virus programs. As their name suggests, this variety of virus is somewhat benign.

A virus attempts to lodge itself within a host program and infect other executable programs (usually COM and EXE files). An increasing number of viruses are turning up in device drivers, such as ANSI.SYS, or even in Microsoft Windows applications.

Viruses tend to come with creative names. You may even have heard of some of the more infamous ones, such as the Pakistani Brain, Hundred Years, Stoned, Dark Avenger, or Jerusalem B (also known as Friday the 13th). The Jerusalem B virus waits until the system clock/calendar indicates that the date is a Friday the 13th and then starts to delete program files without warning.

Understanding How Viruses Manifest and Spread

Three basic types of viruses can infect your system. These come under the general headings of boot infectors, program infectors, and cloaked infectors.

Looking at Boot Infectors

Boot infectors inhabit the areas used by your PC when you boot it up either by turning it on (cold boot) or by pressing Ctrl-Alt-Del (warm boot). As you may remember from Chapter 3, "Understanding How DOS Works with Your Hard Disk," these bootable areas are called the *boot sector* or *partition table*.

To understand how these viruses manifest themselves, consider what happens when you boot up your system. Your computer first checks its memory and other hardware and then decides from where it will load an operating system (usually DOS). The system first looks at drive A and, if a disk isn't found there, then tries the hard disk. Figure 14.1 shows how a virus "inserts" itself into the chain of programs that gets executed at boot time.

The first area the system finds on a hard disk is the partition table sector, which has double duty. It serves as a small program to point to a boot sector and also tells how many logical drives are defined and how big they are. (Floppy disks have only one partition and therefore don't have the partition table, but they do have a boot sector, which your computer accesses to start itself up.) The partition table program runs the boot program, which resides on the first part of logical (or real) drive C.

Boot area viruses can turn up in the partition table of a hard disk or in a boot sector of a hard or floppy disk. A virus usually achieves this feat by substituting itself for either of these programs and moving a copy of the original boot program somewhere else so that it still can be accessed. Because this method infects programs that are not part of DOS, you cannot remove such viruses by deleting or replacing files. A good tip here is to keep a bootable disk with a write-protect tab on it handy for this kind of emergency.

Looking at Program Infectors

Executable programs (COM or EXE) are the most likely targets for *program infectors*. More recently, however, overlay files (OVL), device drivers (SYS), and even Windows drivers (DRV) have become virus targets. The crudest program infectors simply replace a piece of the program or driver with the infector's own code, irreparably damaging the original program. More subtle viruses add their code to the program or driver without interfering in the normal operation, but they do interfere with your system in other, usually much more annoying ways.

The first order of business for these viruses, after being loaded into memory, frequently is to examine the hard or floppy disk in order to infect other noninfected programs, overlays, or drivers. In this situation, your hard disk drive light might come on for no apparent reason. Figure 14.2 is a simplified illustration of how a program infector might establish and reproduce itself.

You often can remove these kinds of viruses by replacing or deleting the infected programs. One simple way to tell whether a program has become infected is if it mysteriously grows in size. Of course, this change is difficult to notice unless you keep a copy of all the directory listings from the uninfected state and compare file sizes when you suspect a virus. And this method is not always foolproof because some viruses affect the DIR command itself and lie about the file sizes! (You learn more about those kinds of viruses in the next section.) Commercially available utilities provide methods to check for file tampering by viruses or other covert means. You learn about these utilities later in this chapter, in "Using Virus Protection and Recovery Utilities."

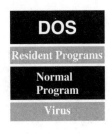
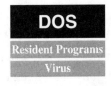
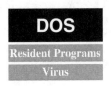

FIG. 14.2

Looking at a program virus's infection cycle.

Looking at Cloaked Infectors

Cloaked infectors also are known as *stealth* viruses and are a special type that actively seek to conceal and defend themselves against detection. They use tricks like encryption (see Chapter 13), relocation, self-modification, and replacing or interfering with DOS commands, such as DIR, CHKDSK, and DOS 5.0's MEM.

The Hundred Years virus, for example, infects any COM and EXE files, including COMMAND.COM, increasing each file's size by 4K and adding 100 years to the date field of infected files (a normal DIR displays only the last two digits of the year). When executed, this virus loads itself into memory and uses up 6K, yet the DOS MEM command displays 6K more than is available. In addition, a DIR of any infected file shows the original file size and not the larger infected size. To make things even worse, the virus encrypts itself so that it doesn't look like a program. It even attaches itself to some data files. Although this action does not spread the virus, it still takes up 4K of disk space per file, which is annoying. Luckily, all the virus-detection programs described in this chapter are capable of combatting this virus.

NOTE In Chapter 7, "Using Batch Files and Macros," you learn about using the ATTRIB DOS command to create read-only (R/O) files. One important thing to note is that read-only files are not safe from all but the simplest of virus programs. Any DOS command such as ATTRIB can be executed by a virus program and remove any protection placed on the file.

A popular misconception is that viruses can infect files on write-protected disks. This thought directly stems from the fact that viruses can affect files in which the ATTRIB is set to read-only. Where the protection afforded by the R/O ATTRIB is controlled by software, the R/O arrangement for a floppy disk is physical. When you use a write-protect tab, a floppy drive is electrically unable to write data to the protected disk. The alteration of the electrical properties of the floppy drive by a piece of software is thus physically impossible.

Preparing a Virus Avoidance Checklist

As more types of media, such as removable hard drives, CD ROM, and optical drives and access to networks and widespread communications improve, the possibility of your PC contracting a virus is increased greatly. To help combat these possible threats, simply applying common sense and some of the following practices may significantly reduce that possibility. At the very least, if a virus attack occurs, you will be able to recover easily.

Try to load software from freshly shrink-wrapped packages. This precaution may not always be foolproof because most retailers accept returned software that may have come in contact with a nonprotected PC. Some malicious individual may deliberately introduce a virus before returning a software package. Many retailers rewrap returned packages and put them out on the shelf without doing any sort of virus check first. So even with shrink-wrapped software, use a virus checker if you have one.

Avoid loading pirated copies of software or programs from unknown sources or allowing others to install applications on your PC without super-vision. Pirated software tends to be handed around frequently with little checking and has a greater chance of collecting viruses along the way.

Make periodic backups of all your files. Backing up at least your data more frequently is one of the best insurance policies against all threats, from viruses to physical abuse of the PC. Chapter 10, "Understanding the

Importance of Backing Up," discusses the importance of making backups and gives you several alternative methods in detail.

Be careful with all programs downloaded from public bulletin board systems (BBSs). Even with some popular BBSs, viruses do slip through the net, especially in new or modified BBSs. Try to stick to using boards that at least declare some sort of virus testing of all files before they are posted for general consumption.

A frequent misconception is that your computer can get a virus if you call an infected BBS. This fear is simply not true because you access the BBS by using a modem and some sort of communication package. The BBS at the other end of the modem cannot write information on your disks because you, the operator, control the file transfer that's handled by the communications software you use. *If you suspect that a BBS you access is infected, however, be extremely wary of any software you download from it.* You may want to run the programs through a virus detector, which is described later in this chapter. Usually, the files you download are in a packed (ZIPped) format, and you have to perform one more step (UNZIPping) before the files can be executed, which is where a potential infection can occur.

Another bulletin board caution is to not be too enthusiastic about getting the latest piece of uploaded software. Unless you absolutely cannot wait, letting newly uploaded files "mature" on a BBS for a few weeks before you download them is a good idea. Keep your eyes on the BBS message area to see whether any problems occur with those files. If no reported problems appear in the first few weeks, go ahead and download the program, and if you have a virus checker, use it.

Checking for Viruses

The following paragraphs give you some general questions that you can use to determine whether you have a virus. Encountering an unusual situation on your system and immediately declaring, "oh, I must have a virus" is all too easy. Before you go out and spend time and money on anti-virus solutions, you might want to consider that your problem can be caused by one of several other situations.

Watching for the Signs

In Chapter 11, "Preventing Trouble," you learn some common causes for disk problems, which often are applicable to both floppy and hard drives. Some of these symptoms also can be caused by a computer virus. The following are some circumstances that might lead you to suspect the presence of a virus:

- Is a program taking longer to load or run?

- Is disk access taking longer than normal?

- Does your drive light come on unexpectedly?

- Has the computer seriously malfunctioned or frozen up, leaving you hanging with a dead disk?

- Have you noticed any unexplained changes in your files on disk?

- Have files that you did not delete suddenly disappeared?

- Have files that you do not recognize suddenly appeared— especially ones with odd file names?

- Did anything odd appear on your screen (such as advertisements, profanity, slogans, or warnings)?

- Does what appears on your screen look odd or appear in different colors, in flashing or reverse video, or with missing characters?

- Did any strange sounds, or even recognizable tunes, come from the speaker unexpectedly?

- Does what you type at the keyboard get misrepresented on-screen?

- Did any keyboard lights activate for no apparent reason?

- Did you notice whether available computer memory decreased or increased after you ran a nonresident program?

- Have you noticed a mysterious change in size for any of your files?

To track down the potential source of the infection, list any and all new disks and applications that have been introduced to your system recently. These new applications should include all commercial software and especially software obtained from bulletin board systems. If you have gathered all this information and still are not sure of the source of a problem, read on to help you decide whether you really have a virus.

Eliminating Other Causes

Strange behaviors by your system may not always indicate a virus. You need to ask yourself some other questions. Have you set your floppy disks near any magnetic fields lately? These fields can be simple household items, such as the telephone, a TV or computer display screen, loudspeakers, and refrigerator magnets. Have you traveled with your floppies on an electric mass-transit (trolley or train) system (especially a veteran one)? If so, you may have sat too near a large electric motor. Excessive heat also can be a factor. Have your disks been in direct sunlight or near another heat source?

Has your hard drive suffered from any physical shocks lately, such as an earthquake? Have you moved your computer from one room to another, or had someone else move the computer unsupervised? If you have a tower case or system unit on the floor, has it fallen over or been kicked?

Simple things often can cause erratic results that at first may seem like a virus. One example can be the result of a static discharge if you dusted your work area recently. Try to remember whether something like tea, coffee, or paper clips dropped into your keyboard. Do you have pets that shed a lot of hair or like to chew cables? Is your computer wired into the same circuit as your washing machine, air conditioner, dishwasher, or refrigerator? Are your computer cables bundled closely together with other appliance cables? If you look down right now, are you on carpet? If so, do you get static electricity shocks from it? Do you live in a dry climate, or do you frequently get electrical storms? Do you have a spike/surge filter between the outlet and your computer?

Often some software may be incompatible with other programs and produce some erratic behavior. Have you run any disk repair or disk optimizing programs lately—especially for the first time? Think about what software you installed recently. Did it modify the AUTOEXEC.BAT or the CONFIG.SYS files? Could you have accidentally deleted or damaged your data files in any way?

If after asking yourself these questions you still have a reasonable amount of doubt, you may indeed have a virus. The rest of this chapter discusses ways of avoiding or protecting yourself from viruses and, in the unfortunate event that you think you have acquired one, confirming its existence and purging it from your system.

Getting Rid of Viruses

Just as you can acquire a computer virus in many ways, you also have a number of ways to remove them. The guaranteed foolproof method is to take your original, write-protected DOS disk, put it in drive A, boot the computer, delete and then re-create your DOS partition by using FDISK, and completely reformat your hard disk by using FORMAT C:/S! Then you have to start reloading all your software.

Although the above steps may sound like a drastic method, they do emphasize the importance of backups, especially of your data. Simply using the DOS COPY command to copy critical data files to a disk or saving files to both the hard disk and a floppy disk takes you a long way toward a painless recovery from disaster. Reloading software from the original disks is relatively straightforward, and if you have the data backed up to floppies, you simply can copy the files back to your data directories afterwards.

Often a virus may not completely cripple your hard disk. Maybe the virus just stops you from booting the hard disk. Then you may still be able to retrieve your data and copy to a floppy disk or two. You need to remember that data is usually safe from infection by viruses, so after securing your data, go ahead and reformat your hard disk.

If you don't have the time, patience, or peace of mind to take the drastic action outlined in the previous paragraphs, commercial products are available to perform recovery for you. In addition, they also offer protection from future virus attacks. You learn about some of these products in the next section.

Using Virus Protection and Recovery Utilities

One thing you need to be aware of is that anti-virus software cannot give you 100 percent protection from viruses. There is no such thing as a foolproof anti-virus program (other than reformatting the hard disk), and the human error factor always can override even the best virus protection system. You could, for example, make a critical mistake when deciding whether to let a "warning" operation continue. Also, as long as people are writing viruses, they will be designed to bypass the latest anti-virus products.

One point cannot be emphasized enough: *The best protection you can have for your system is a good set of backups* (see Chapter 10, "Understanding the Importance of Backing Up"). But you also might want to consider using an anti-virus package that not only gives a good level of protection but also certainly saves you time and effort if you have to reconstruct a hard disk from backups.

Although you have many to choose from, the following paragraphs cover only a few of the major commercial utilities that provide comprehensive virus protection and recovery: Symantec's Norton AntiVirus, Central Point Anti-Virus, Fifth Generation's Untouchable, and a shareware product called McAffee Associates Viruscan Series.

Examining Norton AntiVirus for DOS

Norton AntiVirus is available in DOS and Windows versions, and it also is available as a part of Norton Desktop. This section covers Norton AntiVirus for DOS first and then takes a brief look at the Windows version because there are no discernible differences in the features of the two.

Testing for Viruses while Booting

Without a doubt, the best way to deal with viruses is to avoid them altogether. One of the most likely points of attack by a virus is when your system is booting. To combat this threat, Norton AntiVirus installs a device driver called Virus Intercept before it loads any other drivers or programs. This procedure will effectively alert you to any viruses that occur (or are recognized) during the boot process or anytime that you run a program or copy a file or disk. If the virus is recognized, you will then be given the opportunity to repair damage to programs that the virus has attacked wherever possible.

> If you use Norton AntiVirus, keep a bootable, write-protected diskette with a copy of Virus Intercept on it. This backup will enable you to guarantee a safe bootup and will intercept any illegal attempts to infect other programs. Regardless of which utility you use to protect against viruses, keeping a bootable, write-protected disk handy is definitely a good idea.
>
> **T I P**

Using Norton AntiVirus

Norton AntiVirus is very simple to use and offers a number of protection features, including a disk and memory scan for viruses, a method of specific file protection referred to as Inoculating/Uninoculating, a Virus Clinic to control the inoculations, and ways to provide global settings depending on your security needs.

As an additional level of protection, Norton AntiVirus includes password-protection for the utilities themselves to avoid malicious and undetected loading of viruses on your system. These options can be selected from the Norton AntiVirus Main Menu, as illustrated in figure 14.3. Each of the features available from the main menu is explained in the sections that follow.

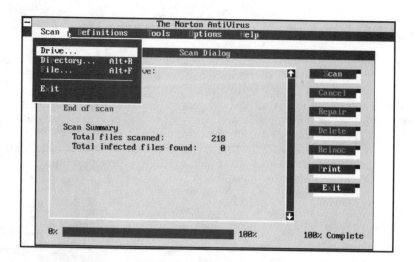

FIG. 14.3

Norton AntiVirus Main Menu.

Scanning for Viruses with Norton AntiVirus

Norton AntiVirus features a manual disk scanning utility to combat the threat of acquiring a virus. You should run a disk scan on a regular basis if your machine is publicly available or just for peace of mind. All of the components of Norton AntiVirus are LAN aware and work on most major network software, including Novell, OS/2 LAN Manager, and 3Com Open LAN. As a further level of protection, Clinic, Intercept, and Global can be additionally protected by using a password.

If you suspect that you have acquired a virus and you have just gone out and purchased Norton AntiVirus for the first time, reboot the system with a noninfected, write-protected DOS diskette. Remove the DOS diskette, and place a protected copy of Disk 1 of the set of Norton AntiVirus disks into drive A: and type **NAV** at the DOS prompt. You will be asked to enter your name, but because you write-protected the disk, you can put anything you like, because it will not be recorded. Because the information cannot be written to disk, you will get an error message that you can ignore for now and press OK.

The Scan menu selection should be selected by pressing the highlighted letter S (because your mouse driver probably has not been loaded) followed by the Drive selection letter D. You can then use the cursor control (or Tab) keys (or the highlighted letter L) and press the space bar to select All Local Drives. Finally, press Enter (or OK) and the scan will begin.

As already suggested, running a virus scan is usually the first task of anyone who acquired a utility to repair a suspect system. Norton AntiVirus first scans the system memory, then it checks all files and compares any suspicious evidence it finds against a list of known viruses. Elimination of any viruses is by way of repairing damaged files, replacement with a *clean* original or in more serious cases, deletion of the file. If somebody gives you a disk containing an unknown program you might want to perform a virus scan, as shown in figure 14.4.

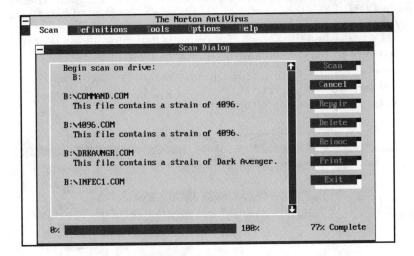

FIG. 14.4

Scan of unknown
diskette in drive B:

In this case, the scan found several viruses present, so you should put a warning label on the disk and take care to not boot from it or execute any of the programs on it. The button selection to the right of the screen in figure 14.4 offers a Repair option. If you select Repair All, the viruses will be removed and if a further scan comes up clean, you should be relatively safe to proceed and copy those files onto your hard disk.

Inoculating/Uninoculating

Inoculation of files takes place during a scan. The inoculation protects files from unknown viruses. An unknown virus is one where Norton AntiVirus does not have a definition. Inoculation takes a unique snapshot of a file and stores this in a special subdirectory. On a subsequent scan or execution of this file, Norton AntiVirus will compare the file with the inoculation data for that file; if there is no match, then a warning message will appear.

In rare cases, you might want to uninoculate a drive if there are files on it constantly modifying themselves legitimately. Uninoculation will avoid having to respond to the virus alert warning message.

Using Virus Clinic

Virus Clinic controls the way the inoculations take place. When a disk is scanned, the clinic settings are used to decide what files are to be inoculated. There are special types of files that can be inoculated by using Virus Clinic, which this section discusses later. Virus Intercept checks these (.COM, .EXE, .DRV, .OVL, .OVR, .BIN, .SYS) inoculated files to see if they change in any way over time. If a change is detected, then a virus alert is signalled on the screen. This change detection allows for the discovery of previously unknown viruses.

Virus Clinic is available from the Options menu selection. There is a comprehensive setup screen that enables you to check the desired protection features, as illustrated in figure 14.5.

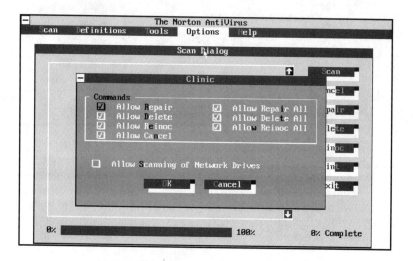

FIG. 14.5

Virus Clinic Setup Screen.

Using Global Settings

Norton AntiVirus enables you to globally set defaults as to how thoroughly you wish to protect against viruses. To what level you go will really depend on the perceived threat to your system and the cost of loss of data. Figure 14.6 illustrates the options available under the global settings of Norton AntiVirus.

Some of the options set as global defaults are particularly useful, especially the detection of unknown viruses. Situations that appear to be a virus at work will cause an alert to appear. Then you can decide whether it could be a virus or simply a coincidence and take appropriate action.

The inoculation directory contains unique values (often referred to as signatures) that correspond with files on your hard drive. This book discusses inoculation later in this chapter. The intercept program compares any file that it executes with the values in the inoculation directory and will alert the user if any discrepancies are found.

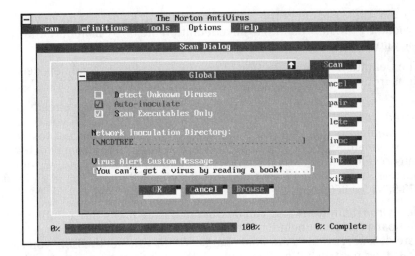

FIG. 14.6

Norton AntiVirus
Global Settings

Using Intercept

Virus Intercept is used as a possible virus-at-work early warning system, informing you if it suspects a file you access contains a virus and enabling you to take appropriate action. Virus Intercept is a runtime virus defense utility. It is loaded as a device driver and can be set up by the Norton AntiVirus installation procedure. After you load Intercept, it will scan for viruses every time you boot the machine by turning it on or by pressing Alt-Ctrl-Del. Virus Intercept also scans any executed program as it is loaded into memory or any file that is moved or copied on your system. A log is maintained of all the virus alerts that are signalled so that you can review any potential problems at a later date.

Using Password-Protection Access

Norton AntiVirus provides an option to add a password in order to protect access to sensitive features, such as Clinic, Intercept, Global, and Uninoculate. Two rules of thumb here are to choose a password that others will find difficult to guess and not to forget it yourself. Avoid obvious words like your name or names of people in your family. Also avoid writing the password down, because these items have a habit of falling into the wrong hands.

Keeping Up with New Viruses

Some experts claim that one new virus is created somewhere in the world every day, so it is likely that Norton AntiVirus will be unable to detect one of these using its list of more than 1,000 known viruses.

Norton AntiVirus offers the capability to add to its list of known viruses by loading the information from a definition file or by manually entering the information.

The Definitions menu selection offers the capability to load new definitions from disk.

Inoculation will provide a level of protection, but if you are already infected, you will need a definition to repair an infected file. If you own a communication package, such as PROCOMM, and have access to a modem, Symantec provides a bulletin board service (BBS) from which you can download new virus definitions (.DEF files). At the time of writing, the telephone numbers are (408) 973-9598 for 300 to 2400 baud and (408) 973-9834 for 9600 baud.

New virus definitions also can be obtained from many other public bulletin board services, including CompuServe. Symantec also offers an update disk service for a nominal charge. When you call the BBS, you can download new definition files and use the Definitions menu option in Norton AntiVirus to load them into your master list.

If you select the Modify List selection under the Definitions menu, you will see a list of all the currently known (by your copy of Norton AntiVirus) viruses and their derivative strains. You can add to or delete from this list, although it is unlikely you would want to delete virus definitions unless they are incorrect.

If you do not have a modem, you can manually enter the definitions by getting information from the Symantec Newsline or by FAX. After you have the definition information, you can select the Add option from the Modify List selection menu. One word of caution is that this can often be a tedious way to update your virus list.

Examining Norton AntiVirus for Windows

Norton AntiVirus for Windows offers identical features as Norton AntiVirus for DOS except that the main AntiVirus utility works in a Windows environment and the screens look and operate a little differently. As in the DOS version, the utilities are split into two areas. Virus Intercept works more or less the same as the DOS version, except that it will pop up a Windows virus alert message. Virus Clinic is a Windows-specific version.

Examining Central Point Anti-Virus

Central Point Anti-Virus (often called CPAV) is offered either separately or bundled as a part of PC Tools 7.1. Central Point Anti-Virus offers a similar set of functions to Norton AntiVirus.

 NOTE A new Windows version of CPAV was due out at the time of this writing. If you're interested, check with your local computer store to see whether the new program is available.

You can create an emergency floppy disk to recover CMOS memory, the boot sector, and the partition table in the event of damage by a virus or other catastrophe. A "bootsafe" utility provided as part of the Anti-Virus package checks the boot programs for viruses every time the system is started.

Central Point's immunization of files is a little different from Norton's AntiVirus inoculation in that Central Point's Anti-Virus adds a small (about 1K) monitor program to each selected file. Immunization works only on executable files, unlike Norton's inoculation, which works on almost all files. Immunization is known to conflict with the operation of some programs. To help you avoid these problems, Central Point wisely has included a de-immunize option. After a file is immunized by Central Point's Anti-Virus, the file is given the capability to check itself for any infection or damage whenever it is executed. If the file feels that it has been modified in some way, a warning message is flashed on-screen.

The main virus management utility can be presented in full graphical menu or Express menu style. The Express menu is useful for selecting bulk file virus detection, cleaning, and logging on entire drives.

The full menu option enables you to perform sophisticated virus detection and cleaning and immunization of individual files and selected directories. You easily can select files for virus scanning, immunization, and cleaning from the full menus. In addition, the activity log, which you access by pressing F7, shows the past history of all the alerts, immunizations, and cleaning that has taken place since CPAV was installed.

Just as in the Norton AntiVirus program, you can update periodically the extensive list of viruses known to CPAV. To update, you can use Central Point's BBS, CompuServe, written bulletins, and a 24-hour hotline.

VSafe, part of the CPAV suite of utilities, comes as either a COM file that can be executed from AUTOEXEC.BAT or as a device driver that can be loaded by CONFIG.SYS. The VSafe resident utility takes up 22K of memory and monitors the system for any suspicious activity. If any violations are noticed, you are provided with a warning screen and an option to accept whatever action caused the alert and thus continue or to terminate it. This feature protects you from a program trying to load a virus resident into memory.

Another CPAV program, VWatch, involves a much smaller overhead than VSafe, with less protection, of course. Taking up only 8K of memory, VWatch checks each executed program for evidence of known viruses. If a virus is found, a warning message is displayed, and the program is halted, enabling you to make a decision about whether to continue. If you decide to terminate the intercepted virus, you then can run CPAV and selectively clean or remove the offending file. The only weakness with this program is that continually updating the virus list is critical; otherwise, you risk being a victim of an unknown virus.

Examining Fifth Generation's Untouchable

Untouchable, produced by Fifth Generation Systems, Inc., is a comprehensive package made up of three programs to detect, remove, and protect a PC system against viruses.

UTRES is a TSR program that checks the system memory for the presence of any viruses. It checks the system at each initial boot, scans each file before execution, and checks every floppy disk inserted in the system. UTRES is tiny and uses less than .09K (900 bytes) when loaded into expanded memory and 5K when loaded into conventional memory.

UTSCAN, a virus scanner and remover, is the second line of defense. It runs during any program installation to ensure a clean environment. UTSCAN is activated as a precursor to adding any new files to Untouchable's database. You can run the UTSCAN program manually from the command line to scan a floppy disk or to check new program disks before installation or file copying.

UT, the final line of defense, uses the principle of file modification to detect known and unknown viruses in the system. UT is the foundation of the Untouchable line of virus protection utilities. During installation, UT registers all files and stores the information in both an on-line and an off-line database. UT automatically performs a check on files and compares them to the register of existing file information in the database to make sure that they haven't changed. If a virus is detected,

Untouchable's method of removal uses the database of registered file information to reconstruct the file to original form.

When you start up your system, Untouchable performs one of three file integrity checks. The Daily Integrity Test checks the boot sector, partition table, and vital system files (DOS and all the drivers and programs executed during startup). If an altered or deleted file is found, Untouchable displays an alert message. The message tells which file has been altered, gives a possible reason for the alteration, and recommends an appropriate action.

The Weekly Integrity Test is run every seven days by Untouchable. A more thorough test, it checks all files on the hard disk that are targeted by viruses (files like BAT, EXE, and COM files). Just as in the daily test, Untouchable is looking for any altered of modified files.

While performing either the Daily or Weekly Integrity Test, Untouchable may display the message Quick Check or Full Check. The program uses two calculations to check a file. The Full Check performs a more extensive scan of the files than the Quick Check, but both checks are secure and fast. As an added precaution, a different sample of the files is scanned each time a Weekly or Daily Integrity Test is done using the Full Check feature.

The third file integrity check, performed every 21 days, is the Safe Test. The Safe Test uses the off-line database on its own bootable disk to check for any file modification. This floppy disk contains a clean copy of DOS. In booting the system from this disk, you prevent any resident viruses from being loaded into the system during the Safe Test. When the time has come to run the Safe Test, Untouchable displays a message and gives you the option to perform the test now or delay the test until next time. If you choose to run the Safe Test, you then turn off the system, insert the Safe Disk into drive A, and turn the system back on. Untouchable runs the test automatically.

Whenever Untouchable finds a file that is new, missing, modified, or infected, the program displays an alert message. The Alert screen displays one line for each type of file found. At the bottom of the screen, Untouchable displays its diagnosis of the problem and recommends a course of action. Untouchable requires that you take some form of action for each modified file in the list. Depending on the problem with the file, you can choose to restore the file, update the file to the database, ignore the alert, exclude the file from the list to be checked, or remove the file from the list to be checked. You generally can rely on the recommended course of action, but the program manual has a chapter dedicated to handling alert messages. The chapter covers possible problems, the possible causes, and recommended actions.

Untouchable comes packaged with a 125-page manual that fully covers all operations. The first chapter is an introduction to viruses, which is helpful to PC users who may not be familiar with viruses and the way they work. The manual also contains a large section describing ways to customize how Untouchable works. Despite the depth of the manual, the first-time user can be up and running with minimal effort.

Examining McAffee Associates Viruscan Series

The McAffee series of virus programs is distributed as shareware for home use. You can download the programs by modem from many local computer bulletin boards. Registration is required, and you must obtain a license to use the programs for business, corporate, organizational, and institutional applications. Information about both procedures accompanies the Viruscan series of programs in a file called REGISTER.DOC.

Each program in the series comes with two separate files called VALIDATE.EXE and VALIDATE.DOC. This program and its accompanying document enable you to check to see whether the program files in the Viruscan series are free of viruses or have been altered in any way. With each program file in the series is included a DOC or document file. Within these DOC files are sections entitled Authenticity, which contain codes for their respective programs. These codes are to be matched to the codes read by the VALIDATE program. Typing **validate scan.exe** brings the codes to the screen. If the on-screen codes match the codes in the SCANV84.DOC file, the program has not been tampered with and is fine to use.

In the following paragraphs, you learn a little more about the individual programs included in the Viruscan series.

Scan

The *Scan* program, for any PC with 256K and DOS 2.0 or greater, detects the presence of any viruses it knows about and identifies them. It works on stand-alone and network PCs but not on file servers. Scan searches the system for patterns unique to computer viruses and can detect the presence of unknown viruses with the use of validation codes. The program does so by calculating a validation code from the contents of EXE and COM files. Scan then matches its recorded code to the current file validation calculation. If the codes do not match, the program has been altered in some way, which may indicate the presence of a virus.

Scan's report contains the name of any discovered known virus as well as the area that the virus occupies (memory, boot section, or file). Along with the name and area, Scan provides an identification code that you use to remove the virus.

Scan currently can identify 301 known computer viruses and their different strains. Many viruses have been modified so that one virus can have several different strains. Despite all these strains, about 20 viruses remain the most common and account for about 98 percent of all reported PC viruses. Scan comes with the file VIRLIST.TXT, which lists all new, public domain, and extinct computer viruses identified by the program.

Scan is easy to use. But remember to write-protect your floppy disk before running the program to prevent any virus from infecting the Viruscan programs. To run Scan, you just type the following command:

     SCAN *d1:,d2:...dn:*

d1:, *d2:*, and so on, refer to the drive or drives to be scanned. The program also has a number of switches that enable you to modify the way Scan checks the system. Suppose, for example, that you want to add validation codes to EXE and COM files. The command is:

     SCAN *d1:* /AV

Scan then goes to the drive specified by *d1:* and places validation codes on all EXE and COM files.

The program comes with the document file SCANV84.DOC, which provides complete information on the different aspects of running Scan.

Scan for Windows (Wscan)

Wscan is a program running under the Windows environment. It is essentially the same program as Scan, except that with Wscan you use two graphic menus rather than DOS commands to set the drives to be scanned and to utilize the many extensions that are available.

Clean

Clean is a virus disinfection program that works on all viruses identified by Scan. Clean searches through a system and removes any virus specified by you. During most virus removals, Clean is able not only to disinfect the virus but also to repair any damage done by it. If the virus is less common, Clean displays a message asking whether you want the program to overwrite and delete the infected file. If you choose this delete option, the file is deleted with no chance of recovery. Clean runs on any PC with at least 256K and DOS 2.0 or above.

To run Clean, you must have the identification code that is provided in the Scan report. The identification code is displayed inside square brackets, as in [***]. This code is important; Clean does not remove a virus unless specifically told the code of the infecting virus. The code for the Friday the 13th virus, for example, is [FRI13]. When entering the code for Clean, you must include the square brackets.

Before running Clean, you need to power down the system and boot from a noninfected system disk. Running Clean from a write-protected disk prevents infection of the Clean program. To run Clean, use the following command:

   CLEAN *d1: d2:...dn* [*virus ID*]

d1:, *d2:*, and so on, refer to the drive or drives to be disinfected. You also can run the program with several different extensions that customize the program for different applications. A complete list of extensions is enclosed in CLEAN84.DOC, which comes with the program.

For each infection, Clean reports when the virus has been removed successfully. After the virus has been removed, power down the system and let the computer boot normally. Check to make sure that the computer has been disinfected by running Scan a second time. Make sure to check any floppy disks that may have been placed in the infected system, because they may have contracted the virus, too.

Vshield

Vshield is a TSR (terminate and stay resident) program that prevents viruses from getting into your system. Vshield checks all programs before they load. When a virus is found, or a program does not match its validation check (provided by Scan), Vshield does not allow the program to load. If Vshield finds a virus while the system is booting, it stops the system from booting and prompts you to insert an uninfected, write-protected boot disk from which to reboot. You then should run Scan to determine the extent of the virus.

Two Vshield programs are available. VSHIELD.EXE checks for both known and unknown viruses by looking for patterns unique to viruses and by using the validation codes provided by Scan. You can run this program in two modes. In nonswap mode it uses 31K. In swap mode the program loads from disk only the programs it needs at that moment and unloads them when not needed. This design saves memory space and uses only 3K of memory. VSHIELD1.EXE does validation code checking only and uses 6K of memory. Both run on IBM PCs and compatibles with 256K of memory and DOS 2.0 or higher.

Vshield contains four levels of protection that you can control. The minimal Level I protection checks the validation codes added to programs by Scan. Level II protection checks programs to see whether they contain a virus signature. Level III protection is simply a combination of Level I and Level II. And Level IV protection enables you to determine which programs can and cannot be run. You must list in a certification file the programs you want to be able to run. Vshield then checks this file before letting any programs run. The following chart lists the commands necessary to run each level of protection:

Level I	VSHIELD1
Level II	VSHIELD
Level III	VSHIELD /CV
Level IV	VSHIELD /CV /CERTIFY EXCPTN.LST

Along with the different levels of protection, you can add other extensions. One extension adapts Vshield for use in the Windows environment, and another removes the program from the computer's resident memory.

For the best protection, McAffee Associates recommends that you add the appropriate Vshield command at the end of the AUTOEXEC.BAT file. The exception is when the computer is running a menu file such as PC Shell. You should place your Vshield command before these types of programs. Also, if you use Vshield on a network, the network drivers should load before Vshield.

Summary

After reading this chapter, you can safely conclude that a computer virus is definitely something to be avoided. This chapter has outlined many of the ways to acquire a virus, how to recognize symptoms, how to eradicate them by using utilities or more drastic manual methods, and finally how to barricade your PC by using protection utilities. The threat is not as great as some of the anti-virus utility makers would have you believe. The danger is real yet not substantial enough to require you to operate your PC in total isolation. As you have learned in this chapter, you can avoid getting a virus by employing some safe practices. And you can avoid loss due to viruses by taking precautions such as backing up data and critical information. In short, viruses can be annoying but can only be as fatal as you allow them to be.

Understanding Data Compression

A common problem encountered at some point by just about every PC user today is the lack of available disk space. One of the major complaints is that no matter how big a drive you get, it always seems to fill up at the worst possible moment. This sudden calamity usually leads to some hasty, and sometimes later regretted, file deletions.

Over the long term, your disk housekeeping efforts can delay the effect of disk clog. After a while, however, even the housekeeping becomes tedious and frequently ineffective, often relying on the storage of occasionally used data and programs on floppy disks. And ultimately the solution to the problem is to buy a new drive altogether.

An alternative way to overcome the dwindling disk space problem involves using one of several inexpensive—or even free—utility programs. These programs tend to offer less disruptive methods of stretching your disk space. By compressing data, such programs normally reduce the size of your files or make the apparent disk space seem larger. The penalty for using the disk-enlarging methods may be a slight reduction in the computer's overall performance or its available memory and may not even be feasible on some slower machines. But you need to know your options.

In this chapter, you take a look at the effects and mechanics of data compression, some of the methods used, and the potential problems or side effects. You also explore some software and hardware disk-compression options.

Defining Data Compression

Compression is a generic term for a method of removing redundant pieces of a file while leaving it unique enough to make the rebuilding of the original possible. After being compressed, a disk or file requires some method of decompression to counteract the compression.

In some cases, you may not even be aware that data compression is taking place. The simplest way to tell whether a file has been compressed is to look at its extension. If the file has a ZIP, an ARC, or a LZH file extension, as in PACKSTUF.ZIP, the file is compressed. (You learn more about ZIP, ARC, and LZH files later in this chapter. These are the most common types of packed files found on MS-DOS systems.) Some programs may include compression in their data files, and some programs may be compressed themselves.

English text has a great deal of redundancy built into it. Most human beings do a good job of compressing text and then expanding as they read it back. Take, for example, this advertisement for a car:

> 89 wht Merc Sbl Wgn, 4 dr, A/C, AT, PB, PS, PW, PL, lic, V6, grgd, lo hwy mls, $8000 OBO, tel 555-1212 dys.

Most people can understand what this message means. In less than two lines, the ad uniquely says what could have been put into the following lengthy message:

> 1989 White Mercury Sable, Four Door Station Wagon. It has Air Conditioning, Automatic Transmission, Power Brakes, Power Steering, Power Windows, and Power Locks. It is currently licensed, has a V6 engine, and has been garaged. It has low freeway mileage, and the sale price is $8,000 or best offer. The daytime telephone number is 555-1212.

A couple of data-packing pioneers named Jacob Ziv and Abraham Lempel first developed a specification for the Universal Algorithm for Sequential Data Compression in the mid-1970s. You often see references to LZ, which, in data-compression terms, stands for Lempel and Ziv. In about 1984, Terry Welch developed some of the first algorithms for compressing and decompressing files from the original LZ specifications. So today, you often also see references to LZW (for Lempel Ziv Welch). Sometimes you even see LZH; the H refers to another compression algorithm frequently referred to as Huffman encoding.

Understanding How Data Compression Works

If you take a look at any text file, you may notice that it contains certain patterns, a great deal of blanks, perhaps many occurrences of common words such as "and," "the," and "or," numbers with lots of zeros, and so on. Each of these patterns can be represented by a single unique value, which is often the method used by compression utilities. This method, called *run-length encoding*, seeks out repetitious patterns and replaces them with a single pattern and a repetition count. A simple example of run-length data compression is illustrated in figure 15.1. In this example, multiple occurrences of characters are replaced with a single character and a repetition number. True run-length data compression does a much more significant level of reduction.

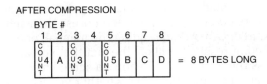

BEFORE COMPRESSION
BYTE #
1 2 3 4 5 6 7 8 9 10 11 12 13 14

A A A A   B B B B B C D   = 14 BYTES LONG

AFTER COMPRESSION
BYTE #
1 2 3 4 5 6 7 8

COUNT 4 | A | COUNT 3 | COUNT 5 | B | C | D   = 8 BYTES LONG

Figure 15.1 shows the original file as 14 bytes or characters long. The compression program scans the file and checks for multiple occurrences of each letter. When discovering the four As, the program changes a small piece of the first occurrence to add a flag indicating that the rest of that character contains a count of the number of occurrences. The following character (2 in fig. 15.1) is a single example of what will be duplicated on decompression the number of times indicated by the count in the first byte. The same effect happens when three blanks and five Bs are counted. The C and the D are left alone because they are single occurrences. The result is a much shorter compressed file. Although this example is an oversimplification of the types of compression used in disk packers, it does give you a general idea of what these programs are trying to achieve.

As a general rule of thumb, writing the compressed data to disk can take significantly longer than reading it. The reason is that the compression utility performs a deterministic scan of the data first and calculates the best type of compression to use before beginning to compress it. When reading a compressed file, the program already knows the decompression method because it was stored as part of the archive.

Being Wary of Multiple Compressions

If you already have many compressed files, performing a disk compression may not gain you much space and could even slow down processing. A second compression is unlikely to recover any further space; in fact, in many cases, this effort may even increase the final file size. Performing data compression only once is the ideal. Determining whether a file has been compressed simply by looking at it, however, is not always easy. Thus a file or program could be compressed several times inadvertently. In the worst case, a user might use a program that compresses its data files, then compress these by using a file archive/packing utility such as PKZIP, then store them on a compressed disk by using Stacker.

A good example of a program using self-compression is Norton Utilities, which has been discussed throughout this book. The programs that make up Norton Utilities are compressed and decompress themselves only when they are executed. Other than reading the manual, one way to tell in this case that the compression exists is the fact that you are given the option to decompress them. Figure 15.2 shows a screen from the Norton Utilities configuration section that asks whether you want to decompress the program files.

Looking at Compression's Effectiveness

The amount of compression carried out on a file varies depending on the type of file. ASCII text files, for example, often contain a great deal of blank space and contain only printable characters that are a small sub-set of all the possible characters a file can have. Databases, especially some of the more structured ones, often can be compressed by as much as 90 percent. Program or executable files contain little blank space, are very random, and use the entire range of characters available. Table 15.1 illustrates the typical amount of compression that can be expected for various types of files.

FIG. 15.2

Deciding whether to decompress Norton Utilities.

Table 15.1 Typical Compression Percentages

File Type	Compression Percentage Reduction
GIF files	0-10%
Programs (EXE, COM, SYS)	0-50%
Word processing files	40-80%
ASCII text files (BAT, TXT)	50-90%
Program source code (C, PAS)	50-90%
Database files (DBF, DB)	40-90%
Spreadsheet files (WKS, WK1, XLS, WKQ)	40-80%
Bitmaps/screen files (TIF, BMP)	60-95%
Graphics program data	50-80%
Compressed data or programs (CMP)	-1-10%

As you can see from table 15.1, with the exception of already com-pressed files that might even get larger, the level of compression that can be achieved usually makes it well worth considering.

Determining When You Should Use Compression

Two disparate approaches to choosing data compression are popular. The first is that you consider compression only when you discover that you are running out of disk space and cannot afford or don't have room for a new hard drive. The second is that you consider performing compression as soon as you get your hard drive, thus extending the time it takes to reach capacity. If you dislike disk housekeeping or are wary of adding layers between your data and DOS, you might want to opt for the first option. If you like to keep your disk strictly ordered and don't mind spending time on housekeeping, then the latter option may prove to be the best for you.

Some other situations might arise, such as the need to keep applications on floppies for security, space restrictions, or other reasons. Compression secures your data by adding another level of protection and in some cases encrypting your files into a single library or archive file. Choosing to compress also may be the only way you can fit a number of files on a single floppy disk. Later in this chapter, you learn a method of using a RAM disk to unpack archived applications temporarily; you can initiate this process from a floppy disk, too.

Examining Software Solutions

Several file compressors are available both commercially and through shareware from bulletin board systems. The major ones covered here are LHARC, ARC, and PKZIP plus two lesser-known archives called PAK and ZOO. PKLITE is a special utility that enables compressed executable program files to decompress themselves. You also learn about two disk compressors, Stacker and SuperStor.

NOTE   Many other effective disk-compression utilities are available that provide similar features to both SuperStor and Stacker. In particular, two of the more popular products worthy of mention are Expanz from InfoChip Systems, Inc., and DoubleDisk from Vertisoft Systems, Inc. You may want to check out those programs too.

Looking at LHARC

LHARC gets its name from the type of compression algorithms it uses, namely Lempel-Ziv and Huffman. One of the most popular compression/archiving utilities in Japan, LHARC is command-line-driven from the DOS prompt and creates a file with an LZH extension. Figure 15.3 is the help screen that appears if you simply type **lharc** at the DOS prompt. LHARC is a copyrighted product but is distributed as freeware, which means that individuals may use and distribute it freely. Commercial use requires contact with the author prior to implementation.

```
LHA version 2.13               Copyright (c) Haruyasu Yoshizaki, 1988-91
=== <<< A High-Performance File-Compression Program >>> ========  07/20/91  ===
Usage: LHA <command> [/option[-+012|WDIR]] <archive[.LZH]> [DIR\] [filenames]
_____
  <command>
    a: Add files           u: Update files        m: Move files
    f: Freshen files       d: Delete files        p: disPlay files
    e: Extract files       x: eXtract files with pathnames
    l: List of files       v: View listing of files with pathnames
    s: make a Self-extracting archive   t: Test the integrity of an archive
  <option>
    r: Recursively collect files      w: assign Work directory
    x: allow eXtended file names      m: no Message for query
    p: distinguish full Path names    c: skip time-stamp Check
    a: allow any Attributes of files  z: Zero compression (only store)
    t: archive's Time-stamp option    h: select Header level (default = 1)
    o: use Old compatible method      n: display No indicator a/o pathname
    i: not Ignore lower case          l: display Long name with indicator
    s: Skip by time is not reported   -: '@' and/or '-' as usual letters
==============================================================================
You may copy or distribute this software free of      Nifty-Serve  SDI00506
charge. For use as a part of commercial or of shared  ASCII-pcs    pcs02846
distributions, see our distribution policy in Manual. PC-VAN       FEM12376
```

FIG. 15.3

LHARC control options.

The current version of LHARC is 2.13. Although in benchmarks it sometimes measures compression time slightly slower than some of the other major archive utilities, it does produce some of the smallest archives. LHARC also offers a wealth of commands, including the capability to create self-extracting files and extensive batch file support. LHARC often is chosen by software developers as an installation method for this reason. LHARC is sophisticated enough to create its own subdirectories on decompression and copy the appropriate files to each one.

Judging by the accompanying documentation, LHARC appears to be aimed at experts. The material is chock full of detailed technical information. LHARC and LZH files are not prolific in the U.S. and Europe, but the utility is freely available and handy to have in case you need to decompress an LZH file. If you live in Japan, plan to go there, or use a Japanese bulletin board, then LHARC is a must.

Looking at ARC

Compressed archives started with Seaware's ARC. It was the first program to combine the capability to compress files and the power to collect the related files into one group. This feature makes cataloging, archiving, and distributing complete applications or series of files an easy task. Before ARC, in the early 1980s, individual file squeezers and separate librarian programs were offered. The general trend was to squeeze each file and then combine the files into a LIB file by using a librarian program. In pre-ARC days, the letter Q usually was the last character in the file extension. TEST.CQ, for example, would be the squeezed version of TEST.C.

Ever since the advent of ARC in the mid-1980s, the majority of bulletin board systems have used it as the mainstay of their file collections. In recent years, a distinct movement toward ZIP files as the standard has been noted.

ARC 6.0 from Seaware is the latest available release. The program has improved steadily in performance over the years. ARC archives tend to be slightly larger than their ZIP, LZH, and ZOO counterparts, but the differences may be offset by a faster turnaround time and some excellent accompanying documentation.

ARC 6.0 contains most of the features considered by many users to be the basic requirements for an archiving utility. Although ARC has the capability to include subdirectories when archiving, it does not re-create subdirectory structures on decompression as PKZIP and LHARC can.

Looking at PKZIP

PKWare currently offers Version 1.93 of PKZIP, which consists of a series of files in a self-extracting archive called PK193A.ZIP. (At the time of this writing, the utility had been issued in a preliminary release, or "Alpha" stage. By the time this book is printed, Version 1.93 should be the current release.)

PKZIP/PKUNZIP Version 1.01 first was released following the legal wrangling between PKWare and System Enhancement Associates on the ownership of the ARC file extension and format. The most popular version of PKZIP that is generally available on most public bulletin board systems is 1.10. (Archiving programs tend not to be upgraded by users as frequently as other commercial utility programs, on a variation of the theme of "if it ain't broke, don't fix it.")

PKZIP is one of the fastest general-purpose archiving utilities and performs an excellent job with both text and executable files of all shapes, sizes, and formats. PKUNZIP is a stripped-down version of PKZIP that can unarchive only ZIP files.

The 1.10 production version of the PKZIP package usually includes a series of programs as follows:

PKZIP.EXE	The all-purpose archiver
PKUNZIP.EXE	The main decompression program
PKSFX.PGM	Used to perform self-extraction
ZIP2EXE.EXE	Makes a self-extracting archive
REZIP.EXE	Updates previous ZIP files to the latest ZIP format

Version 1.93 offers many improvements over the earlier releases. Some of the most notable improvements include new compression algorithms—in fact, a series of eight different types. This new process allows a high level of data compression and is extremely fast. You even have a way to specify the type of compression method to be used. The three available methods are Fast, which does not create the smallest archives but runs quickly; Extra, which spends more time squeezing every last piece of available space from a file; and Normal, which does somewhat of a balancing act between these two extremes.

Perhaps the most significant addition to the latest version is the support of multivolume archives, which means that PKZIP can create and extract ZIP files that span more than one physical disk. In some respects, this process resembles a DOS backup. When you specify the multivolume option, a ZIP file being created on removable media such as a floppy disk or removable hard disk can overcommit to space. When a ZIP file reaches the point at which it would exceed the capacity of the storage device, you are prompted to insert another one. In the case of standard floppy disks (360K/720K/1.2M/1.44M), you can format them on-the-fly—that is, if an unformatted disk is inserted, PKZIP formats it before continuing to write the archive.

One other significant improvement is that expanded memory (EMS) is fully supported, which greatly reduces the amount of conventional RAM needed to run PKZIP. When sufficient EMS is available, PKZIP now requires only 85K of conventional memory to run. Without EMS, PKZIP requires 183K. PKUNZIP requires approximately 75K if EMS is present and approximately 81K without EMS. What this change means is that if you shell out from a large application program to perform some DOS command line work, you often have only a small DOS workspace in which to operate but still enough to run PKZIP.

Another feature of PKZIP enables you to create an ASCII archive control file containing the particular file names that you want to compress or exclude from an operation. This feature can enable you to drive a PKZIP operation from another application or by using a batch file.

Figure 15.4 illustrates the options screen that appears when you type **pkzip** at the DOS prompt with no file options. This screen lists all the basic controls needed to run the utility, obviating the need to refer constantly to the documentation.

```
PKZIP (R)  FAST!  Create/Update Utility  Version 1.93  ALPHA  10-15-91
Copr. 1989-1991 PKWARE Inc.  All Rights Reserved.  PKZIP/h for help
PKZIP Reg. U.S. Pat. and Tm. Off.   Patent No. 5,051,745

Usage: PKZIP [-b[path]] [options] zipfile [@list] [files...]
Options summary - consult the PKWARE documentation for additional information
  -x<filespec¦@list> = eXclude filespec(s)        -z = add zipfile comment
  -d = delete files             -f = freshen files      -i = add changed files
  -l = display license info     -u = update files       -m[u,f] = move files
  -a = add files                -b = create temp zipfile on alternate drive
  -c = add/edit file comments   -C = add comments to new files only
  -k = keep same ZIP date       -o = set ZIP date to latest file
  -q = enable ANSI comments     -s<pwd> = Scramble files with password
  -r = recurse subdirs          -$[drive] = save volume label
  -<T¦t>[mmddyy] = Compress files before¦after specified date (default=today)
  -e[x,n,s] = maXimal compression/Normal compression/Speed(fast) compression
  -<p¦P> = store pathnames ¦ p=recursed into ¦ P=specified & recursed into
  -<w¦W><H,S> = ¦ w=include ¦ W=don't include ¦ Hidden/System files
  -<j¦J><H,S,R> = ¦ j=mask ¦ J=don't mask ¦ Hidden/System/Readonly attributes
  -v[b,c,d,e,n,p,s,r,t] = view ZIP [Brief listing/show Comments/sort by -
     Date/Ext/Name/Percentage/Size/sort Reverse/Technical (long) listing]
zipfile = ZIP file name.  Default extension is .ZIP
file    = Names of files to compress. Wildcards *,? ok. Default is ALL files.
@list   = listfile containing names of files to add or view etc.
Press any key to continue


NOTICE: THIS IS PRE-RELEASE SOFTWARE AND, AS SUCH, HAS NOT BEEN COMPLETELY
TESTED.  PERSONS USING THIS SOFTWARE MAY ENCOUNTER PROBLEMS AND IT IS LIKELY
THAT YOU MAY LOSE OR DESTROY DATA.  YOU MUST BACKUP YOUR SYSTEM PRIOR
TO USING THIS SOFTWARE, AND SHOULD DO SO OFTEN DURING SUBSEQUENT USE.

PKWARE, Inc.
9025 N. Deerwood Drive
Brown Deer, WI 53223
```

FIG. 15.4

The PKZIP options screen.

Looking at PAK

PAK Version 2.1 was one of the first compression utilities to support the OS/2 environment. Currently, this program uses a less frequently found compression method that seems to still have some strongholds of usage, particularly with some diehard OS/2 users.

The interesting feature of the PAK utility is that it does particularly well in compressing very large files. Both OS/2 and Windows 3.X are employing larger and larger files, so the PAK archiver is likely to survive for quite some time to come. Because most BBS downloads are growing in size and because OS/2 BBS systems are beginning to appear, the need for PAK might even increase.

One other major feature of PAK is that it is one of the easiest-to-use archive programs. The help option is extensive and fills two screens with information on how to use PAK, with a brief line of information on what each command does.

One other attractive feature of PAK is the well-written documentation, which enables beginners and experts to become proficient PAK users quickly. The expert can find comprehensive technical information on the structure and composition of PAK format files. Program developers can purchase a "programmer's version" of PAK that contains utilities and libraries that enable you to write your own archive by using the same algorithms as PAK.

The PAK options are extensive, including options to create EXE self-extracting files, turn these same EXE files into standard archives, sort files, include subdirectories in archive creation, and create subdirectories upon decompression. Similar to LHARC in this respect, PAK can be used to self-install a commercial software package.

If you have older PAK or ARC files, you can convert them to the latest PAK file format. PAK also includes a level of security against file tampering by programs such as viruses. The utility protects files by keeping tabs on file sizes and dates. A change can indicate to you that a file has been modified while in an archive file.

From a documentation standpoint, PAK also includes the capability to place comments on each file in an archive, as well as a comment on the entire archive. Again, this feature can be important from a software developer's viewpoint as useful supplementary documentation for installation.

Looking at ZOO

The initial, generally available release of ZOO was Version 1.5 and first appeared on a network called Usenet sometime in the summer of 1987. The current ZOO Version is 2.11.

A specialized archiving tool, ZOO's main feature is the fact that it is the only method presently supported by some mainframes and most UNIX derivatives such as XENIX. ZOO also currently is supported on VAX/VMS, Amiga DOS, and PC DOS. Unfortunately, although ZOO provides a reasonably fast archiving method, it has proved to be one of the least efficient in terms of the final archive compression size.

As with many other archive utilities you have explored in this chapter, ZOO uses a derivative of the Lempel-Ziv compression algorithm that appears to provide space savings between 20 and 80 percent, depending on the file type. For historical archiving, ZOO can store and selectively extract multiple generations of the same file. This feature makes it an excellent candidate for program source code and anything where a general release of related files is required. The number of generations to be stored can be controlled by a user-defined parameter. ZOO also offers an archive-patching feature that enables you to recover lost data from damaged archives by skipping the damaged portion and locating undamaged data in current and previous generations.

The help and on-line documentation features of ZOO are adequate. The printable ZOO manual itself is fairly cryptic and difficult to understand for both novice and advanced users. Figure 15.5 shows the on-line help available. To get on-line help, you need to type the command **zoo h** to get the summary of options.

```
Zoo archiver, Version 2.00 (1988/02/06 21:24:14)
(C) Copyright 1988 Rahul Dhesi — Noncommercial use permitted
Usage: zoo {acDeglLPTuUvx}[aAcCdEfInmMNoOpPqu1:/.@n] archive file
("zoo h" for help)

Choose a command from within {} and zero or more modifiers from within [].
E.g.:  'zoo a save /bin/*' will archive all files in /bin into save.zoo.
(Please see the user manual for a complete description of commands.)

Commands in {} mean:              ¦Modifiers in [] mean:
  a      add files                ¦ a      show archive name(s) in listing
  c      update comments          ¦ A      apply g or c to archive
  D      delete stored files      ¦ c      add/list comments
  e,x    extract files            ¦ d      extract/list deleted files too
  g      adj. gen. limit/count    ¦ dd     extract/list only deleted files
  l,L,v,V list filenames          ¦ E      erase backup after packing
  P      pack archive             ¦ f      fast add (no compression) or list
  T      fix archive datestamp    ¦ M      move when adding (erase original)
  u      add only newer files     ¦ n      add only files not already in archive
  U      undelete stored files    ¦ N      send extracted data to Neverland
  — — — — — — — — — — — — —         O      don't ask "Overwrite?"
  q      be quiet                   p      pipe extracted data to standard output
  :      don't store dir names      /,//   extract full pathnames
  .      pack to current dir        I      add filenames read from stdin
  C      show file CRC value        +/-    enable/disable generations
  S      overwrite newer files      g      list generation limits
  P      pack after adding         @n      start extract/list at position n

Novice usage: zoo -cmd archive[.zoo] file... where -cmd is one of these:
-add -extract -move -test -print -delete -list -update -freshen -comment
```

FIG. 15.5

Viewing ZOO's on-line help.

ZOO offers two types of command levels: expert and novice. Expert commands consist of one command letter that can be followed by one or more characters if needed to modify the selection further. Novice commands consist of a hyphen (-) followed by a command word that can be abbreviated. Expert commands are case-sensitive, but novice commands are not.

Overall, ZOO is too specialized for exclusive use on PCs. Unlike most of the other archive programs described in this chapter, ZOO does not offer important features such as the capability to create self-extracting files, selective multiple compression methods, and directory structure rebuilding. The primary reason you would use this program is if you use a mainframe or UNIX system and need to exchange compressed files. From the PC perspective, however, if someone gives you a file with a ZOO file extension, you need this program to decompress the file.

Looking at PKLITE

PKLITE is a method of compressing programs such as COM and EXE files. PKLITE compresses and enhances these executable files so that they require much less disk space yet still run normally.

PKLITE compresses your files in much the same way that PKZIP does, but PKLITE adds a small extraction program at the beginning of the executable file. When you run an application that has been compressed with PKLITE, the program expands itself before loading into memory and then runs normally. The compressing process does not change the operation of the program at all but merely reduces the disk space required to store the program. In some cases, especially with large executable files, compressing speeds up the load time. No additional memory is needed to run most programs compressed with PKLITE.

Of course, you may need to decompress some application files if, for example, they need to be patched or upgraded. PKLITE also has the capability to expand your files back to their original size.

PKLITE runs on any IBM PC or compatible with DOS 2.0 or higher. Running a program that has been compressed with PKLITE requires roughly an additional 4K of memory beyond the normal requirement for that program to load. After the program is loaded, memory available to the application remains the same as before it was compressed.

Figure 15.6 illustrates the typical help screen that you access by simply entering **pklite** at the DOS command line prompt.

Looking at SuperStor

SuperStor 1.3 uses on-the-fly compression to pack considerably more space on the hard disk than its physical size would normally allow. The amount of compression you get depends on the type of files on the disk; text, word processing, database, spreadsheet, and bitmap graphics files compress more significantly than executable and other binary files.

Referring back to table 15.1, you can get an idea of the typical compression ratios that can be achieved by SuperStor with different types of files. In addition to the basic function of SuperStor, a caching program and defragmentation utility are provided.

```
PKLITE (tm)   Executable File Compressor   Version 1.13   8-01-91
Copyright 1990-1991 PKWARE Inc. All Rights Reserved. Patent Pending

Usage: PKLITE [options] [d:][/path]Infile [[d:][/path]Outfile]
Options are:
  -a = always compress files with overlays and optimize relocations
  -b = make backup .BAK file of original
  -e = make compressed file unextractable (* commercial version only *)
  -l = display software license screen
  -n = never compress files with overlays or optimize relocations
  -o = overwrite output file if it exists
  -r = remove overlay data
  -u = update file time/date to current time/date
  -x = expand a compressed file

(*) See documentation and license screen for more information

If you find PKLITE easy and convenient to use, a registration of $46.00
would be appreciated. Registration includes one free upgrade to the
software and a printed manual. Please state the version of the software
that you currently have. Send check or money order to:
                    PKWARE, Inc.
                    9025 N. Deerwood Drive
                    Brown Deer, WI 53223
```

FIG. 15.6

The PKLITE help screen.

SuperStor works by creating a large file on your disk that effectively becomes just another disk. The device driver enables the operating system to see this large file as another drive. Without the device driver loaded, this file appears to be what it is: a huge file.

If you want to add SuperStor to your bootable drive, you must retain a small space to enable the underlying DOS to boot up. When setting up SuperStor, you need to back up your hard disk prior to creating any SuperStor drives, especially on the bootable disk. Having done your backup, you can create a SuperStor disk and let it move any existing files out of the way and onto the new SuperStor drive.

Figure 15.7 illustrates the effects of SuperStor more clearly. The first part of figure 15.7 shows a standard 40M drive with just a system area and some critical parts of DOS installed. As you can see, 39M of disk space is available. The second part of figure 15.7 shows the creation of a large (39M) SuperStor file. If DOS is booted without SuperStor loaded, a single drive is found, and the SuperStor disk shows up as a large file taking up all the available space on drive C. With SuperStor loaded, the device driver recognizes the SuperStor file and pretends to DOS that an additional 78M hard disk is attached. One further option is to enable SuperStor to exchange the C drive with the D (SuperStor) drive, making the SuperStor drive appear to be the main drive.

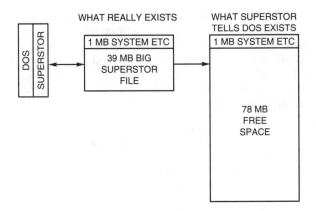

FIG. 15.7

Examining SuperStor's
structure.

(The same space-saving mechanism applies to another disk-compression utility called Stacker, which is covered in detail in the next section of this chapter.)

Another space optimization feature of SuperStor is its tendency to save files in 512-byte chunks, whereas DOS may be using 2,048- or 4,096-byte chunks (also known as allocation units). A small 128-byte file, for example, occupies one allocation unit (the smallest available) or 512 bytes on the SuperStor drive. This same small file could take up 4,096 bytes of disk space by using typical DOS allocation units.

SuperStor can handle up to eight partitions, each up to 512M, on your system. One important caveat is that although SuperStor is claimed to be compatible with existing disk-management utilities, avoidance of third-party defragmentation programs is recommended. As you can imagine, a defragmentation utility may ignore the SuperStor structure and simply optimize the space as if it contained normal DOS files. In the SuperStor structure, the files may be organized completely differently and become degraded in performance after defragmentation. SuperStor provides its own defragmentation utility to maintain the program's special format in an optimum configuration.

To provide on-the-fly compression, the SuperStor manager is loaded as a device driver. Typically the device driver takes up 53K of RAM. Because of the size of the SuperStor device driver and the cache buffer workspace it requires, you cannot load SuperStor in high memory, so the 53K is taken from conventional memory. In most cases, this situation does not cause a problem, but if your applications require as close to the maximum 640K as possible, SuperStor probably will not work for you.

You need to follow several precautions when installing SuperStor—or any other disk-compression utility for that matter. These steps include backing up your system, deinstalling any copy-protected software, removing any Windows permanent swap files, and making sure that you have at least 1.5M of free disk space available. If you reboot, lose power, or suffer a disk error during the installation and conversion process, you have a good chance of a catastrophic data loss.

Version 1.3 of SuperStor is provided as a standard file-compression utility under DR DOS 6.0. This trend may continue into the other operating systems, and a file-compression utility may become just another standard component of an operating system.

Looking at Stacker

Stacker from Stac Electronics is a disk-compression utility that easily can double available hard disk capacity. As with SuperStor, Stacker offers compression on-the-fly. Unlike SuperStor, however, Stacker offers an optional, half-sized, 8-bit hardware coprocessor board to perform the compression and decompression without taxing your PC's processor. This board is particularly noticeable in use on slower, older machines such as 8088 and 80286 systems. The coprocessor board itself is a compact, well-designed card that can fit into any ISA or EISA 8- or 16-bit slot. The nice feature is that you have no jumpers, DIP switches, or cables to mess with, and you can install the utility in minutes. A microchannel version of this board also is available for use in IBM PS/2s and other compatible machines.

From a performance standpoint, benchmarks have shown that Stacker running with the coprocessor board is faster than regular, unenhanced DOS. And considering the features that Stacker offers, it requires little overhead. Typically, any IBM compatible running DOS 3.0 or higher with at least 512K of available RAM and at least 1M of free hard disk space can use Stacker. The type of hard disk you use seems irrelevant whether you have an MFM, RLL, EDSI, IDE, or SCSI type.

Because of Stacker's high degree of compatibility, when the program is installed you will be totally unaware of its presence. You should not notice any strange files, and everything appears to be in DOS format only larger. As with SuperStor, the data is stored in a hidden, compressed format, so you should not run certain utilities, such as low-level formatters and optimizers. Instead, Stacker provides its own defragmenting utility called SDEFRAG.

Stacker 2.0 works on some LAN servers running LAN operating systems such as LANtastic and also operates on Bernoulli Boxes, Plus Passport drives, and floppy disks. The resident program for Stacker is a mere 26K and, unlike SuperStor, can be loaded into high memory on 386 machines, using DOS 5.0's DEVICEHIGH option, QEMM-386's LOADHI device driver, or Qualitas 386MAX. If you select to allocate buffering to expanded memory (EMS), you can further reduce the space taken by the device driver to 18K with only a slight decrease in disk performance.

The same warnings given for SuperStor apply to Stacker, too. Before performing any type of disk compression, you first should back up your entire hard disk. You also need to uninstall any copy-protected software and remove any Windows permanent swap files. The time taken to perform compression on a drive depends on how many files are there and how easy they are to compress. The easiest are text, spreadsheets, bitmap graphics, and database data. The more difficult are executable programs, printer fonts, device drivers, and files that have some sort of compression already applied. In a test run with the card loaded on a 486, Stacker compressed just under 40M of data in about 16 minutes. In another 10 minutes, the utility performed the defragmentation of existing space.

Stacker is supplied on 5 1/4-inch and 3 1/2-inch media and comes with a compact 200-page manual that is easy to read and contains many illustrations. Installation is a breeze if you closely follow the directions, which consist of a series of simple steps and a few questions.

An additional Stacker feature is the inclusive disk cache, which helps to improve disk performance dramatically.

Using Data Compression with a RAM Disk

One method you can use when you're either running out of disk space or want to move infrequently used programs is to create a temporary disk or RAM disk and unzip your application to it just for one session. After completing the session, you can update the archive and delete the files in the temporary disk. The whole operation is ideally controlled from within a batch file.

Consider the following example of a BAT file used to unpack an application on a 2M RAM disk, run the application, and then repack it back to the original ZIP file:

```
@ECHO OFF
REM UNZIP CIM TO RAM DRIVE E:
E:
CD \
MD CIM
CD CIM
PKUNZIP -D C:CIM.ZIP
CIM
PKZIP -UPR C:CIM *.*
```

This BAT file creates a subdirectory called CIM, which in this case stands for CompuServe Information Manager, on the RAM drive E. The file then proceeds to decompress the files, using the PKUNZIP -D C:CIM.ZIP line. The -D tells PKUNZIP to create any new directories it finds in the ZIP file. Then the program is executed with the CIM command. Finally, when the CIM session is over, PKZIP is used to check the CIM.ZIP file and update any files and directories that changed during the session. In the last line, PKZIP -UPR C:CIM *.*, the -UPR stands for Update files, Process directories, and Recurse directories. Because this drive is a RAM drive, deleting the files afterwards is fairly redundant, but if you use this file to create temporary space on a real hard disk, then deleting your work directory after updating the archive is good practice. You might even want to delete files on the RAM drive if you have other applications that you plan on expanding and running in it.

Exploring Hardware Options

As outlined in the previous section on Stacker, you can use a coprocessor board with the Stacker software to increase disk throughput by as much as 50 percent. The coprocessor board comes in 3 versions: an 8-bit XT model, a 16-bit AT through 486 model, and a 16-bit Microchannel (MCA) or PS/2 type. After the board is installed, no setup is required because the Stacker software simply registers the board's presence and starts to use it.

RLL disk controllers, as mentioned in Chapter 1, "A Hard Disk Primer," do in fact provide a limited amount of data compression and were among the first offerings with any kind of data-compression features. An RLL controller is a card that interfaces with MEM/ST506 drives and formats them in a special way to give more available space. RLL controllers usually work only with MFM- or RLL-supported drives.

One word of warning is in order here: in rare cases, if you have an RLL controller and a regular MFM drive, you run the risk of pushing the MFM drive outside its critical design parameters and thus causing it to fail. In fact, some MFM drive manufacturers often label their higher tolerance products as being "RLL capable." Checking with the manufacturer of your MFM drive to make sure that it can be "pushed" to RLL specifications is a good idea before you buy the RLL controller card.

Perstor Systems, Inc., manufactures some high-performance hard disk controllers that offer an alternative to the standard MFM- or RLL-type controllers. Perstor claims that replacing your current hard disk controller with one of their PC hard disk controllers can almost double the amount of storage on your existing drive. These controllers reportedly work with most standard hard disk drives (MFM or RLL). You should note, however, that these controllers do not currently work with drives such as IDE, ESDI, and SCSI.

The Perstor controllers store data by using a proprietary disk-coding method called Advanced Data Recording Technology (ADRT). The effect of ADRT is to increase the number of sectors per track. The increased density also should improve the throughput of data between the drive and controller. In theory, both disk capacity and performance are improved significantly. Perstor claims a 90 percent improvement in disk storage and between 10 and 100 percent improvement in overall performance. Perstor emphasizes that this technique is not data compression. Thus you can achieve further storage gains by using a disk-compression utility such as Stacker or SuperStor.

The two controller cards that Perstor provides to improve hard disk performance are models PS9008 and PS180-16FN. The PS9008 supports MS-DOS V3.0 and higher and works with both MFM and RLL drives. The PS9008 requires only an 8-bit slot and is primarily aimed at the older XT market but works on an AT-style 80286, 386, or even 486 system with some loss of performance. The PS180-16FN HDC, the faster 16-bit version, is designed to work with most 286, 386, and 486 systems. It requires at least DOS 3.0 but also can currently support Novell, SCO XENIX, and OS/2. The PS180-16 requires a 16-bit ISA slot.

Summary

In this chapter, you have looked at the problem of dwindling disk space and learned about some things to consider when you decide that you need to increase the available size of your hard disk. More importantly, you have discovered ways to avoid having to buy yourself another hard disk. The chapter has outlined some data-compression fundamentals, explored how effective compression can be, and explained how it was developed in the first place. You have explored both software and hardware solutions and in one case a bit of both. Some of the solutions provide methods for compressing the entire hard disk. Other utilities are aimed directly at compressing individual files or groups of files.

DOS Commands

This appendix serves as a handy reference to DOS commands. Many of these commands are covered more fully throughout the book. Unless otherwise noted, all commands are for Version 5.0 of DOS.

APPEND

APPEND is an external command that tells the operating system where to look for data files not in the current directory. This command is similar to the PATH command, except that PATH is used for executable (program and batch) files, and APPEND is used for nonexecutable files.

Syntax

APPEND   (to display the current APPEND list)

APPEND;   (to disable APPEND)

APPEND [*d:path1;*]\[*d:path2;*]...[*switches*]

d:path\ are the drives and directories you want DOS to search.

Switches

/?	Displays on-line help
/E	Places the disk drive paths in the environment

/X	Redirects programs that use the DOS function calls SEARCH FIRST, FIND FIRST, and EXEC
/X:ON	Same as /X (DOS 4.0 and later)
/X:OFF	Turns off the X search (DOS 4.0 and later)
/PATH:ON	Turns on a search for files that have a drive or path specified (DOS 4.0 and later)
/PATH:OFF	Turns off the search for files that have a drive or path specified (DOS 4.0 and later)

Notes

File names from appended directories do not show up in directory listings produced by the DIR command.

You should not use the DOS BACKUP or RESTORE commands when APPEND is activated. If APPEND is in use, you must remove it by typing **append;** before you attempt to use BACKUP or RESTORE. If you use the /N or /M switch with RESTORE, it may not process the correct files if you haven't deactivated APPEND.

If you use the APPEND command with the ASSIGN command, you should use the APPEND command first.

If you use the /E and /X switches with APPEND, using the command is a two-part process because you cannot include any path names with those switches. You have to type **append /e /x** first and then type in the directories you want to search, as in

APPEND C:\DOS;C:\DOS\UTILS

ASSIGN

ASSIGN is an external command used to reassign or reroute a drive. If DOS typically looks for something on a floppy drive, for example, you can reassign the hard drive in its place.

Syntax

ASSIGN *d1=d2* . . .

d1 is the letter of the disk drive DOS would normally use. *d2* is the letter of the disk drive that you want DOS to use instead.

Switch

/?   Displays on-line help

Notes

ASSIGN causes DOS or some other program to use a drive that's different from the one it thinks it's using. If you have a program that for some reason works only with drive A, for example, but you want it to work with drive C, you type the following command:

ASSIGN A=C

You can use more than one assignment on the same line, so if you want both the B drive and the A drive to be reassigned to drive C, you type the following:

ASSIGN A=C B=C

To remove the command after reassigning drives, you simply type **assign** at the prompt.

You must not use the ASSIGN command to assign the drive letter of your hard disk to another drive, nor should you use ASSIGN for a drive that is being used by a program.

Do not use ASSIGN with commands that require drive information, such as BACKUP, JOIN, LABEL, RESTORE, or SUBST.

Do not use ASSIGN with the DISKCOPY or FORMAT commands, because they ignore drive reassignments.

In fact, Microsoft recommends that you not use ASSIGN at all for typical uses of MS-DOS, unless a program cannot read or write files on the specified drive.

ATTRIB

ATTRIB is an external command used to view or change a file's attributes, such as read-only, system, archive, and hidden. Making a file a read-only file is a handy security precaution if you share a machine with other people.

Syntax

ATTRIB   (to display all attributes of all files in the current directory)

ATTRIB [+/-*attribute*] [*d:*][*path*][*filename*][*extension*]

Switches

/?   Displays on-line help

+R   Sets the read-only file attribute on

-R   Clears the read-only file attribute

+A   Sets the archive attribute on

-A   Clears the archive attribute

+S   Sets the file as a system file

-S   Clears the system file attribute

+H   Sets the file as a hidden file

-H   Clears the hidden file attribute

/S   Processes files in the current directory and all its subdirectories

Notes

You can use ATTRIB with groups of files by using wild cards (* and ?). If a file has the system or hidden attribute set, you must clear that attribute before you can change any other attributes for the file.

The archive attribute is used to mark files that have changed since they were previously backed up. This attribute is used by the BACKUP, RESTORE, and XCOPY commands.

The read-only attribute means that a file cannot be changed or deleted. To make a file called REPORT.DOC in the current directory a read-only file, type the following command at the DOS prompt:

ATTRIB +R REPORT.DOC

You can use as many switches as you want with ATTRIB. You can set both the read-only and archive attributes to on, for example, by typing

ATTRIB +R +A REPORT.DOC

BACKUP

BACKUP is an external command used to back up one or more files to a different disk drive (typically from the hard disk to floppy disks).

Syntax

BACKUP *d:*[*path*][*filename*][*extension*] *d:*[*path*] *d2:*[*switches*]

d:[*path*] are the drives and directories to be backed up. [*filename*][*extension*] are the specific files you want to back up. You can use wild cards (* or ?) to back up groups of files. *d2:* is the drive that receives the backup files.

Switches

/?	Displays on-line help.
/S	Backs up all subdirectories, beginning at the current or specified subdirectory.
/M	Backs up only the files that have changed since the last backup and clears the archive attribute of the original files.
/A	Adds backup files to an existing backup disk without deleting existing files.
/F[*size*]	Formats the backup disk to a size you specify.
/D:*date*	Backs up only files that were changed on or after the specified date.
/T:*time*	Backs up only files that were changed on or after the specified time. (Do not use /T without /D.)
/L:[:[*drive:*][*path*][*logfilename*]	Creates a log file. If you do not specify a location, BACKUP puts the log file in the root directory of the source drive. If you do not specify a name for the log file, BACKUP names it BACKUP.LOG.

Notes

Suppose that you want to back up everything in your FILES subdirectory to a formatted disk in drive A. Type the following at the DOS prompt:

BACKUP C:\FILES*.* A:

If you want to format the disk as you perform the backup, and it's a 720K disk, type the following at the prompt:

BACKUP C:\FILES*.* A: /F:720K

Now suppose that you want to back up only the files that were changed or created on or after January 1, 1992. Type this command:

BACKUP C:\FILES*.* A: /F:720K /D:01/01/92

After a backup is finished, BACKUP gives you exit codes to let you know how everything went.

0 means that the backup was successful.

1 means that the command couldn't find any files to back up.

2 means that some files weren't backed up because of file-sharing conflicts.

3 means that the user pressed Ctrl-C to stop the backup process.

4 means that the process stopped because of an error.

If you do not use the /A switch, BACKUP deletes all the old files and logs from a backup disk before adding new files.

Log files are important because they help you find the files you want to restore. In a backup log file, the date and time of the backup are on the first line. Each file name appears on a separate line with the number of the backup disk that contains the file.

Labeling and numbering backup disks consecutively is important. As one disk is filled, BACKUP prompts you for the next disk. When you use BACKUP's companion program RESTORE to restore backed-up files, you need to insert the disks in the same sequence you used to back them up. You can use the DIR command (if you have DOS 3.3 or later) to check the backup disk number.

You should not use BACKUP with drives that have been reassigned using the ASSIGN, JOIN, or SUBST commands. RESTORE may not be able to restore files if you do.

You cannot use the BACKUP command to back up DOS system files (MSDOS.SYS, IO.SYS, and COMMAND.COM). To copy these files to a floppy disk, use the SYS command.

You cannot use older versions of RESTORE (DOS 3.2 or earlier) with newer versions of BACKUP (DOS 3.3 or later) because the formats don't match. If you try it, DOS gives you the following message: Source does not contain backup files.

BREAK

BREAK is an internal command that sets or clears the Ctrl-C (or Ctrl-Break) checking. You can press Ctrl-C to stop a program or activity. You can use BREAK from the command line or in the CONFIG.SYS file.

Syntax

BREAK [ON][OFF]   (from the command line)

BREAK=ON   (from the CONFIG.SYS file)

Switch

/?   Displays on-line help

Note

If BREAK is turned off, DOS checks for the Ctrl-C key sequence only while reading from the keyboard or writing to the printer or screen. If you turn BREAK on, DOS extends its search for the Ctrl-C combination to other functions such as disk reads or writes.

BUFFERS

BUFFERS is an internal command that specifies the amount of memory to be allocated for disk buffers. Each buffer holds the contents of one sector, 512 bytes. DOS uses the reserved buffer memory to hold data during disk reads and writes. The more memory you have set aside for buffers, the less memory you have available to run programs.

The BUFFERS command is contained in the CONFIG.SYS file. For more information on working with BUFFERS and CONFIG.SYS, see Chapter 8, "Using Memory To Speed Up Your Disk."

Syntax

BUFFERS=n[,m]

n is the number of disk buffers (1 through 99). m specifies the number of buffers in the secondary buffer cache (1 through 8).

Notes

If you use many subdirectories, Microsoft recommends increasing the number of buffers to 20 or 30. The default setting for buffers varies with the configuration of the system. On machines with 512K to 640K of RAM, the default setting for buffers is 15.

If DOS is loaded into the high memory area (HMA), the buffers are also in HMA, leaving more conventional memory free to run programs.

CALL

CALL is an internal command that transfers temporary control from one batch file to another without causing the parent batch program to stop. CALL is used only with batch files. For more information on batch files, see Chapter 7, "Using Batch Files and Macros."

Syntax

CALL [*d:path*][*filename*][*batch parameters*]

[*d:path*][*filename*] specifies the location and name of the batch program you want to call. [*batch parameters*] specifies the command-line information required by the batch program. These parameters can be any parameters used by batch programs.

Switch

/?   Displays on-line help

CHDIR or CD

CHDIR or CD is an internal command that displays the current directory or changes the current directory. For more information on directories, see Chapter 6, "Working with Directories on Your Hard Disk."

Syntax

CHDIR or CD   (to display the current directory)

CHDIR *d:path* or CD *d:path*   (to change to a specified drive and directory)

CHDIR.. or CD..   (to change from a subdirectory back to the parent directory)

d:path represents drive and directory names.

Switch

/?   Displays on-line help

Notes

The root directory is the top of the directory hierarchy. To change to the root directory, type **chdir ** or **cd **. If you want to change to a directory called FINANCES, type **chdir \finances** or **cd \finances**.

You also can use CD to change to a subdirectory. If you want to change to the FINANCE subdirectory AUGUST, type this command:

CHDIR \FINANCES\AUGUST

or

CD \FINANCES\AUGUST

CHKDSK

CHKDSK is an external command that creates and displays a status report for a disk.

Syntax

CHKDSK [*d:path*][*filename*][*extension*][*switches*]

[*d:path*][*filename*][*extension*] represents the location and name of the files to be analyzed.

Switches

/?   Displays on-line help

/F   Fixes errors on the disk

/V   Displays the name of each file on the directory as the disk is checked

Notes

CHKDSK displays a report screen similar to the one shown in figure A.1.

```
C:\
chkdsk

Volume DR C 911029 created 10-29-1991 6:20p
Volume Serial Number is 1773-630C

 130279424 bytes total disk space
     77824 bytes in 4 hidden files
     83968 bytes in 30 directories
  51617792 bytes in 1339 user files
  78499840 bytes available on disk

      2048 bytes in each allocation unit
     63613 total allocation units on disk
     38330 available allocation units on disk

    655360 total bytes memory
    476608 bytes free

C:\
```

Using CHKDSK.

The command lets you know how much disk space is allocated in addition to letting you know how much memory is in use.

If you specify the /F switch, CHKDSK asks you to confirm that you want repairs made if it finds any problems. It gives a message similar to this one:

```
12 lost allocation units found in 4 chains.
Convert lost chains to files?
```

If you press Y, CHKDSK saves each lost chain as a file with the new name FILEnnnn.CHK. If you press N, CHKDSK fixes the disk but doesn't save the contents of the lost allocation units (clusters).

You can use CHKDSK C: /V | MORE to list all files on drive C one page at a time, and CHKDSK :: /V >PRN to print out all files on the drive.

COMP

COMP is an external command that compares the contents of two files or sets of files. It can compare files on the same drive or on different drives, in the same directory or in different directories.

Syntax

dc:pathc\COMP[*d:path1*][*filename1*][*extension1*][*d:path2*][*filename2*][*extension2*][*switches*]

dc:pathc\ represents the drive and directory containing the command. [*d:path1*][*filename1*][*extension1*] are the location and name of the first file to be compared. [*d:path2*][*filename2*][*extension2*] are the location and name of the second file to be compared.

You can use wild cards (* and ?) to compare groups of files.

Switches

/?	Displays on-line help
/D	Displays differences in decimal format (default format is hexadecimal)
/A	Displays differences as characters
/L	Displays the number of the line on which a difference occurs
/N=*number*	Displays the first number of lines of both files
/C	Performs a comparison that is not case-sensitive (FILE matches file)

Notes

You can compare files with the same name if they are in different directories or different drives. If you don't specify a file name for *filename2*, COMP looks for a file with the same name as *filename1*. If you don't specify a *filename1*, COMP compares all the files in the specified directory (*.*) to the contents of *filename2*.

To compare the file LETTER in drive C with the file LETTER in drive A, for example, type the following:

COMP C:LETTER A:LETTER

If you want to compare all the files in the subdirectory LETTERS on drive C to all the files in drive A, type the following:

COMP C:\LETTERS*.* A:*.*

Files that have the same name but different lengths are not checked. COMP gives you a message telling you that the files are different.

After 10 mismatches, COMP gives up. It displays a message letting you know that it is ending the compare process.

COMP is a good way to verify the COPY command and also is a good way to check a program that's starting to act squirrelly. You can compare a strangely acting program to a backup copy of the program that is in good working order.

COPY

COPY is an internal command that copies one or more files to a different location.

Syntax

COPY [*d:source*][*path*][*filename*][*extension*]. . .
[*d:destination*][*path*][*filename*][*extension*][*switches*]

[*d:source*][*path*][*filename*][*extension*] represent the location and name of the file you want to copy. The source can be a drive letter, directory, file name, or a combination. You also can use wild cards. The . . . indicates that you can copy several files from the source directory into one file in the destination directory.

Switches

/?   Displays on-line help.

/A   Indicates an ASCII (text) file. If you use the /A switch to precede a
            list of files, they all are copied as ASCII files until you indicate a
            binary file by using the /B switch.

/B   Indicates a binary file. When the /B switch precedes a list of file
            names, they all are copied as binary files until you indicate an /A
            switch, at which point all the files following are copied as ASCII
            files. The /B switch is the default value unless COPY is combining
            files.

/V   Verifies that the new files are written correctly.

Notes

You can substitute device names such as COM1 (a serial port, which
may be attached to a modem) or LPT1 (a printer port, which is attached
to a printer) for the source or destination.

If you use the + sign to specify more than one source, COPY combines
the files and creates a single destination file. If you use wild cards in the
source but specify a single file in the destination, COPY combines all the
matching files in the source and creates a single file in the destination. If
you want to combine the REPORT.JAN, REPORT.FEB, and REPORT.MAR
files into a single file called REPORTS, for example, type the following:

COPY REPORT.JAN + REPORT.FEB + REPORT.MAR REPORTS

This command creates a new file called REPORTS in the same directory
that contains the three original files. To copy the three original files from
the current directory on the hard drive to a new file REPORTS on the A
drive, type the following:

COPY REPORT.JAN + REPORT.FEB + REPORT.MAR A:REPORTS

DEL (ERASE)

DEL and ERASE are interchangeable internal commands. Either one
deletes a specified file or files. For more information on DEL and ERASE,
see Chapter 5, "Keeping Files Organized."

Syntax

DEL (ERASE) [*d:*][*path*][*filename*][*extension*][*switches*]

[*d:*][*path*] are the drive and directory holding the file or files to be deleted. You can use wild cards * and ? with DEL (ERASE).

Switches

/?   Displays on-line help

/P   Prompts you for confirmation before deleting the specified file or files

Notes

If you want to delete all the files in a directory, use *.*. If you want to empty out your REPORTS directory, for example, either make that the current directory or type REPORTS in the PATH. If REPORTS is the current directory, simply type **del *.*** or **erase *.*** at the prompt. You also can type **del c:\reports** or **erase c:\reports**.

The /P switch is a great way to avoid deleting the wrong file if you're daydreaming at the keyboard. Using this switch is also a good idea if you're deleting a group of files but want to check to make sure that you want to get rid of all of them. When you use the /P switch, DOS deletes the files one at a time, displaying for each file the file name and the prompt Delete (Y/N)? and asking you to confirm you each deletion.

DEL (ERASE) does not work on directories. To remove a directory, you must use the RMDIR (RD) command.

> *CAUTION:* If you notice that you accidentally deleted a file you want to keep, you must use the UNDELETE command right away. If you save other files to the disk before you use the UNDELETE command, you risk overwriting and thus losing your accidentally deleted file.

DIR

DIR is an internal command that displays the files and subdirectories in a disk directory. For more information on DIR, see Chapter 5, "Keeping Files Organized."

Syntax

DIR [*d:*][*path*][*filename*][*extension*][*switches*]

[*d:*][*path*] are the drive and directory you want to view.
[*filename*][*extension*] are file names. You can use wild cards.

Switches

/?	Displays on-line help.
/P	Pauses when the screen is full until you press any key to scroll down.
/W	Gives a wide display of file and directory names without the date, size, and time information.
/A	Displays all files, including hidden and system files.
/A[*attributes*]	Displays only the names of the directories and files with attributes you specify. If you omit this switch, DOS displays all files except hidden and system files. For *attributes*, you can use any of the following:

	H	Hidden files
	-H	Files that are not hidden
	S	System files
	-S	Files that are not system files
	D	Directories only
	-D	Files only
	A	Files ready for archiving (backing up)
	-A	Files that have not changed since the last backup
	R	Read-only files
	-R	Files that are not read-only

/O[*sortorder*]	Controls the order in which DIR sorts and displays directory names and file names. If you omit this switch, DIR displays directory and file names in the order in which they occur. If you use the /O switch without specifying the order, DIR sorts the directories and files in alphabetical order. For *sortorder*, you can use any of the following:

	N	Alphabetic order by name
	-N	Reverse alphabetic order (Z through A)

E	Alphabetic order by extension
-E	Reverse alphabetic order by extension
D	By date and time with the earliest first
-D	By date and time with the most recent first
S	By size with smallest first
-S	By size with largest first
G	With directories grouped before files
-G	With files grouped before directories

/S	Lists every occurrence of a specified file name in both the specified directory and subdirectories.
/B	Lists every directory name or file name, one per line, without heading information or summary (overrides the /W switch).
/L	Displays unsorted directory names and file names in lowercase.

Notes

You can use any combination of switches, but don't use spaces to separate them.

SETDIRCMD=[*switches*] is a new command with DOS 5.0 that you can use to change the default settings for your directory display. You can execute this command from the DOS command line or a batch file. (If you put the command in your AUTOEXEC.BAT file, the command installs automatically every time you start the computer. For more information on AUTOEXEC.BAT, see Chapter 7, "Using Batch Files and Macros.")

If you want the default setting for your directories to be in alphabetical order, for example, you use this command:

    SET DIRCMD=/O:N

If your directory is too large for one screen, and you want the list to pause automatically, you add the /P switch, and your command looks like this:

    SET DIRCMD=/O:N/P

Notice that you don't use any spaces.

DOSKEY

DOSKEY is an external command that starts the DOSKEY program, which recalls DOS commands, creates macros, and edits command lines. DOSKEY is new to DOS 5.0.

Syntax

DOSKEY [*switches*]

Switches

/REINSTALL	Installs a new copy of the DOSKEY program.
/BUFSIZE=*size*	Specifies the size of the buffer that DOSKEY uses to store commands and DOSKEY macros. The default size is 512 bytes.
/MACROS	Displays a list of all DOSKEY macros. Can be abbreviated as /M.
/HISTORY	Displays a list of all commands stored in memory. Can be abbreviated as /H.
/INSERT/OVERSTRIKE	Specifies whether the text you type will replace old text. INSERT inserts text as if you had used the Ins key. OVERSTRIKE (the default setting) replaces old text.

Note

For more details on using DOSKEY and creating macros, refer to Chap-ter 7, "Using Batch Files and Macros."

FASTOPEN

FASTOPEN is an external command that provides quick access to recently used subdirectories and files by caching their names. The FASTOPEN command is added to the CONFIG.SYS file.

Syntax

dc:pathc\FASTOPEN *d:*=[*nnn*][*mmm*][*switch*]

dc:pathc\ represents the disk drive and directory containing the command. *d:* is the name of the drive containing the directory information to be cached in memory. *nnn* is the number of directory entries to be held in memory (10 to 999). The default value is 48. *mmm* is the number of fragmented entries (1 to 999).

Switches

/?   Displays on-line help

/X   Creates the name cache in expanded memory rather than conventional memory

Notes

Do not use FASTOPEN from the DOS Shell. Doing so may cause your machine to lock up.

If you want to keep up to 65 files from the C drive in memory, you type **fastopen c:=65**.

FC

FC, an external command that is like a newer, better version of COMP, enables you to compare two files or sets of files.

Syntax

dc:pathc\FC [*d:*][*path*][*filename1*][*d:*][*path*][*filename2*][*switches*]

dc:pathc\ are the drive and directory that contain the command. [*d:*][*path*][*filename1*] are the location and first file or set of files to be compared. [*d:*][*path*][*filename2*] are the location and path of the second file or set of files to be compared.

You can use wild cards (* or ?) with FC.

Switches

/A	Abbreviates the output of an ASCII comparison.
/B	Uses binary mode to compare the files. This mode is the default mode for comparing files with EXE, COM, SYS, OBJ, LIB, or BIN extensions.
/C	Disregards case (upper or lower).
/L	Compares files in ASCII mode. This mode is the default mode for files that don't have EXE, COM, SYS, OBJ, LIB, or BIN extensions. FC attempts to synchronize the files when it finds a mismatch.
/LB[n]	Sets the number of lines for the internal file buffer. The default length is 100 lines. If the files to be compared have more than 100 lines, FC cancels the comparison.
/N	Displays line numbers for ASCII comparisons.
/T	Does not expand tabs as spaces.
/W	Compresses tabs and spaces.
/$nnnn$	Specifies the number of consecutive lines that have to match before FC considers the files resynchronized. If the number of matching lines is less than this number, FC displays the matching lines as differences. The default value is 2.

Notes

If you want to compare two text files in the same directory that are named REPORT.JUN and SALES.JUN, you type

FC REPORT.JUN SALES.JUN

at the prompt.

To abbreviate the results of the comparison, you add the /A switch, as in

FC /A REPORT.JUN SALES.JUN

FDISK

FDISK is an external command that partitions a disk so that it is ready to work with DOS. FDISK is discussed in detail in Chapter 3, "Understanding How DOS Works with the Hard Disk."

Syntax

FDISK

Switch

/?   Displays limited on-line help

Note

FDISK doesn't work on drives created by ASSIGN, SUBST, or JOIN.

FIND

FIND is an external command with which you can search for specified words or phrases in a text file.

Syntax

dc:pathc\FIND [*switches*] "*searchtext*" [*d:*][*path*][*filename*][*extension*]

dc:pathc\ are the drive and directory containing the command.
"*searchtext*" is the word or phrase you want to find.
[*d:*][*path*][*filename*][*extension*] are the drive, directory, and file you want to search.

Switches

/?   Displays on-line help

/V   Displays all lines not containing the word or phrase

/C   Counts the number of times the word or phrase occurs and displays that number on-screen

/N   Displays the number of the line that contains the phrase at the beginning of that line

/I   Specifies that the search is not case-sensitive

Notes

If you do not use the /I switch, you must match the case of the phrase or word exactly. FIND does not think that "nora" and "Nora" match, for example, if you have not used the /I switch.

FIND does not work with wild cards.

You must use double quotes ("") around the text to be searched. To find each occurrence of the word *inventory* in a file named REPORT in the current directory, for example, you type

FIND "inventory" REPORT

FORMAT

FORMAT is an external command that initializes a hard or floppy disk so that it can be used by DOS. Formatting takes place after partitioning.

Syntax

FORMAT *d:* [*switches*]

d: is the drive you want to format.

Switches

/V:*labelname*	Specifies volume label, which identifies the disk. You can use up to 11 characters.
/Q	Deletes FAT and root directory of previously formatted disk but does not scan disk for bad areas. Use only on disks in good condition.
/U	Specifies unconditional format.
/S	Copies system files from start-up drive.

(Other switches are available, but they apply to floppy drives only. The switches shown here are the ones you are most likely to use with your hard drive.)

Note

FORMAT is discussed in detail in Chapter 3, "Understanding How DOS Works with the Hard Disk."

HELP

HELP, an external command, is new to DOS 5.0. You may have noticed that every command contains the optional /? switch, which displays on-line help for that command. HELP gives you another way to get help.

Syntax

HELP [*commandname*]

[*commandname*] is the name of the command on which you want to get help.

Notes

You can type **help copy**, for example, instead of typing **copy /?**. Using the COPY /? version is faster, however, than using HELP COPY.

HELP contains help only for DOS commands; help for DOS Shell functions is contained within the DOS Shell itself.

JOIN

JOIN is an external command that links a physical or logical drive to a subdirectory on another drive.

Syntax

*dc:pathc*JOIN *d1: d2:\\directoryname*

dc:pathc are the drive and directory containing the command. *d1:* is the drive to be connected (called the guest disk drive). *d2:* is the disk drive to which *d1:* will be connected (called the host drive). *directoryname* is a subdirectory in the host drive (called the host subdirectory).

Switches

/?   Displays on-line help

/D   Cancels any previous join commands

Notes

If you want to join the A drive to a subdirectory called FILES on the C drive, you type this command:

JOIN A: C\FILES

To cancel the current JOIN command for the A drive, you type

JOIN A:/D

Using the JOIN command invalidates the guest drive. If you try to access the A drive after joining it to a subdirectory in the C drive, you get an `Invalid drive specification` message.

Use the JOIN command with care. The following commands do not work with drives formed by the JOIN command:

ASSIGN
BACKUP
CHKDSK
DISKCOMP
DISKCOPY
FDISK
FORMAT
LABEL
MIRROR
RECOVER
RESTORE
SYS

LABEL

LABEL is an external command that creates, changes, or deletes a disk's volume label (name). The volume label is displayed as part of the directory listing.

Syntax

LABEL [*d:*][*volumename*]

d: is the disk drive whose label is to be changed. *volumename* is the new name.

Notes

To see the volume label of the current drive, simply type **label** at the prompt. You see the following message:

```
Volume in drive C is xxxxxx
Volume serial number is xxx-xxx
Volume label (11 characters, ENTER for none)?
```

(The second line is not displayed if no serial number exists.)

If you press Enter, the current label is deleted.

To give a drive a new label, you type **label** followed by the drive letter and the name you want to use. To change the label of drive C to DISK, for example, type

LABEL C:DISK

You cannot use the following symbols in volume labels:

* ? / \ | . , ; : + = [] ( ) & ^ <> "

LABEL does not work with drives created using the JOIN, ASSIGN, or SUBST commands.

MEM

MEM is an external command that displays the amount of used and free memory in your system.

Syntax

MEM [*switch*]

(You can use only one switch at a time.)

Switches

/?	Displays on-line help.
/PROGRAM	Displays the status of programs that currently are loaded into memory. Also displays the amount of free memory available. Cannot be used in conjunction with the other switches.
/DEBUG	Displays the status of currently loaded programs and device drivers. Also displays the amount of free memory available. Cannot be used in conjunction with the other switches.
/CLASSIFY	Displays the status of programs loaded into conventional memory and the upper memory area. Also lists the largest memory blocks that are available. Cannot be used in conjunction with the other switches.

Notes

Using MEM without the switches displays how much memory is available and how much is in use without going into the program specifics. The command displays the status of extended memory only if your system has extended memory. The command displays the status of expanded memory only if it conforms to Version 4.0 of the LIM EMS (Lotus-Intel-Microsoft Expanded Memory Specification).

You may want to use MEM /C | MORE because the listing may be too long. With MORE, you can view one screenful at a time.

MIRROR

MIRROR is an external command new to DOS 5.0. MIRROR records data about one or more disks for use with the UNDELETE and UNFORMAT commands. MIRROR is described in Chapter 12, "Raiders of the Lost Data."

Syntax

MIRROR [*d:*] [*switches*]

[*d:*] is the drive that you want mirrored.

Switches

/?	Displays on-line help.
/1	Retains only the most recent disk information.
/T*drive*[-*entries*]	Loads a memory-resident tracking program that records information used by the UNDELETE command. The required *drive* parameter specifies the drive containing the disk you want MIRROR to track. The optional *entries* parameter specifies the maximum number of entries for the deletion-tracking file (1 through 999). The default number of entries varies with drive size. For a 20M drive, the default number of entries is 101. On a 32M drive, the default is 202, and on drives above 32M, the default is 303.
/U	Unloads the deletion-tracking program from memory. (You cannot unload it if you have installed other memory-resident programs after you loaded it.)
/PARTN	Saves partition information to a floppy disk. The UNFORMAT command can use this information to rebuild disk partitions.

Notes

MIRROR creates image files of the file allocation table, the partition table, and the root directory. The more current the information, the less you lose if you have to unformat the disk. For that reason, putting MIRROR in the AUTOEXEC.BAT file is a good idea.

To save the FAT and root directory for drive C and install deletion tracking, you type the following:

MIRROR C:/TC

To save the partition information, you type

MIRROR/PARTN

MIRROR then prompts you to insert a floppy disk.

CAUTION: Do not use the deletion-tracking feature for any drive that you have redirected with the JOIN or SUBST command. If you plan to use the ASSIGN command, you must run it before using MIRROR to install deletion tracking.

MKDIR (MD)

MKDIR or MD is an internal command that creates a subdirectory. It is discussed in more detail in Chapter 6, "Working with Directories on Your Hard Disk."

Syntax

MKDIR *d:*[*path*] or MD *d:*[*path*]

d: is the disk drive for the subdirectory. [*path*] is the path to the directory that holds the subdirectory being created.

Notes

You can create as many subdirectories as you want, but the path name is limited to 63 characters.

To create a subdirectory called ARTICLES on the current drive, for example, you type **md \articles** and press Enter at the DOS prompt.

PATH

PATH is an internal command that tells DOS which directories to search for executable files. PATH typically is found in the AUTOEXEC.BAT file, both of which are discussed in more detail in Chapter 7, "Using Batch Files and Macros." PATH helps DOS get through the directory hierarchy more quickly and saves you from always having to switch to certain directories.

Often, when you get the message Bad command or file name, the reason is that DOS has given up after searching the current directory. Suppose that you want to start WordPerfect from the DOS prompt. To do so, you must include the directory that contains the WP.EXE command in DOS's search path; otherwise, you have to make that directory the current directory before you can start WordPerfect.

Syntax

PATH [*d:*][*pathname*];[*d:*][*pathname*]; . . .

[*d:*][*pathname*] are valid disk drive names and path names. The ellipsis indicates that you can include additional path names.

Switch

/?   Displays on-line help

Notes

At installation, many programs update the AUTOEXEC.BAT file and add themselves to the PATH command contained in that file.

To place a program in DOS's search path, you type the program in the PATH command. Suppose that you want to be able to start WordPerfect and Lotus 1-2-3 from the DOS prompt, without having to switch to their directories first. The WordPerfect directory is called WP51, and the Lotus directory is called 123. You type the following:

PATH C:\WP51;C:\123

To display the current path setting, simply type **path** and press Enter at the prompt.

You can use PATH only for executable files.

The maximum length for the PATH command is 127 characters.

RENAME (REN)

RENAME is an internal command used to rename a file or files. For more on this command, see Chapter 5, "Keeping Files Organized."

Syntax

RENAME [*d:*][*path*][*oldname*][*extension*][*newname*][*extension*]

d:[*path*] are the drive and path of the file to be renamed. [*oldname*] represents the old file name. [*newname*] is the new name you're giving the file.

Switch

/?   Displays on-line help

Notes

You can use wild cards (* and ?) with either the old file name or the new file name.

If you want to use RENAME to change extensions for all the files in a directory, for example, you type this command:

REN *.DOC *.OLD

If you try to rename a file with a name that's already in use, RENAME gives you this message: Duplicate file name or file not found.

REPLACE

REPLACE is an external command used to replace files on a destination directory with files of the same name from a source directory. You also can use REPLACE to add unique file names to the destination directory.

Syntax

REPLACE [*d:*][*path*][*filename*][*extension*][*d2:*][*path2*][*switches*]

[*d:*][*path*][*filename*][*extension*] indicates the source of the file or set of files. [*d2:*][*path2*] indicates the location of the destination directory. You don't specify a name for the destination.

Switches

/?   Displays on-line help.

/A   Adds new files instead of replacing existing files. You cannot use this switch with the /S or /U switch.

/P   Prompts for confirmation before replacing a destination file or adding a source file.

/R   Replaces read-only files as well as unprotected files.

/S   Searches all subdirectories of the destination directory. Does not work with the /A switch.

/W   Causes REPLACE to wait for you to insert a disk.

/U   Replaces only the files in the destination directory that are older than those in the source directory.

Notes

REPLACE searches only on the basis of names, not file content. Using this command is a quick way to update files, although you cannot use it to update hidden files or system files.

REPLACE comes in handy if you have several versions of the same file in different directories. Suppose that you have a directory called TAPE from which you back files up to a tape drive, but the latest version of your document CHAPTER2 is in your word processing directory. To replace the older version in your TAPE directory, you type

REPLACE C:\WP51\CHAPTER2 C:\TAPE

REPLACE shows you the following exit codes when it is finished:

0 means that REPLACE was successful.

2 means that REPLACE couldn't find the source files.

3 means that REPLACE couldn't find the source or destination path.

5 means that you don't have access to the files you want to replace.

8 means that you have insufficient system memory to carry out the command.

11 means that you used the wrong syntax.

RESTORE

RESTORE is an external command for restoring files that were backed up with the BACKUP command. RESTORE is covered in Chapter 10, "Understanding the Importance of Backing Up."

Syntax

RESTORE *d1:*[*d2:*][*path*][*filename*][*extension*][*switches*]

d1: is the disk drive holding the backup files. *d2:* specifies the drive to which the backup files will be restored. [*path*] specifies the directory to which the backup files will be restored. It has to be the same directory from which they were backed up. [*filename*] and [*extension*] specify the names and extensions of the backup files you want to restore.

Switches

/?	Displays on-line help
/S	Restores all subdirectories
/P	Prompts you for permission to restore files that are read-only or that have changed since the last backup
/M	Restores all files that have been modified or deleted since the last backup
/N	Restores all files that no longer exist on the destination disk
/B:*date*	Restores all files that were created or changed on or before the date you specify
/L:*time*	Restores all files that were created or changed at or later than the time you specify
/E:*time*	Restores all files that were created or changed at or earlier than the time you specify

Notes

To restore a file called CATTLE from the A drive to a subdirectory called FARM on the C drive, for example, you type the following:

RESTORE A: C:\FARM\CATTLE

RESTORE, like BACKUP, uses exit codes to let you know whether it was successful.

0 means that RESTORE was successful.

1 means that RESTORE couldn't find the files to restore.

3 means that you pressed Ctrl-C to stop the operation.

4 means that RESTORE stopped because of an error.

RESTORE works only on files that were backed up with the BACKUP command. RESTORE prompts you to insert the backup disks in order.

Be careful if you use RESTORE on files that were backed up while ASSIGN, JOIN, or SUBST were in effect. You also should disable APPEND by typing **append;** before attempting to use RESTORE.

DOS 5.0 RESTORE can work with all old versions of DOS, but be careful when mixing old versions of BACKUP and RESTORE.

RMDIR (RD)

RMDIR is an internal command that removes directories. For more information, see Chapter 6, "Working with Directories on Your Hard Disk."

Syntax

RMDIR [*d:*][*path*][*directory*] or RD [*d:*][*path*][*directory*]

[*d:*] is the drive holding the subdirectory. [*path*] is the path to the subdirectory. [*directory*] is the directory you want to remove.

Switch

/?   Displays on-line help

Notes

When you remove a subdirectory, it must be empty except for the current directory file (.) and any parent directories (..).

To remove a directory called ARTICLES from the current drive, you type the following:

RD ARTICLES

or

RMDIR ARTICLES

If the directory you want to remove isn't in the current drive or directory, you need to use the CD command to change to that directory first.

SUBST

SUBST is an external command that creates a virtual (pretend) disk drive name that can be associated with a path.

Syntax

SUBST *d1: d2:pathname*

d1: is a name for the virtual drive. *d2:* and *pathname* are the drive and path that will go by the name of the virtual drive.

Switches

/?   Displays on-line help

/D   Deletes the virtual drive

Notes

To display the name of any virtual drives currently in effect, simply type **subst** and press Enter at the DOS prompt.

If you want to create a virtual drive X for the path C:\FARM\CATTLE, you use this command:

      SUBST X: C:\FARM\CATTLE

To delete the virtual drive, you use this command:

      SUBST X:/D

SUBST is one of those commands you have to use with care. The following commands either do not work or should not be used with drives used in the SUBST command:

      ASSIGN
      BACKUP
      CHKDSK
      DISKCOMP
      DISKCOPY
      FDISK
      FORMAT
      LABEL

MIRROR
RECOVER
RESTORE
SYS

TREE

TREE is an external command that displays a tree structure of the directory path on a specified drive.

Syntax

TREE *d:*[*path*][*switch*]

d: is the disk drive you want to examine. [*path*] is the directory for which you want to display the structure.

Switches

/? Displays on-line help

/F Displays the names of files in each directory

/A Uses text characters rather than graphics characters to show the lines linking subdirectories (typically used with printers)

Note

If you don't specify a path or drive, TREE starts with the current directory of the current drive.

UNDELETE

UNDELETE is an external command new to DOS 5.0. The command restores files that were deleted with the DEL or ERASE command and is explained in depth in Chapter 12, "Raiders of the Lost Data."

Syntax

UNDELETE [*d:*][*path*][*switches*]

[*d:*] is the drive that contains the file or files you want to recover. [*path*] is the path for the file or files you want to recover.

Switches

/LIST	Lists the deleted files that are available but does not recover them.
/ALL	Recovers deleted files without prompting for confirmation on each file.
/DOS	Recovers only the files that are listed as deleted by DOS and ignores the deletion-tracking file if it is present. Prompts for confirmation after each file.
/DT	Recovers only the files listed as deleted in the deletion-tracking file created by the MIRROR command.

Notes

If you do not specify a switch, UNDELETE uses the deletion-tracking file if it is available. If you simply type **undelete** at the DOS prompt, the command recovers all deleted files in the current directory and prompts you for confirmation.

You can use wild cards with UNDELETE. If you want to recover all deleted files with the DOC extension in the root directory of drive C and don't want to be prompted for each file, you type the following:

UNDELETE C:\ *.DOC /ALL

CAUTION: After you have deleted a file, you may not be able to get it back. UNDELETE works safely only if no other files have been saved to the disk. If you accidentally delete a file, use UNDELETE IMMEDIATELY.

UNFORMAT

UNFORMAT is an external command new to DOS 5.0. The command restores hard or floppy disks that have been reformatted accidentally. For more information, see Chapter 12, "Raiders of the Lost Data."

Syntax

UNFORMAT d: [switches]

d: is the drive you want to recover.

Switches

/?	Displays on-line help.
/J	Verifies that the file created by MIRROR agrees with the system information on the disk but does not rebuild the disk. You cannot use the /J switch used with other switches.
/U	Unformats a disk without using the MIRROR file.
/L	When used without the /PARTN switch, lists all the files and subdirectories found by UNFORMAT.
/P	Sends all output to the printer.
/TEST	Shows how UNFORMAT would re-create the disk information but does not perform any repairs.
/PARTN	Restores a hard drive's partition table. Requires a file that was created by MIRROR and saved to a floppy disk.

Notes

DOS 5.0 now performs a safe format by default, which enables UNFORMAT to recover information. If you used the /U switch with FORMAT, however, UNFORMAT is not able to restore the disk.

UNFORMAT attempts to restore the root directory and FAT to the condition they were in when the MIRROR file was created. For that reason, you should update the MIRROR file frequently. One of the best ways to do so is to have MIRROR in your AUTOEXEC.BAT file; then MIRROR updates the DOS structures every time you boot the computer.

You can use UNFORMAT without MIRROR, but the command will be less reliable.

To determine whether UNFORMAT will be able to re-create a disk based on information in the MIRROR image file, use this command:

UNFORMAT C:/J

To restore the hard disk, you use this command:

UNFORMAT C:

To restore a hard disk without a MIRROR file, listing all files and subdirectories, you use this command:

UNFORMAT C:/L

Some Program Files You Can Live Without

One of the easiest ways to free up space on your hard disk is to remove unnecessary programs or not install them in the first place. Programs are becoming larger all the time; luckily, they're also becoming smarter and more considerate. Many popular software packages contain optional programs such as tutorials that you can skip during the installation process.

Some programs, such as Lotus 1-2-3 Release 2.3 and Systems Compatibility Corporation's The Complete Writer's Toolkit, tell you up front exactly how much disk space each module needs. Others, such as WordPerfect, don't spell it out that specifically but still let you know that a particular module is optional and that you can save disk space by not installing it.

Tutorials are a good candidate for programs not to install or to remove after you have used them and become comfortable with the program. WordPerfect, Microsoft Word, and Lotus 1-2-3 all contain tutorials, called Learn, Learning Word, and 1-2-3 Go!, respectively.

The optional WYSIWYG component of Lotus 1-2-3 also has a tutorial called WYSIWYG-Go!. WYSIWYG, which stands for What You See Is What You Get, is a graphics and desktop publishing term. 1-2-3's WYSIWYG program enables you to add graphic elements to spreadsheets. It's nice, but it takes up more than 2M of disk space, and you can live without it in a crunch.

Other optional programs in 1-2-3 cater to specialized needs. If you don't have those needs, you don't have to install programs such as PrintGraph and Translate. PrintGraph, for example, isn't necessary unless you plan to use a pen plotter or print several graphs at the same time. Translate isn't necessary unless you plan to convert worksheets from other spreadsheet or database programs into 1-2-3 or convert 1-2-3 documents to other programs.

In addition to its tutorial, WordPerfect contains a number of optional graphics images with WPG extensions that are not necessary unless you plan to enhance documents.

Windows also contains a number of graphics image files called BMP files. If you don't plan on using them, save your valuable disk space by removing them.

If you use your computer primarily to bring work home from the office and don't have a printer, you don't need to install any printer device drivers. Some programs, such as Windows, automatically detect the absence of a printer and don't even attempt to install the printer files.

Some Common Errors

This chapter lists some common DOS error messages you might see—ranging from easy-to-fix to scary problems—describes why these messages appear, and gives you some tips on how to handle them. You also learn what to do when some other types of problems occur.

Looking at Some DOS Error Messages

DOS contains quite a bevy of error messages. The one most of you probably learn first is the ever-popular Bad command or file name, which you see often while you're learning to navigate directories. This message usually translates to one of two things: you have made a typographical error, or you have issued a command from the wrong directory. Either way, the message has pilot error written all over it.

Some of DOS's error messages, however, point the finger at the computer, at the hard drive in particular. The following section explores some of the messages you may encounter and gives some possible causes. Notice that usually more than one potential cause underlies a single message. This appendix can help you identify some potential sources of trouble.

Abort, Retry, Ignore?

The system area (boot record, FAT, or root directory) may be damaged. If you suspect that the system area is damaged, you can use the DOS

UNFORMAT command or one of the unformat commands contained in PC Tools on the Norton Utilities.

Access Denied

You (or a program) tried to change or erase a file that is marked read-only or is in use. If the file is read-only, use the ATTRIB command with the /-R switch to turn off the read-only attribute.

Allocation Error, Size Adjusted

The contents of a file have been truncated because the amount of data in the file is not the same as the size indicated in the file's directory entry. Use CHKDSK/F to correct the discrepancy.

APPEND Already Installed

You tried using APPEND with the /X or /E switch after using APPEND earlier. You can use the /X or /E switch only the first time you use APPEND. To change the switch, reboot the computer.

Bad Command or File Name

You may have mistyped a command or file name or neglected to specify the path for a command. Try it again.

Bad or Missing Command Interpreter

Reboot, using a system floppy disk or DOS Uninstall disk. You may need to reinstall COMMAND.COM.

Bad Sector

Having a bad sector isn't necessarily critical on "regular" drives but can be a sign of trouble on an IDE drive. Mark the sectors as bad in the FAT by using a utility program. Bad sectors may indicate that the drive's life is nearing an end, so start shopping for a new drive and back everything up if you aren't in the habit of doing so.

Drive Not Ready Reading Drive C

You may get this message if you install an IDE drive on a machine with an older BIOS. The problem occurs frequently with AMI BIOS prior to 4/9/90 but also can happen with older BIOS versions from other manufacturers. You may need to upgrade the BIOS. If you get this message on a machine with a new BIOS, try using one of the disk utilities, such as PC Tools DiskFix, to examine and repair the drive.

File Allocation Table Bad, Drive X

This message may indicate a virus infection, a defective drive or controller, or a RAM or CMOS error. Use a diagnostic tool such as the Norton Disk Doctor to diagnose the FAT.

`General Failure Reading/Writing Drive C`

When you see this message, you should be afraid. Usually DOS can give you an idea of the kind of problem that has occurred, as in the `Bad` or `Missing Command Interpreter` message. When you see `General Failure Reading/Writing Drive C`, however, even the operating system is stumped. This message can indicate a failed hard disk controller or drive, disconnected cables, an overheated system, a RAM failure, or a virus.

Turn the machine off and let it sit for a few minutes. Remove the cover and look under the hood to make sure that none of the connecting cables or the controller card has come loose. If you can reboot the machine, run a diagnostic utility or CHKDSK. If the diagnostic utility encounters problems, you may need to use advanced diagnostics. Call your dealer, unless you're willing to tackle this situation yourself.

`Invalid Drive Specification`

The specified drive doesn't exist or hasn't been initialized, or the partition table is damaged. First make sure that the message hasn't been caused by pilot error. (You may have typed **d:** when you meant to type **c:**). If you suddenly get this message on a C drive that has been working fine up until that point, the latter situation is the probable cause.

If the drive hasn't been initialized yet, you need to partition and format it. If you suspect a damaged partition table, use the DOS UNFORMAT/PARTN command to restore the original partition table. (Your ability to use this command depends on your having backed up the partition information onto a floppy by using the MIRROR command.)

To use UNFORMAT, first you use the DOS install disk to bring up the computer from the floppy drive. This disk contains the UNFORMAT command, so after you get the DOS prompt, you can type **unformat/partn** and press Enter. You then are prompted to insert the floppy disk that contains the PARTNSAV.FIL file created by MIRROR and to enter the letter of the floppy disk drive. After you do so, UNFORMAT checks the drive parameters saved in the PARTNSAV.FIL against the true parameters. If they don't match, UNFORMAT does not restore the information. UNFORMAT also prompts you to insert a system disk and press Enter to restart. This step lets the system know that the partition information has changed. Then use UNFORMAT without PARTNSAV.FIL.

`Non-System Disk or Disk Error`

You may have left a floppy disk in your floppy drive, and the system may be trying to boot from that disk.

```
Sector Not Found
```

This message can mean that the disk wasn't formatted properly. It also can indicate that the disk has sustained physical damage. Use one of the diagnostic programs to see what's going on.

```
Numbered Error Messages
```

You also may get numbered error messages. Messages in the 1700s indicate hardware problems. Some of the numbered messages you may encounter include the following:

1701	Power-On Self-Test error
1702	Controller error
1703	Controller/cabling/drive error
1704	Disk 0 failure
1705	Disk 1 failure
1782	Controller failure
17xx	Other hard drive failure or CMOS failure

(Messages numbered 01x, 102, 103, 162, or 163 also may indicate CMOS problems.) If you see any of these messages, call your dealer.

Encountering Other Problems

You also may encounter some other types of problems, not necessarily indicated by a DOS error message. In this section, you learn how to handle some of these troublesome situations.

When you first start your computer, it sounds like a sick vacuum cleaner for the first minute or so and then settles down. Take the computer in so that the dealer can look at it. The power supply probably needs replacing.

Your drive makes a high-pitched, constant whine. The heads may have crashed, or the drive may be dying. Take it to the shop.

You boot up and get no sign of activity from either the disk drive light or the display screen. The system emits a series of beeps or a long beep. Your CMOS battery may be going out. Contact your dealer about replacing the battery.

Glossary

Address. A memory location, much like a house's street address.

Address space. The amount of memory a computer can address. A computer may have more addresses available than it has memory to fill them. The amount of address space a computer has is determined by the type of microprocessor it contains.

Application. Software that is used to perform a specified task. This term applies to almost every kind of computer program with the exception of operating system software.

Archive bit. The file attribute used to mark files that have changed since the last backup.

ASCII (American Standard Code for Information Interchange). The character-coding system used by most computer systems. It converts the 1s and 0s of the computer's native tongue (binary) to the characters and numerals used by people.

ASCII file. An unformatted text file, which means that it doesn't contain any special coding for a particular software program. ASCII files typically use the extension TXT.

Assign. The DOS command that redirects requests for disk operations from one drive to a different drive.

ATTRIB. The DOS command used to display or change file attributes (characteristics such as read-only, archive, or hidden).

AUTOEXEC.BAT. A batch program that defines the characteristics of the devices connected to the system and also can execute any DOS command. After carrying out the CONFIG.SYS commands, DOS looks for an AUTOEXEC.BAT file.

Average access time. The average amount of time a read/write head takes to access a random area of a disk.

Backfilling. A process used by expanded memory to fill in gaps in conventional memory, bringing it up to 640K.

Backup. A copy of a floppy disk, hard drive, personal work, or program intended to ensure against the loss of data.

Bank switching. A process used by expanded memory that enables a computer to address more space than it has room for, by switching 16K chunks of memory into a 16K page, or bank, as needed.

Batch file. A program that can carry out a sequence of commands.

Baud rate. A measure of data-transmission speed used with modems.

Binary file. A file such as a program file that contains raw data in binary language.

BIOS (Basic Input Output System). The system responsible for communicating with the computer's hardware. Also contains information the computer needs to boot up (start).

Bits. Short for binary digits, which are either 1 or 0. The smallest unit of information handled by a computer.

Boot record. The portion of the hard disk that stores information the computer needs to get up and running.

Buffers. Temporary storage areas that are established by DOS in the computer's RAM to hold data that has been read from a disk. Each buffer uses 512 bytes of memory. The more buffers used, the larger the amount of data read from a disk, and the less available free memory. The BUFFERS command is in CONFIG.SYS.

Bug. A programming glitch in software or a hardware error. Corrected by "debugging."

Bus. The set of lines within a computer system used to transfer data and other information. Serves as an electronic highway connecting the hard drive, for example, to the other parts of the system.

Bytes. A unit of information containing eight bits. One byte stores a character.

CAD/CAM (Computer-Aided Drafting/design). The use of computers to aid mechanical, architectural, or industrial design, or software programs that perform these tasks. Autodesk Inc.'s AutoCAD is probably the most widely known CAD program.

CD ROM. A storage device that uses compact disk technology for data storage.

Chain. The string of clusters that makes up a file.

Character-based interface. Also known as a text-based interface. A nongraphical interface that uses characters typed at the keyboard as the primary means of communication. The DOS prompt is a character-based interface.

CHKDSK. The DOS command that checks a specified disk for errors and displays a status report for the disk.

Clock speed. The computer's operational speed. Clock speed is measured in megahertz (MHz), or millions of cycles per second.

Cluster. Also known as a file allocation unit. DOS's basic unit of allocation for disk space. A cluster is a group of sectors. When a file is stored, it is broken down into clusters.

Cold boot. Starting the computer by flipping the computer switch. See warm boot.

COMMAND.COM. The portion of DOS that interprets commands.

Command interpreter. The part of the operating system that you use directly. DOS's command interpreter is called COMMAND.COM.

Command line. The place where you enter DOS commands. The prompt (C>) is the primary command line, but Windows and the DOS Shell also contain command lines.

CONFIG.SYS. A file that DOS looks for (before it looks for AUTOEXEC. BAT) to control how DOS starts. CONFIG.SYS contains commands that load installable device drivers such as mouse drivers and also contains the BUFFER and FILES commands. CONFIG.SYS is created by the DOS setup program and is in the root directory of your hard disk.

Conventional memory. The amount of memory that DOS can use to run programs. Conventional memory addresses range from 0K to 640K.

CP/M (Control Program for Microcomputers). An early operating system used on personal computers.

CPU (Central Processing Unit). The part of the computer that executes instructions. Often referred to as the brain of the computer.

Cross-linked files. Two or more files that claim ownership of the same file allocation unit.

Cyclic redundancy check. A method of checking for data-transmission errors.

Cylinder. A vertical column of aligned tracks. Cylinder 0, for example, is made up of track 0 on the top of platter 1 and track 0 from the bottom of platter 1. If the drive has two platters, cylinder 0 also includes track 0 from the top of platter 2 and track 0 from the bottom of platter 2.

Data bus. The channel across which data is carried throughout the computer.

Data compression. A method of compressing data so that it can be stored in less space or transmitted across a modem in less time.

Data file. A file that you create. In addition to information, data files typically contain coding specific to the program that created them.

Data transfer rate. The speed at which a hard disk transfers data to the CPU.

Database. A type of applications software used to store records such as address lists. Databases have become sophisticated and are able to use selected criteria to generate reports on the data they contain.

DES (Data Encryption Standard). A standard developed for the Department of Defense and normally available for use only in the U.S. Packages containing the DES algorithm cannot be exported from the U.S.

Device driver. Special software that tells DOS how to communicate with hardware devices. Mice and CD-ROM drives, for example, come with device drivers.

Differential backup. A backup procedure that is similar to an incremental backup but doesn't change the setting.

Directory. A way of organizing related files. Serves as an electronic "folder."

Directory tree. Displays the structure of the directories and subdirectories of the current drive.

Disk cache. A portion of memory set aside to speed access to the hard disk by holding frequently requested information. Accessing the cache is much quicker than accessing the mechanical hard disk.

Disk controller. The chip and circuitry that transfers data between the drive and the computer's memory. In some systems, the controller resides on a separate add-in card that you install in one of the PC's expansion slots. In others, the controller is built directly into the drive.

Disk locking. A protection method that does not enable a user to look at a hard or floppy disk without pressing the appropriate key.

DISKCOPY. The DOS command that copies contents from one floppy disk to another.

DMA (Direct Memory Access). A method of data transfer that bypasses the CPU. Commercial backup programs use DMA channels to transfer data.

DOS (Disk Operating System). The operating system used by most PCs. DOS was developed by Microsoft.

DOS Shell. The graphical user interface used in DOS Versions 4 and 5. See GUI.

Drive bay. The area of the computer that holds a hard disk drive, floppy disk drive, or tape drive.

Drive latency. The length of time a bit of data takes to pass underneath the read/write head.

Echo messages. Messages displayed on-screen by DOS.

EDLIN. A line-oriented text editor contained in DOS.

Encryption. Making data secure by adding special coding that converts the data from understandable to meaningless while preserving its integrity. Software programs and special hardware both can be used to encrypt data. Encrypted (scrambled) files cannot be accessed without the descrambling key code.

ESDI (Enhanced Small Device Interface). A type of hard drive interface used by IBM PS/2s and IBM-compatible PCs. The ESDI interface is faster than the ST-506/412 interface. (See also Interface and ST-506/412.)

Expanded memory. Memory that exists outside DOS's addressable limits and borrows addresses within DOS's range so that DOS can use the memory. Can be used by any type of computer.

Extended memory. A linear continuation of memory beyond 1M. XTs (PCs based on 8088 microprocessors) do not contain and cannot use extended memory.

Extension. The three-letter part of the file name that typically describes a file's function. DOC is the three-letter extension for Microsoft Word files; for example, your letter to Mom might be called LETTER.DOC.

FASTOPEN. A DOS command that speeds access to recently used subdirectories and files by caching their names.

FAT (File Allocation Table). The portion of the hard disk that acts as an index to the location of files. It is basically a map of all the different clusters on the disk.

FDISK. The DOS command used to partition a disk.

File. A collection of related information. May be a document or a set of program instructions.

File allocation unit. A synonym for cluster. The term file allocation unit is new to DOS 5.0. Before version 5.0, the file allocation unit was known as the cluster, and most books and product manuals still refer to clusters rather than file allocation units. The DOS 5.0 manual, however, refers to file allocation units.

File name. Common parlance for the full file name, including the root name and extension.

FILES. A command in CONFIG.SYS that sets the number of files that can be open simultaneously.

Floppy disk. A removable disk used to store data. Currently come in 3 1/2-inch and 5 1/4-inch versions.

FORMAT. The DOS command used to prepare the hard disk to accept DOS files.

Form factor. The dimensions of a hard drive mechanism, including the casing or computer system.

Fragmentation. Occurs when data, instead of being stored in neighboring (contiguous) clusters, is stored in clusters in many different places on the disk. Does not compromise the integrity of the data but cuts the efficiency of the drive because it must search the entire disk to bring up the file.

Full backup. A procedure that backs up the entire contents of the hard disk.

GUI (Graphical User Interface). An interface that replaces the command line with visual elements, such as icons (symbols) and pull-down menus, and works with a mouse, a small pointing device. The DOS Shell and Microsoft Windows are GUIs.

Hard disk. A fixed, unremovable disk drive.

Hard disk card. Storage contained on an adapter card.

Head actuator. The movement mechanism responsible for moving the read/write heads across the disk drive's platters. Two types of head actuators exist: stepper motor actuators and voice-coil actuators.

Hidden file. A file not shown in a normal directory listing.

High density. A type of floppy disk that holds more information than a double-density disk. High-density 5 1/4-inch disks hold 1.2M; high-density 3 1/2-inch disks hold 1.44M.

High-level format. Also called the logical format. The process that creates the boot record, file allocation table, and root directory on the disk.

HMA (High Memory Area). The first 64K block of extended memory, minus 16 bytes, that can be used by DOS 5.0 and memory managers such as Quarterdeck's DESQView.

Icon. A symbol that represents a program or a file.

IDE (Integrated Drive Electronics) drive. A type of drive found in most newer PCs. In an IDE drive, the disk controller is built directly into the drive, thereby freeing up expansion slots for other use.

Incremental backup. A backup that records only the files that have changed since the last full backup.

Initialization. Starting up a disk or preparing it for use.

Installation program. A program that installs another program.

Interface. In hard disk parlance, the circuitry that communicates between the hard disk and the rest of the computer.

Interleave. The way sectors are organized on the disk surface.

Interleave factor. The arrangement of sectors on a disk so that they aren't necessarily sequential.

Internal command. A command that is loaded into memory when the computer is booted up.

Kilobytes. 1,024 bytes. Abbreviated K or Kb.

Label. An identifier given to a disk. Also called a volume label.

Loop. A set of statements in a program that are executed repeatedly.

Local area network (LAN). A group of computers connected by cabling and a special operating system. Each PC contains a card that enables it to communicate over the network.

Logical drive. A partitioned section of a hard disk that looks like an additional hard disk to DOS.

Low-level format. Also called the physical format. The imprinting of sectors and tracks on a hard disk. The low-level format also establishes the disk interleave.

Macro. A set of commands that can be executed by typing the macro's name. Macros are used to simplify keystrokes that may be long and drawn out or to perform functions that are repeated frequently.

Magneto-optical drive. A storage device that combines magnetic and optical technology.

Megabytes. 1,048,576 bytes. Often rounded off to a million bytes. Abbreviated M or Mb.

MTBF (Mean Time Between Failures). A manufacturer's estimate of the amount of time before a hard drive fails and requires service.

Memory. The fast electronic storage that a computer uses when a program is loaded.

Microprocessor. The computer's main information-processing chip.

Microsoft Windows. Microsoft's graphical user interface that works with DOS.

Motherboard. A computer's main circuit board.

Mouse. A small device used with GUIs. You use a mouse to point at areas on-screen and select items from pull-down menus instead of having to type instructions on the keyboard. Mice also are highly effective for producing graphics.

MS-DOS. Microsoft's operating system for personal computers.

Multitasking. The capability to run more than one program at a time.

Operating system. The software program that controls the computer's basic functions and also acts as a liaison between you, your software, and the computer. Examples of operating systems include DOS, OS/2, and UNIX.

Optical disk. A storage device that uses optical rather than magnetic technology.

Orphaned cluster. A phrase used to describe an empty cluster that is marked as being in use.

OS/2 (Operating System/2). A graphical operating system developed by IBM and Microsoft and now marketed by IBM. The latest version is a 32-bit operating system.

Parameters. A set of guidelines in programming. Parameters let you know what you can and cannot do. In DOS, for example, you cannot use file names with more than eight characters.

Partitions. Sections of the hard disk that are allocated for use by DOS (or other operating systems).

Password. A key word that you may be asked to type in order to gain access to a computer.

Path. A full description of a file's location, such as \WP51\BOOK\ CHAPTER5, which indicates that the file CHAPTER5 is located in the subdirectory BOOK, which is contained in the WP51 subdirectory. The PATH command tells DOS which directories to search when it looks for a file. The PATH command typically resides in the AUTOEXEC.BAT file.

Platters. The individual metal storage disks contained in a hard disk system.

POR (Power-On Reset). The clearing of RAM, the microprocessor, and the other circuits that takes place when the computer's power is turned on. The POR immediately precedes the POST (see POST).

POST (Power-On Self Test). A test that the computer runs every time it boots up, to make sure that everything is functioning normally.

Program file. A file that is used by an application program. WP.EXE, for example, is the program file that executes (runs) WordPerfect.

Prompt. The on-screen symbol where you enter DOS commands when not in the DOS Shell or Windows. Also called the command line.

Pull-down menu. A list of options that appears under a menu heading (the heading is typically part of a menu bar across the top of the screen) when you select that menu by clicking the mouse button, holding it down, and dragging it down the list.

RAM (Random-Access Memory). Also known as system memory. The electronic memory the computer uses for temporary storage of data and programs as they're being used. When the computer is shut off, the contents of RAM are lost.

RAM disk. A portion of RAM reserved for use as an alternate hard disk.

Read/write head. The magnetized mechanism that reads data from or writes it to the surface of the hard disk platter.

RECOVER. The DOS command that recovers data from a defective disk.

Removable media. A term that covers every type of storage medium that can be removed from a system, ranging from a floppy disk to a removable hard drive or tape cartridge.

RESTORE. The DOS command used to bring back files that were backed up with the DOS BACKUP command.

ROM (Read-Only Memory). Unlike RAM, memory that is burned directly into a microchip. The contents of ROM are not lost when the computer is shut off. For that reason, ROM contains vital start-up information.

Root directory. The hard disk's main directory where all other directories and files are stored. The root directory is created by DOS during the high-level format.

Root name. The file's "first name"; also known as the base name. Typically used to describe the file's contents.

SCSI (Small Computer Systems Interface). An interface used for a wide variety of peripherals, including hard drives. Pronounced "scuzzy."

Sector. An area of the disk that holds 512 bytes of data.

Security. Protecting a computer and data from accidental loss or harm.

ST-506/412. The original technology for disk controller cards. It rapidly is being replaced by IDE on drives with a capacity of 300M or less, and by ESDI or SCSI on larger-capacity drives.

Stepper-motor actuator. A movement mechanism used in some disk drives. See also voice-coil actuator.

Subdirectory. A directory that resides within another directory.

Tape backup unit. A storage device that uses magnetic tape as the storage medium. Tape cartridges typically hold more data than hard drives can.

Text file. Used synonymously with ASCII file.

Track. A concentric ring on a disk's surface that is further subdivided into sectors. Tracks are numbered from the outside in, with the outermost track being 0.

Track-to-track seek time. The amount of time a read/write head takes to get from one track to an adjacent track.

TSR (Terminate and Stay Resident). Also called RAM-resident or pop-up. Programs that stay in memory until the user presses a designated key or keys that bring the resident program to the screen.

User-friendly. Easy to use and learn.

Utility program. A program that performs routine maintenance, such as backup or recovery.

Upper memory blocks. The area of memory between 640K and 1M that traditionally was reserved for use by hardware. (Upper memory blocks are sometimes referred to as upper memory, high DOS, or UMBs.)

Virtual memory. Memory simulated by the hard disk.

Virus. A program like any other, except that its purpose is to infect other programs in order to inhibit the computer's efficiency or capability to function.

Voice-coil actuator. A movement mechanism that uses an electromagnetic wire coil. See also stepper-motor actuator.

Warm boot. Restarting the computer when the power is on by pressing either the Ctrl-Alt-Del key combination or the reset button if the computer has one.

Wipe. Another way to delete files from a disk. Wiping differs from deleting in that wiping scrambles the data on the disk rather than simply rendering it free to be overwritten. Wiping a file or disk is more secure and permanent.

WORM (Write-Once, Read-Many) drive. A type of optical storage device that can be written to only once. Then it becomes a read-only device.

Write-protect. Prevent the writing of information to a disk.

WYSIWYG. What-You-See-Is-What-You-Get. A display method in which the on-screen appearance matches the printed output.

XCOPY. The DOS command that enables you to copy directory and subdirectory structures as well as files.

Symbols

* (asterisk) wild card, 100
* (EDLIN prompt), 150
+ (expandable branches), 134
? (question mark) wild card, 100
286-class PCs, 12
    addressable memory, 181
    extended memory, 185
386-class PCs, 12
    addressable memory, 181
    extended memory, 185
386DX chip, 12
486-class PCs, 13
    addressable memory, 181
    extended memory, 185
486DX chip, 13
80286 chip, 12
80386 chip, 12
80386SX chip, 12
80486 chip, 13
80486SX chip, 13
8086 chips, 12
8088 chips, 12

A

Abort, Retry, Ignore? error
    message, 393-394
absolute paths, 132
Access Denied error
    message, 394

actuators
    head, 19
    stepper-motor, 19-20, 33
    voice -coil, 19-20, 33
add-in cards, 10
add-on cards, 25
addressable memory, 180-181
addresses, 397
    bus, 10
    space, 397
Advanced run-length-limited
    (ARLL) data-encoding, 24
Alarmcard, security option, 306
All Files command, 80
allocating space on
    hard disks, 202-206
Alter menu option, 219
ALU (Arithmetic Logic Unit), 11
American Standard Code for
    Information Interchange, see
    ASCII
ANSI bomb virus, 310
APPEND (DOS) command,
    353-354
APPEND Already Installed
    error message, 394
Apple Macintosh computers, 12
ARC, data compression
    program, 340
archive bit, 397
Arithmetic Logic Unit (ALU), 11

ARLL (Advanced run-length-limited) data-encoding, 24
ASCII (American Standard Code for Information Interchange, 13, 95, 397
  creating batch files, 152
  viewing files, 106
ASSIGN (DOS) command, 354-355, 397
AST Research Inc., security features, 305
asterisk wild card (*), 100
AT bus Attachment (ATA) interface, 26
AT chip, 12
ATA (AT bus Attachment) interface, 26
ATTRIB (DOS) command, 51, 96, 252-254, 355-356, 397
attributes, file
  archive bit, 397
  changing, 355-356
  displaying, 256
  modifying with DOS Shell, 255-256
  modifying with File Manager (Windows), 256-257
AUTOEXEC.BAT file, 66, 131, 144, 164-169, 397
Automenu, DOS menu program, 170

B

Back-It 4, backup program, 237-239
backfilling, 184, 398
back ups, 315, 357-359
  Back-It 4 program, 237-239
  Central Point Backup program, 243-244
  FastBack Plus program, 234-236
  floppy disk requirements, 231
  frequency of backups, 226

  Norton Backup program, 240-243
  prior to optimization, 200
  restoring files, 382-384
  tape drives, 244-245
  where to keep backups, 225-226
  with DOS
    BACKUP command, 230-234
    COPY command, 227
    RESTORE command, 230-234
    XCOPY command, 228-230
BACKUP (DOS) command, 230-234, 357-359
  switches, 233
Bad Command or File Name error message, 394
Bad Sector error message, 394
bad sectors, recovering data, 284-285
bank switching, 183, 398
base names, see root names
Basic Input/Output System (BIOS), 21, 51
batch files, 50-56, 95, 141
  alternatives, 169-171
  AUTOEXEC.BAT, 164-169, 397
  commands
    CALL, 154
    DO, 154, 160
    ECHO, 154-157
    ECHO OFF, 154-157
    FOR, 154, 160
    GOTO, 154
    IF, 154, 158-159
    IF NOT, 154, 159-160
    IN, 154, 160
    PAUSE, 154, 158
    REM, 154-157
    SHIFT, 154, 159-160
  creating, 145-153
    with COPY CON, 145-147
    with DOSKEY, 174
    with EDIT, 151-152

with EDLIN, 147-151
with third-party text
editors, 152-153
parameters, 155-156
manipulating, 160
shifting, 159-160
purpose, 143-145
running, 153
structure, 142-143
uses
housekeeping chores, 162
menu systems, creating,
163-164
organizing disks, 161-162
baud rate, 398
BBSs, (bulletin board
systems), 315
Bernoulli Box, 42
binary
digits, 13
files, 398
math, 13
BIOS (Basic Input/Output
System), 21, 39, 51, 65, 398
bits, 13, 398
bomb virus, 310
boot records, 64-66, 398
boot sector, 311-312
booting, 51, 65
area viruses, 312
cold, 65, 311, 399
infector virus, 311-312
protecting against
(Watchdog), 303
warm, 311
branches
+ (expandable branches), 134
collapsing, 133
expanding, 133
BREAK (DOS) command, 359
BRIEF, text editor, 152
buffers, 35-37, 398
adjusting, 187-188
full-track, 37
read-ahead, 37

BUFFERS (DOS) command,
359-360
bugs, 398
bulletin board systems (BBS),
315
buses, 9-11, 398
address, 10
control, 10
data, 10, 400
expansion, 10, 25
I/O, 10
bytes, 13, 96, 398
testing hard disks, 212

C

caches
delayed-write, 197
disk, 192-193, 400
SMARTDrive, 194-195
hardware, 196-197
read-ahead, 196-197
write-back, 197
write-through, 197
CAD (computer-aided
design), 58
CAD/CAM (Computer-Aided
Drafting/design), 398
CALL (batch file) command, 154
CALL (DOS) command, 360
cards
add-in, 10
add-on, 25
controller, 10
daughtercards, 10
hard disk, 29, 41-42
host adapter, 25-26, 39
video, 10, 102
wild, 100-101
CD (DOS) command, 132, 361
CD-ROM drives, 43, 398
Central Point Anti-Virus
program, 324-326
Central Point Backup, backup
program, 243-244

Central Processing Unit
  (CPU), 12
chaining, 266-267
Change Directory (CD/CHDIR)
  command, 132
character-based interfaces, 399
CHDIR (DOS) command, 132,
  361
chips, 11-13
  AT, 12
  CISC (Complex Instruction
    Set Computing), 58
  DMA (Direct Memory
    Access), 36
  Intel, 12
  memory, 10
  Motorola, 12
  RISC (Reduced Instruction
    Set Computing), 58
  XT, 12
CHKDSK (DOS) command, 53,
  257-258, 361-363, 399
CISC (Complex Instruction Set
  Computing) chips, 58
Clean virus disinfection
  program, 330-331
clear screen (CLS) command,
  154
Clipboard Viewer (system
  program), 83
clock speeds, 11, 399
closed-loop systems, 19
CLS (clear screen) command,
  154
clusters, 399
  orphaned, 404
coated platters, 17
cold boots, 65, 311, 399
collapsing branches, 133
command files, 94, 405
command interpreters, 52-53,
  399
command line, 72, 399
COMMAND.COM file, 52-53

commands
  All Files, 80
  batch file
    CALL, 154
    DO, 154, 160
    ECHO, 154, 156-157
    ECHO OFF, 146, 154-157
    FOR, 154, 160
    GOTO, 154
    IF, 154, 158-159
    IF NOT, 154, 159-160
    IN, 154, 160
    PAUSE, 154, 158
    REM, 154-157
    SHIFT, 154, 159-160
  CLS (clear screen), 154
  Confirmation, 119
  Copy, 106, 110, 114
  COPY CON, 145-147
  Create Directory, 135
  DEBUG, 40
  Delete, 118-119, 138
  Deselect All, 104
  Display, 102
  DOS
    APPEND, 353-354
    ASSIGN, 354-355, 397
    ATTRIB, 51, 96, 252-254,
      355-356, 397
    BACKUP, 230-234, 357-359
    BREAK, 359
    BUFFERS, 359-360
    CALL, 360
    CD, 132, 361
    CHDIR, 132, 361
    CHKDSK, 53, 217, 257-258,
      361-363, 399
    COMP, 363-364
    COPY, 227, 364-365
    DEL, 365-366
    DIR, 56, 99, 108-110, 124,
      366-368
    DISKCOPY, 400
    DOSKEY, 369
    ERASE, 120, 365-366

FASTOPEN, 369-370, 401
FC, 370-371
FDISK, 53, 61, 371-373, 401
FORMAT, 63-64, 373-374, 402
HELP, 374
JOIN, 374-375
LABEL, 375-376
MD, 379
MEM, 376-377
MIRROR, 62, 264, 269, 283-284, 377-378
MKDIR, 379
MORE, 108
PATH, 167-169, 379-380
RD, 384
RECOVER, 284-285, 405
REN, 380-381
RENAME, 138, 380-381
REPLACE, 381-382
RESTORE, 230-234, 382-384, 405
RMDIR, 384
SHARE, 55
SUBST, 385-386
TREE, 133-135, 386
TYPE, 108
UNDELETE, 55, 270-273, 386-387
UNFORMAT, 55, 273-278, 388-389
XCOPY, 228-230, 406
DOSKEY, 171-172
Dual File List, 78, 112
EDLIN, 148-149
Expand All, 134
Expand Branch, 134
external, 53
internal, 52, 403
Move, 117
Open, 131
Program List, 80
Program/File List, 80
Rename, 120, 137
Repaint Screen, 80

Save, 131
Search, 108
Select Across Directories, 106
Select All, 104
Single File List, 78
View File Contents, 106-107
COMP (DOS) command, 363-364
Compact Disc Read-Only Memory, *see* CD-ROM
Compaq, security features, 304-305
Complex Instruction Set Computing (CISC) chips, 58
compressed files, downloading with RAM disk, 192
CompuServe, downloading files, 192
computer systems
Apple Macintosh, 12
buses, 9
microprocessors, 9
motherboards, 9-10
computer-aided design (CAD), 58
CONFIG.SYS file, 66, 399
buffers, changing, 187-188
Confirmation command, 119
consoles, 145
control bus, 10
Control Panel (system program), 83
controller cards, 10
controller compatibility, testing, 218
conventional memory, 182, 399
in RAM disk, 190
COPY (DOS) command, 227, 364-365
Copy command, 106-114
COPY CON command, 145-147
copying files, 110-116, 364-365
to RAM disk, 191-192
CP/M (Control Program for Microcomputers), 399

CPAV (Central Point
Anti-Virus), 324-326
CPU (Central Processing
Unit), 12, 399
CRC (cyclic redundancy
check), 20
Create Directory command, 135
creating
  batch files, 145-153
    with COPY CON, 145-147
    with DOSKEY, 174
    with EDIT, 151-152
    with EDLIN, 147-151
    with third-party text
      editors, 152-153
  contiguous files, 205
  directories, 135-136
  DOSKEY macros, 172-174
  RAM disks, 189-191
  subdirectories, 379
  virus avoidance checklist,
    314-315
cross-linked files, 399
current directory, 130-131
cursors, selection, 77
cyclic redundancy check
  (CRC), 20, 399
cylinders, 17-18, 399

D

data
  entering, 80
  loading, 21
  saving, 21
data bus, 10, 400
data compression, 334-337
  effectiveness, 336-337
  hardware options, 350-351
  programs, 338
    ARC, 340
    LHARC, 339-340
    PAK, 342-343
    PKLITE, 345
    PKZIP, 340-342

    Stacker, 348-349
    SuperStor, 345-348
    ZOO, 343-345
  when to use, 338
  with RAM disks, 349-350
data errors, detecting, 218
data exchange, improving, 218
data files, 94, 400
  finding, 353-354
Data Monitor (PC Tools),
  program, 263-264, 297-298
data protection programs, 295
  Data Monitor (PC Tools),
    263-264, 297-298
  Disk Monitor (Norton
    Utilities), 298-299
  DiskLock (Fifth Generation
    System), 300-301
  Diskreet (Norton Utilities),
    299-300
  PC Secure (PC Tools), 296-297
  Watchdog, 301-303
data separation, 20
data space, moving to front of
  disk, 210
data storage, 19-23
data transfer rate, 31, 40, 400
data-encoding schemes
  ARLL (Advanced run-length-
    limited), 24
  MFM (Modified Frequency
    Modulation), 24
  RLL (Run Length Limited), 24
databases, 400
daughtercards, 10
dBASE files, repairing, 284
DEBUG command, 40
decimal math, 13
default directory, 130-131
Definitions menu, 324
defragmentation, 205
defragmenting files, 210
DEL (DOS) command, 365-366
delayed-write caches, 197
Delete command, 118-119, 138

deleting
  directories, 384
  files, 118-120, 289-291, 365-366
    permanently, 291-294
    restoring, 266-267, 386-387
    unneeded program files,
      391-392
  program infector virus, 312
  viruses, 317-318, 323-328
DES (Data Encryption
  Standard), 400
Deselect All command, 104
DESQView (shell program),
  84-87
destination drives, 116
detecting
  bulk file virus, 325
  viruses, 315-316, 323-329
    with Norton AntiVirus,
      320-321
device drivers, 40-43, 95, 400
  viruses, 312
device-level interfaces, 23
differential backups, 400
DIR (DOS) command, 56, 99,
  108-110, 124, 366-368
Direct Access, DOS menu
  program, 170
Direct Memory Access (DMA)
  chip, 11, 36
directories, 123, 400
  activating, 101
  changing, 361
  creating, 135-136
  current, 130-131
  damaged, recovering data,
    284-285
  deleting, 384
  directory tree, 75, 133
  displaying current, 361
  files, displaying, 366-368
  moving, 209
  navigating, 132
  removing, 138-139
  renaming, 137-138

  root, 68, 127, 405
  subdirectories, 127
  tree structure, displaying, 386
  viewing, 129
disk access time, 211
disk caches, 36-37, 192-193, 400
  hardware, 36
  SMARTDrive, 194-195
  software, 36
disk controller, 400
Disk Error error message, 395
disk locking, 400
Disk Monitor (Norton Utilities),
  data protection, 298-299
disk space, optimizing, 210
disk surface, scanning, 218
disk utilities, 35, 76, 209-220
disk-drive controller, 20-21
DISKCOPY (DOS) command, 400
DiskFix (PC Tools), 281-282
DiskFix (PC Tools) diagnostic
  program, 261-263
DiskLock (Fifth Generation
  Systems), data protection,
  300-301
Diskreet (Norton Utilities), data
  protection, 299-300
disks
  floppy
    as security measure, 288
    formatting, 373-374
    high density, 402
    requirements for
      backups, 231
    unformatting, 388-389
  formatting , 51
  hard
    diagnostic utility
      programs, 257-264
    formatting, 373-374
    heat, protecting against,
      249
    impact, protecting against,
      250

increasing speed, 187-197
leaving on versus turning
off, 251-252
magnetic fields, protecting
against, 251
nonparked heads,
protecting against, 249
organizing with batch files,
161-162
partitioning, 371-372
power fluctuations,
protecting against,
250-251
removable, 289
unformatting, 268-269,
388-389
vibration, protecting
against, 249-250
wiping, 291-293
optical, 404
repairing, 330-331
status reports, displaying,
361
volume labels, modifying,
375-376
display adapters, 10, 102
Display command, 102
display monitors, 9
displaying
directory tree structure, 386
files, 366-368
attributes, 256
lists, 97-99
free memory, 376-377
DMA (Direct Memory Access)
chip, 36, 400
DO (batch file) command, 154,
160
DOS
backing up files, 226-227
BACKUP command,
230-234
COPY command, 227
RESTORE command,
230-234
XCOPY command, 228-230
buffers, adjusting, 187-188

commands
APPEND, 353-354
ASSIGN, 354-355
ATTRIB, 252-254, 355-356
BACKUP, 230-234, 357-359
BREAK, 359
BUFFERS, 359-360
CALL, 360
CD, 132, 361
CHDIR, 361
CHKDSK, 132, 217, 257-258,
361-363, 399
CLS (clear screen), 154
COMP, 363-364
COPY, 227, 364-365
COPY CON, 145-147
DEL, 120, 365-366
DIR, 108-110, 124, 366-368
DISKCOPY, 400
DOSKEY, 369
ECHO OFF, 146
ERASE, 120, 365-366
FASTOPEN, 369-370, 401
FC, 370-371
FDISK, 371-373, 401
FORMAT, 373-374, 402
HELP, 374
JOIN, 374-375
LABEL, 375-376
MD, 379
MEM, 376-377
MIRROR, 264, 269, 283-284,
377-378
MKDIR, 379
MORE, 108
PATH, 167-169, 379-380
RD, 384
RECOVER, 284-285, 405
REN, 120, 380-381
RENAME, 138, 380-381
REPLACE, 381-382
RESTORE, 230-234,
382-384, 405
RMDIR, 384
SUBST, 385-386
TREE, 133-135, 386
TYPE, 108

UNDELETE, 270-273, 386-387
UNFORMAT, 273-278, 388-389
XCOPY, 228-230, 406
EMM386.EXE memory manager, 186-187
error messages, 393-396
HIMEM.SYS memory manager, 185-186
history, 54-55
memory management improvements, version 5.0, 185-187
SMARTDrive disk cache, 194-195
structures, repairing, 278
 DiskFix (PC Tools), 281-282
 error messages, 279
 FAT symptoms, 279
 MIRROR (DOS) command, 283-284
 Norton Disk Doctor (Norton Utilitites), 282-283
DOS command line, 116
DOS Shell, 71-73
 basics, 74-76
 file attributes, modifying, 255-256
 modifying, 78-80
 navigating, 76-77
DOSKEY (DOS) command, 369
DOSKEY macro program, 56
 batch files, creating, 174
 commands, accessing, 171-172
 macros
  alternatives to, 175-176
  creating, 172-174
double-clicking mouse, 83
downloading, compressed files with RAM disk, 192
dragging mouse, 77
drive area, 75
drive bays, 41, 401
drive latency, 32, 401

Drive Not Ready Reading Drive C error message, 394
drives
 activating, 75
 CD-ROM, 43
 destination, 116
 full-height, 41
 half-height, 41
 IDE (Integrated Drive Electronics), 402
  formatting, 200
 linking to subdirectories, 374-375
 logical, 403
 magneto-optical, 403
 one-third height, 41
 performance, measuring, 218
 reassigning, 354-355
 rewritable optical, 43
 source, 116
 status, analyzing, 211
 surface, testing, 217
 tape, 25
  backing up files, 244-245
  helical scan, 244-245
  QIC (quarter-inch cartridge), 244-245
 WORM (Write-Once, Read-Many), 406
Dual File List command, 78, 112
dumb terminals, 58

E

ECHO (batch file) command, 154-157
echo messages, 401
ECHO OFF (batch file) command, 154-157
ECHO OFF command, 146
EDIT program, 151-152
editing hard disks, low-level formats, 215
Editor, 75-77
EDLIN (LINe EDitor), 147-151
 commands, 148-149
 prompt (*), 150

EMM386.EXE memory manager, 186-187
encryption, 313, 401
Enhanced Small Device Interface (ESDI), 25
ERASE (DOS) command, 120, 365-366
error messages, DOS, 393-396
   structure damage, 279
ESDI (Enhanced Small Device Interface), 25, 37-39, 401
Expand All command, 134
Expand Branch command, 134
expanded memory, 401
   backfilling, 184
   bank switching, 183, 398
   RAM disks, 189-192
expanding branches, 133
expansion bus, 10, 25
expansion slots, 10
extended memory, 184-185, 401
   RAM disks, 189-192
extended partitions, 61
external
   commands, 53
   drives, 37

F

/F option, CHKDSK (DOS) command, 258
FastBack Plus, backup program, 234-236
FASTOPEN (DOS) command, 369-370, 401
FastTrax, 213-215
FAT (File Allocation Table), 66-68, 202, 401
   chaining, 266-267
FC (DOS) command, 370-371
FDISK (DOS) command, 53, 61, 371-373, 401
file allocation table (FAT), 66-68, 202, 401
   chaining, 266-267
File Allocation Table Bad, Drive X error message, 394

file attributes
   archive bit, 397
   changing, 355-356
   displaying, 256
   modifying with DOS Shell, 255-256
   modifying with File Manager (Windows), 256-257
File Fix (Norton Utilities) program, 284
File Fix (PC Tools) program, 284
File Manager (Windows), 83
   file attributes, modifying, 256-257
File menu (DOS Shell), 74
   Copy, 110, 114
   Create Directory, 135
   Delete, 118-119, 138
   Deselect All, 104
   Move, 117
   Open, 131
   Rename, 120, 137
   Save, 131
   Search, 108
   Select All, 104
   View File Contents, 106-107
files, 92
   arranging during optimization, 209
   ASCII, 95
   AUTOEXEC.BAT, 66, 131, 144, 164-169, 397
   backing up, 226-227, 315, 357-359
      Back-It 4 program, 237-239
      BACKUP (DOS) command, 230-234
      Central Point Backup, 243-244
      COPY (DOS) command, 227
      FastBack Plus program, 234-236
      floppy disk requirements, 231
      frequency of backups, 226
      Norton Backup, 240-243

RESTORE (DOS) command, 230-234

restoring, 382-384

tape drives, 244-245

where to keep backups, 225-226

XCOPY (DOS) command, 228-230

batch, 50-53, 95, 141

  altenatives, 169-171

  AUTOEXEC.BAT, 164-169, 397

  creating, 145-153, 174

  housekeeping chores, 162

  menu systems, creating, 163-164

  organizing hard disks, 161-162

  parameters, 155-156

  running, 153

  structure, 142-143

binary, 398

comparing, 363-364, 370-371

compressed, downloading with RAM disk, 192

CONFIG.SYS, 66, 399

  buffers, changing, 187-188

copying, 110-116, 364-365

  to RAM disk, 191-192

cross-linked, 399

data, 94, 400

defragmenting, 210

deleting, 118-120, 289-291, 365-366

  permanently, 291-294

  restoring, 266-267, 386-387

  unneeded program files, 391-392

displaying, 366-368

finding, 108-110, 379-380

fragmenting, 266

graphics, 95

hidden, 402

  IO.SYS, 40, 51

  MSDOS.SYS, 51

image, 269

immunization, 325

inoculating, 321-322

integrity checks, 327

lists, 75

  displaying, 97-99

modifying, 96

moving, 116-118

multiple, selecting, 102-104

naming, 92-93

opening with FASTOPEN, 369-370

PCTRACKR.DEL, 269

prioritizing, 214

program, 94, 405

protecting

  hiding files, 253-254

  making files read-only, 252-253

  Watchdog program, 302

read-only, 96

  viruses, 314

renaming, 120-121, 380-381

replacing, 381-382

selecting, 101-106

spreadsheet, repairing, 284

system, 95

text, 94, 406

  repairing, 284

uninoculating, 321-322

viewing, 106-108

finding files, 353-354, 379-380

Flash program (Software Matters), 195

floppy disks, 15-16, 402

  as security measure, 288

  formatting, 373-374

  high density, 402

  requirements for backups, 231

  unformatting, 388-389

flux changes, 22

FOR (batch file) command, 154, 160

form factor, 41

FORMAT (DOS) command, 63-64, 373-374, 402

FORMAT switches, 63

formats
  accidental, recovering
    from, 273-278
  high-level, 63-68, 402
  low-level, 17, 60, 403
  physical, 17
  protecting against
    (Watchdog), 303
formatting, 51, 94
  floppy disks, 373-374
  hard disks, 59-60, 373-374
  IDE drives, 200
  partitioning disks, 60-62
    extended partitions, 61
    primary, 61
fragmentation, 202-206, 266, 402
  causes, 202
  reducing, 209-210
Full Optimization option, 210
full-height drives, 41
full-stroke time, 211
full-track buffers, 37

G

General Failure Reading/
  Writing Drive C error
  message, 395
GOTO (batch file) command,
  154
graphical user interface (GUI),
  71, 80-81, 402
graphics files, 95
graphics modes, selecting, 102
GUI (Graphical User Interface),
  71, 80-81, 402

H

half-height drives, 41
hard disks, 15-16
hardware
  data compression, 350-351
  disk caches, 36, 196-197
  security options, 306-307
head actuator, 19, 402

headers, sector, 18
heads
  crashes, 22
  nonparked, protecting
    against, 249
  parking hard drive, 220
  read/write, 19-21, 32
heat, protecting against, 249
helical scan tape drives, 244-245
HELP (DOS) command, 374
Help menu, 74
hexadecimal (hex) viewer, 106
hidden files, 253-254, 402
  IO.SYS, 40, 51
  MSDOS.SYS, 51
high density floppy disks, 402
high DOS, *see* UMB
High Memory Area, *see* HMA
High Performance File
  System (HPFS), 57
high-level format, 63-68, 402
HIMEM.SYS memory manager,
  185-186
HMA (High Memory Area), 183,
  402
host adapter cards, 25-26, 39
HPFS (High Performance File
  System), 57
Hundred Years virus, 313

I

I/O bus, 10
IBM, security features, 305
icons, 402
IDE (Integrated Drive
  Electronics) interface, 24-26,
  37-39, 402
  formatting, 200
  interleave requirements, 206
IF (batch file) command, 154-159
IF NOT (batch file) command,
  154, 159-160
image files, 269
immunization of files, 325
impact, protecting against, 250

IN (batch file) command, 154, 160
incremental backups, 403
infecting programs, 310
initialization, 403
inoculation of files, 321-322
input/output bus, 10
inputting data, 80
integrated circuits, 11
Integrated Drive Electronics (IDE) interface, *see* IDE
Intel chips, 12
interfaces, 403
    AT bus Attachment (ATA), 26
    character-based, 399
    device-level, 23
    ESDI (Enhanced Small Device Interface), 25, 401
    GUI (Graphical User Interface), 71, 402
    IDE (Integrated Drive Electronics), 24-26
    SCSI (Small Computer Systems Interface), 25-26, 405
    serial, 24
    ST-506/412, 24
    system-level, 23
    user, 71
interleaves, 33-35, 215, 403
    adjusting, 212
    requirements, 206
    settings, 207-208
internal
    commands, 52, 403
    drives, 37
Invalid Drive Specification error message, 395
IO.SYS files, 40, 51, 64
Iomega Corporation, 42

J-K

JOIN (DOS) command, 374-375

KEDIT, text editor, 152
kernels, 51
keyboard shortcuts, Ctrl-Alt-Del (reboot), 65, 131
keyboards, 9
Keyworks Advanced, macro utility program, 175
Keyworks, macro utility program, 175
kilobytes, 14, 403

L

LABEL (DOS) command, 375-376
labels, volume, 125
LamaLock Security System, 306
LAN (local area network), 403
LapGuard, security option, 306-307
Lazy Susan, DOS menu program, 170
LHARC, data compression program, 339-340
LIM/EMS, 184
LINe EDitor, *see* EDLIN
linking drives to subdirectories, 374-375
lists, files, 97-99
loading
    data, 21
    programs, 51
    software, 314
logical drives, 403
    linking to subdirectories, 374-375
logical format, *see* high-level format
loops, 403
Lotus 1-2-3 files, repairing, 284
Lotus Symphony files, repairing, 284
Lotus-style command menus, 85
low-level format, 17, 60, 403
    editing hard disks, 215
    restoring hard disks, 217

M

Macintosh operating system, 58-59
macro programs, 87, 403
    DOSKEY, 171
        accessing commands, 171-172
        alternatives to, 175-176
        batch files, creating, 174
        creating, 172-174
magnetic domains, 22
magnetic fields, protecting against, 251
magneto-optical drive, 43, 403
mainframes, 14
math
    binary, 13
    decimal, 13
McAffee Associates Viruscan Series, 328-329
MD (DOS) command, 379
mean time between failures (MTBF), 33
Media Player (accessory program), 83
megabytes, 14, 403
MegaHertz, 11, 24
MEM (DOS) command, 376-377
memory
    addressable, 180-181
    conventional, 182, 399
        in RAM disk, 190
    displaying free amount, 376-377
    DOS 5.0 improvements, 185-187
    expanded, 401
        backfilling, 184
        bank switching, 183, 398
        RAM disks, 189-192
    extended, 184-185, 401
        RAM disks, 189-192
    managing, 51
    upper, 182-183
    virtual, 406

memory chips, 10
menu bar, 74
menu programs, *see* shell programs
menus, 74
    creating with batch files, 163-164
    Definitions, 324
    Express, 325
    Lotus-style, 85
    opening, 76
    pull-down, 76, 405
MFM (Modified Frequency Modulation) data-encoding, 24
microprocessors, 9-13, 403
Microsoft Windows, 81-83
milliseconds, 32
Minesweeper (game program), 82
miniprograms, *see* batch files
MIRROR (DOS) command, 62, 264, 269, 283-284, 377-378
Mirror (PC Tools) diagnostic program, 263
MKDIR (DOS) command, 379
modes, graphics, 102
Modified Frequency Modulation (MFM) data-encoding, 24
MORE command, 108
motherboards, 9-10, 404
Motorola chips, 12
mouse, 57, 77, 404
    advantages, 80-81
    copying files, 114-115
    cost, 80
    moving files, 117
Move command, 117
moving files, 116-118
MSDOS.SYS file, 51, 64
MTBF (Mean Time Between Failures), 33, 403
multiple files, selecting, 102-104
multitasking, 404

N

names, root, 405
naming files, 92-93, 380-381
navigating
    directories, 132
    DOS Shell, 76-77
NEAT chip set, 185
Non-System Disk error
    message, 395
nonparked heads, protecting
    against, 249
Norton AntiVirus, 318-324
    global defaults, 322
    viruses, detecting, 320-321
Norton Backup (Norton
    Utilities), 240-243
Norton Disk Doctor (Norton
    Utilities), 258-261, 282-283
Norton Utilities(Symantec), 195
    Disk Monitor, 298-299
    Diskreet, 299-300
    File Fix, 284
    Norton Backup, 240-243
    Norton Disk Doctor, 258-261,
        282-283
    WipeInfo, 291-292
Notepad (Windows), 152

O

Object Packager (accessory
    program), 83
Open command, 131
open-loop systems, 19
opening files, 369-370
operating systems, 404
    components, 50-53
    CP/M (Control Program for
        Microcomputers), 399
    OS/2, 404
    role, 49-50
optical disks, 404
optimizating hard disks
        automatic, 200
        benefits, 201

disk space, 210
    manual, 200
    Norton Utilities
        Speeddisk, 212
    sector interleave, 218
Optune utility, 215-216
orphaned cluster, 404
OS/2 operating system, 56-57,
    404
overlay (OVL) files, 312

P

paddleboards, 26, 39
page frames, 184
PAK, data compression
    program, 342-343
parameters, 155-156, 404
    manipulating, 160
    shifting, 159-160
parking hard drive heads, 220
partition table sector, 311-312
partitioning disks, 60-62
    FDISK, 371-372
Password-Protection
    Access, 323
passwords, 294-295, 404
    adding, 323
PATH (DOS) command, 167-169,
    379-380
paths, 129-130, 404
    absolute, 132
    relative, 132
PAUSE (batch file) command,
    154, 158
PC Tools 7.1 (Central Point
    Software), 195, 261-264
    Data Monitor, 297-298
    DiskFix, 211-212, 281-282
    File Fix, 284
    PC Secure, 296-297
    Wipe, 293-294
PCTRACKR.DEL file, 269
physical formats, 17
PKLITE, data compression
    program, 345

PKZIP, data compression
program, 340-342
platters, 16-17, 404
POR (Power-On Reset), 65, 404
POST (Power-On Self Test), 65,
404
power fluctuations, protecting
against, 250-251
PreCursor, DOS menu
program, 170
Presentation Manager (graphic
interface), 56-59
Print Manager (system
program), 83
Prodigy, downloading files, 192
program area, 75
program files, 94, 405
program infector virus, 312
Program Manager, 82
programs
backup, 234
Back-It 4, 237-239
Central Point Backup,
243-244
FastBack Plus, 234-236
Norton Backup, 240-243
data compression, 338
ARC, 340
LHARC, 339, 340
PAK, 342-343
PKLITE, 345
PKZIP, 340-342
Stacker, 348-349
SuperStor, 345-348
ZOO, 343-345
data protection, 295
Data Monitor (PC Tools),
297-298
Disk Monitor (Norton
Utilities), 298-299
DiskLock (Fifth Generation
System), 300-301
Diskreet (Norton Utilities),
299-300
PC Secure (PC Tools),
296-297
Watchdog, 301-303

data recovery, 280
DiskFix (PC Tools), 281-282
MIRROR (DOS) command,
283-284
Norton Disk Doctor
(Norton Utilities), 282-283
diagnostic utility, 257-258
MIRROR (DOS) command,
264
Norton Utilities, 258-261
PC Tools, 261-264
disk caching, 195-196
disk utility, 35
infecting, 310
loading, 51
macro
DOSKEY, 171-176
Keyworks, 175
Keyworks Advanced, 175
ProKey Plus, 175-176
SuperKey, 176
memory management, 184
EMM386.EXE (DOS 5.0),
186-187
HIMEM.SYS (DOS 5.0),
185-186
running, 51
shell, 84
TSR, 80, 217
ProKey Plus, macro utility
program, 175-176
prompts, 405
changing, 131
pull-down menus, 76, 405

Q

Q-DOS 3 (shell program), 84-86
QIC (quarter-inch cartridge)
tape drives, 244-245
question mark (?) wild card, 100
Quick Surface Scan menu
option, 218

R

RAM, 15, 65, 180, 405
RAM disk, 189, 405
  copying files to, 191-192
  creating, 189-191
  data compression, 349-350
random-access memory, *see* RAM
RD (DOS) command, 384
read-ahead buffers, 37
read-ahead caches, 196-197
read-only files, 96, 252-253
  viruses, 314
read-only memory, *see* ROM
read/write heads, 19-21, 32, 405
RECOVER (DOS) command, 284-285, 405
Reduced Instruction Set Computing (RISC) chips, 13, 58
relative paths, 132
REM (batch file) command, 154-157
removable
  hard disks, 42
  media, 405
REN (DOS) command, 380-381
RENAME (DOS) command, 138, 380-381
Rename command, 120, 137
renaming
  directories, 137-138
  files, 120-121
Repaint Screen command, 80
repairing
  disks, 330-331
  hard disks, 211-212
REPLACE (DOS) command, 381-382
RESTORE (DOS) command, 230-234, 382-384, 405
restoring
  backed up files, 382-384
  deleted files, 266-267, 386-387
  formatted hard/floppy disks, 388-389
    low-level format, 217

revolutions per minute (RPM), 19
rewritable optical drives, 43
RISC (Reduced Instruction Set Computing) chips, 13, 58
RLL (Run Length Limited) data-encoding scheme, 24
RMDIR (DOS) command, 384
ROM (read-only memory), 65, 180, 405
root directory, 68, 127, 405
root names, 92, 405
RPM (revolutions per minute), 19
Run Length Limited (RLL) data-encoding scheme, 24
run-length encoding, 335
running
  batch files, 153
  programs, 51

S

Save command, 131
saving data, 21
Scan for Windows (Wscan), 330
Scan program, 329-330
scroll bars, 77
scrubbing hard disks, 219
SCSI (Small Computer Systems Interface), 25-26, 405
Seagate Technology, 14
Search command, 108
sector headers, 18
sector interleave, optimizing, 218
Sector Not Found error message, 396
sectors, 17-18, 405
  recovering data from, 284-285
security
  built-in protection
    AST Research Inc., 305
    Compaq, 304-305
    IBM, 305

data protection programs, 295
  Data Monitor (PC Tools), 297-298
  Disk Monitor (Norton Utilities), 298-299
  DiskLock (Fifth Generation System), 300-301
  Diskreet (Norton Utilities), 299-300
  PC Secure (PC Tools), 296-297
  Watchdog, 301-303
  deleting files permanently, 291-294
  floppy disks, 288
  hardware options, 306-307
  passwords, 294-295
  removable hard disks, 289
Select Across Directories command, 106
Select All command, 104
selecting
  files, 101-106
  graphics modes, 102
  multiple files, 102-104
selection cursor, 77
serial interfaces, 24
SHARE command, 55
shell programs
  DESQView, 84-87
  DOS, 71
  PC Shell, 84
  Q-DOS 3, 84-86
  XTree Gold, 84
SHIFT (batch file) command, 154, 159-160
Shugart Technology, 14
Single File List command, 78
slots, expansion, 10
Small Computer Systems Interface (SCSI), 25-26
SMARTDrive, disk cache, 194-195
snapshots, 269
software disk caches, 36

Solitaire (game program), 82
Sound Recorder (accessory program), 83
source drives, 116
SpinRite II Version 2.0, 216-220
  benefits, 217
  DOS CHKDSK command, 217
  exiting, 219
  menu options, 218-219
  operation reports, printing, 219
  pattern testing, 219
spreadsheet files, repairing, 284
sputtering, 17
ST-412 hard drive, 24
ST-506 hard drive, 24
ST-506/412 interface, 24
Stacker, data compression program, 348-349
status bar, 76
stepper-motor actuators, 19-20, 33, 405
storing data, 19-23
structures, DOS
  batch files, 142-143
  hard disks, 16
  repairing, 278
    DiskFix (PC Tools), 281-282
    error messages, 279
    FAT symptoms, 279
    MIRROR (DOS) command, 283-284
    Norton Disk Doctor (Norton Utilities), 282-283
subdirectories, 127, 406
  creating, 379
  linking drives, 374-375
  opening with FASTOPEN, 369-370
SUBST (DOS) command, 385-386
Super PC-Kwik program (Multisoft), 195
SuperKey, macro utility program, 176
SuperStor, data compression program, 345-348

switches
  BACKUP (DOS) command, 233
  FORMAT (DOS) command, 63
  RESTORE (DOS) command, 233
  UNDELETE (DOS) command, 270-275
  UNFORMAT (DOS) command, 274-275
  XCOPY (DOS) command, 229-230
SYSEDIT.EXE file (Windows), 152
system files, 95
system-level interfaces, 23
systems, 19

T

tape backup unit, 406
tape drives, 25
  backing up files, 244-245
  helical scan, 244-245
  QIC (quarter-inch cartridge), 244-245
terminate and stay resident programs, *see* TSR
testing
  controller compatibility, 217-218
  drives, 217
  hard disks
    bytes, 212
  viruses, 315, 331
    while booting, 319
text files, 94, 406
  repairing, 284
thin-film media, 17
title bar, 74
track buffering controller, 196
track-to-track seek time, 33, 406
track-to-track timing, 211
tracks, 17-18, 406
TREE (DOS) command, 133-135, 386

Tree menu, 75
  Expand All, 134
  Expand Branch, 134
Trojan horse virus, 309-310
TSR (terminate and stay resident) programs, 56, 80, 406
  avoiding, 217
  Vshield, 331
TYPE command, 108

U

UMB (Upper Memory Block), 183-184
UNDELETE (DOS) command, 270-275, 386-387
undeleting files, 386-387
UNFORMAT (DOS) command, 55, 273-278, 388-389
unformatting
  hard disks, 268-269
    with MIRROR, 275-277
    without MIRROR, 277-278
uninoculation of files, 321-322
UNIX (operating system), 57-58
Untouchable programs, 327-328
upper memory, 182-183
Upper Memory Block, *see* UMB
user interfaces, 71
UTRES program, 327
UTSCAN (Untouchable) program, 327

V

V shield (TSR) program, 331
VCache program (Golden Bow Systems), 195
vibration, protecting against, 249-250
video cards, 10, 102
View File Contents command, 106-107

viewing
  ASCII files, 106
  directory tree, 129
  files, 106-108
virtual drives, *see* RAM disks
virtual memory, 406
Virus Clinic, 322
Virus Intercept, 323
Virus Intercept device driver, 319
viruses, 406
  avoidance checklist, 314-315
  bomb, 310
  boot area, 312
  boot infector, 311-312
  cloaked infector, 313
  deleting, 317-318, 323, 327-328
  detecting, 315-316, 323-329
    bulk file, 325
    with Norton AntiVirus, 320-321
  device drivers, 312
  "do-nothing", 310
  eliminating, 329-331
  encryption, 313
  Hundred Years, 313
  overlay files (OVL), 312
  program infector, 312
  programs, infecting, 310
  protecting against, Watchdog program, 303
  read-only files, 314
  relocation, 313
  self-modification, 313
  software, loading, 314
  testing, 315
    while booting, 319
  Trojan horse, 309-310
  Windows drivers, 312
  Worms, 310
voice-coil actuators, 19-20, 33, 406
volume labels, 125
volume serial number, 125

W

warm boots, 65, 311, 406
Watchdog, data protection program, 301-303
wild cards, 100-101
Windows
  batch files, creating with Notepad, 152
  drivers, viruses, 312
  File Manager, modifying file attributes, 256-257
  SMARTDrive disk cache, 194-195
Wipe (PC Tools), 293-294
WipeInfo (Norton Utilities), 291-292
wiping hard disks, 291-293
WORM (Write-Once, Read-Many) drive, 43, 406
Worms virus, 310
write-back caches, 197
write-through caches, 197
writes, 21
WYSIWYG (What-You-See-Is-What-You-Get), 406

X-Y-Z

XCOPY (DOS) command, 228-230, 406
XT chips, 12
XTree Gold (shell program), 84

ZOO, data compression program, 343-345

Computer Books from Que Mean PC Performance!

Spreadsheets

1-2-3 Beyond the Basics	$24.95
1-2-3 for DOS Release 2.3 Quick Reference	$ 9.95
1-2-3 for DOS Release 2.3 QuickStart	$19.95
1-2-3 for DOS Release 3.1+ Quick Reference	$ 9.95
1-2-3 for DOS Release 3.1+ QuickStart	$19.95
1-2-3 for Windows Quick Reference	$ 9.95
1-2-3 for Windows QuickStart	$19.95
1-2-3 Personal Money Manager	$29.95
1-2-3 Power Macros	$39.95
1-2-3 Release 2.2 QueCards	$19.95
Easy 1-2-3	$19.95
Easy Excel	$19.95
Easy Quattro Pro	$19.95
Excel 3 for Windows QuickStart	$19.95
Excel for Windows Quick Reference	$ 9.95
Look Your Best with 1-2-3	$24.95
Quattro Pro 3 QuickStart	$19.95
Quattro Pro Quick Reference	$ 9.95
Using 1-2-3 for DOS Release 2.3, Special Edition	$29.95
Using 1-2-3 for Windows	$29.95
Using 1-2-3 for DOS Release 3.1+, Special Edition	$29.95
Using Excel 4 for Windows, Special Edition	$29.95
Using Quattro Pro 4, Special Edition	$27.95
Using Quattro Pro for Windows	$24.95
Using SuperCalc5, 2nd Edition	$29.95

Databases

dBASE III Plus Handbook, 2nd Edition	$24.95
dBASE IV 1.1 Quick Reference	$ 9.95
dBASE IV 1.1 QuickStart	$19.95
Introduction to Databases	$19.95
Paradox 3.5 Quick Reference	$ 9.95
Paradox Quick Reference, 2nd Edition	$ 9.95
Using AlphaFOUR	$24.95
Using Clipper, 3rd Edition	$29.95
Using DataEase	$24.95
Using dBASE IV	$29.95
Using FoxPro 2	$29.95
Using ORACLE	$29.95
Using Paradox 3.5, Special Edition	$29.95
Using Paradox for Windows	$26.95
Using Paradox, Special Edition	$29.95
Using PC-File	$24.95
Using R:BASE	$29.95

Business Applications

CheckFree Quick Reference	$ 9.95
Easy Quicken	$19.95
Microsoft Works Quick Reference	$ 9.95
Norton Utilities 6 Quick Reference	$ 9.95
PC Tools 7 Quick Reference	$ 9.95
Q&A 4 Database Techniques	$29.95
Q&A 4 Quick Reference	$ 9.95
Q&A 4 QuickStart	$19.95
Q&A 4 Que Cards	$19.95
Que's Computer User's Dictionary, 2nd Edition	$10.95
Que's Using Enable	$29.95
Quicken 5 Quick Reference	$ 9.95
SmartWare Tips, Tricks, and Traps, 2nd Edition	$26.95
Using DacEasy, 2nd Edition	$24.95
Using Microsoft Money	$19.95
Using Microsoft Works: IBM Version	$22.95
Using Microsoft Works for Windows, Special Edition	$24.95
Using MoneyCounts	$19.95
Using Pacioli 2000	$19.95
Using Norton Utilities 6	$24.95
Using PC Tools Deluxe 7	$24.95
Using PFS: First Choice	$22.95
Using PFS: WindowWorks	$24.95
Using Q&A 4	$27.95
Using Quicken 5	$19.95
Using Quicken for Windows	$19.95
Using Smart	$29.95
Using TimeLine	$24.95
Using TurboTax: 1992 Edition	$19.95

CAD

AutoCAD Quick Reference, 2nd Edition	$ 8.95
Using AutoCAD, 3rd Edition	$29.95

Word Processing

Easy WordPerfect	$19.95
Easy WordPerfect for Windows	$19.95

Look Your Best with WordPerfect 5.1	$24.95
Look Your Best with WordPerfect for Windows	$24.95
Microsoft Word Quick Reference	$ 9.95
Using Ami Pro	$24.95
Using LetterPerfect	$22.95
Using Microsoft Word 5.5: IBM Version, 2nd Edition	$24.95
Using MultiMate	$24.95
Using PC-Write	$22.95
Using Professional Write	$22.95
Using Professional Write Plus for Windows	$24.95
Using Word for Windows 2, Special Edition	$27.95
Using WordPerfect 5	$27.95
Using WordPerfect 5.1, Special Edition	$27.95
Using WordPerfect for Windows, Special Edition	$29.95
Using WordStar 7	$19.95
Using WordStar, 3rd Edition	$27.95
WordPerfect 5.1 Power Macros	$39.95
WordPerfect 5.1 QueCards	$19.95
WordPerfect 5.1 Quick Reference	$ 9.95
WordPerfect 5.1 QuickStart	$19.95
WordPerfect 5.1 Tips, Tricks, and Traps	$24.95
WordPerfect for Windows Power Pack	$39.95
WordPerfect for Windows Quick Reference	$ 9.95
WordPerfect for Windows Quick Start	$19.95
WordPerfect Power Pack	$39.95
WordPerfect Quick Reference	$ 9.95

Hardware/Systems

Batch File and Macros Quick Reference	$ 9.95
Computerizing Your Small Business	$19.95
DR DOS 6 Quick Reference	$ 9.95
Easy DOS	$19.95
Easy Windows	$19.95
Fastback Quick Reference	$ 8.95
Hard Disk Quick Reference	$ 8.95
Hard Disk Quick Reference, 1992 Edition	$ 9.95
Introduction to Hard Disk Management	$24.95
Introduction to Networking	$24.95
Introduction to PC Communications	$24.95
Introduction to Personal Computers, 2nd Edition	$19.95
Introduction to UNIX	$24.95
Laplink Quick Reference	$ 9.95
MS-DOS 5 Que Cards	$19.95
MS-DOS 5 Quick Reference	$ 9.95
MS-DOS 5 QuickStart	$19.95
MS-DOS Quick Reference	$ 8.95
MS-DOS QuickStart, 2nd Edition	$19.95
Networking Personal Computers, 3rd Edition	$24.95
Que's Computer Buyer's Guide, 1992 Edition	$14.95
Que's Guide to CompuServe	$12.95
Que's Guide to DataRecovery	$29.95
Que's Guide to XTree	$12.95
Que's MS-DOS User's Guide, Special Edition	$29.95
Que's PS/1 Book	$22.95
TurboCharging MS-DOS	$24.95
Upgrading and Repairing PCs	$29.95
Upgrading and Repairing PCs, 2nd Edition	$29.95
Upgrading to MS-DOS 5	$14.95
Using GeoWorks Pro	$24.95
Using Microsoft Windows 3, 2nd Edition	$24.95
Using MS-DOS 5	$24.95
Using Novell NetWare, 2nd Edition	$29.95
Using OS/2 2.0	$24.95
Using PC DOS, 3rd Edition	$27.95
Using Prodigy	$19.95
Using UNIX	$29.95
Using Windows 3.1	$26.95
Using Your Hard Disk	$29.95
Windows 3 Quick Reference	$ 8.95
Windows 3 QuickStart	$19.95
Windows 3.1 Quick Reference	$ 9.95
Windows 3.1 QuickStart	$19.95

Desktop Publishing/Graphics

CorelDRAW! Quick Reference	$ 8.95
Harvard Graphics 3 Quick Reference	$ 9.95
Harvard Graphics Quick Reference	$ 9.95
Que's Using Ventura Publisher	$24.95
Using DrawPerfect	$24.95
Using Freelance Plus	$24.95
Using Harvard Graphics 3	$29.95
Using Harvard Graphics for Windows	$24.95
Using Harvard Graphics, 2nd Edition	$24.95
Using Microsoft Publisher	$22.95
Using PageMaker 4 for Windows	$29.95
Using PFS: First Publisher, 2nd Edition	$24.95
Using PowerPoint	$24.95
Using Publish It!	$24.95

Macintosh/Apple II

Easy Macintosh	$19.95
HyperCard 2 QuickStart	$19.95
PageMaker 4 for the Mac Quick Reference	$ 9.95
The Big Mac Book, 2nd Edition	$29.95
The Little Mac Book	$12.95
QuarkXPress 3.1 Quick Reference	$ 9.95
Que's Big Mac Book, 3rd Edition	$29.95
Que's Little Mac Book, 2nd Edition	$12.95
Que's Mac Classic Book	$24.95
Que's Macintosh Multimedia Handbook	$24.95
System 7 Quick Reference	$ 9.95
Using 1-2-3 for the Mac	$24.95
Using AppleWorks, 3rd Edition	$24.95
Using Excel 3 for the Macintosh	$24.95
Using FileMaker Pro	$24.95
Using MacDraw Pro	$24.95
Using MacroMind Director	$29.95
Using MacWrite Pro	$24.95
Using Microsoft Word 5 for the Mac	$27.95
Using Microsoft Works: Macintosh Version, 2nd Edition	$24.95
Using Microsoft Works for the Mac	$24.95
Using PageMaker 4 for the Macintosh	$24.95
Using Quicken 3 for the Mac	$19.95
Using the Macintosh with System 7	$24.95
Using Word for the Mac, Special Edition	$24.95
Using WordPerfect 2 for the Mac	$24.95
Word for the Mac Quick Reference	$ 9.95

Programming/Technical

Borland C++ 3 By Example	$21.95
Borland C++ Programmer's Reference	$29.95
C By Example	$21.95
C Programmer's Toolkit, 2nd Edition	$39.95
Clipper Programmer's Reference	$29.95
DOS Programmer's Reference, 3rd Edition	$29.95
FoxPro Programmer's Reference	$29.95
Network Programming in C	$49.95
Paradox Programmer's Reference	$29.95
Programming in Windows 3.1	$39.95
QBasic By Example	$21.95
Turbo Pascal 6 By Example	$21.95
Turbo Pascal 6 Programmer's Reference	$29.95
UNIX Programmer's Reference	$29.95
UNIX Shell Commands Quick Reference	$ 8.95
Using Assembly Language, 2nd Edition	$29.95
Using Assembly Language, 3rd Edition	$29.95
Using BASIC	$24.95
Using Borland C++	$29.95
Using Borland C++ 3, 2nd Edition	$29.95
Using C	$29.95
Using Microsoft C	$29.95
Using QBasic	$24.95
Using QuickBASIC 4	$24.95
Using QuickC for Windows	$29.95
Using Turbo Pascal 6, 2nd Edition	$29.95
Using Turbo Pascal for Windows	$29.95
Using Visual Basic	$29.95
Visual Basic by Example	$21.95
Visual Basic Programmer's Reference	$29.95
Windows 3.1 Programmer's Reference	$39.95

For More Information,
Call Toll Free!
1-800-428-5331

All prices and titles subject to change without notice.
Non-U.S. prices may be higher. Printed in the U.S.A.

Personal computing is easy
when you're using Que!

Using 1-2-3 for DOS Release 2.3, Special Edition
$29.95 USA
0-88022-727-8, 584 pp., $7^3/_8$ x $9^1/_4$

Using 1-2-3 for DOS Release 3.1+, Special Edition
$29.95 USA
0-88022-843-1, 584 pp., $7^3/_8$ x $9^1/_4$

Using 1-2-3 for Windows
$29.95 USA
0-88022-724-9, 584 pp., $7^3/_8$ x $9^1/_4$

Using 1-2-3/G
$29.95 USA
0-88022-549-7, 584 pp., $7^3/_8$ x $9^1/_4$

Using AlphaFOUR
$24.95 USA
0-88022-890-3, 500 pp., $7^3/_8$ x $9^1/_4$

Using AmiPro
$24.95 USA
0-88022-738-9, 584 pp., $7^3/_8$ x $9^1/_4$

Using Assembly Language, 3rd Edition
$29.95 USA
0-88022-884-9, 900 pp., $7^3/_8$ x $9^1/_4$

Using BASIC
$24.95 USA
0-88022-537-8, 584 pp., $7^3/_8$ x $9^1/_4$

Using Borland C++, 2nd Edition
$29.95 USA
0-88022-901-2, 1,300 pp., $7^3/_8$ x $9^1/_4$

Using C
$29.95 USA
0-88022-571-8, 950 pp., $7^3/_8$ x $9^1/_4$

Using Clipper, 3rd Edition
$29.95 USA
0-88022-885-7, 750 pp., $7^3/_8$ x $9^1/_4$

Using DacEasy, 2nd Edition
$24.95 USA
0-88022-510-6, 584 pp., $7^3/_8$ x $9^1/_4$

Using DataEase
$24.95 USA
0-88022-465-7, 584 pp., $7^3/_8$ x $9^1/_4$

Using dBASE IV
$24.95 USA
0-88022-551-3, 584 pp., $7^3/_8$ x $9^1/_4$

Using Excel 3 for Windows, Special Edition
$24.95 USA
0-88022-685-4, 584 pp., $7^3/_8$ x $9^1/_4$

Using FoxPro 2
$24.95 USA
0-88022-703-6, 584 pp., $7^3/_8$ x $9^1/_4$

Using Freelance Plus
$24.95 USA
0-88022-528-9, 584 pp., $7^3/_8$ x $9^1/_4$

Using GeoWorks Ensemble
$24.95 USA
0-88022-748-6, 584 pp., $7^3/_8$ x $9^1/_4$

Using Harvard Graphics 3
$24.95 USA
0-88022-735-4, 584 pp., $7^3/_8$ x $9^1/_4$

Using Harvard Graphics for Windows
$24.95 USA
0-88022-755-9, 700 pp., $7^3/_8$ x $9^1/_4$

Using LetterPoerfect
$24.95 USA
0-88022-667-6, 584 pp., $7^3/_8$ x $9^1/_4$

Using Microsoft C
$24.95 USA
0-88022-809-1, 584 pp., $7^3/_8$ x $9^1/_4$

Using Microsoft Money
$19.95 USA
0-88022-914-4, 400 pp., $7^3/_8$ x $9^1/_4$

Using Microsoft Publisher
$22.95 USA
0-88022-915-2, 450 pp., $7^3/_8$ x $9^1/_4$

Using Microsoft Windows 3, 2nd Edition
$24.95 USA
0-88022-509-2, 584 pp., $7^3/_8$ x $9^1/_4$

Using Microsoft Word 5.5: IBM Version, 2nd Edition
$24.95 USA
0-88022-642-0, 584 pp., $7^3/_8$ x $9^1/_4$

Using Microsoft Works for Windows, Special Edition
$24.95 USA
0-88022-757-5, 584 pp., $7^3/_8$ x $9^1/_4$

Using Microsoft Works: IBM Version
$24.95 USA
0-88022-467-3, 584 pp., $7^3/_8$ x $9^1/_4$

Using MoneyCounts
$24.95 USA
0-88022-696-X, 584 pp., $7^3/_8$ x $9^1/_4$

Using MS-DOS 5
$24.95 USA
0-88022-668-4, 584 pp., $7^3/_8$ x $9^1/_4$

Using Norton Utilities 6
$24.95 USA
0-88022-861-X, 584 pp., $7^3/_8$ x $9^1/_4$

Using Novell NetWare, 2nd Edition
$24.95 USA
0-88022-756-7, 584 pp., $7^3/_8$ x $9^1/_4$

Using ORACLE
$24.95 USA
0-88022-506-8, 584 pp., $7^3/_8$ x $9^1/_4$

Using OS/2 2.0
$24.95 USA
0-88022-863-6, 584 pp., $7^3/_8$ x $9^1/_4$

Using Pacioli 2000
$24.95 USA
0-88022-780-X, 584 pp., $7^3/_8$ x $9^1/_4$

Using PageMaker 4 for Windows
$24.95 USA
0-88022-607-2, 584 pp., $7^3/_8$ x $9^1/_4$

Using Paradox 4, Special Edition
$29.95 USA
0-88022-822-9, 900 pp., $7^3/_8$ x $9^1/_4$

Using Paradox for Windows, Special Edition
$29.95 USA
0-88022-823-7, 750 pp., $7^3/_8$ x $9^1/_4$

Using PC DOS, 3rd Edition
$24.95 USA
0-88022-409-3, 584 pp., $7^3/_8$ x $9^1/_4$

Using PC Tools 7
$24.95 USA
0-88022-733-8, 584 pp., $7^3/_8$ x $9^1/_4$

Using PC-File
$24.95 USA
0-88022-695-1, 584 pp., $7^3/_8$ x $9^1/_4$

Using PC-Write
$24.95 USA
0-88022-654-4, 584 pp., $7^3/_8$ x $9^1/_4$

Using PFS: First Choice
$24.95 USA
0-88022-454-1, 584 pp., $7^3/_8$ x $9^1/_4$

Using PFS: First Publisher, 2nd Edition
$24.95 USA
0-88022-591-2, 584 pp., $7^3/_8$ x $9^1/_4$

Using PFS: WindowWorks
$24.95 USA
0-88022-751-6, 584 pp., $7^3/_8$ x $9^1/_4$

Using PowerPoint
$24.95 USA
0-88022-698-6, 584 pp., $7^3/_8$ x $9^1/_4$

Using Prodigy
$24.95 USA
0-88022-658-7, 584 pp., $7^3/_8$ x $9^1/_4$

Using Professional Write
$24.95 USA
0-88022-490-8, 584 pp., $7^3/_8$ x $9^1/_4$

Using Professional Write Plus for Windows
$24.95 USA
0-88022-754-0, 584 pp., $7^3/_8$ x $9^1/_4$

Using Publish It!
$24.95 USA
0-88022-660-9, 584 pp., $7^3/_8$ x $9^1/_4$

Using Q&A 4
$24.95 USA
0-88022-643-9, 584 pp., $7^3/_8$ x $9^1/_4$

Using QBasic
$24.95 USA
0-88022-713-3, 584 pp., $7^3/_8$ x $9^1/_4$

Using Quattro Pro 3, Special Edition
$24.95 USA
0-88022-721-4, 584 pp., $7^3/_8$ x $9^1/_4$

Using Quattro Pro for Windows, Special Edition
$27.95 USA
0-88022-889-X, 900 pp., $7^3/_8$ x $9^1/_4$

Using Quick BASIC 4
$24.95 USA
0-88022-378-2, 713 pp., $7^3/_8$ x $9^1/_4$

Using QuickC for Windows
$29.95 USA
0-88022-810-5, 584 pp., $7^3/_8$ x $9^1/_4$

Using Quicken 5
$19.95 USA
0-88022-888-1, 550 pp., $7^3/_8$ x $9^1/_4$

Using Quicken for Windows
$19.95 USA
0-88022-907-1, 550 pp., $7^3/_8$ x $9^1/_4$

Using R:BASE
$24.95 USA
0-88022-603-X, 584 pp., $7^3/_8$ x $9^1/_4$

Using Smart
$24.95 USA
0-88022-229-8, 584 pp., $7^3/_8$ x $9^1/_4$

Using SuperCalc5, 2nd Edition
$24.95 USA
0-88022-404-5, 584 pp., $7^3/_8$ x $9^1/_4$

Using TimeLine
$24.95 USA
0-88022-602-1, 584 pp., $7^3/_8$ x $9^1/_4$

Using Turbo Pascal 6, 2nd Edition
$29.95 USA
0-88022-700-1, 800 pp., $7^3/_8$ x $9^1/_4$

Using Turbo Pascal for Windows
$29.95 USA
0-88022-806-7, 584 pp., $7^3/_8$ x $9^1/_4$

Using Turbo Tax: 1992 Edition Tax Advice & Planning
$24.95 USA
0-88022-839-3, 584 pp., $7^3/_8$ x $9^1/_4$

Using UNIX
$29.95 USA
0-88022-519-X, 584 pp., $7^3/_8$ x $9^1/_4$

Using Visual Basic
$29.95 USA
0-88022-763-X, 584 pp., $7^3/_8$ x $9^1/_4$

Using Windows 3.1
$27.95 USA
0-88022-731-1, 584 pp., $7^3/_8$ x $9^1/_4$

Using Word for Windows 2, Special Edition
$27.95 USA
0-88022-832-6, 584 pp., $7^3/_8$ x $9^1/_4$

Using WordPerfect 5
$27.95 USA
0-88022-351-0, 584 pp., $7^3/_8$ x $9^1/_4$

Using WordPerfect 5.1, Special Edition
$27.95 USA
0-88022-554-8, 584 pp., $7^3/_8$ x $9^1/_4$

Using WordStar 7
$19.95 USA
0-88022-909-8, 550 pp., $7^3/_8$ x $9^1/_4$

Using Your Hard Disk
$29.95 USA
0-88022-583-1, 584 pp., $7^3/_8$ x $9^1/_4$

Find It Fast with Que's Quick References!

Que's Quick References are the compact, easy-to-use guides to essential application information. Written for all users, Quick References include vital command information under easy-to-find alphabetical listings. Quick References are a must for anyone who needs command information fast!

To Order, Call: (800) 428-5331
OR (317) 573-2500

Free Catalog!

Mail us this registration form today, and we'll send you a free catalog featuring Que's complete line of best-selling books.

Name of Book _____

Name _____

Title _____

Phone (___) _____

Company _____

Address _____

City _____

State _____ ZIP _____

Please check the appropriate answers:

1. Where did you buy your Que book?
   - ☐ Bookstore (name: _____)
   - ☐ Computer store (name: _____)
   - ☐ Catalog (name: _____)
   - ☐ Direct from Que
   - ☐ Other: _____

2. How many computer books do you buy a year?
   - ☐ 1 or less
   - ☐ 2-5
   - ☐ 6-10
   - ☐ More than 10

3. How many Que books do you own?
   - ☐ 1
   - ☐ 2-5
   - ☐ 6-10
   - ☐ More than 10

4. How long have you been using this software?
   - ☐ Less than 6 months
   - ☐ 6 months to 1 year
   - ☐ 1-3 years
   - ☐ More than 3 years

5. What influenced your purchase of this Que book?
   - ☐ Personal recommendation
   - ☐ Advertisement
   - ☐ In-store display
   - ☐ Price
   - ☐ Que catalog
   - ☐ Que mailing
   - ☐ Que's reputation
   - ☐ Other: _____

6. How would you rate the overall content of the book?
   - ☐ Very good
   - ☐ Good
   - ☐ Satisfactory
   - ☐ Poor

7. What do you like *best* about this Que book?
   _____
   _____

8. What do you like *least* about this Que book?
   _____
   _____

9. Did you buy this book with your personal funds?
   ☐ Yes   ☐ No

10. Please feel free to list any other comments you may have about this Que book.
    _____
    _____
    _____

que

Order Your Que Books Today!

Name _____

Title _____

Company _____

City _____

State _____ ZIP _____

Phone No. (___) _____

Method of Payment:

Check ☐ (Please enclose in envelope.)

Charge My: VISA ☐   MasterCard ☐

American Express ☐

Charge # _____

Expiration Date _____

Order No.	Title	Qty.	Price	Total

You can **FAX** your order to **1-317-573-2583**. Or call **1-800-428-5331, ext. ORDR** to order direct.
Please add $2.50 per title for shipping and handling.

Subtotal _____

Shipping & Handling _____

Total _____

que

BUSINESS REPLY MAIL

First Class Permit No. 9918   Indianapolis, IN

Postage will be paid by addressee

11711 N. College
Carmel, IN 46032

NO POSTAGE
NECESSARY
IF MAILED
IN THE
UNITED STATES

BUSINESS REPLY MAIL

First Class Permit No. 9918   Indianapolis, IN

Postage will be paid by addressee

11711 N. College
Carmel, IN 46032